AN

Nanthangle
Crouhen
lly Vcha
Per Euch
Tü'yny Llwyn
Aberbrynant
Lloyd Esq
Mynydd
Carn
Munech
Maen Arthur
Dole y Rhyadergony
Gores Aberystwith
Lead
Mines

Funnon
Drindod
Cum Newidion
Pont Rheidol
G

Parke Brook
Coffinwood

Vifcount Lifburn
Crofinwood Park

Klon
Bicch
Llangwon

Yftruth R.

LA

20.7

Llanihangle
Lledred
Tüyny Graig
Foesyblydded
Llanunai
Cum Elis

Lloyd Gent
Ystraed
Myrick
Hen
Ddrinen
Peny Bryn

Pentre inued
Vendiged
Tary
Ystraed
ftnr
at

The Abby
in ruin
Strata Florida
Stedman Esq.

Pont yr
landawr

U

Maen Sultean
Llyn Vathey
Cringlace

N
D
R
E
D

Castell
Fleming
Indu

bridge

Castell
nnon

Craig
Grim
Berwin

Berin R.

N

Llwyn Gaig
Panty Cory

Craig
Berwin

Traw

Cum
Berwin

That part of the Road that
goes over the Marsh or Bogg
is generally out of Repair tho
it might be kept in good Order
and made pafable without
Danger at a small Yearly
Expence.

ARO

Craig y
Vndir

Dale Goch
Williams Esq.

B

Llandderry
Brevy Tregaron 10
Llanymddovery

19.5

R

HUN
DRE
D

E
A

R

Nescob

Forest

Llandderry
Abergwefin

apel
Ylin

R.

DANIEL ROWLAND

and the Great Evangelical Awakening in Wales

DANIEL ROWLAND

*and the Great Evangelical Awakening
in Wales*

Eifion Evans

THE BANNER OF TRUTH TRUST

THE BANNER OF TRUTH TRUST
3 Murrayfield Road, Edinburgh EH12 6EL
PO Box 621, Carlisle, Pennsylvania 17013, USA

*

© Eifion Evans 1985
First published 1985
ISBN 0 85151 446 4

*

Set in Linotron Sabon 10 on 12 pt
at The Spartan Press Limited, Lymington
and printed and bound at The Camelot Press Ltd, Southampton

TO MEIRA

Contents

Illustrations

Illustrations 6, 13, 15 and 23 reproduced at the National Library of Wales by courtesy of the Historical Society of the Presbyterian Church of Wales.

Illustration 18 is reproduced by courtesy of the Bodleian Library, Oxford.

Illustration 19 is reproduced by courtesy of the Ulster Museum, Belfast.

All the others are reproduced by courtesy of the National Library of Wales.

Preface

Many years ago I was introduced to the eighteenth-century Welsh Methodists by the discovery of one of their letters in a London library. Although my field of study at the time was the rich Puritan theology of the previous century, I was immediately drawn to read accounts of the Methodist Revival and the wider Great Awakening of that period. Shortly afterwards Rev. Derek O. Swann, a friend from college days, expressed an interest in Daniel Rowland. When he realised that for a comprehensive study of Rowland a knowledge of Welsh was essential, he suggested that I, as one who spoke Welsh, should undertake this task. In pursuing this objective I received considerable and repeated encouragement from one who admired Rowland greatly, the late Dr D. Martyn Lloyd-Jones. Over the years, in spite of many difficulties, I have never regretted accepting that challenge, and gladly acknowledge the stimulus of it.

The main difficulty was the almost total loss of Rowland's papers. It is a loss which is only partially compensated for by the availability of other contemporary records, particularly those of Howel Harris of Trefeca and William Williams of Pantycelyn. As a result, the amount of research has been far greater, generalisations have been more frequent, and some conclusions have to be less dogmatic. Nevertheless, even though the picture which emerges is blurred at some of the edges, the overall impression is clear and definite: Rowland was a man of God whose ministry was both powerful and glorious. In this respect he was the embodiment of The Great Awakening's most prominent features. To turn to Rowland's life and work, therefore, is to breathe the very atmosphere of that mighty work of God. What Dr Lloyd-Jones has said of this era in the history of the church, and of Whitefield in particular, could equally have been said of Rowland: 'When I get discouraged and over-tired and weary I invariably go to the eighteenth century. I have never found George Whitefield to fail me. Go to the eighteenth century! In other words read the stories of the great tides and movements of the Spirit experienced in that century. It is the most exhilarating experience, the finest tonic you will ever know.'

The year 1985 affords a special reason for the appearance of a book on Rowland. Both he and Howel Harris came to faith in Christ during 1735, 250 years ago. From that time until his death Rowland was God's chief instrument of revival in Wales. In writing the book I have sought to keep before me the maxim of John Owen, another of Rowland's biographers, 'The design of every biographer should be, not to exalt the man, but the grace of God displayed in him'. Rowland was a self-effacing man who vigorously shunned all appearance of publicity for himself, and consistently owned the cross of Christ to be his only glory. I have sought to respect Rowland's desire, and affirm my own, by aiming at the Psalmist's ideal: 'This shall be written for the generation to come: and the people which shall be created shall praise the Lord' (Psalm 102:18).

I am indebted to many for counsel and assistance. Dr Geoffrey F. Nuttall and Rev. Gomer M. Roberts have helped me as much with their friendship as with their expertise. Staff at many libraries have served me with courtesy and efficiency, especially at The National Library of Wales, Aberystwyth. During the period of writing the book my Abergavenny Pastorate has generously given me time and practical help. In particular, I am thankful to my colleague Rev. Geraint D. Fielder who ministered to the congregation on the occasions of my absence, and to Mrs Anne Evans and Mrs Anthea Price who helped with the typing. The Rev. Sulwyn Jones, by his fellowship and discussion while we walked the Brecon Beacons together, often spurred me to perseverance and brought many new insights. To the Rev. Iain H. Murray and Mr S. M. Houghton of The Banner of Truth Trust I owe an incalculable debt for their careful and far-sighted comments on the manuscript.

Finally, I am deeply grateful to my family for their unfailing support and patience. They have lived, so to speak, with Daniel Rowland for many years, and I know that the appearance of this book will provide tangible evidence that his usefulness in God's kingdom lives on. My son, Jonathan, deserves separate mention as the one who enthusiastically guided me through the intricacies of Word Processing. More than any other, my wife is the one who knows how much this study of Rowland has influenced me. She also shares with me fully the longing that its appearance in print will glorify the God of Daniel Rowland, who has made us 'heirs together of the grace of life'. For that reason the book is affectionately dedicated to her.

November 1984   Eifion Evans

Sources

Manuscript material relating to Welsh Methodism is found at The National Library of Wales, Aberystwyth. The main Collections are (1) Calvinistic Methodist Archives (CMA). These include the Howel Harris Diaries, over 280 in all, and 'The Trevecka Letters', of which there are more than 3,000. A List of the Diaries appears in xxvii. 45–55; and an Inventory of most of the Letters is found in M. H. Jones, *The Trevecka Letters*, 1932.
(2) Church in Wales Records, especially the St David's Episcopal Records.

The main printed sources are listed in the Abbreviations.

The orthography has been modernised throughout in the hope that what has been lost may in some measure be compensated for by clarity.

Abbreviations

Small Roman numerals refer to the Journal of the Historical Society of the Presbyterian Church of Wales (Cylchgrawn Cymdeithas Hanes Eglwys Methodistiaid Calfinaidd Cymru) up to 1976 (vol. lx). From 1977 it appears as CH, with the relevant year. MS refers to Manuscript Supplements of this Journal, issued periodically in two series with consecutive pagination in each.

BCM Richard Bennett, *The Early Life of Howel Harris*, 1962

CMHO D. E. Jenkins, *Calvinistic Methodist Holy Orders*, 1911

CYN N. Cynhafal Jones, *Gweithiau Williams Pant-y- celyn*, cyf. i, 1887; cyf. ii, 1891

DAL Arnold A. Dallimore, *George Whitefield*, vol. 1, 1970; vol. 2, 1980

DWB *Dictionary of Welsh Biography*, 1959

GWL *A Select Collection of Letters of . . . George Whitefield*, 3 vols. 1772

GWP1 Gomer M. Roberts, (gol.) *Gweithiau William Williams Pantycelyn*, cyf. i, 1964

GWP2 Garfield H. Hughes, *Gweithiau William Williams Pant-ycelyn*, cyf. ii, 1967

HH Edward Morgan, *The Life and Times of Howel Harris*, 1852

HMGC Gomer M. Roberts (gol.), *Hanes Methodistiaeth Galfinaidd Cymru*, cyf. i, 1973; Cyf. ii, 1978

HRS Tom Beynon, *Howell Harris, Reformer and Soldier*, 1958

HVL id. *Howell Harris's Visits to London*, 1960

HVP id. *Howell Harris's Visit to Pembrokeshire*, 1966

JO John Owen, *A Memoir of Daniel Rowlands of Llangeitho*, Banner of Truth Issues 215–216, August–September 1981. This is based on the 1848 (English) edition of John Owen's *Memoir*.

MC John Hughes, *Methodistiaeth Cymru*, cyf. i, 1851; cyf. ii,

1854; cyf. iii, 1856

MR   E. Morgan, *Ministerial Records of . . . the Rev. D. Rowlands*, 1840

MTU   Richard Bennett, *Methodistiaeth Trefaldwyn Uchaf*, 1929

STL   Gomer M. Roberts, *Selected Trevecka Letters* (1742–1747), 1956; (1747–1794), 1962

TGW   Luke Tyerman, *The Life of the Rev. George Whitefield*, vols. i and ii, 1890

TM   John Morgan Jones a William Morgan, *Y Tadau Methodistaidd*, cyf. i, 1895

WW   Gomer M. Roberts, *Y Per Ganiedydd*, cyf. i, 1949; cyf. ii. 1958

'It is a faithful saying, and worthy of all remembrance, that the ministry which exalts Christ crucified most, is the ministry which produces most lasting effects. Never, perhaps, did any preacher exalt Christ more than Rowland did, and never did preacher leave behind him such deep and abiding marks in the isolated corner of the world where he laboured.'

BISHOP J. C. RYLE

I

'God is There'

For at least two Church of England clergymen in the later years of the eighteenth century, Daniel Rowland was 'the greatest minister in the whole world'. One of the men was William Romaine, the highly esteemed English evangelical leader, the other was Thomas Jones, who came from West Wales. Such a statement might well be regarded as naïve, partisan, or patently foolish. After all, how many today have heard of Daniel Rowland? When Christians think of the great ministers and preachers of the church, a cluster of names come readily to mind. In the early centuries of the church, Ambrose, Chrysostom, and Augustine excelled in this way. During the Protestant Reformation, they had their counterparts in Luther, Calvin, and Latimer. Likewise, in subsequent centuries, Bunyan, Whitefield, Wesley, Spurgeon, and Moody were outstanding preachers, but who was Rowland?

Significantly, two of those just named, Whitefield and Wesley, were Rowland's contemporaries. They knew one another quite well, on occasions they had preached together, and they commonly went under the name of 'Methodists'. Whitefield, certainly, would have understood the sentiments of Romaine and Jones. Under Rowland's ministry he had often felt his 'heart burn within him', and had never forgotten the sight of some ten thousand people during the preaching of a sermon by Rowland 'crying "glory!", "praise", and ready to leap for joy'. Other contemporary estimates of Rowland were just as enthusiastic. After ten years of his evangelical ministry one person said of him, 'In his pulpit he is a second Paul.' Writing nearly thirty years later in 1773, another reliable witness claimed, 'Surely he is the greatest preacher in Europe'.[1]

A similar assessment was given by Christmas Evans, who lived on

[1] JO, 4, 59; STL.i.164; (A. C. H. Seymour), *The Life and Times of Selina Countess of Huntingdon*, vol. 11, 1844, p. 118.

into another century and belonged to a Nonconformist denomination: 'Rowland was a star of the greatest magnitude that appeared the last century in the Principality, and perhaps there has not been his like in Wales since the days of the apostles.'[1] What is it, then, that accounts for this prevailing ignorance and neglect of Daniel Rowland at the present time?

The most obvious explanation is that Rowland laboured in a Welsh-speaking community, and that his work scarcely touched other parts of the British Isles. It is true that he undertook some journeys into England for preaching purposes, but he had a decidedly Welsh bias in the matters of language and sphere of ministry. That ministry lasted for over fifty years and was centred on the comparatively remote village of Llangeitho in West Wales. Frequent preaching tours took him throughout his homeland but Rowland's reputation was chiefly associated with Llangeitho.

Then, paradoxically, the very success attending Rowland's ministry contributed to the failure of posterity to record its history. A glorious change had come to Wales, and for many years to come a great harvest was to be reaped. His successors, closest to him, were simply too busy with the work to find time to write his biography. The years following his passing witnessed further seasons of extraordinary spiritual success, calling for yet more preaching and spiritual oversight. The very scale of the Holy Spirit's operations stretched ministerial resources to the limits. Even allowing for this, however, there seems to have been an unwarranted negligence in the matter on the part of the Welsh leaders.

True, some eleven elegies were written in Rowland's memory, and attempts were made to secure a biography. One such attempt was reported by Rowland's son, Nathaniel:

'Soon after the death of Rowland, Lady Huntingdon, who had long been acquainted with him, requested that all information respecting him should be collected and sent to her, as she intended to write his life. This request was complied with, but before she made use of the materials, she was removed to another and a happier world. There was no inquiry made for these documents for some years, and when it was made, they could not be found.'[2]

All subsequent efforts to recover these manuscripts have hitherto

---

[1] MR, 130.   [2] JO, 9.

been in vain. Biographers have therefore laboured under grave disadvantages. They have had to rely on the accounts of Rowland's contemporaries. Furthermore, details of Rowland's personal and domestic life which have survived have been regrettably sparse.

Lady Huntingdon would hardly have contemplated writing the biography herself. Apart from her advanced age, for she was 83 when Rowland died, she had no knowledge of Welsh, and much of the material would be in that language. This is another reason why many are unfamiliar with Rowland's story.

As Nathaniel Rowland evidently declined the work, the most eligible biographers would have been David Jones of Llangan and Thomas Charles of Bala. Both men were highly esteemed by Lady Huntingdon, and both were bilingual. Jones' ministry in the South Wales counties meant that he had worked in close association with Rowland for some twenty years. Charles looked on Rowland as his spiritual father, and a Catechism by him had already appeared in print. Yet neither undertook the task, possibly believing that Nathaniel Rowland and Lady Huntingdon had already arranged for someone else to do the work.

Rowland died in 1790. Before the close of the century, Charles had encouraged another to write about Rowland: 'Describe with pen and ink as best you can, his solemn appearance, the depth of his ideas, the extent of his gifts, the power of the Holy Spirit working through him, and his great success in the ministry.' The response to that appeal was meagre, a few paragraphs in a Welsh work that appeared thirty years after Rowland had passed away. Early in 1811, Charles himself was urged to bring out a new edition of Rowland's sermons in an English translation, 'with a short account of the author's life, and the efficacy and power the Word had upon his hearers'.[1] This did not materialise, but he wrote a little about Rowland's ministry in his periodical, *Trysorfa Ysprydol* (Spiritual Treasury), more by way of an appreciation than of history.

The first attempt at biography appeared in the *Evangelical and Missionary Magazine* for November, 1825. John Owen's fuller account *Coffhâd*, appeared in 1839. An English translation was issued in the following year, under the title *A Memoir*, a second edition being called for in 1848. Edward Morgan's *Ministerial*

[1] D. E. Jenkins, *The Life of the Rev. Thomas Charles B.A. of Bala*, vol. ii. 1908, p. 202; vol. iii. p. 382. The Welsh work was: Robert Jones, *Drych yr Amseroedd* (Ail Argraffiad, 1841), tt. 75–82.

Records of Rowland also appeared in 1840, using Owen's Welsh biography and other material which he himself had collected. Later works have drawn extensively on these. The last biography appeared in Welsh in 1938.[1]

For many the measure of great preaching in Rowland's century was set by George Whitefield. Certainly Whitefield's excellence in this respect was widely and consistently acknowledged both at the time and since. One writer, Edward Morgan, gives this account of both men:

'A friend once asked an old gentleman of considerable intelligence, now dead, who had often heard both Whitefield and Rowland, respecting their comparative merits as preachers. He decidedly gave the preference on the whole to the latter. Whitefield, he said, was greater perhaps in the power of alarming the unconcerned. But Rowland excelled in building up, strengthening, and comforting the Christian. His sermons were more methodical, and contained more matter and more point. Whitefield's sermons would be soon forgotten; but those of Rowland would be remembered and retained through life. This I believe, was true; for I have heard old people often mention what they heard from Mr. Rowland though he has been now dead nearly forty years. There is another point in which the superiority, according to this old gentleman's opinion, belonged to Mr. Rowland. Whitefield, at times, when much animated, lost his matter, his feelings impeding the operations of his mind. But this was never the case with Rowland; the more animated he was, the greater was his matter, the more weighty was what he said.'

This assessment of Rowland is borne out by Thomas Jones, for whom Rowland's peculiar excellences as a preacher were 'depth and fervour'. Thomas Charles' appreciation speaks of the 'loftiness and grandeur' in Rowland's endowments, his 'profound thoughts, strength and sweetness of voice, clearness and lively energy in proclaiming the deep things of God'. He continues: 'The gifts of Mr. Rowland, and the power that accompanied his ministry, were such, that no hearers in the present age can form any adequate idea of

[1] The other English works are: J. C. Ryle, *The Christian Leaders of England in the Eighteenth Century*, 1868; and Owen Jones, *Some of the Great Preachers of Wales*, 1885. 'A Historical Sketch' of *Welsh Calvinistic Methodism* by William Williams appeared in 1872. The principal Welsh biographies are: *Goleuad Cymru*, Ionawr 1826; TM.i.pennod IV; D. Worthington, *Cofiant Daniel Rowland*, 1905 (Ail Argraffiad 1923); D. J. Odwyn Jones, *Daniel Rowland Llangeitho*, 1938.

them. There is no one who has not heard him, that can imagine anything equal to what they were. Oh! how wonderful the authority and light that accompanied his ministry, and how wonderful the effects on the hearers!'[1]

One of Rowland's closest colleagues was Howel Harris. At an early stage in his Christian life, Harris resolved to keep a diary. He also corresponded with many of the religious leaders, in England as well as in Wales. These contemporary records of events are an invaluable source for Rowland material. Although Harris was generally ready with his pen, even he found it difficult at times to describe Rowland's ministry. 'I was last Sunday at the Ordinance with Brother Rowland where I saw, felt, and heard such things as I can't send on paper any idea of. The power that continues with him is uncommon.' He then tries to picture the scene, yet obviously feels he has failed. Of one thing he is sure, that 'a spiritual eye must see and acknowledge that God is there. This is but a very faint idea of it, for what words can express spiritual things?'[2]

The hand of God on the ministry of the Word during the eighteenth century is brought out very clearly by Lady Huntingdon's chief biographer. Rowland and another colleague, Howel Davies, are referred to as 'these apostolic men', 'indefatigable labourers', who 'went about continually preaching the doctrines of the Cross'. And the source of their power? 'Conscious that no human persuasion could prevail with man to accept a free and plenteous redemption, with earnest supplication they recommend those whom they addressed to the Spirit of Grace, and to the efficacious influences of His power.' The reason why 'whole congregations became melted, borne down, and overcome' under their ministry was not brilliant oratory, or polished phrases, or convincing arguments.[3] They would have been the first to insist that it had nothing to do with a skilful use of human resources. Their dependence was entirely upon God's Spirit, and any success which followed their labours was to be ascribed to the Triune God, and to Him alone.

For an understanding of the foundation of Rowland's reputation it is safest to rely on the words of those who knew him best. Foremost among such men was William Williams of Pantycelyn, scarcely known outside Wales today except for his hymn, 'Guide me, O Thou

[1] JO, 29, 59, 61.   [2] STL.i.81, 82.
[3] Seymour, *op. cit.* ii.373, 374.

great Jehovah.' In explaining the revival of religion in Rowland's day, which has come to be known as 'The Great Awakening', Williams makes one of his characters say this:

'You know, dear Sir, that hundreds, yes, thousands, that I know of, possess this flame apart from me. Was there as much of God's authority in His glorious church for some time past as there is in these days? . . . A summer's day has dawned on the land; many of the ungodly are brought from the world to make a clear path for the Gospel of the Lamb. The Spirit that has now shone on the Church is like a blazing fire. . . . When God pours down His presence, it is as the days of the apostles . . . so that multitudes have to confess, "This is most certainly the work of God."'[1]

Note the words: 'God's authority', 'the Spirit like a blazing fire', 'God pours down His presence', 'as the days of the apostles', 'the work of God'. When people thought of Rowland, these were the categories which came to mind. Under his preaching the awareness of God excluded all thoughts of human learning or gifts.

Williams highlights this in one of his long poems, as he tries to present the ideal preacher:

> Though education's precious, I see this every day,
> That only the experienced will preach the Gospel way;
> The Spirit makes a preacher, and heaven's choicest sound
> Is heard with power wherever the Spirit's work is found.[2]

In another of his writings, Williams asserts that if reputation is not established by the Spirit's endowment of power, men often seek it from motives of selfish ambition, with consequences damaging to themselves and to the church:

'The pride of preachers of the Word, in wanting a name for themselves alive and after their death, is the cause of attracting men to themselves, rather than to the Lord of the harvest. Men are so prone to make idols of one another . . . and ordinary people, when they hear a good orator, and have but a little taste of his doctrine, are ready to set him up as Herod of old, in the place of God; then his heart is so taken with this promotion, and with the people's allegiance, that he begins to boast of, and flaunt this new name which he wishes to perpetuate, and which others readily ascribe to him. This new sect both he and they conclude is better than all those old sleepy sects whose names have rusted.'

[1] GWP.ii.3–4, 5.   [2] GWP.i.385.

[6]

Rowland's reputation was made, not on the numbers of followers he drew after himself, but on the manifestation of God's glory in his ministry. 'He reckoned his chief work on earth to be doing good to God's Church.'[1] So much for Williams' oblique portrayal. It is relevant because Rowland was, in many ways, the very embodiment of a Methodist preacher.

Rowland's burning passion to bring men to Christ, saints to heaven, and glory to God, is epitomised in one of his sayings. The words, first spoken as a spontaneous exclamation in the pulpit in a time of revival, are now carved on the monument to his memory at Llangeitho. He is depicted with the Bible in his left hand, and his right hand inviting to heaven, while below is the inscription:

> O Heaven! Heaven! Heaven!
> Your mansions would be empty enough
> if Zion did not nurture children for you on earth!

[1]GWP.ii.146–7, 140.

'God was a stranger in the land . . . and even though there were
many trumpets – and some of them silver trumpets – hardly
anyone heeded their sound from one end of Wales to the other.'

WILLIAM WILLIAMS
of Pantycelyn

'When the Spirit shall be poured forth plentifully . . . I believe
you will hear much other kind of sermons . . . than you are
wont to do now-a-days. Souls will surely be dealt with at
another kind of rate. It is plain, too sadly plain, there is a great
retraction of the Spirit of God even from us. We know not how
to speak living sense unto souls, how to get within you: our
words die in our mouths, or drop and die between you and us.'

JOHN HOWE
in a sermon on 'The Outpouring of the Spirit.'

2

'Silver Trumpets Unheeded'

At much the same time on two continents, events were taking place which marked the beginning of the eighteenth-century 'Great Awakening' or 'Revival' of religion. Within a five-year period a new galaxy of men whose lives God had amazingly changed was to appear in the religious firmament. Between 1734 and 1739 such men as Jonathan Edwards in America, George Whitefield, John and Charles Wesley in England, Daniel Rowland and Howel Harris in Wales, were to come into prominence for their extraordinary experiences and labours in preaching the Word of life. The scope of that Awakening was vast in terms of geographical spread, numerical success, great personalities, and lasting significance. The entire direction of the Christian church was to be fundamentally changed, from decline to prosperity, from deadness to vitality, and from recession to expansion.

In the providence of God, it is true, several factors, in the realm of ideals as well as ideas, influenced that great movement. There was an interplay of social, theological, and ecclesiastical forces, contributory and reactionary. To transform a situation which was beyond human remedy, however, as also to transform one human life, God Himself must 'come down', His Spirit must be 'poured forth plentifully'. The spiritual activity which followed such a manifestation of God's presence was in no sense an organised or predictable outcome. There was often chaos as well as growth; there were tensions as well as opportunities. But from this vast cauldron of spiritual upheaval and change came results which were both creative and beneficial.

Nothing in the Wales of 1735 would have held out the prospect of such a dramatic transformation. Social conditions were characterised by poverty. 'The Welsh people in the eighteenth century were almost entirely a peasant people . . . engaged in either sheep-farming in the hilly regions, or in cattle-farming on the plains, or in mixed husbandry . . . Wales was poor and backward; its agriculture was primitive and its mineral resources as yet unrecognised.'[1] The social and economic changes of the Industrial Revolution were still two generations away.

From the time of King Henry VIII Wales and England had been unified. The same Parliamentary, legal, and ecclesiastical arrangements obtained throughout the kingdom. The Welsh, however, preserved their distinct cultural and historical traditions. For this reason, life in Wales still retained a certain air of independence and remoteness from that of England. Communication between the two countries was not easy. Roads were notoriously hazardous, dirty, and dangerous. They were described in 1767 as 'mere rocky lanes, full of huge stones as big as one's horse, and abominable holes'. This could well have explained George Whitefield's complaint after a preaching tour some ten years earlier: 'The Welsh roads have almost demolished my open one-horse chaise, as well as me.'[2] The bad state of the roads gave the impression of an inhospitable country, adding to the inhabitants' sense of isolation.

Another aspect of Welsh isolation was the widespread use of the Welsh language. Daniel Rowland's preference for Welsh, especially in the early years of his ministry, was abundantly evident. One Methodist in Bristol apologised in 1742 for his seeming rudeness to Rowland, giving as his reason that 'he talked so bad English I could not understand him'.[3] Three years later, Rowland's fellow-worker, Howel Harris, reported of the Welsh converts, 'Most of our societies understand no English.'[4] Contemporary correspondence with the Society for Promoting Christian Knowledge bristles with protestations of the monoglot nature of vast numbers of the population: 'The vulgar understand not English books and people are generally so poor that little help can be expected of them. . . . There are in the four Welsh Dioceses upwards of 500 parishes in which the generality of the people understand no other language.'[5]

One man whom this state of affairs affected profoundly was the

[1] M. G. Jones, *The Charity School Movement*, 1938, pp. 268, 269.
[2] Arthur Young, *Six Weeks' Tour Through England and Wales*, 1768, p. 120; GWL.iii.236.
[3] Emory University, Atlanta, Georgia, U.S.A. (Special Collections, Wesleyana), Letter of John Cennick to Howel Harris, July 28, 1742.
[4] STL.i.177.
[5] Mary Clement (ed.), *Correspondence and Minutes of the S.P.C.K. Relating to Wales*, 1952, pp. 5, 334.

active Anglican clergyman, Griffith Jones. He was passionately concerned to evangelise the Welsh people, and established free, 'circulating' schools with this very aim in mind. He argued the case for supporting his venture in this way:

'I am not at present concerned what becomes of the language, abstractedly considered. . . . The thing to be cleared up is, whether the chief and greatest end of all, viz. the glory of God, the interests of religion, and the salvation of the poor Welsh people, is most likely to be promoted by continuing or abandoning it. . . . Consider the weight and importance of saving four or five hundred thousand souls (more or less) now living in Wales. . . . There are some advantages peculiar to the Welsh tongue favourable to religion, as being perhaps the chastest in Europe. Its books and writings are free from the infection and deadly venom of Atheism, Deism, Infidelity, Arianism, Popery, lewd plays, immodest romances, and love intrigues; which poison the minds, captivate all the senses, and prejudice so many . . . against their duty to God, and due care of their own souls; and which, by too many books in English and some other languages, are this day grievously propagated.'[1]

Evidently, Jones recognised the prior claim of the Gospel over that of material or even cultural considerations. It would have been tempting to teach English, with its accompanying enticements of personal betterment or social elevation. Concern for his fellow-countrymen, however, would not allow him to abdicate the clear responsibility to teach and preach God's Word in the only language commonly understood by so many of them.

Their speaking in the Welsh language was not a matter of nationalism, but of cultural heritage. Nationalism did not crystallise until another century had dawned, and although it is possible to speak of a 'renaissance' in Welsh culture during the eighteenth century, what it achieved was not nationalism, but a 'cultural patriotism . . . a new sense of Welshness'.[2]

Significantly, however, in order to achieve this cultural goal, two conflicting forces were at work. One was humanism, as expressed in the literary aspirations of writers such as the Morris brothers of Anglesey and Edward Williams (*Iolo Morgannwg*). These men imposed rigid standards of literary form and criticism, but there is little evidence of moral restraint in their literary output. In a letter to the

---

[1] W. Moses Williams, *Selections from the Welch Piety*, 1938, pp. 38, 39, 43.
[2] Prys Morgan, *The Eighteenth-Century Renaissance*, 1981, p. 161.

schoolmaster Edward Richard (who had been at school with Daniel Rowland), Lewis Morris speaks of the 'qualifications of a modern Welsh poet': 'Is he in raptures with a cup of good ale? . . . Does he affect low company and greedily swallow the praises of tinkers and cobblers? . . . Is he naturally inclined to buffoonery, dirty language, and indecent expressions?'[1] Clearly, Welsh culture as well as Welsh souls needed to be transformed by the Gospel. Nevertheless, the Methodists did not set out to influence the former by programmed organisation, as the Society for the Reformation of Manners had done at the end of the seventeenth century. They recognised that a transformed society would be the fruit rather than the cause of a true Reformation.

Consequently, the other force was the Christian literary witness of the Welsh Methodists. It was one of their number, William Williams of Pantycelyn, who produced the 'best-sellers' of the day. It was said of them, 'that by creating a nation of readers of classical Welsh, they were primarily responsible for the literary renaissance of the eighteenth and nineteenth centuries'.[2] Griffith Jones' aim had been not merely to combat illiteracy but also ignorance, not so much to perpetuate the Welsh language as to change Welsh hearts. Between the Catechism of Griffith Jones, the sermons of Rowland, and the hymns of Williams, Pantycelyn, Wales came to have not merely words to sing, but a heart with which to sing them.

Before the Great Awakening the song was a very different one. Attendance at church was generally sparse and frequently irreverent. Outside, the churchyard would be the scene of any number of sports and pastimes: football and other ball-games, wrestling, bowls, skittles, cock-fighting, dancing to the tunes of pipes, fiddlers, harpists and minstrels. Inside the church, the scene left much to be desired. In 1703 Ellis Wynne had published his famous *Gweledigaethau y Bardd Cwsg* (Visions of the Sleeping Bard). One of these is of people at worship: 'There I saw some whispering, some laughing; others eyeing young maidens; yet others surveying the dress of their neighbours from head to toe; some fighting and quarrelling about privileged positions, some asleep, others diligent in their devotion, and some of these even were hypocrites.'[3]

[1] Hugh Owen (ed.), *Additional Letters of the Morrises of Anglesey*, Part II, 1949, p. 525.
[2] M. G. Jones, *op. cit.*, p. 324.
[3] 1960 edition, p. 36.

Such a state of affairs is not altogether surprising in the light of the famous statement by Bishop Butler in his *Analogy of Religion*, which appeared in 1736, that 'Christianity is not so much a subject of enquiry, but . . . discovered to be fictitious . . . a principal subject of mirth and ridicule'. The sermons of the clergy were usually rational and ethical, rather than Scriptural and evangelical, and the great concern in preaching was for sedate propriety, moderation, and a smooth style. As to their frequency, in Rowland's Archdeaconry of Cardigan in 1733, of 62 parishes that supplied information, 25 had a weekly Sunday sermon, 27 a sermon on alternate Sundays, and the remainder less frequently.[1] Few of the clergy could preach in Welsh. Some churches were 'totally neglected', serving only 'for the solitary habitations of owls and jackdaws'.[2]

The diocese of St David's, in which Rowland laboured, covered nearly half of Wales, and included over three hundred parishes. This undoubtedly presented difficulties of administration and communication for its bishops. It was the least popular diocese in the country, its financial inadequacy resulting in the bishops seeking preferment to other more lucrative sees. The parish clergy were also under great financial strain, and often found themselves living in unfit accommodation. For these ills the classical remedy was to serve several churches, necessitating a hasty schedule on Sundays. The cleric vividly portrayed in *A View of the State of Religion in the Diocese of St. David's*, published in 1721, 'abruptly huddles over as many prayers as may be in half an hour's time, and then returns again to his road, fasting'.[3] The clergy's intellectual, not to mention biblical, attainments often fell short of that of their people. There is a profusion of evidence in the diocesan records of clergy being charged with wantonness, drunkenness, neglect of duty, impure conversation, and the performing of clandestine marriages.[4]

Contemporary evidence from Griffith Jones bears out this picture. He had been cited to the Church authorities for such 'irregularities' as extra-parochial activities and attracting crowds! In a long defence,

[1] NLW Church in Wales MS SD/Misc.B/132, pp. 14–15, 20–23, quoted in Geraint Jenkins, *Literature, Religion and Society in Wales 1660–1730*, 1980, p. 12.
[2] Erasmus Saunders, *A View of the State of Religion in the Diocese of St. David's About the Beginning of the Eighteenth Century* (1721), 1949 edn., pp. 23–4.
[3] 1949 edn., p. 36.
[4] HMGC.i.69.

he expresses his grief at the serious inadequacies of so many of the clergy.

''Tis far from me to revile any of them or to deny that there are several pious and painstaking divines . . . that endeavour to do their duty; but several more there are that I am afraid do not. Some cannot for the plurality of their cures. . . . Others because of their non-residence. . . . Others . . . that understand not our language. . . . Many others make a shift to frame their discourse as it were in an unknown language to the people . . . empty speculations, high and lofty quaint phrases, scholastical or controversial divinity above the reach of ordinary capabilities. . . . At the least one can hear from many but a little sober morality . . . without any intimation of repentance, regeneration, etc. The next sort . . . are the carnal, covetous, profane and voluptuous, whose lives give the lie to their doctrines. . . . Many profane and sottish persons steal into the ministry. . . . True piety is not a little impaired, which calls for the most vigorous endeavours for the recovering of its practice and purity.'

So much for the clergy. As to the constant sniping at him for his evangelistic fervour, Griffith Jones added, 'None can cultivate a wilderness without being sometimes scratched by the thorns and briars; we can't . . . think that we are rightly sowing God's pearls unless some dogs turn again and rend us.'[1]

Rowland was soon to be equally forthright in regard to the prevailing decline in religion. In a sermon on Matthew 2:8–9, 'Good News to the Gentiles', he tells his hearers that it was a 'heavy judgment',

'to have such ministers among you as will countenance you in your sloth and neglect of Jesus; as depreciate His merits and speak lightly of His grace as a sanctifying principle; as run with you into every excess of riot, are the foremost to lead the dance, to circulate the glass, to promote your time-killing pastimes, and to encourage every kind of dissipation. . . . All ministers do not fall under this censure. I only speak of the unawakened among them, who have had no call to the ministry but the capricious design of partial friends or fond parents; and have received no gifts but the tithes. Of all such, to whatever denomination they may belong, or over whatever congregations they may preside, I may safely say with the old Welsh bard, that

> To set the blind to lead the blind,
> To set the dull t'instruct mankind,

[1] NLW Ottley Papers, No. 100.

To set th' unskilled to show the way
From dark despair to perfect day;
Is not the Spirit's ordination,
But mere human innovation,
Which loudly calls for reformation.[1]

Actually, Rowland might well have been referring to his own experience before the mighty change wrought in him by the Spirit of God.

The indictment was also largely true of ministers in the other section of Protestantism, outside the Established Church, the Dissenters. Here, too, there were the 'awakened' and the 'unawakened', and in similar proportions. Early in the century Presbyterians, Independents, and Particular Baptists in Wales together totalled nearly 18,000, most of them in the South.[2]

Of the 'awakened' ministers, the Baptist Enoch Francis exercised a lively ministry within twenty miles of both Griffith Jones and Daniel Rowland. 'Wherever he went vast crowds would assemble. The sum of his preaching was free salvation to sinners through the amazing love of Christ. He would hardly ever preach without tears streaming down his face from love to God and men. His ministry was exceedingly melting.' A sermon preached by him in 1723 on Ephesians 5:14, 'Awake, thou that sleepest', bears witness to the painful heart-searching caused by the lethargy of Dissenters. In it he acknowledged that 'even the godly have a tendency to spiritual sleep'. The reasons he gave for this were, 'a kind of mist arising in the heart, Lk. 21:34; weariness; fleshly ease, so in a time of peace and prosperity the Lord's people forget God; and keeping company with men who are asleep'.[3]

Another Welsh Dissenter, the Presbyterian Jeremy Owen, writing in 1733, bemoaned the spiritual barrenness of the day and called for earnest prayer. 'At present the cause of Christ is low in the world. It is now night in the Church. The friends of the Bridegroom are uneasy. . . . The language of each heart is, "Come, my Beloved . . . return, return in greater glory than ever, to enlighten and quicken our present state". . . . Who knows whether this is not the time for

---

[1] *Eight Sermons*, 1774, pp. 173–4. 'The old Welsh Bard' was Rhys Prichard (1579?–1644) of Llandovery, s.v.DWB.
[2] Michael R. Watts, *The Dissenters, from the Reformation to the French Revolution*, 1978, pp. 270, 272–4.
[3] Joshua Thomas, *Hanes y Bedyddwyr*, 1778, tud. 386; NLW MS 10589A.

the Lord to break in upon us in a powerful manner?'[1] He could not have known that the answer to those prayers was near.

Glimpses of the forthcoming Great Awakening were afforded to such men from time to time, and so hope was kept alive. Edmund Jones of Pontypool, a Dissenting friend of Howel Harris later, could say of one preaching occasion that 'the fire of God went through the house', and could say of some preachers, 'Such men seem to be . . . on the borders of glory. . . . The tide of glory seems to be coming up the river of grace in their souls.'[2] Men such as Francis, Owen, and Edmund Jones, although few in number and scattered almost to the point of insignificance, made up a fervent, if weak remnant.

In England, Isaac Watts welcomed news of the revival in New England, and Philip Doddridge could say of Dissent in 1740, 'There is a secret strength.' It was found in such lesser-known men as Joseph Williams of Kidderminster and Timothy Thomas of Pershore. Even before 1725, at a time of spiritual decline, Williams' observations testify to a warm devotion: 'Never did I experience such a flame of divine love as was kindled in me. The word came to me with life and power.' Thomas died in 1720 after only three years' ministry at Pershore, and his diary was published in 1752 as *The Hidden Life of a Christian*, an apt title for the sentiments of close, heartfelt dealings with God which it includes.[3] God's people were being refreshed even in the spiritual wilderness of the early years of the eighteenth century.

When Rowland and others depicted Wales before the Great Awakening in this way they were not exaggerating. They were merely making an assessment in the light of biblical criteria. Although their evaluation of other similar periods in the history of the church might have been more objective, it would have been no different. Indeed, Williams of Pantycelyn refers to parallel experiences in the church's story at the time of Constantine ('deadness came in'), and the Middle Ages ('all the errors of Rome'). In contrast, the

[1] *Traethawd i Brofi ac i Gymmell*, tt.iv, 18, 60.
[2] Geoffrey F. Nuttall, *Howel Harris*, 1965, p. 48. For Edmund Jones, see DWB; the Countess of Huntingdon referred to him as 'the dear good old prophet . . . what a blessed saint of God! how devoted! how lively! how active! always athirst for full communion with the Father of Light!' (Seymour, *op. cit.*, ii.117–18).
[3] David Fountain, *Isaac Watts Remembered*, 1974, Chapter 10 'Revival'; Geoffrey F. Nuttall, 'Methodism and the Older Dissent: Some Perspectives', in The United Reformed Church Historical Society *Journal*, vol. ii. pp. 261–4.

great effusions of God's Spirit in Apostolic days, at the time of the Reformation, and in Rowland's day, are referred to as 'the bold, pleasant, zealous spirit', 'the fiery spirit', 'the breaking forth of the light', 'the shining of the Sun' which dispels darkness and lukewarmness alike.[1]

The Methodists were being realistic. They painted a dark picture of their contemporaries, much as Christ had done of His. Then, too, religious power and prominence had been in the hands of 'hypocrites' who consistently used them for their own ends (Matt. 23:13–33). Christ had referred to His generation as 'faithless and perverse', 'evil and adulterous', even though there were those in His day, like Simeon and Anna, who were 'waiting for the consolation of Israel' and 'looking for redemption in Jerusalem' (Matt. 17:17; 12:39; Lk. 2:25, 38). When Rowland was converted the 'Simeons' of his day were very much a despised and impotent minority, and as their numbers grew they were relentlessly opposed by the 'faithless and perverse' majority. The 'silver trumpets' of the land were largely unheeded. Unbelief seemed to hold almost universal sway.

[1] GWP.ii.22–3.

'The wise men came in quest of Jesus . . . to Jerusalem, not indeed by the direction of the star, but by the guidance of their own reasonings . . . and therefore they found Him not, whom they sought after. He cannot be discovered but by the light of His own illuminations. Reason indeed is a goodly gift, and of royal extraction; but, since the fall, it is like Mephibosheth, lame in both its feet.'

DANIEL ROWLAND
in a sermon on Matthew 2:8–9

'I appeal to the experience of the most learned disputer against divine revelation, whether he does not find in himself, that he is naturally proud, angry, revengeful, and full of other passions contrary to the purity, holiness, and long-suffering of God. And is not this a demonstration that some way or other he is fallen from God? . . . Here then, God by His Word steps in, and opens to his view such a scene of divine love and infinite goodness in the Holy Scriptures, that none but men of such corrupt and reprobate minds as our modern deists, would shut their eyes against it.'

GEORGE WHITEFIELD
in a sermon on John 5:39

3

'Lame in Both Feet'

In the realm of ideas, the eighteenth century was dominated by what were considered to be two self-evident principles. One was the belief that reason governs all truth and goodness, and the other was that the pursuit of pleasure should be paramount. Popular thinking had been influenced, directly or indirectly, by philosophical rationalism. The result had been an abandonment of divine revelation in favour of human reason. Its practical effect can be traced through contemporary literature and art, which provide an illuminating commentary on the morality of the times. Thus, the works of the dramatist William Congreve, Henry Fielding the novelist, and William Hogarth the artist depict a society adrift from its moral moorings.

As there were some 'silver trumpets' endeavouring to sound an alarm against the prevailing decline, so also there was a steady stream of good Welsh literature. Rowland was familiar with the work of Rhys Prichard, whose catchy, homely hymns under the title *Canwyll y Cymry* (The Welshman's Candle), had gone through fourteen Welsh editions between 1658 and 1730. The collection came to be known affectionately as 'The Vicar's Book', and was intended as a popular handbook of sound Protestant theology. In 1738 Howel Harris discerned 'hopeful signs of grace in a boy that was touched in reading the Vicar's book'.[1] The book brought conviction of sin to Ioan Thomas in his youth, and the account of his spiritual pilgrimage, *Rhad Ras* (Free Grace) is a classical example of Methodist autobiography.[2]

Several Puritan works were translated into Welsh during this same period. They were used for the purposes of evangelism and edification by the 'awakened' clergy of Anglicanism and Dissent

---

[1] xxxiv.33.
[2] Reprinted in 1949. References to the Vicar's book are on pp. 22 and 51 of this edition.

alike. Among the most popular were Joseph Alleine's *An Alarm to the Unconverted*, Richard Baxter's *Call to the Unconverted*, John Bunyan's *Pilgrim's Progress* and *Come and Welcome to Jesus Christ*, and Thomas Shepard's *The Sincere Convert*. As their titles suggest, these books were characterised by simplicity, directness, and warmth in their appeal for personal, close dealings with God.

How widely they were read, however, must be assessed by factors other than their availability. Ninety per cent of the population was illiterate, a situation which Griffith Jones sought to remedy by his Schools. In terms of attendance at these schools he achieved staggering success. Between 1737 and 1761 there were 3225 Schools in 1600 different locations, made up of more than 200,000 scholars, that is, nearly half the total population.[1] The general poverty of the people was another factor which militated against a wide readership. Griffith Jones wrote in one financially testing time, 1747, 'Very few of the Welsh people, even of the farmers, and scarce any at all of the labourers, can at present afford to buy books; all the lower ranks of people here being much reduced in their circumstances.'[2] Such facts show why unbelief held sway for at least the first four decades of the century. As a result, the popular teaching which passed for truth in the churches was a travesty of the pure Gospel of Christ.

One widespread influence responsible for this state of affairs was Deism. Its leading representatives and propagators were John Locke, John Toland, and Matthew Tindal. For these men, human reason was the measure of both truth and reality. Revelation, Scripture, the mysteries of the Christian Faith, miracles, the atonement, and human destiny were all subjected to its evaluation. Whatever was unacceptable or incomprehensible by that standard was deemed to be superstitious or false. Christ's coming was presented in terms of buttressing natural reasonableness and morality, as reflected in the titles of their books: Locke's *The Reasonableness of Christianity* (1695); Toland's *Christianity Not Mysterious* (1696); and Tindal's *Christianity as old as the Creation* (1730). The direct tendency, if not intention, of such principles was to produce the loss of a sense of God and of a sense of sin. Sadly, many religious leaders adopted these ideas, creating throughout the land an aversion to divine truth. In this way many were led astray into the maze of theoretical speculation if not into downright scepticism.

[1] Geraint H. Jenkins, *Hen Filwr Dros Grist*, 1983, tt. 18, 17.
[2] *Welch Piety* (1747), p. 4.

There were debates on these issues in Wales, too. Parts of Cardiganshire, Rowland's sphere of labour, witnessed a ferment of theological
discussion on them, especially after 1745. It was inevitable, therefore,
that before long the Methodists sought to expose the inadequacy of
reason, and the danger of rationalism, in matters of faith. Williams of
Pantycelyn does so relentlessly in Song 1 of his Welsh 'Poetical Relics'.
His treatment of the subject views man in his first state of innocence,
and then in his present state of sinful corruption. Of the former he
claims that man's reason could not fathom one part of a thousand in
the reality of nature around him. Apart from divine revelation he
could not name the animals, nor discern the mystery of conjugal union
with his wife. How much more necessary is that revelation now that
the divine image is in ruins after man's disastrous fall! Sin has
perverted and twisted every part of man's personality: intellect,
desire, will, temperament, conscience, gifts, memory, they are all 'in
Egyptian error, knowing nothing of God'.

> The crooked, straight appears, the truth he cannot see;
> He loves what's vile and tainted, and hates all purity;
> Indulges every pleasure, embraces every lust,
> Delights in total darkness; reject the light he must.

> So that man's highest reason, which now he boasts with might
> But sends him even further from heaven's pure shining light. . . .

> Nor can the light of nature, nor eye, nor hand supply
> Safe guide to heaven's glory, on them can none rely;
> Desire with all its branches, the instinct that's so strong,
> Drags reason's mightiest power relentlessly along.

With this last couplet Williams had demonstrated the most basic flaw
in the rationalists' position. Apart from God's grace, man's reason is
dominated by desire. Consequently, in the absence of the Gospel
revelation, 'the light of nature' leads to the carnal perversions and
superstitions of idolatry, culminating in the philosophical Athenians'
pathetic altar 'To the Unknown God'. Mercifully, however, God had
given man 'a shining light to lead him to heaven, a short while after his
fall'. That light, of course, was divine revelation, shining repeatedly in
promise and prophecy throughout the Old Testament, from the
reference in Genesis to 'the woman's seed' onwards.[1]

---

[1] CYN.i.629–33. For a discussion in Welsh of 'Rationalism' and related
issues in the period, see John Gwili Jenkins, *Hanfod Duw a Pherson Crist*,
1931; and R. Tudur Jones, *Hanes Annibynwyr Cymru*, 1966, tt. 136–40.

In his long poem *Golwg ar Deyrnas Christ* (A View of Christ's Kingdom), published in 1756, Williams approaches the matter from a different angle. Basing the work on Colossians 3:11 and 1 Corinthians 15:25, his concern is to show the futility of any teaching which by-passes Christ. The Son of God is at the centre of all things, from the eternal counsels of God to the realms of creation and providence, revelation and redemption. By contrast, the Deists 'give little place to Christ's merits, the efficacy of His blood, the excellence of His Person, as the only way of salvation'.[1] Between Deist and Methodist there could be no compromise, and the Great Awakening can only be fully understood as being a restoration of the authority of divine revelation.

A more subtle influence against vital Christianity in the eighteenth century was formalism, with its hatred of 'enthusiasm'. In effect, formalism was a denial of the place of emotion in religious experience. It created an image of piety which was sterile, theoretical, and impersonal. The charge of 'enthusiasm' was a favourite indictment ranged against the Awakening's leaders and subjects. Sometimes it was used to imply that Methodist preaching had abandoned reasoned exposition, and was nothing more than an inflated emotional exercise. This was shown to be demonstrably false in Rowland's case with the appearance of his soundly argued sermons in English in 1774. John Davies, the translator, stated in his 'Preface' that one reason for undertaking the work was because 'the Methodists in Wales have been represented as a set of ignorant, hot-headed Enthusiasts'.[2]

On other occasions the word was used as a synonym for 'extremism', or 'pretended inspiration'. Both usages betrayed a gross ignorance of the leaders' concern for experimental religion. To them life, light, power, authority, fire, and unction were the hallmarks of biblical Christianity. In controversy the lines were drawn on the difference between a 'head' and a 'heart' knowledge of Christ, between a merely 'intellectual' and a full-orbed 'spiritual' response to the Gospel message.

A notable defence of experimental religion was issued by Jonathan Edwards in 1746 under the title *The Religious Affections*. An early paragraph crystallises his argument:

'I am bold to assert that there never was any considerable change wrought in the mind or conversation of any person, by anything of a

---

[1] CYN.i.90; cf. Derec Llwyd Morgan, *Y Diwygiad Mawr*, 1981, tt. 219–20.
[2] *Eight Sermons*, 'To the Reader.'

religious nature that ever he read, heard, or saw, that had not his affections moved. Never was a natural man engaged earnestly to seek his salvation; never were any such brought to cry after wisdom, and lift up their voice for understanding, and to wrestle with God in prayer for mercy; and never was one humbled and brought to the foot of God, from anything that ever he heard or imagined of his own unworthiness and deservings of God's displeasure; nor was ever one induced to fly for refuge unto Christ, while his heart remained unaffected. Nor was there ever a saint awakened out of a cold, lifeless frame, or recovered from a declining state in religion, and brought back from a lamentable departure from God, without having his heart affected. . . . The holy Scriptures do everywhere place religion very much in the affection; such as fear, hope, love, hatred, desire, joy, sorrow, gratitude, compassion, and zeal.'[1]

This was not to say that the Gospel appeal ignored a man's mind. On the contrary, access to men's hearts was through their minds. The rationalists and religious formalists, however, stopped short of the Gospel method when they confined religion to the mind. Furthermore, a desire to see such signs of genuine spiritual change did not mean that they could be brought about by a premeditated and humanly engineered plan of action. They were acknowledged to be solely the result of the Spirit's activity, at once profuse and powerful.

Under such divine impressions the leaders preached with extraordinary penetration and effect, with burning conviction and urgency. It was this immediacy and fervency in their dealings as they preached that often brought upon them from their opponents the charge of spiritual delusion and anarchy. For the leaders, however, this was no worked-up fanaticism or hysteria. The views afforded them of the sinner's predicament and danger affected them deeply, and this, together with the Spirit's unction, compelled them to deal closely and passionately with men's souls.

This was in sharp contrast to the cold detachment and objectivity of the sermons of most of their contemporaries. The latter had produced an age of lifeless, formal religion in which eternal destinies seemed to be of no consequence. Their ideal was Archbishop Tillotson (1630–94), whose polished, stylish sermons were widely admired. In the diocese of St David's they were held out as the supreme example of pulpit erudition and oratory.[2] However, such

---

[1] *Select Works of Jonathan Edwards*, vol. iii, 1961, pp. 30–31.
[2] Geraint H. Jenkins, *Literature, Religion and Society in Wales 1660–1730*, 1980, p. 16.

sermons seldom touched men's hearts. They failed to do so not merely because their form was aesthetically too pleasing, but mainly because their content was less than evangelical, as Whitefield realised. He brought upon himself a veritable hornet's nest of abuse when he publicly criticised Tillotson in 1740 as one who 'knew of no other than a bare historical faith', and was 'ignorant' of 'our justification by faith alone'.[1]

Somehow men felt an irresistible constraint, an inner and inexplicable attraction, to hear the preachers of the Great Awakening. There was a plainness and directness about their dealing with souls, a simplicity and homeliness about their style, which was compelling and attractive. They would go away, many of them, with a lasting impression on their hearts and a new direction in their lives. Take the testimony of Ioan Thomas to Howel Harris's preaching:

'I was led to go in spite of all reasoning, even though I could not think nor know what carried me, nor what purpose I had in going, but that I went with as ardent a desire as I had gone many times to my favourite pleasures; which desire I had never before felt in going to hear a sermon. . . . The sight of him won my affections; in my view, at times his countenance shone as an angel. . . . I remember he said words such as these: "You may often have turned the pages of the Bible for forty years, and yet you know no more of God than a dog or a pig; you may have been often on your knees praying, a very religious man as you thought, but you have not once prayed from your heart; and except God has your heart, He will yet see the devils tearing your soul and body apart in the hour of death, and at the day of judgment; my arrows are sharp; May God send His words like bullets to shoot through your heart!" As I considered these words, I realised that I was that man.'[2]

Note the frequent allusions to the 'heart' in this passage. To understand the full significance of this it is useful to turn to the classical defence of the Awakening by Williams of Pantycelyn, *Ateb Philo Evangelius* (Philo Evangelius's Answer):

'With the heart man believes to salvation. Although a man has believed some body of divinity, unless those principles which he has believed in his head have taken root in his heart so that he loves God's Son, rejoices in His salvation, denies himself, takes up his cross, follows the Lamb through all manner of reproach, his knowledge only makes him boast. He is blind and cannot see far. He

---

[1] DAL, 482–4; *The Daily Advertiser*, No. 2942, Thursday, June 26, 1740.
[2] J. Dyfnallt Owen (gol.), *Rhad Râs Ioan Thomas*, 1949, tt. 28–9.

has never felt the authority of God's grace within, and how can such a person love the Saviour of the world?'[1]

Before a man's life can be changed the Gospel must penetrate the very citadel of his personality; its message must take root in his 'heart'. The 'authority of God's grace' must be 'felt . . . within'. This was the distinguishing characteristic of the Great Awakening. In Wales, Rowland was one of the first to prove its reality.

[1] GWP.ii.24–5.

'Never was the world fuller of hindrances to the good work of stirring ourselves up to lay hold on God; and yet this work was never more necessary, since we have reason to fear that God is now about leaving our land and departing from us. It is now, if ever, we should stir ourselves up to lay hold on Him, as the prophet says, and by earnest resolution, fixed thoughts, and flaming affections, solicit His return and stay with us.'

GRIFFITH JONES
in August, 1735

'Conscious of the importance of the vocation wherewith he was called, he applied all his time and attention to that one great concern, which came upon him daily, the care of the churches. In his preaching he inculcated the plainest and most obvious duties of Christianity, which he enforced upon the minds of his hearers with a truly Christian zeal, and in so interesting a manner, that none could depart unaffected or unedified.'

MEMORIAL TO GRIFFITH JONES IN LLANDDOWROR CHURCH

4

'Begotten to the New Gospel'

When Daniel Rowland's godly grandfather died, he seems to have sensed a glorious entrance into another world. He is reputed to have said, 'I am now in the air among the chariots',[1] a direct allusion to the manner of the prophet Elijah's departure from this life. The next member of the family to prove such fiery experiences in the tradition of Elijah was to be Rowland himself. Certainly the comparison was fitting when applied to his Elijah-like ministry of powerful words and remarkable events.

Although both Daniel Rowland's father and his brother were clergymen, neither of them seems to have been distinguished for godliness. Daniel Rowland senior had been ordained deacon on 19 September 1695 when 36 years of age, serving as curate of Llanbadarn Trefeglwys in the south-west corner of Cardiganshire. He was ordained priest on May 30, 1697, and two weeks later moved to Llangeitho to become rector of the parish church. Within a year he was in trouble with the authorities over the payment of ecclesiastical dues. With two sons and four daughters to raise, he must have been glad of extra income provided him in 1708 when the curacies of Llangybi and Llanfair Clydogau, and the vicarage of Nantcwnlle were added to his charge. His ministerial usefulness remains a matter of speculation, although both his sons followed him into the ministry. He died on April 24, 1731, having resigned from Llangeitho on September 4, 1730. His wife, Jennett, was nearly ten years younger than her husband. She was the daughter of a local farmer, Rhys Thomas of Wenallt. She died in 1736 at the age of 68.[2]

The father was succeeded in the Rectory at Llangeitho by his older

[1] xxix.96.
[2] NLW Church in Wales, SD/BR/4, pp. 14, 196; NLW MS 1626; xxxvi.24; lix.32; HMGC.i.124–5; D. Worthington, *Cofiant y Parch. Daniel Rowland*, 1923, 'Pedigree of the Rowlands of Nantcwnlle and Llangeitho.'

son, John. Born probably in 1703, John's ministerial career began
with his ordination as deacon to serve under his father at Llangeitho
and Nantcwnlle on 11 September 1726. For some reason he moved
to North Wales in the following year, serving as curate in the two
small parishes of Llanenddwyn and Llanddwywe in Merioneth-
shire. Possibly on account of failing health his father desired his
return, and on September 1, 1728, John Rowland was ordained
priest by the Bishop of St David's to serve once more at Llangeitho
and Nantcwnlle. John duly replaced his father, at Llangeitho in
1730 and at Nantcwnlle in the following year.[1] By 1733 the
curacies of Llanddewibrefi and Llanbadarn Odwyn had been added
to his charge. His Sunday schedule was a busy one, with the
Rectory at Llangeitho serving as his base.

'He would this Sunday set out three miles west to Nantcwnlle for
prayers at 8.0 a.m., return to Llangeitho for prayers at 10, then a
mile's tramp eastwards to Llanbadarn Odwyn, with a steep hill to
reach it, for service at noon. The afternoon service at 4.0 o'clock at
Llanddewibrefi involved a return journey of 10 miles. That makes 18
miles of hard going with no motor-car. The following Sunday he
would vary his schedule by beginning at Llanbadarn at 8.0,
Llangeitho as usual at 10, Nantcwnlle at 12, and then probably
straight across the valley for seven miles to Llanddewibrefi by 4
o'clock. The total on this Sunday might be two miles less. It is little
wonder that he could only manage a sermon on alternate Sundays at
each of his four churches, the sermon being scheduled an hour later
than the usual time for prayers.[2]

The 1733 Deanery Returns note that the rectory at Llangeitho was
'new built and not quite finished', but that the 'minister resides in it'.
John did not stay there much longer. His marriage in August of 1735
to Anne Jenkins took them to her native village of Llanddewibrefi to
a house of their own. They had two sons, one of whom, also called
John, became a clergyman with Methodist sympathies and translated into Welsh Whitefield's last sermon in Britain.[3]

[1] NLW Church in Wales, SD/BR/4, pp. 162–3, 176, 196, 201; vii.34–5;
HMGC.i.127–8
[2] NLW MS 9145F; E. D. Jones on 'Llangeitho' in *Archaeologia Cambrensis*,
vol. xcix.152.
[3] NLW 9145F; HMGC.i.129; D. Worthington, *ibid.*; HMGC.ii.102;
*Pregeth a bregethwyd gan y Parchedig George Whitefield . . . Awst 30,
1769, ar ei ymadawiad i Georgia.* Cyfieithwyd gan y Parchedig Mr. John
Rowlands, 1771; xxxix.74.

There is some uncertainty as to the date of Daniel Rowland's birth. Most writers have accepted 1713, but the carefully reasoned arguments of E. D. Jones in favour of 1711 are convincing. In favour of that date are the two gravestones, the second of which is the one now to be seen in Llangeitho parish church. The other was placed as a hearth stone in Troed-y-rhiw, Nantcwnlle. Both of these state that Rowland was 79 when he died in 1790. Similar testimony to Rowland's age is borne by one of his Methodist fellow-workers, Peter Williams, on the title-page of his elegy to Rowland. Another consideration is the fact that ecclesiastical law did not normally allow men to be ordained under 23 years of age. Whitefield was surprised that the Bishop of Gloucester had waived the rule in his own case, ordaining him at the age of 21. Exemption might have been granted to Whitefield because he had an Oxford education behind him. Much evidently depended on the bishop and on the candidate. Nicholas Clagett was Bishop of St David's when Rowland sought ordination, and he was known to be strict on this issue.[1]

At the time of Rowland's birth the family was living at a house called Pantybeudy in Nantcwnlle, a mere three miles from where he spent his entire ministry. Edward Morgan, in his biography of Rowland, tells of a remarkable deliverance which spared Daniel's life when he was a child. 'A large stone fell down from the top of the chimney, directly upon the spot where he had been sitting by the fire only a few minutes before.'[2] Such an escape from injury or even death would have been acknowledged by Rowland in later life in terms of God's sovereign and merciful control.

For his early education Rowland went to Pontygido near Llanarth in Cardiganshire to study under a very able schoolmaster 'by the name of Pugh, who was a distinguished Greek scholar'. The evidence of familiarity with classical works which appears in Rowland's sermons might be traced to his influence. Rowland frequently wrote Latin inscriptions on the books in his possession, and Latin books were included in his library. Another source of classical allusions for Rowland, as J. C. Ryle points out, would have been the many Puritan authors he treasured so much. Before his ordination in 1734, Rowland also spent some time at Hereford

[1] HMGC.i.130–1; MS.i.85. For Nicholas Clagett see *Dictionary of National Biography*.
[2] HMGC.i.131; MR,10.

Grammar School.[1]

From personal acquaintance with some who had known Rowland, John Owen, writing in 1839, gives this picture of Rowland as
a young man: 'He possessed very quick parts, and made rapid
progress in his learning. . . . He was remarkable for natural vivacity,
and very adroit in all the sports and corrupting amusements of the
age. He was of the middle size, of a firm make, quick and nimble in
his action, and foremost in all the youthful feats of the day.' Others
add that he was active and energetic, that he had a light complexion,
and always moved and spoke with great rapidity. The testimony of
one of his daughters confirmed that impression. 'My father was short
and of an iron constitution.' 'He never spared himself.' 'He was very
swift of foot.' 'He was very passionate. His heat was intense at times,
and in that intense heat he was awful.'[2]

It is difficult to ascertain when Rowland finished his education. He
may have been involved in running his mother's old farm of
Wennallt, next to the church at Llangeitho, for some time before his
ordination. The date of this last event, however, is certain. Rowland
was ordained deacon by the Bishop of St David's at Duke Street
Chapel in Westminster (London) on Sunday the 10th of March,
1734.[3] For the ceremony he walked all the way from Llangeitho to
the English capital and back, an indication of his physical fitness. He
may have been the only ordinand in the company of drovers from
nearby Tregaron who frequently made the same journey to sell their
cattle in the metropolis. On his return he carried with him the
bishop's licence to serve the curacies of Llangeitho and Nantcwnlle
for £10 per annum.

Less than two miles to the north of Llangeitho lay the Davies farm
of Caerllugest. It was here that Rowland found a wife, Elinor, whom

---

[1] D. Edwardes, *Plwyf Nantcwnlle Hen a Diweddar* (1913), tud. 3; See also
Edward Richard in DWB; J. C. Ryle, *The Christian Leaders in the
Eighteenth Century*, 1902, p. 199. For details of the books in Rowland's
library see xxxiv.86; xxxv.31; xxxvi.29; xxxviii.25–8; xl.24, 44. One of the
Latin books was Peter Martyr's commentary on 1 Corinthians. Another
book, Edmund Leigh's *Critica Sacra*, assumed a knowledge of Latin,
Hebrew and Greek. D. J. Odwyn Jones, *Daniel Rowland Llangeitho*, 1938,
tud. 6.
[2] JO, 8, 9; D. Davies, *Amddiffyniad y Parch. Daniel Rowland* (1906),
tt. 110–111; JO, 66.
[3] NLW Church in Wales, SD/BR/4, p. 211. For Duke Street Chapel see
xxxv.80–83.

he married before the end of 1734. They lived there for about a year, until the rectory at Llangeitho became vacant on John's removal to Llanddewibrefi. The birth of their first son, John, on October 14, 1735, is recorded in a Latin commentary by Wolfgang Musculus.[1] As this was kept at Caerllugest, they must have been living there at that time.

During the period of these great changes in his domestic affairs a great change came over Rowland's spiritual state, and this inevitably affected his ministry. Until that time he, as well as his brother, had been a stranger to God's grace. John was notorious for his drinking, Daniel for his levity and worldliness. Their sermons would have been, at best, about striving for human 'goodness' by keeping God's law, their churches only sparsely attended.

Some thirty miles to the south, at Llanddowror, Griffith Jones was exercising a very different ministry by his evangelical preaching. He seemed 'to have a spring of thirst in him for the salvation of souls', compelling him to preach wherever he had opportunity. His fame was widespread, his preaching lively, and his congregations large. It was said of him, that 'a sacred pathos distinguished his address. He spoke naturally, for he spoke feelingly. Everything he uttered bore the stamp of sincerity. Great was the power of the Divine Spirit that accompanied the word . . . CHRIST was ALL to him; and it was his greatest delight to publish and exalt the unsearchable riches of his Redeemer.'[2] He was the instrument of Rowland's spiritual awakening. In the words of one critic, ridiculing the Methodists, Rowland was 'begotten to the new Gospel by our own dear Daddy, Griffith Jones'.[3]

Very little is known of the manner of Jones' conversion to Christ. Howel Harris once heard someone 'saying of Mr. Griffith Jones' conversion, how he was dead two hours in body, quite dead, yet in soul the same as usual, and when he awoke, he said if he should have another fit, he should go to heaven'.[4] Evidently, the Spirit's influences upon him at the time were powerful. They also proved

---

[1] HMGC.i.133–4.
[2] Mary Clement (ed.), *Correspondence and Minutes of the S.P.C.K. Relating to Wales*, 1952, p. 336; *A Collection of Valuable Tracts . . . A Summary of the Life and Character of the Rev. Mr. Griffith Jones*, 1780, pp. 33–4.
[3] *A Second Letter to the Rev. George Whitefield*, 1751, pp. 4–5.
[4] HVP, 22.

lasting and fruitful. Throughout his life he suffered from asthma, but he used to say 'that all sickness was more tolerable than one sin'.

Like Amos the prophet, Jones was called from the sheepfold to minister God's Word. A grammar school at Carmarthen provided him with education. One of his early appointments was as curate at Laugharne in Carmarthenshire, made famous in this century as the scene of Dylan Thomas's literary efforts. At one time he felt drawn to missionary service in India, but after consultation on the matter with the Society for Promoting Christian Knowledge, he decided against it. 'The extremely miserable blindness of his own country', and 'the prospect of doing more service to religion in his native country' were the reasons he gave for his decision.[1]

At Laugharne in 1713 there were evident tokens of blessing on his ministry. He began preaching outside his own parish, a practice which displeased some of the clergy, and elicited from Jones the defence to the bishop which has already been noted. In his elegy to Jones, William Williams describes him at this period as 'crowding the churches to capacity, transforming graveyards into churches.' A contemporary account vividly mirrors this picture: 'When Mr. Jones is invited to preach anywhere, and also when he preaches in his own church, in which there does not belong (as parishioners) save 10 or 12 small families, it is to be admired what a numerous congregation he has to administer to . . . having generally above five or six hundred auditors, nay, sometimes 1,000.' Another estimate speaks of three or four thousand following him, many of them Nonconformists, a testimony to both the orthodoxy and the power of his preaching. The crowds came mostly from South Wales, with some from the English borders. When they arrived at Laugharne, some of them were unable to gain access to the church on account of the numbers present.[2] Two years later he was presented with the living of Llanddowror, a mere five miles to the West, and here he was to remain for the rest of his life.

Jones preached feelingly, often with tears running down his cheeks, terrifying the ungodly with the evil and danger of sin, persuading his hearers to flee to Christ for salvation. 'You may be

[1] For Griffith Jones, see DWB; xxvi.10; Mary Clement, *op. cit.*, pp. 57, 62.
[2] CYN.i.439; xxix.3; Thomas Levi, *Casgliad o Hen Farwnadau Cymreig*, 1872, tud. 53; (John Evans), *Some Account of the Welch Charity Schools* (1752), pp. 17–19, 32–33.

poor, and stay poor, and yet go to heaven at last; you may be in sickness or in prison and stay that way, and yet get to heaven after you die; you may be without much education or learning, and yet go to heaven when you leave this world; but without this change, without being a new creature [he was preaching on Galatians 6:15], it is impossible for you ever to get to heaven.' With such plainness in mind, William Williams wrote of him, 'Here's the man who broke forth a little before the break of dawn . . . a bright, glorious star, shining amid the night's threatening clouds', a man whose 'clear trumpet call' was heard by many, Rowland among them.[1] In time, Jones' home at Llanddowror became a virtual 'school of the prophets', a fact which drew upon him the wrath of a neighbouring clergyman:

'Daniel Rowland, Howel Davies, clerk, and Howel Harris, layman (and gentleman taylor, if I am not misinformed) were the first preachers of Methodism in our county. . . . All three came out of Mr. Jones' shop with their heads turned exactly the same way. How long Rowland was his pupil before he was in orders, I know not, but it is certain, that as soon as he was admitted deacon, he came to Llanddowror, and stayed some months with Mr. Jones, and preached in his church often, if not every Sunday during his stay there.'[2]

Rowland would hardly have associated with Jones, who was so notorious for his evangelistic zeal, unless God's grace had wrought a marvellous change in his life. After such a change it would have been both desirable and profitable to spend time under instruction from Jones.

A graphic account of that momentous event in Rowland's life, although written in 1818, recognises its centrality to his subsequent life and ministry.

'One time when he (Jones) was preaching in a churchyard, he saw a young man in the crowd, who appeared restless and rebellious. He observed him for a moment, pointed at him, and with an expression of gentle compassion, exclaimed, "Oh for a word to reach your heart, young man!" Soon it was evident that his restlessness had ceased, and he listened earnestly for the rest of the sermon; and who was this, but Daniel Rowland, the curate of the parish. That was the place, and the way this great man was convicted: great before, in his hostility to

---

[1] Griffith Jones's sermon is quoted by Geraint H. Jenkins in *Hen Filwr Dros Grist*, 1983, tud. 11; CYN.i.440, 438.
[2] (John Evans), *Some Account of the Welch Charity Schools*, pp. 78–9.

Christ's Gospel and Kingdom, great after that in godliness, and one of the most eminent ministers that Wales ever saw.'[1]

According to this statement, the place was either Llangeitho or Nantcwnlle, but other biographers of Rowland have located the scene at Llanddewibrefi, five miles to the east. Daniel may have preached there on occasions, but strictly speaking he was not curate of that parish. The fact that the scene was set in the churchyard may be accounted for either because the crowds were too great, or because the use of the church itself had been refused by the Rowland brothers. As Rowland is represented as having been hostile to the Gospel for some time, and as being the curate of the parish, this preaching occasion must have taken place in the winter of 1734–35. The result, however, is not in question. From that time Daniel Rowland became a changed man, and he sought the company and counsel of Griffith Jones at Llanddowror.

Neither his domestic nor his parish circumstances would have allowed Rowland a prolonged stay with Jones. The distance of some thirty miles between Llangeitho and Llanddowror, however, would not have made regular visits impractical, and both men would have benefited from such an arrangement. It gave Rowland the opportunity to learn from Jones the basic elements of the evangelical faith, and to observe his faithful ministerial labours. Jones, in turn, was glad of help from Rowland. Since 1731 he had become increasingly more involved with free ('charity') schools in the Llanddowror area, a project which he himself had initiated. Now he was responsible for the supervision of their teachers and the provision of their books.[2]

Another aspect of their association during this time would have made a lasting impression on Rowland. For the success of his endeavours, Jones relied on the Holy Spirit. This is clear from something he had written in 1733.

'I wish I had more of the unction of this Holy Spirit to carry me through the work of my day, and to assist me to live in a closer communion with God. It has sometimes refreshed my soul to consider that among all the precious promises in the Holy Scriptures, there is not one more full, and worded in stronger terms of assurance,

[1] John Owen, *Golygiad ar Adfywiad Crefydd yn yr Eglwys Sefydledig oddeutu y flwyddyn 1737*, 1818, tud. 4–5 (nodyn).
[2] F. A. Cavenagh, *The Life and Work of Griffith Jones, Llanddowror*, 1930, pp. 36, 37.

than that of the heavenly Father giving the Holy Spirit to them that ask Him, Luke 11:13. And this should put us upon asking in faith, which can never fail to succeed.'[1]

Rowland still had much to learn of Gospel principles and of ministerial duties, but the experience at Llanddowror provided a strong foundation for future usefulness.

The time to his ordination as priest would have passed all too quickly. He was ordained by the Bishop of St David's at his chapel in Abergwili, near Carmarthen, on August 31, 1735.[2] He was now in full orders. An even greater change, however, had taken place in his preaching. On account of both content and style it was attracting notice beyond the bounds of the remote parish of Llangeitho. The hand of God, as well as that of the bishop, had evidently come upon him.

[1] Edward Morgan (ed.), *Letters of the Rev. Griffith Jones*, 1832, p. 27.
[2] NLW Church in Wales, SD/BR/4, p. 225.

'When men don't preach much about the danger of damnation, there is want of good preaching. . . . If sinners don't hear often of Judgment and Damnation, few will be converted. . . . Ministers should be sons of thunder: Men had need have storms in their hearts, before they will betake themselves to Christ for refuge. . . . If they be but thoroughly convinced of their danger, that will make them go to God and take pains.'

SAMUEL STODDARD
(the predecessor of Jonathan Edwards)
in a sermon at Northampton, Massachusetts, 1723

'When men feel in themselves the heavy burden of sin, see damnation to be the reward of it, behold with the eye of their mind the horror of hell, they tremble, they quake, and are inwardly touched with sorrowfulness of heart, and cannot but accuse themselves, and open their grief unto Almighty God, and call unto Him for mercy. This being done seriously, their mind is so occupied, partly with sorrow and heaviness, partly with an earnest desire to be delivered from this danger of hell and damnation, that all desire of meat and drink is laid apart, and loathing of all worldly things and pleasures comes in its place. So that nothing then likes them more than to weep, to lament, to mourn; and both with words and behaviour of body to show themselves weary of life.'

JOHN WESLEY
in 1746, quoting the Homilies of the Church of England

5

'The Needle of the Law'

During the winter months of 1735 Rowland had much to occupy his mind. With the birth of his son John in October and the prospect of moving house there were extra responsibilities requiring his attention. In addition, according to one writer, he had 'two small farms, one on each side of Llangeitho. The parsonage where he lived, was attached to one of these farms, Wenallt. The other, Meidrim, was a little way off.' For convenience, he brought all the farm produce to the more accessible Wenallt storehouses.[1]

Rowland now devoted every spare moment to diligent study. In this he was prompted by the example and advice of Griffith Jones, but even more by a new thirst for the Scripture in his own heart. The Word of God so mastered his attention that many years later his son could affirm that he 'knew almost the whole Bible, as the expression is, by heart; so that hardly a passage could be mentioned to him, that he could not tell the chapter and verse where it was to be found'. When at home, he spent most of his time in his study, and it was almost impossible to get him out of it, according to the testimony of his daughter.[2] Early in 1738 Howel Harris heard that Rowland was studying so hard that he 'lost his hair and sleep'.

Such dedication to study by Rowland would not have been possible without the encouragement and help of his wife, Elinor. Her family heritage included a strong Puritan strain of piety. Her grandfather had been a Nonconformist minister in the area, whose dying words, 'I now begin to have foretastes of the country to which I am going', were reported on one occasion to Howel Harris.[3] Rowland's spiritual awakening would have gladdened the hearts of

[1] Owen Jones, *Some of the Great Preachers of Wales*, 1886, p. 55.
[2] JO, 64, 66; cf. D. Davies, *Amddiffyniad y Parch. Daniel Rowland* (1906), tud. 111.
[3] xxix.95, 96.

this Nonconformist remnant, not least the heart of their minister, Philip Pugh. His interest and support proved invaluable to Rowland during the period when his life and preaching were so radically transformed.

Charity, piety, and diligence characterised Pugh's life and ministry. Having had a thoroughly Nonconformist education, he had been called to minister with others in a very wide area of Cardiganshire which included Rowland's parishes. Nonconformity taught him to monitor carefully his inner life and maintain a scripturally balanced God-centredness. 'Two things are represented to us in Scripture as worth buying, truth (as Proverbs 23:23), and time (Ephesians 5:16).'

In Pugh's ministry there was both fervency and urgency. 'With this I felt as if a divine power came upon my mind, and those words blazed through my heart, "Be not afraid, I am with you". I had immense liberty to declare the words of eternal life to my fellow-men.' At the same time, he feared lest at any time he should be unfruitful. 'I do not feel for the salvation of my fellow-men', was his frequent complaint. He longed for more of God, and for more effectiveness on the Lord's day. 'O! may God be pleased to take me in His hand this day, and bring me into His banqueting-house, and draw me from every vain thing which saps my faith, cools my love, and makes me unfit for His holy work.'

During Pugh's long ministry of fifty years he had to contend much for the faith. The particular controversies which disturbed the peace of his congregations included Arminianism (which made salvation a partnership between God and man), Arianism (which denied the Deity of Christ), and Antinomianism (which claimed that Christians did not have to obey God's law as a rule of life). He was often misunderstood because of his eirenic spirit. 'I stand alone, blamed by many for my leaning towards the Methodists', he wrote in 1744, 'and by them I am not altogether acceptable because I am not for them in all things. Lord, I long to be thine, to be led in thy way . . . whatever may be man's opinion. Let me live by the light I have and love each one who loves Christ.'

Symbolic of Pugh's all-round Christianity was a copy of James Ussher's *Body of Divinity*, in which he wrote his name in 1724, and which Rowland also autographed in 1740.[1] Its evangelical Calvinism typified both men. It also suggested the close links between

[1] For Philip Pugh, see DWB; and in Welsh, Eifion Evans, 'Phylip Pugh 1679–1760' in *Y Cylchgrawn Efengylaidd*, Medi-Hydref, 1979, tt. 140–45.

them. When Rowland was as yet under early Gospel impressions, Pugh seems to have been instrumental in giving him counsel as to personal faith and public ministry.

At this period of his life, Rowland's preaching brought upon him the nickname of 'the angry clergyman' (*y ffeiriad crac*). The reason for this is given by John Owen in this way:

'What he preached at first was the law, in its high and minute demands, and in its awful threatenings. He stood, as it were, on Mount Sinai, and loudly proclaimed eternal perdition to a sinful world. Awful and extremely terrific was his message; nothing but the consuming flashes and dreadful thunders of the law, with hardly anything like the joyful sound of the Gospel. Endless condemnation, deserved by sinners, was what he set forth with unusual power and energy. His own spirit seemed to have been filled with great and awful terror. He appeared as if he wished to kindle the fire of hell around the transgressors of God's law, that he might terrify them. He unfolded the indignation of heaven against sin with amazing clearness, earnestness, and vigour.'[1]

Edward Morgan says that the texts he chose at this time were those which warn and threaten sinners with God's displeasure, 'The wicked shall be turned into hell', 'These shall go away into everlasting punishment', 'The great day of His wrath is come'. Ryle's explanation for this strain of preaching still stands, 'He began to preach like a man in earnest, and to speak and act like one who had found out that sin, and death, and judgment, and heaven, and hell, were great realities.'[2] God's law in all its holiness and spirituality had been applied to his own heart. Condemnatory Scriptures took on personal meaning with great conviction. The realisation which this had brought to his own soul he sought to communicate to others.

This kind of preaching contrasted greatly with what had gone before in his ministry. Now there was directness, urgency, and purpose. There was great solemnity in his manner, and a more biblical content in his matter. The majesty of God seemed to consume him with zeal and compassion. He saw the souls of men as unutterably precious, and judgment as alarmingly imminent. The

[1] JO, 18, 15, cf. the Welsh account in John Owen, *Coffhad am y Parch. Daniel Rowlands*, 1839, tud. 17. The use of the Welsh 'crac' in Cardiganshire and Carmarthenshire signifies 'angry', 'annoyed', 'cross'. The references to Rowland as 'the mad clergyman' is derived from this, as in the phrase 'he was mad with them'.
[2] MR, 11; J. C. Ryle, *The Christian Leaders of England in the Eighteenth Century*, 1902, p. 184.

Holy Spirit's energies attended his endeavours in such a way that the whole neighbourhood was stirred.

'The excitement made on the minds of the people under his preaching from the very beginning of his conversion was most surprising. The impression on the hearts of most persons was so awful and distressing, as if they saw the end of the world drawing near, or as if they perceived hell ready to swallow them up! His fame went through all the country, and the people went from all parts to hear him. Not only the churches were filled, but also the churchyards too. It is said that the people were under such deep convictions under his sermons, that numbers of them, unable to stand, lay down on the ground in the churchyard of Nantcwnlle, which is very large. They were so thick on the ground that it would not be easy for a person to pass by without stumbling against some of them.'[1]

Before this time, the understanding of the people relating to God's law must have been superficial and they would have assumed their own abilities to meet its demands. To the real meaning of sin, in all its inward ugliness, power, and corruption, they were total strangers. Now, however, at the sight of their guilt, impotence, and danger their fears were aroused.

A close exposition and application of God's law in its spiritual comprehensiveness, though unpremeditated in the case of Rowland, was part of the Protestant tradition of preaching. Later in his ministry, he would have subscribed to the saying of the English Reformer, John Bradford, that 'the right way to go unto heaven is to sail by hell'. John Bunyan's 'Interpreter' in *Pilgrim's Progress* demonstrates to Christian the use of the law and the necessity for the Gospel. Sweeping a dusty room without first sprinkling water merely disturbs and redistributes the particles of dust. 'The Law, instead of cleansing the heart from sin, doth revive, put strength into, and increase it in the soul, even as it doth reveal and forbid it, but doth not give power to subdue. . . . When the Gospel comes in . . . so is sin vanquished and subdued, and the soul made clean, through the faith of it, and consequently fit for the King of Glory to inhabit.' Another Puritan, George Swinnock, sums up their relationship to one another in preaching thus: 'Use the needle of the Law to make way for the thread of the Gospel.'[2]

[1] MR, 14.
[2] Bradford is quoted in Ian Brewer (ed.), *William Perkins*, 1970, p. 336; Bunyan in *Pilgrim's Progress*, 1977, pp. 26–7; and Swinnock in *Works*, vol. i, 1868, p. 326.

William Williams, of Pantycelyn, depicts this period in Rowland's life in his elegy:

> His name was Boanerges,
> Son of thunder, flaming, true;
> Shaking heaven and earth together
> With a voice both strong and new;
> 'Come! Awake!' his voice in echo
> Calls to all, 'our town's ablaze.
> Flee this moment without turning;
> God to ashes all will raze.'
>
> These were days like Sinai's glory,
> Sound of trumpet, sight of smoke,
> Storm and lightning, fire and tempest,
> Voice of God that terror spoke.
>
> Five Welsh counties heard the thunder,
> And with awesome, fearful dread,
> Fell with slaughter and with terror
> On the ground, in heaps as dead.[1]

Williams also makes it clear that what began thus at Llangeitho continued 'for some years', and spread over the hills in an easterly direction to Ystrad-ffin in the neighbouring county of Carmarthen, attracting people from other counties. The 'five Welsh counties' he mentions were Cardiganshire, Carmarthenshire, Glamorganshire, Breconshire, and Montgomeryshire (this latter accounts for Williams' reference to 'the North' in the elegy). Even at this early date of 1735–36 the crowds were making their way to Llangeitho, attracted irresistibly by the manifestation of God's presence.

The urgency which Rowland felt with regard to men's spiritual danger was compelling enough to induce him to preach outside his own parish. In doing so he had the practice of Griffith Joncs as a precedent, and that consideration might have set his mind at ease with regard to possible ecclesiastical repercussions.

Williams specifically mentions Ystrad-ffin in his elegy as one of the early scenes of Rowland's extra-parochial labours. John Owen heard from Rowland's son 'the circumstance that led him first to go and preach out of his own neighbourhood'. It seems that a farmer's wife, living in Ystrad-ffin, was visiting her sister who lived near

[1] CYN.i.582, 583.

Llangeitho. Out of curiosity she went to listen to 'the angry clergyman' preaching. To the surprise of her sister, she returned again the following Sunday, explaining that something Rowland had said in his sermon had been on her mind night and day in the intervening period. She persisted in undertaking the same journey of some twenty miles for many months. Eventually she ventured to approach Rowland with a request that he would come to Ystrad-ffin. 'Sir', she pleaded, 'if what you say to us is true, there are many in my neighbourhood in a most dangerous condition, going fast to eternal misery. For the sake of their souls, come over to preach to them.' Rowland agreed, provided permission could be obtained for him to do so. This was duly granted, and Rowland's first sermon there was blessed to the conversion of some thirty people.[1]

One prominent man whose life was changed through Rowland's ministry at Ystrad-ffin was a local landowner. Edward Morgan relates the following incident concerning him.

'A country squire of very loose and ungodly habits resided in that parish. He would go out with his hounds to hunt sometimes even on the Lord's day, and he went purposely, with some of his tenants, to hunt early that Sunday morning Rowland was to preach there. However, he returned home before time, and then prepared to go to church, with his companions in wickedness, in the most undaunted manner, for he had heard that some strange preacher was to be there that morning. He stood up in his pew, which was opposite the pulpit, in the most bold and independent manner possible, in order to put the minister out of countenance, as he thought. But Rowland soon entered into his subject in his usual way, which was most awful and terrific, and the people were filled with astonishment and alarm. The consequence was, that the stout-hearted man began to blush, fear, and quake exceedingly. . . . The poor, dejected, broken-hearted man was obliged to come down as soon as he could, and sit in a corner of the pew, ashamed and confounded, hanging down his head, and weeping most bitterly. He went to Rowland after the sermon was over, and confessed to him his great wickedness, and humbly entreated him to enter his house that day, and dine with him, which the servant of the Lord did. . . . All this took place in the presence of servants and ungodly friends. He afterwards manifested by his life and conversation a true change of heart, and regularly went to Llangeitho every sacrament Sunday at least.'[2]

In this way a pattern of regular visits was established by Rowland,

[1] JO, 18.
[2] MR, 15–16.

until permission was withdrawn.

Preaching abroad did not curtail Rowland's reforming activities at Llangeitho. There were still those who persisted in assembling for godless purposes on the Lord's day. On one occasion he resolved to take his message to them, as they showed no intention of attending church. 'He proclaimed the truth to them with great faithfulness and with great power,' says his biographer, 'and such was the effect, that there was no more assembling there.'[1]

As Rowland was now busy at Llangeitho, his journeys to Llanddowror would have been less frequent. For fellowship and counsel he would have turned, inevitably, to Philip Pugh, who was more accessible than Jones, and of similar evangelical principles and zeal. He was also a man of compassion and wisdom. Pugh had observed the alarm and despair which was common among many of the people under Rowland's ministry, and felt that the full offer of God's grace should be made to them. Morgan recounts the excellent advice which Pugh offered to Rowland in the light of this:

' "Preach the Gospel to the people, dear Sir, and apply the Balm of Gilead, the blood of Christ, to their spiritual wounds, and show the necessity of faith in the crucified Saviour." "I am afraid", said Rowland, "that I have not that faith myself in its vigour and full exercise." "Preach on it", said Pugh, "till you feel it in that way; no doubt it will come. If you go on preaching the law in this manner, you will kill half the people in the country, for you thunder out the curses of the law, and preach in such a terrific manner, that no-one can stand before you." '[2]

Pugh's sensitivity to Rowland's spiritual state proved invaluable. The advice was heeded, and the result was as Pugh had predicted.

Neither Rowland nor Pugh, however, could have foreseen how powerful and widespread the outcome would prove. 'The success which at this time attended Rowland's ministry', said Owen, 'was very remarkable.' Allowing for Rowland's preaching of the law to have lasted two years, from about 1737 he preached God's saving grace as well.

> He declared the law's strong terror
> For some years with great alarm;
> Many wounds were thus inflicted,
> Then he sang with Gospel charm;

[1] JO, 20.   [2] MR, 18–19.

He proclaimed divine salvation,
Full, complete, sufficient, free
Through the death of the Messiah
Once for ever on the Tree.

Now the power of his doctrines
Nourished faith in sinners' hearts,
By revealing the Atonement,
Ground of all salvation's parts;
God in manhood true residing,
Buying, by His anguish sore,
All of highest heaven's treasures
For believers evermore.[1]

As Rowland advanced in the Christian life, so he advanced in his understanding of Gospel principles. Already there were signs that he was being 'taught of God', deeply and solidly.

In the long poem, *Theomemphus*, Williams Pantycelyn recounts the experiences of the typical Methodist convert. The title character first comes under severe conviction of sin through the preaching of 'Boanerges', and is eventually brought to full Gospel liberty under the preaching of 'Evangelius'. The words of the former 'were like swords', and 'his eyes were like fire'. His preaching so pierced the conscience with the accusations of God's law that Theomemphus trembled, and his thoughts were in turmoil for 'more than sixty days'.

His words were claps of thunder, diverse and threatening all,
Or like the final trumpet, sent forth the dead to call;
Creating awful terror throughout the country round,
Some thousands heard his preaching, and fainted at the sound.

The latter, Evangelius, effectively applies the balm of God's grace. This is how he begins:

You listened to Boanerges, no mean, false prophet he,
Who warned of retribution to those who sinful be. . . .

Now I from heaven's counsels am also sent by grace,
By no means to dismantle the words he set in place;
But to the enslaved and broken, to say that they are free,
And tell with awesome wonder redemption's Jubilee.

[1] CYN.i.583.

In the imagery of Williams, Rowland was now both Boanerges and Evangelius, the complete Gospel preacher. He had still much to learn, but to his hearers the way of salvation had become clear:

> The Gospel that I'm preaching, none else will satisfy;
> Presenting this before you, that Jesus had to die,
> Declaring God's great promise, Christ's anguish and His woe,
> The death of all corruption to those who trust Him now.[1]

So Rowland's preaching now invited sinners to Christ, freely offered in the Gospel and embraced in personal faith.

By 1737 Rowland was travelling further afield for the purpose of preaching. A contemporary account of his early itinerant preaching is given by the Baptist historian, Joshua Thomas. 'I remember hearing him about 1737 in Carmarthenshire. There was a great crowd listening to him, and I heard some of the Nonconformists talking about the sermon on the way home. I remember some of their remarks, "We never heard the like in the Church of England except Mr. Griffith Jones. In our day there has not been such light in the Established Church".'[2]

The comparison with Griffith Jones by a Nonconformist writer is interesting. Evidently Rowland's sermon had impressed the Nonconformists as being evangelical, fervent, and solid. Already his orthodoxy was being recognised, and his usefulness extolled. The influence of both Philip Pugh and Jones was unmistakable. More than this, the power of God in his ministry was leaving a deep impression upon the lives of individuals and on a whole community.

[1] GWP.i.206, 207, 210, 240, 242.
[2] *Hanes y Bedyddwyr*, 1778, tud. 53.

'It appears to me that there is very little preaching of a lively kind in the kingdom. . . . Preaching ought not to be lifeless but lively, to teach, to exhort, to reprove, as Saint Paul says. . . . You are also aware how he speaks of the lively power and energy with which they ought to speak, who would approve themselves as good and faithful ministers of God, who must not make a parade of rhetoric only to gain esteem for themselves; but the Spirit of God ought to sound forth by their voice, so as to work with mighty energy.'

JOHN CALVIN
to the Protector Somerset, 1548

'Christ the text, and Christ the sermon.'

WILLIAM WILLIAMS
of Methodist preaching

6

'Glory in the Pulpit'

From the earliest days of his being wrought upon by God's Spirit, Rowland sought every opportunity to preach. Doors opened for him in neighbouring counties, and the circle of his ministry gradually widened. Consultation with Griffith Jones and Philip Pugh on the matter of extra-parochial activities would have strengthened his inclination and satisfied his conscience.

That Rowland consulted much with these men, with Jones particularly as a fellow Anglican, can hardly be questioned. Whom else could he have relied on for sympathetic understanding of his new experience and wise guidance for his very different ministry? Certainly not on his ecclesiastical superior. The bishop was very much an Establishment figure, satisfied with the generality of his clergy, abhorrent of 'enthusiasm' of the Griffith Jones variety, and hoping for preferment. When Howel Harris, on the advice of Griffith Jones, sought ordination in July 1736, the bishop refused 'with an offended look' and 'a severe check' for his evangelistic zeal.[1]

Inevitably, therefore, Rowland's early piety and ministry relied much on the influence of Griffith Jones. It was a piety which flourished within the framework of Scripture and prayer. In a treatise which was printed in 1738, Jones wrote that the great purpose for which Scripture was written was 'to teach us the way to heaven and make us wise to salvation, so that we might know God's will', and 'the accurate yardstick by which to measure every teaching'. In the same work, prayer is held out as the only means 'to receive guidance, help, and success in any undertaking'.[2] These were the foundational principles of the Christian life which Rowland heard from Jones.

From the time of his conversion Rowland evidently took the view that any reformation must begin at home. Equally, there was an

---

[1] BCM, 68.
[2] *Galwad at Orseddfaingc y Gras*, tt. 9, 11, 15.

awareness that God alone could prosper his labours and make his preaching fruitful. As well as applying himself to study, therefore, he applied himself to prayer.

'He used to go, in the beginning of his ministry, to the tops of the Aeron hills, to see the country around. . . . His mind was exceedingly affected with the still awful state of it, and he exclaimed most feelingly, "Alas, alas, I can see not so much as one house where prayer is offered." And then he interceded for them by prayer to his heavenly Father in the most powerful and affectionate manner. . . . He was viewing some time afterwards that vast country from the same place, but the aspect of things was quite changed, by God's blessing on the Word, and the effect on his mind was very different. "O! blessed be God", he cried, "I see *no* house today in all that country in which someone has not raised an altar to the Lord God Almighty."'[1]

This reformation in the religious aspects of Llangeitho did not happen overnight. It was brought about by sustained preaching coupled with the agonising prayer to which Rowland testified.

Another influence upon Rowland was the example of Jones' indefatigable labour. At Llanddowror in 1736 there was an increasing number coming to Jones for schooling. He was obliged to order a thousand copies, both of the Church catechisms and Psalms in Welsh to meet the demand.[2] In the winter of 1737–38 the schools were organised on a 'circulating' basis, the schoolmasters trained by Jones moving from one place to another. They were located in the counties of Cardigan, Carmarthen, Pembroke, and Brecon, and totalled 37 in number. Children and adults alike attended, the schools being set up by Jones from a realisation of 'how deplorably ignorant the poor people are who cannot read, even where constant preaching is not wanting, while catechising is omitted'.[3] As early as

[1] MR, 141, 142.
[2] Mary Clement (ed.), *Correspondence and Minutes of the S.P.C.K. Relating to Wales 1699–1740*, p. 309.
[3] W. Moses Williams (ed.), *Selections From the Welch Piety*, 1938, pp. 20, 21. This lamentable state of affairs stimulated his conscience and spurred him to action. 'General ignorance in things pertaining to salvation gave great thoughts of heart and painful concern.' The first 'school' for the poor and ignorant of the parish stemmed from this concern as an attempt to meet both their material and spiritual needs. 'A dole of bread', says Jones, was 'provided for them with part of the money the communicants gave at the sacrament'. As the schools grew and proliferated, he adds, 'Divine Providence was not wanting to bring in benefactions to support them'. The teachers were trained by Jones himself, and moved from place to place, each school

1738 schools were established at Llangeitho and Llanddewibrefi, recording respectively 106 and 91 scholars in attendance.[1] This conviction of evangelism through literacy belonged to Jones, but the labours of such an experienced soldier of Christ could not have failed to impress the Llangeitho curate only half his age!

Rowland, however, directed his zeal and energy almost exclusively to preaching. Evidences of God's working through that preaching were to be seen initially at Llangeitho itself.

'The light of divine truth now shone upon his mind with increasing brightness, and he had the pleasure of witnessing a great revival of religion among his people. Their souls were often filled with the joy of salvation, and seemed irresistibly led to prolong the time of divine service by singing and praising God. This gave rise to those rejoicings among the Welsh Methodists which have often called forth the censures of some and the apologies of others. . . . At one time, in particular, when assembled for morning service (probably at a late hour), they continued together nearly the whole afternoon! Mr. Rowland was so far led out in his discourse, the attention of his hearers was so fixed, and their affections so much engaged, that time passed away unperceived. While employed, therefore, in their usual manner, at the close of the service, they were surprised to behold the sun from the western door of the church, in consequence of which the congregation was suddenly dismissed!'[2]

That very message of salvation which had been virtually buried out of sight in the land was now powerfully proclaimed as though from the housetops. Those who before were so averse to preaching were now eager for it. The Son of God who before was despised and rejected of men was now the subject of praise and delight. Who would have believed the change was possible? Such a transformation in a remote village, among an ignorant people through an insignificant and unlikely instrument could be ascribed only to God.

During each great reformation in the history of the Church, God

lasting three or four months, during the winter usually when the poor people could best afford the requisite time. In them both adults and children were taught to read and were catechised. Many of the schools were staffed by Methodist converts, and their location often coincided with a Methodist society, so that they were at once both an instrument and a product of the Great Awakening. By 1764 their fame had spread as far as Russia. See W. Moses Williams, *op. cit.*, pp. 20, 19; M. G. Jones, *The Charity School Movement*, 1938, pp. 313–14.

[1] HVP, 222.

[2] *The Evangelical and Missionary Chronicle*, November 1825, p. 450.

has restored to preaching its divinely appointed lustre and authority. This same pattern now began to emerge at Llangeitho, as God's Spirit attended Rowland's preaching with unction and success. Soon the church building could not contain the numbers that came to Llangeitho. On hearing God's Word preached with clarity, purity, and liveliness, people realised that God was visiting the land.

Rowland also began to encourage those who professed to be the subjects of spiritual impressions to meet together. Such meetings provided a measure of stability and permanence. One tradition locates Rowland's first 'society' between Nantcwnlle and Llangeitho in a narrow, secluded valley. Another tradition makes Llangeitho church at mid-day on Wednesday the setting. It is not really necessary to choose between them, as there may have been several small groups meeting in different places for convenience, and the distinction of being first was hardly important.

Their existence and purpose is far more significant. Initially, says Edward Morgan, Rowland 'was induced to call the professors together in order to hear them relate their various experiences, and by that means to encourage or to correct them, as the circumstances required'.[1] This was the way in which the work of reformation at Llangeitho was to be consolidated. From the earliest times, these 'societies' proved to be heavenly occasions, their experimental emphasis complementing the biblical instruction which Rowland provided.

Another remarkable manifestation of God's power in this early period of Rowland's ministry seems to have occurred while he was reading the Anglican Prayer Book Litany. Here is Edward Morgan's account of the event:

'While he was engaged one Sunday morning in reading the church service, his mind was more than usually occupied with the prayers. An overwhelming force came upon his soul as he was praying in those most melting and evangelical words, – "By thine agony and bloody sweat, by thy cross and passion, by thy precious death and burial, by thy glorious resurrection and ascension, and by the coming of the Holy Ghost." This passage is more emphatic in the Welsh language, by reason of an adjective going before the word "agony",

[1] i.56; The Origin and Growth of the Welsh Methodist 'Private Society' or 'Seiat' is traced by M. H. Jones in *The Trevecka Letters*, 1932, pp. 206–256. See also Eifion Evans, 'Adding to the Church – in the Teaching of the Calvinistic Methodists', in *Adding to the Church*, Papers read at the Westminster Conference, 1973, pp. 52–55; HMGC.i.141; MR, 21, 23–4.

signifying "extreme". The words, if translated would run thus, – "by thine extreme agony". As he uttered these words, a sudden amazing power seized his whole frame; and no sooner did it seize on him, than it ran instantly, like an electrifying shock, through all the people in the church, so that many of them fell down on the ground they had been standing on in a large mass together, there being no pews in the church.'[1]

God's visitation at Llangeitho was nothing if not powerful. The message of the cross, embodied so poignantly in the Litany, was being owned by God in an extraordinary manner.

Opportunities to preach this liberating message in other parishes increased. One of these proved to be immensely significant to the Great Awakening in Wales. In August, 1737, Rowland preached at a small Breconshire village called Defynnog, some thirty miles to the east of Llangeitho. His contact with that parish was probably through Griffith Jones. As early as October, 1734, Jones had preached at Defynnog. More recently, in November 1736, the curate of the parish had requested Jones to set up one of his schools there. Negotiations continued during 1737, with the result that 110 scholars joined in 1738–39, and Jones again preached there in 1739.[2] Evidently the Defynnog clergy were sympathetic to Jones' message and labours, and the way was open for Rowland's preaching visit.

One of Rowland's congregation that day was Howel Harris. This was their first meeting, as unexpected as it was memorable, and for it Harris had travelled fifteen miles in a westerly direction from his home at Trefeca. Harris had been to Defynnog before, and had written in his diary at the end of the summer of 1736, 'Defynnog. N.B. John Prichard when I did not expect, was converted, and in hopes of converting many more there in the neighbourhood.'[3] Rowland's visit therefore coincided with a measure of spiritual activity in the area.

The exact date is given in Harris's *Itinerary* as being August 13,

[1] MR, 38–9. The authenticity of this tradition is disputed by D. Davies, whose recollection of memories of Rowland stretched back to the mid-nineteenth century. *Y. Parch. Daniel Rowland, Llangeitho, a Diwygwyr Methodistaidd eraill . . . Amddiffyniad* (1906), tt. 56–8.
[2] ix.55; cf. NLW Addit. MS. 24B; W. Moses Williams, *The Friends of Griffith Jones*, 1939, p. 27; Edward Morgan, *Letters of the Rev. Griffith Jones*, 1832, pp. 188–9; HVP, 173; MS.i.170.
[3] viii (No. 3), The Itinerary of Howell Harris, Instalment 1, pp. 14, 17; HH Diary No. 15.

1737.[1] An early biographical account written by Harris in 1744 gives his impressions of that occasion.

'As for the other Minister and great man of God, Mr. Daniel Rowland, he was awakened about the same time with myself, but in another part of Wales, viz. in Cardiganshire, where by reason of there being but little correspondence between it and Breconshire, he went on gradually growing in gifts and power without knowing anything of me, as I did the same time without knowing anything of him, until by Providence in 1737 I came to hear him in Defynnog church in the upper part of our county, where, on hearing the uncommon gifts given him and the amazing power and authority by which he spoke and the effects it had on the people, I was made indeed thankful, and my heart burst with love to God and to him. Here began my acquaintance with him and to all eternity it shall never end.'[2]

Writing a quarter of a century after the event, Harris still remembered the exceptional measure of unction which Rowland had enjoyed that day, 'The first time I saw him he was surrounded with glory in the pulpit in Defynnog.'[3] Had the phrase 'surrounded with glory in the pulpit' been expressed at the time, it would have been prophetic; uttered in 1763 it was an astute distillation of Rowland's great ministry.

What was it that brought Harris to Defynnog that day, and to make such an evaluation of Rowland's ministry? Harris was only three years younger than Rowland and their early life without Christ was similar in many respects. Further, as Harris commented, they had been brought to a saving knowledge of Christ at much the same time. The *Brief Account* of Harris's life begins in this way:

'I was born at Trefeca, in the parish of Talgarth, in the county of Brecon, on January 23rd. 1714. My parents kept me at school till I was eighteen years old. . . . I was soon carried away with the stream of vanity, pride, and youthful diversions, which got the ascendant in my soul. . . . On March 30th. 1735 our parish minister was using arguments to prove the necessity of receiving the Sacrament. . . . By his saying, "if you are not fit to come to the Lord's Table, you are not fit to live, nor fit to die", I was convinced, and resolved to leave my outward vanities.'

A spiritual struggle began in him whereby he became increasingly aware of inward corruption. Attempts at self-reformation and improvement proved futile and only brought home to him the

---

[1] Itinerary, Instalment 1, p. 17. The source of information for this date is not clear.
[2] NLW CMA Trefecca 3186.   [3] HRS, 187.

realisation that he was 'all this while in a damnable state, and in danger of final destruction'. Deliverance, however, was not long delayed;

'One day in prayer I felt a strong impression on my mind to give myself to God as I was, and to leave all to follow Him. But presently felt a strong opposition to it, backed with reasons, that if I would give myself to the Lord, I should lose my liberty, and would then be not my own, or in my own power; but after a great conflict for some time, I was made willing to bid adieu to all things temporal, and chose the Lord for my portion. I believe I was then effectually called to be a follower of the Lamb.'

More was to come. On Whit Sunday, 1735, he was again at the Lord's Table, 'simply believing in the Lord Jesus Christ', and it was here that he had evidence of his acceptance with God: 'I was now acquitted at the bar of Justice, and in my conscience. This evidenced itself to be true faith by the peace, joy, watchfulness, hatred to sin, and fear of offending God, that followed it.'

Harris felt very much on his own. He knew of no-one to whom he could turn for counsel in spiritual matters. God alone taught him and led him, assuring him of His faithfulness in spite of failure on his part and derision on the part of others. Three weeks later, however, he experienced another manifestation of God to his soul.

'June 18th. 1735, being in secret prayer, I felt suddenly my heart melting within me like wax before the fire with love to God my Saviour; and also felt not only love, peace, etc., but longing to be dissolved, and to be with Christ. Then was a cry in my inmost soul, which I was totally unacquainted with before, Abba, Father! Abba, Father! I could not help calling God my Father; I knew that I was His child, and that He loved me and heard me. My soul being filled and satiated, crying, "Tis enough, I am satisfied. Give me strength, and I will follow Thee through fire and water." I could say I was happy indeed. There was in me a well of water, springing up to everlasting life, John 4:14. The love of God was shed abroad in my heart by the Holy Ghost, Rom. 5:5.'

This private ministry of the Holy Spirit to his soul, in the seclusion of Llangasty Tal-y-llyn church near Trefeca, proved to be a memorable anointing for Harris's public activities.

At home, he set up family worship with his mother and some of their neighbours. With spontaneous fervour he also began to talk to others about salvation.

'Now the fire of God did so burn in my soul, that I could not rest day nor night, without doing something for my God and Saviour; nor could I go with satisfaction to sleep, if I had not done something for His glory that day. Time was so precious, that I knew not how to improve it entirely to the glory of God and the good of others. When alone I was taken up wholly in reading, praying, or writing, etc., and also continued to go on exhorting the poor people, and they flocked to hear me every Sunday evening.'

That had been his experience during the summer months of 1735. In November he went to enrol at Oxford University, with a view to taking holy orders, but he was back home within a week, 'having no taste for the entertainments there'.

Neither the censure of his vicar nor his responsibilities as a schoolmaster could quench his thirst for souls as he now widened the sphere of his Gospel preaching. Soon he found himself 'discoursing generally three or four, and sometimes five and six times a day, to crowded auditories'. 'I took no particular texts', he adds, 'but discoursed freely as the Lord gave me utterance.'[1] He travelled incessantly, 'exhorted' at every conceivable opportunity, feverishly wrote his extensive diary, was diligent in reading and correspondence, and established fruitful friendships wherever possible with men of evangelical sympathies. In addition, he maintained contact with those who gave evidence of spiritual awakening, forming them into 'religious societies'. The drain on his mental, physical, and emotional energy was enormous. By the time he met Rowland he had visited Griffith Jones at Llanddowror more than once for fellowship and counsel, and had undertaken still more labours in connection with his schools.

One outcome of the Defynnog meeting was an arrangement for Harris to visit Llangeitho as soon as possible. Their plan was realised with Harris's arrival at Rowland's house on Saturday night, October 15, 1737. Travelling westward from Trefeca, the journey of fifty miles to Llangeitho had taken two days. He was extremely tired from loss of sleep and his usual strenuous activities.

Not surprisingly, therefore, in church the next morning, he was 'dull and sleepy like a stick'. On the way to 'another church' his mind was in a turmoil about the meeting he was to address later. 'When on horseback, I saw pride enough and a great concern because now so deserted lest God would not give assistance tonight, but found it was not out of a concern for God's glory, but lest I should lose any of

[1] *A Brief Account of the Life of Howell Harris Esq.*, 1791, pp. 9, ff.

mine.' He was 'comforted from the sermon' shortly afterwards, and when he spoke to the 'congregated multitude' he had 'great and unexpected help'. Further discourse and prayer at an alehouse followed 'to past 11', and then he and Rowland talked on into the night, retiring to bed at 2 a.m.[1] Their joint labours had begun.

[1] HH Diary No. 25; xxix. 94.

'He so tasted the love of God for a whole week, that he could not hear one word of the world. He did everything for Christ, and to His glory. When he did eat, he did not taste what taste the meat had; in singing, it was as if his mouth and heart was with the cherubim.'

HOWEL HARRIS
writing of Howel Davies in 1738

'The faith that God has planted, a principle divine,
A witness by its nature which cannot hence decline;
It firmly grasps what's living, believes the Blood that's shed,
Shall never lose its power, is living and not dead.'

WILLIAM WILLIAMS OF PANTYCELYN

7

'Reforming Days'

When Rowland entertained Howel Harris for the first time at Llangeitho in October 1737 they had a great deal to talk about. There was much common ground between them. Their indebtedness to Griffith Jones would have been freely acknowledged. They both delighted in his message and shared his zeal for the salvation of their countrymen. His unashamed, uncompromising efforts to preach beyond the limits of his own parish they found an attractive precedent for imitation.

While they were both in their middle twenties, Jones was very much a father figure, and an old campaigner at fifty-four. By comparison both Rowland and Harris were novices, and had a lot to learn from his mature judgment. Any plans they might make would have to meet with the projected approval of Griffith Jones.

Both Rowland and Harris had experienced a measure of success in their Gospel labours already. At Llangeitho the crowds attending Rowland's preaching were large, and the societies were multiplying. Similarly, crowds were attracted to the Scripture-based, if spontaneous and homely, discourses of Harris. He, too, could count several societies under his supervision. The spiritual experience of both men was lively, their missionary zeal and concern was ablaze.

There was, however, one major difference between them. Rowland was in the happy position of being a fully ordained clergyman, while Harris was still a layman. Having been refused ordination in the summer of 1736, it was still his hope, but meanwhile he could not remain silent.

'As to the lawfulness of laymen's preaching, in some cases and at times of necessity, I saw in the Acts of the Apostles the account of Apollos, and others, who were scattered by the death of Stephen, having no other mission than being moved by the Holy Ghost and love to the immortal souls of their fellow creatures. I thought a greater time of necessity could hardly be than at present, when the whole country, in a cursory sense, lay in a lukewarm, dead condition. . . . Where an intelligible sermon was preached, it was so legal, in the language of the Old Covenant, and advancing men's works, etc., not treating of a Mediator, that should any give heed to it, they could easily perceive that they were far from being led thereby to Christ, the only new and living way to God. Seeing this, and feeling the love of Christ in my heart, I saw an absolute necessity of going about to propagate the Gospel of my dear Master and Redeemer.'[1]

Rowland evidently accepted Harris's lay ministry, in spite of its ecclesiastical irregularity. Consequently, he allowed Harris to address the crowd at Llangeitho, in spite of the fact that such activities were likely to result in a further refusal of ordination to Harris by the bishop. They would have concurred with Richard Baxter's evaluation of priorities in the previous century. Justifying occasional irregularity and answering the fear that 'every brain-sick proud opinionist will think that there is a necessity of his preaching', Baxter argued, 'it's better that men should be disorderly saved, than orderly damned, and that the Church be disorderly preserved than orderly destroyed'.[2] If a choice must be made, life comes before order. As they saw things in 1737 that choice could not easily be avoided without incurring the most reprehensible guilt. Further consideration of principles and of consequences was to come later. For the present it was sufficient that both shared a burning zeal for the souls of men.

The news that Harris brought to Llangeitho gave real cause for praise. He had discovered others who preached a pure Gospel. One of these was Thomas Jones, curate of Cwm-iou in the narrow Llanthony valley near the border with England. Harris had known of him since May, 1736, and always found the twenty-mile journey from Trefeca to hear him, 'one of the most experienced, solid ministers', to be highly profitable. Furthermore, young men were being converted under Harris's ministry, the most recent being Howel Davies, who before long became one of the Methodist leaders in Wales. Davies had family connections near Brecon, and he first appears in the Harris diaries as a schoolmaster in Talgarth, when the

[1] *A Brief Account*, pp. 41–4; cf. Eifion Evans, *Howel Harris Evangelist (1714–1773)*, 1974, pp. 13–14.
[2] Richard Baxter, *Five Disputations* (1659), p. 165, quoted in Geoffrey F. Nuttall, *Howel Harris*, 1965, p. 42.

need for his conversion was recorded as a matter for prayer. That was on February 21, 1737. By September Harris's prayer had been answered, and God had made their friendship as that of David and Jonathan. Davies spent some time with Griffith Jones at Llanddowror, eventually settling in West Wales for his life's ministry as 'the Apostle of Pembrokeshire'.[1] Rowland and Harris were not alone in the work of reformation.

Before leaving Llangeitho Harris had invited Rowland to Breconshire. Rowland's response came two weeks later, and on Thursday, November 3, 1737, Harris was praying, 'O Lord, today speak through the mouth of Thy servant Mr. Rowland', and feeling 'great thankfulness that God sends him to us'. His prayer was answered, Rowland 'had help'. However, on another occasion in the same county later that month, Harris heard that 'Mr. Rowland was stopped [that is, prevented from going] to Bronllys'.[2] Rising success was mixed with stiffening opposition.

Nevertheless, in the closing months of 1737, Harris found that crowds flocked everywhere to hear the Word. He mentions numbers between 400 and 2,000.[3] Llangeitho was no exception. On his second visit to Rowland, December 6th, he addressed an estimated congregation of between 1,500 and 2,000 at an early morning meeting. Under the subject 'The marks of grace', he referred to Abel, David, and Mary Magdalene, and went on to speak 'of Judgment Day, Hell, Heaven, Eternity, self-examination and glorifying God'.[4]

As Christmas was approaching, Rowland set himself the task of writing a Welsh carol extolling the Incarnation of the Son of God. It was in a recognised and popular Welsh literary form, the 'halsing'. According to the contemporary commentator, Erasmus Saunders, a 'halsing' was intended to make 'private instruction more agreeable and effectual'. He adds:

'It is not to be expressed, what a particular delight and pleasure the young people take to get these hymns by heart, and to sing them with a great deal of emulation of excelling each other. . . . Before and after divine service . . . eight or ten will commonly divide themselves to

[1] For Thomas Jones see BCM, 56–9; CH. 1985; Trefeca Letter no. 743, Howel Harris to Bro. Harcourt. This is also in *Account of the Progress of the Gospel*, 1743, vol. ii. No. 2, p. 29; For Howel Davies see DWB.
[2] HH Diary No. 25, November 3 and December 1, 1737.
[3] BCM, 142.
[4] xxix. 95.

four or five a side, and so forming themselves . . . one party first begins, and then by way of alternate responses, the other repeats the same stanza, and so proceed until they have finished their halsing, and then conclude with a chorus.'

Rowland recounts Scriptural material from Isaiah and the Gospels with an emphasis on the wonder of the occasion.

> This wonderful day, so great every way,
> Atonement was paid, for mankind was made;
> Satan was conquered, bondage was shattered,
> From prison release to men, and great peace;
> News for rejoicing, sharing, believing,
> News of His coming, Jesus so loving;
> With this none compares, no land, gold, or shares,
> Christ our possession, the Hope of Salvation.

It is a long poem of 119 lines, whose 'comforting words will awake from sleep' and put the greatest issues of life in their real perspective.[1] While this modest attempt by Rowland to express the Gospel in song was not without merit, its real significance lay in the conviction that the message of the Great Awakening was eminently worthy of propagation and celebration.

At the close, Rowland modestly describes himself as 'the weak clergyman who tries to serve three churches', Llangeitho, Nant-cwnlle, and Llanbadarn Odwyn. According to the Rural Dean's Returns for both 1733 and 1745 his brother John served all three and Llanddewibrefi as well.[2] When Rowland ministered at Llanbadarn, and later at Llanddewi, it would have been as a private arrangement rather than in a settled, official capacity.

On Wednesday, February 8, 1738, Rowland was preaching once more in Breconshire. This was at a village called Gwenddwr some ten miles from Trefeca. Harris was in the congregation, and it proved a significant occasion for his spiritual pilgrimage.

'Prayed for assistance to Mr. Rowland and Oh! Lord! send Rowland strength and prudence from above! O! stand today for Thy glory, that Satan's turrets may be drawn down for myself and all others. In

[1] *A View of the State of Religion*, 1949 edn., p. 33. The halsing is printed in full in xxxiii.13–15. Further information about this literary form is given by Geraint H. Jenkins in *Literature, Religion and Society in Wales, 1660–1730*, 1978, pp. 158–161.
[2] For the Rural Dean Returns see NLW MS 9145 F.

hearing him pray, I saw myself a nothing creature. In hearing of Christ's love, Proverbs 8:31–32 ("Rejoicing in the habitable parts of his earth, and my delights were with the sons of men. Now therefore hearken unto me, O ye children; for blessed are they that keep my ways"), I was made sick of love. . . . The clouds of doubt were taken away . . . I resolved thus, that as I saw Christ is all in all, pleading for me in heaven, having never before seen His love in His Word and Promises so far, had understanding cleared and heart yielded, will surrendered . . . I found self entirely weaned from all chains, willing to go about and leave and entirely surrender self to Christ. . . . Had a clearer witness of the Covenant than ever. . . . Having a true sense of His love is a foundation of my trust and faith. . . . Today was an extraordinary day to my soul; I see myself more on Christ, by seeing that His love originates from Himself and not from any deserts in us.'

From Rowland that day Harris received confirmation of the sovereignty of God's grace in salvation.

This truth had first dawned on him under the preaching of another curate, Thomas Lewis of Merthyr Cynog in Breconshire, the previous November. Later, Harris wrote of his growing appreciation of this teaching:

'Mr. Thomas Lewis preaching from John 1:12 . . . showed me clearly that I had received Christ. (It is one thing to possess faith; it is quite another thing to [exercise it; it is one thing to be in the Covenant, it is another thing to] know it.). . . But now I came to see the difference between unbelief and humility, and between faith and presumption. But at Gwenddwr . . . my eyes were opened to the light when I heard Mr. Rowland preaching on Proverbs 8:32. He was the means whereby I was brought to the knowledge of the truth about Christ.'[1]

Gradually both Rowland and Harris were being taught of God. Their understanding of Christian truth was deepened, but they were also given greater insights into their own hearts. Harris's diary for January, 1738, for instance, records his inner conflicts: 'Jan. 6, prayer renewed for Mr. Rowland, that God's Spirit may guide and protect him'; 'Jan. 27, inward envy to Mr. Daniel Rowland'; 'Jan. 30, I see spiritual pride inwardly, the heart comparing itself with Mr. Rowland and Mr. Griffith Jones etc . . . praising God for the grace given to Mr. Rowland and others.'[2] Both men were learning the necessary lesson, that while grace in the believer is sovereignly

---

[1] HH Diary 25; BCM, 134, 153.
[2] HH Diary No. 25.

bestowed it is also experimentally progressive.

According to Thomas Charles of Bala, another of the future Methodist leaders was 'converted in 1738. This was William Williams, Pantycelyn, the hymn-writer. He hailed from the same county as Charles and Griffith Jones, Carmarthenshire. 'Pantycelyn' was the name of his mother's old home where he went to live after his marriage in 1748, and it is the name which usually identifies him in the Welsh Great Awakening. It was while he was studying for a career in medicine that he heard Harris preaching in Talgarth churchyard. He was twenty years of age at the time, and of that occasion and Harris's preaching he later wrote:

> This the morning, still remembered,
> That I first heard heaven's sound;
> And the summons straight from glory,
> By his voice my heart did wound.
>
> That's the spot, for ever treasured,
> Where I first his visage spied;
> At the church's portly entrance,
> With no path on any side;
> In a solemn, serious spirit,
> With eternity in sight;
> Urging, pleading with the people
> From God's wrath to take their flight.[1]

While the sermon was instrumental in changing his life, there seems to have been little contact with Harris for the next few years.

After a short time Williams's career also took a different course. He was ordained deacon in 1740 by the Bishop of St David's. The 'irregularity' of his compulsive, itinerant preaching subsequently provided the Bishop with an excuse for refusing to ordain him priest, and by 1744 he had left his curacy in order to work with Rowland and Harris. His special, though not exclusive, gift was the writing of hymns, spiritual poetry and prose for the Methodist converts. His letters to Lady Huntingdon later in the century reveal something of the urgency with which he viewed preaching, and the extent of his travels for that purpose. On one occasion Williams writes: 'I have promised to write to your Ladyship before this, but neglected it, by reason of my roving and ranging over the rough mountains and wild

[1] CYN.i.492, 498–9.

precipices of Wales, in search of poor, illiterate souls chained in the dens of darkness and infidelity.' Other letters convey a similar sense of urgent activity: 'being in such a hurry to reach home, so that I might set out once again immediately on a tour around Carmarthenshire for three or four days'; 'I have been of late through all the north, and travelled about 600 miles in 22 days, and preached constantly twice a day, and often kept a private society.' In all he wrote some 860 hymns, claimed to have travelled 111,800 miles, and his name appears on the title page of over 90 books.

Williams' literature displays a profound understanding of orthodox, evangelical theology, and his greatest contribution lies in the realm of experimental hymnody and revival apologetic. While he learnt a great deal from Puritan authors, the source of his imagery is biblical, and his genius finds expression within a biblical framework. On his death in 1791 Thomas Charles paid him this tribute:

'Putting everything together, he was one of the most gifted, respected and useful men of his age. His gift of poetry was naturally and abundantly given him by the Lord. He would frequently mount on very strong wings, which would lift him into heights of splendour. The cross and its great sacrifice are the chief topics and substance of his writings. . . . His hymns wrought a remarkable change in the religious aspect of Wales, and in public worship. Some verses in his hymns are like coals of fire, warming and firing every passion when sung, and impelling the people to repeat them many times, until they break forth, shouting and leaping for joy. . . . Mr. Daniel Rowland's sermons, and the hymns of Mr. William Williams, made the age in which they lived more remarkable than almost any age in the history of Wales.'[1]

Together with Rowland and Harris, Williams and Howel Davies made up the four leaders of the Great Awakening in Wales, and they were to work together in that capacity for many years.

During 1738 Rowland was taking every opportunity to preach. His extra-parochial activities had to be carried on in defiance of ecclesiastical restraints, as Griffith Jones had found before him. Henry Davies, one of Harris's Nonconformist contacts in

---

[1] WW.i.44–5, 66, 164; liii, 56, 58, 59; D. E. Jenkins, *The Life of the Rev. Thomas Charles*, vol. ii, 1908, pp. 56, 57. For William Williams see DWB. In addition to the bibliography listed there, the following works on Williams deal with literary criticism: John Gwilym Jones, *William Williams Pantycelyn*, 1969 (bilingual); Glyn Tegai Hughes, *Williams Pantycelyn*, 1983 (English); and Derec Llwyd Morgan, *Williams Pantycelyn*, 1983 (Welsh).

Glamorganshire, sought his aid in securing the services of Rowland in his area. Writing on July 28, 1738, he says, 'I desire you to procure Mr. Griffith Jones' letters from Mr. Rowland, and if you can, prevail with him to come to these parts to preach the everlasting Gospel. I shall endeavour to have a letter of consent from one of our clergy if he will come.' A year later Rowland's excursions into the area were sufficiently well established for Henry Davies to write, 'Mr. Rowland – that pious, zealous man – I had his good company for a night when he was at Llanwynno.'[1]

Rowland seems to have carried his episcopal licence with him on such preaching journeys. An entry in a Carmarthenshire parish register of the same period copied the details of Rowland's licence from the Bishop: 'The Revd. Daniel Rowland, curate, ordained priest by the Reverend Father in God, Nicholas, Lord Bishop of St. David's, on Sunday the 31st. of August 1735 at his Lordship's Chapel in Abergwily. Officiated in the Parish Church of Llandybie on Wednesday, August 23rd. 1738.'[2]

Rowland's preaching journeys were undertaken in the face of great inconvenience, and often opposition. 'We had but a poor reception and a poor fare while travelling over hills and mountains on our little nags, without anything to eat but the bread and cheese we carried in our pockets, and without anything to drink but water from the springs; and if we had a little buttermilk in some cottages, we thought that a great thing.'[3] When permission to preach in the church was refused, Rowland had no hesitation in preaching in the open air, in a churchyard, on a horse-stand or table, in a field or in a house, anywhere convenient for a crowd to gather. He had initially ventured into the fields to rebuke Sabbath-breakers at Llangeitho. With Harris it was common practice to discourse in 'unconsecrated' places, and the crowds which attended their preaching occasions would often have necessitated field-preaching.

Certain areas were more sympathetic than others, and these in time became Methodist strongholds. The area around Defynnog was one of these. A nearby church, Llywel, provided Rowland with a pulpit on November 29, 1738, when he preached a sermon in Welsh of great encouragement to young Christians. The text was Luke 12:32, 'Fear not, little flock, for it is your Father's good pleasure to

[1] Hugh J. Hughes, *Life of Howell Harris*, 1892, p. 55; MS.i.211.
[2] Gomer M. Roberts, *Methodistiaeth fy Mro*, 1938, tud. 45.
[3] JO, 76.

give you the kingdom.'

'Doctrine: 1. God's people should fear nothing; 2. God's people are few in number; 3. God's people will receive a prize. Why should not God's people fear when they are under such crosses? Because this is God's goodness and will. About Abraham being tried (after the promise) in the matter of Isaac's being offered. Moses was cast down when tried by the sea, pursued by Pharaoh with malice, but he drowned. Shadrach, Meshach, Abednego.

'Fear not as long as you may go to God in prayer, but fear what stands between us and God, that is, sin, rather than persecution etc. Consider God's deliverances of His people, past and present. Noah floats while others drown; Lot escapes while others burn. He who is least in his own sight is the one most highly esteemed by God. He fears more at the gate of heaven than the other fears at the gate of hell.

'Christ's flock is little in its own eyes, is little in the eyes of the world. . . . God's people fear on account of Satan's wrath, who is greater in his malice than his wisdom: why does he take Job's goods? It was to see whether poverty would discourage him. Satan's subtlety, using the drowned swine to stir up opposition to Christ's teaching; the deceitfulness of evil men placing hindrances in the way of God's people; David's near acquaintance becomes his enemy; Job's wife also.

'Use: 1. None should be more secure than the Lord's people, since it is not their neighbour or their child who tells them "be not afraid". 2. A reproof: let the ungodly consider that every man here below is either most blessed or most miserable. God holds before us heaven as full of glory, and the other as a place of woe; 3. An enquiry: what have we gained here today? Not merely the answer of the tongue, but that of the conscience. Have you left the heart open?'

As well as these sermon notes, Harris gives his own response: 'I saw a tendency in me to go and admire the man, Mr. Rowland, but was melted and guided to look to Jesus. In hearing the text, I was filled with heavenly sweetness of assuring love. . . . I can't have any true delight now to talk of anything but Christ. Great fear as I am going to talk tonight after they heard such powerful doctrine today. Helped to give all to Jesus.'[1]

Only a week previously, Harris had written to a friend in Bristol, 'Oh how should our souls rejoice that our days are reforming days! There is a hopeful prospect in some places that would rejoice your soul. We have several societies, in this and other counties, of young

[1] HH Diary 35; xxvi.1.

people meeting together to pray and converse etc. which are hopeful; some are of a year's standing, and some more. . . . You have heard of the Rev. Mr. Griffith Jones of Carmarthenshire, and the Rev. Mr. Daniel Rowland of Cardiganshire, and some other clergymen in this county, who preach Christ powerfully.'[1] Already, in the eyes of its leaders, the Great Awakening in Wales was becoming an identifiable and cohesive movement of God's Spirit.

[1] *A Brief Account*, pp. 109, 110.

'If then the general spirit of the Bible be in favour of revivals; if the prayers which holy and inspired men have offered for them are here recorded; if there be many instances here mentioned of their actual occurrence; and if the spirit of prophecy has been exercised in describing and predicting them; then we may consider the objection that they are unscriptural as fairly set aside; nay, we may regard them as having the sanction of divine authority in the highest and clearest possible manner.'

W. B. SPRAGUE
in *Lectures on Revivals of Religion* (1832)

'Whence is it that we hear of so much of these things now, but from the more plentiful effusion of the blessed Spirit? – Whence is it that this blessed work has spread so extensively, far and near, among young and old; and there are so many crying out under the burden of their sins; and so earnestly enquiring after the way of salvation? – Is not human nature the same now that it used to be? – Whence is it that the Ordinances, that were before but as a dead letter, do now make such a lively impression? Certainly this is the Lord's doing, and it is marvellous in our eyes.'

JONATHAN DICKINSON
in *A Display of God's Special Grace*, 1742

8

'A Great Revival'

While Rowland and Harris were together in Breconshire in November 1738, Harris made a significant comment about the work. 'Sure the time here now is like New England.' The comparison was based on Jonathan Edwards' account of events under his ministry at Northampton, Massachusetts. This account had appeared in England late in 1737 under the title *A Narrative of Surprising Conversions*, and was published with the recommendation of Isaac Watts and John Guyse. The book had been in Harris's possession since February, 1738, and its contents would have stirred his heart and that of Rowland.[1]

Edwards was born at East Windsor, Connecticut, in a home with a distinctly Puritan atmosphere, and educated at Yale. In his conversion experience the words of I Timothy 1:17, 'Now unto the King eternal, immortal, invisible, the only wise God, be honour and glory for ever and ever', came to have special meaning to him:

'As I read, there came into my soul, and was as it were diffused through it, a sense of the glory of the Divine Being; a new sense, quite different from anything I ever experienced before. . . . From about that time I began to have a new kind of apprehensions and ideas of Christ, and the work of redemption, and the glorious way of salvation by Him. An inward, sweet sense of these things, at times, came into my heart; and my soul was led away in pleasant views and contemplations of them. And my mind was greatly engaged to spend my time in reading and meditating on Christ, and on the beauty and excellency of His person, and the lovely way of salvation by free grace in Him.'[2]

[1] HH Diary No. 35; s.v. Feb. 22, 23; Nov. 27, 1738; The *Narrative* was published by The Banner of Truth Trust in 1958 and 1965 in *The Select Works of Jonathan Edwards*, volume 1. Unless otherwise indicated, the extracts which follow are from the 1965 edition. 'A Memoir of Jonathan Edwards' by Iain Murray appeared in the 1958 edition.
[2] *The Select Works of Jonathan Edwards*, vol. 1, 1958, p. 15.

He was licensed to preach in 1722, and settled at Northampton five years later.

After seven years in this pastorate Edwards witnessed some astonishing scenes. Northampton 'seemed to be full of the presence of God'. At that time, says Edwards, 'our public assemblies were then beautiful: the congregation was alive in God's service, every one earnestly intent on the public worship, every hearer eager to drink in the words of the minister as they came from his mouth; the assembly in general were, from time to time, in tears while the word was preached, some weeping with sorrow and distress, others with joy and love, others with pity and concern for the souls of their neighbours'.

For Edwards, the authenticity of this extraordinary, divine work could be deduced from several facts: its clear effects upon all sorts of people, young and old, rich and poor; the large numbers converted; its rapid progress in terms of suddenly changed lives; and the strength of the spiritual impressions experienced. These considerations together convinced Edwards that 'this amazing work' was 'indeed divine'. As a trained theologian with a brilliant mind, Edwards was hardly given to gullibility or emotional excess. He was as careful in describing what happened in the revival as he was in expounding Scripture when preaching. His account of events showed evidence of painstaking accuracy, and his carefully reasoned interpretation carried conviction.

In their preface to the book, Watts and Guyse use the language of revival to speak of the New England events. First they set out in summary the salient facts.

'Never did we hear or read, since the first ages of Christianity, any event of this kind so surprising as the present Narrative hath set before us. . . . Within the compass of thirty miles, wherein it pleased God, two years ago, to display his free and sovereign mercy in the conversion of a great multitude of souls in a short space of time, turning them from a formal, cold, and careless profession of Christianity, to the lively exercise of every Christian grace, and the powerful practice of our holy religion. The great God has seemed to act over again the miracle of Gideon's fleece, which was plentifully watered with the dew of heaven, while the rest of the earth round about it was dry, and had no such remarkable blessing.'

Next comes an attempt to set the events in a biblical framework.

'As the gospel is the same divine instrument of grace still, as ever it was in the days of the apostles, so our ascended Saviour now and then takes a special occasion to manifest the divinity of this gospel by a plentiful effusion of his Spirit where it is preached: then sinners are turned into saints in numbers, and there is a new face of things spread over a town or a country. *The wilderness and the solitary places are glad, the desert rejoices and blossoms as the rose....* Certainly it becomes us, who profess the religion of Christ, to take notice of such astonishing exercises of his power and mercy, and give him the glory which is due, when he begins to accomplish any of his promises concerning the latter days.'

A call to prayer is included in the recommendation.

'It gives us further encouragement to pray, and wait, and hope for the like display of his power in the midst of us. . . . "Return, O Lord, and visit thy churches, and revive thine own work in the midst of us". . . . May the numerous subjects of this surprising work hold fast what they have received, and increase in every Christian grace and blessing! May a plentiful effusion of the blessed Spirit, also, descend on the British Isles. . . .'

Rowland, Harris, Williams, and others saw the Welsh work in similar biblical categories. It could not be adequately explained or described in terms of ordinary ministerial success, or unusual human activity. The events which they were witnessing were beyond human instigation and control.

Several things evidenced this: Rowland and Harris had seen extraordinary and widespread instances of conversion independently of each other early in their ministries. There was a spontaneous element in the gathering and concern of the crowds which met them wherever they went. The very scale of the transformation wrought in the lives of so many signalled an outpouring of the Spirit rather than a deliberate strategy on their part, however thoroughly orchestrated. Nor could the awareness of God and of sin which was apparent among the people have been induced by human means, it was too intense, too universal. Spiritual concerns were paramount, and spiritual experiences were heightened. They took on an urgency and reality which swallowed up all other pursuits and gripped the most unlikely people.

Reading the *Narrative*, the Welsh leaders would have immediately identified with Edwards' situation and experiences. They could happily and honestly echo such important, telling phrases as, 'a considerable revival of religion'; 'an unusual religious concern'; 'no small effusion of the Spirit of God'; 'a general awakening'; 'here, in

this corner of the world, God dwells, and manifests his glory'. They
had witnessed effects similar to those spoken of by Edwards: 'the
Spirit of God began extraordinarily to set in, and wonderfully to
work amongst us'; 'the town seemed to be full of the presence of
God'. Such was the similarity in the character of the work that
Edwards' description of the one would have served equally well for
the other:

'The work in this town, and others about us, has been extraordinary
on account of the universality of it, affecting all sorts, sober and
vicious, high and low, rich and poor, wise and unwise. . . . Many . . .
have, of their own accord, formed themselves into religious societies. . . . Persons are first awakened with a sense of their miserable
condition by nature, the danger they are in of perishing eternally, and
that it is of great importance to them that they escape and get into a
better state. Those who before were secure and senseless, are made
sensible how much they were in the way to ruin, in their former
courses. . . . Persons, after their conversion, often speak of religious
things as seeming new to them; that preaching is a new thing; that it
seems to them they never heard preaching before; that the Bible is a
new book: they find there new chapters, new psalms, new histories,
because they see them in a new light.'

Small wonder, then, that when Harris first read the *Narrative*, he felt
his heart 'boiling with love to Christ', and prayed, 'O go on with Thy
work there and here'. Such sentiments would undoubtedly have been
shared with, and by, Rowland in 1738.

The end of that year brought news from George Whitefield of 'a
great pouring out of the Spirit at London'. Harris did not receive
Whitefield's first letter to him until January 7, 1739. He replied the
next day, and his response was both warm and excited.

'Oh how ravishing is it to hear of such demonstrations of the divine
love and favour to London! and to make your joy greater still, I have
some more good news to send you from Wales. There is a great
revival in Cardiganshire, through one Mr. D. Rowland, a Church
clergyman, and he has been much owned and blessed in
Carmarthenshire also. We have also a sweet prospect in Breconshire,
and part of Monmouthshire; and in this county where I am now, the
revival prospers. . . . In Montgomeryshire . . . there seems to be
some shining beams of the Gospel of grace . . . but enemies are many
and powerful.'[1]

[1] BA, 110, 111, 113. Also in DAL, 233–4.

Referring to this period many years later, Williams of Pantycelyn adds his testimony to the character and reality of the work:

'Ignorance covered the face of Wales, hardly any Gospel privilege could stand against the corruptions of the day, until about 1738 light broke forth as the dawn in many parts of the world ... and O wonderful day! the Sun shone on Wales. God raised these instruments from the dust and set us with the princes of His people. The net was cast into the sea, and all kinds of fish were caught, great and small. The six southerly counties soon embraced the Word. . . . And this lasted for some years.'[1]

Such was the retrospective view given of those days by one of the Welsh leaders.

The factual basis for Williams' assessment of those early years was provided by Rowland's ministry. Phrases like 'uncommon power', 'God was among us indeed', 'amazing power', tumble over one another in Harris's diaries as he seeks to describe the occasions when Rowland ministered. Often the scene was one of Rowland's own parishes, as on December 14, 1740, at Nantcwnlle, when Rowland was preaching on John 5:6, 'When Jesus saw him lie, and knew that he had been now a long time in that case, he saith to him, Wilt thou be made whole?' Harris writes:

'He had vast power to call all to Christ. Never did I hear such calling, such earnest striving to call all to Christ. Many cried out. Showing that God's love is eternal and unchangeable. Blessed be God for the amazing gifts and power given to dear Brother Rowland. Surely there is no such ministry in Wales. I never heard of like.'[2]

Rowland was by no means the only human instrument proving much of God's anointing upon him, but when Harris wrote of those times, he singled him out as being the one who was exceptionally used of God to carry on the work.

The spiritual appetite of the crowds attending Rowland's ministry confirmed the strong impression that God's hand was upon him in an extraordinary measure. On his way to Llanddewibrefi one Sunday in November, 1741, Harris tells of 'seeing some running to hear the Word' at five in the morning! In July 1741 three 'dear sisters' travelled the 40 or so miles from Llanidloes to Ystrad-ffin to hear

---

[1] GWP.ii.23–4.
[2] August 31, 1741 (MS.i.486); November 6, 1741 (MS.ii.155, 156); MS.i.492.

Rowland preaching, crossing some of the wildest and roughest terrain in Wales to do so.[1] The intensity of such religious affections allowed of some variation, but early in 1743 their vigour was far from abated, as Rowland wrote in a letter of 2nd February to Whitefield:

'There is a general, fresh, and uncommon stirring in most places. Many come anew under convictions, especially old, worldly professors, and backsliders return. And there is such power as I never felt before given me in preaching and administering the Lord's Supper. The Lord comes down amongst us in such a manner as words can give no idea of. Though I have, to prevent nature mixing with the work, openly discountenanced all crying out, yet such is the light, view, and power that God gives very many in the Ordinance, that they cannot possibly help crying out, praising and adoring Jesus, being quite swallowed up in God. And thus I was obliged to leave my whole congregation, being many hundreds, in a flame, the one catching it from the other. It would have set your heart in a flame to see them, and to feel the flame that runs through; and this is our condition generally every Sabbath! The convictions are now more deep and solid than formerly.'[2]

Whitefield himself had an opportunity 'to feel the flame that runs through' shortly afterwards, and reported: 'The power of God at the sacrament, under the ministry of Mr. Rowland, was enough to make a person's heart burn within him. At seven in the morning I have seen, perhaps, ten thousand from different parts, in the midst of the sermon, crying 'glory', 'praise', ready to leap for joy.'[3] By attributing such a manifestation to 'the power of God' he was affirming his conviction that the Spirit had been poured out in great effusion upon the church.

It was important for the leaders to come to a biblical understanding of this work of God in their midst. The most obvious parallel was the Spirit's outpouring on the Day of Pentecost, and contemporary writers repeatedly drew on the second chapter of Acts for an adequate base for their theology of the revival. Thus in Williams Pantycelyn's view, the days of 'heavenly authority' in Wales were 'like the time of the Apostles, when the Spirit descended from on high on a handful of people. . . . As it was then, so it was here now.' And

[1] xxvi.75; MS.ii.94.
[2] HH, 130.
[3] John Gillies, *Memoirs of the Late Reverend George Whitefield*, 1811, pp. 119–20, n.

the result was just as impressive:

'Now the tone of whole districts was changed; instead of playing games on the Sabbath, dancing, cursing, swearing, blaspheming the name of God, singing unworthy songs, empty talk, gossiping, collecting stories, lying and persecuting God's people – instead of all this . . . the shepherds would sing hymns in the valleys, the plough-men and the driver of his oxen often sing psalms and spiritual songs together in the fields; the maidens, the children and the old men together discoursing happily about the works of the Spirit of grace. . . . To the flesh and the natural man this wonderful work of heaven was as full of awe and as fearful as blood and vapour, smoke and fire to timid men.'[1]

Across the Atlantic in 1741 William Cooper was preparing a 'Preface' for another of Jonathan Edwards' works, *The Distinguishing Marks of a Work of the Spirit of God*. Again the comparison is made with the Day of Pentecost.

'What a dead and barren time has it now been, for a great while, with all the churches of the Reformation? The golden showers have been restrained; the influences of the Spirit suspended, and the consequence has been that the Gospel has not had any eminent success. Conversions have been rare and dubious; few sons and daughters have been born to God; and the hearts of Christians not so quickened, warmed, and refreshed under the ordinances, as they have been. . . . And *now*, – "Behold! the Lord whom we have sought, has suddenly come to his temple." The dispensation or grace we are now under, is certainly such as neither we nor our fathers have seen; and in some circumstances so wonderful, that I believe there has not been the like since the extraordinary pouring out of the Spirit immediately after our Lord's ascension. The apostolic times seem to have returned upon us.'[2]

One more account must suffice. A revival in the northern part of the Netherlands in 1749 was reported as 'a perfect commentary on the 2d. of the Acts'. In this instance, as in Wales in the early days of Rowland's ministry, there was deep conviction of sin. 'There was a great lamentation; rivers of tears gushed out, and several fell trembling and astonished to the earth unable to stand by reason of the agony and agitation of their spirits, arising from the sudden, strong impression made upon them of the dreadful state and crying necessity of their souls.'[3]

[1] William Williams, *The Experience Meeting*, 1973, pp. 9, 10.
[2] *Select Works of Jonathan Edwards*, vol. i. 1965, p. 77,
[3] John Gillies, *Historical Collections*, 1845, pp. 490, 491.

In terms of initial fulfilment of Joel's prophecy, Pentecost was a unique occasion. In terms of historic realisation in the life of the church during the Day of Grace it was the first of many. Around the year 1738, Rowland and Harris experienced one such visitation of the Holy Spirit in saving activity and blessed profusion. Its powerful effects persisted for some years, with large crowds, experiences of deep conviction and ecstatic joy, and frequent conversions. There was no innovation in the doctrines or the methods: God was simply owning the familiar 'foolishness of preaching' of the orthodox message of 'Christ crucified', but in a manner unprecedented in living memory.

The Scriptures provide ample material for an understanding of revival. There are predictions and examples, prayers and instructions relating to it. In the Old Testament, the familiar figures of restoration and profusion spoke of the extraordinary blessings of the Gospel day, as in Isaiah 35:1, 'The desert shall rejoice, and blossom as the rose'; and Isaiah 66:8, 'Shall the earth be made to bring forth in one day? or shall a nation be born at once?' It was compared to a springtime, the breaking forth of life after the deadness and barrenness of a hard winter, as in Song of Solomon 2:12, 'The flowers appear on the earth; the time of the singing of birds is come, and the voice of the turtle is heard in our land.' Above all, perhaps, it was spoken of as the manifestation of God's presence in the midst of His people, a coming down of God among men with unmistakable reality and irresistible power, as in Isaiah 64:1, 'Oh that thou wouldest rend the heavens, that thou wouldest come down, that the mountains might flow down at thy presence.' Prayers found in the Psalms often express this desire of the godly for the Lord's return in restoring grace: 'shine forth', 'come and save us', 'return', 'turn us again', as in Psalms 80 and 85. There are descriptive prayers, too, for God's visitation after withdrawal, as in Psalm 74:11, 'Why withdrawest thou thy hand, even thy right hand? pluck it out of thy bosom.'

That the Gospel Day is to see the realisation of this profusion is evident from the New Testament documents. They speak of large numbers converted, and of insignificant human agencies being instrumental in transforming seemingly impossible situations, as at Jerusalem on the day of Pentecost, or in Samaria according to Acts chapter eight. Subsequent chapters of Acts provide evidence of remarkable spiritual activity under the preaching of the Gospel among non-Jewish communities from Syrian Antioch to Thessalonica. The New Testament letters testify to the fact that the change wrought in men's lives as a result of such revivals was both profound and lasting.

To Rowland and Harris in 1738, Jonathan Edwards' *Narrative* must have seemed like another 'commentary on the 2d. of Acts'. Its appearance was timely, and it came to have deep significance for their work. It strengthened their biblical understanding of 'this remarkable pouring out of the Spirit of God'. It virtually provided them with a 'text-book of revival', a safe and tried frame of reference, by which to measure and describe the parallel events they were witnessing in Wales. It served to confirm the authenticity of God's work in their midst: there were the same wonderful evidences of God's extraordinary activity in Wales as in New England. Did Edwards report that 'a great and earnest concern about the great things of religion and the eternal world became universal'? So could Rowland. Was religion 'the great concern, and the world was a thing only by the bye' at Northampton? So also at Llangeitho. Was the astonishing manner of conversion witnessed by Edwards best described by saying that 'souls did as it were come by flocks to Jesus Christ'? Both Rowland and Harris knew by experience what he meant. Finally, they would have benefited enormously from Edwards' perceptive analysis of the workings of grace and its fruits in personal godliness during a season of revival, when the quality as well as the quantity of conversions is remarkably high. In effect, this part of the *Narrative* set out reliable guidelines for the evaluation and consolidation of the work. Consequently, echoes of Edwards' ideas and phraseology are repeatedly found in the documents and writings of the Welsh leaders.

Amid the scenes of extraordinary success which accompanied the labours of Rowland and Harris in those early years their thoughts would inevitably have turned to the means of maintaining spiritual life and growth. Foremost among these was preaching. Then followed prayerful consultation with each other and with the converts which the Lord had given them. Their lot had been cast in unusually pleasant places. The universal, and powerful sense of God in wide areas testified to the reality of God's visitation in revival. A regular, faithful ministry of the Word yields fruit as God 'gives the increase' upon the 'planting' and 'watering' of the divine 'seed'. By the end of 1738, however, the depth of conviction, together with the frequency and reality of conversions, which so generally attended their labours were such as to convince them that God had 'come down'. 'The strong man' had been bound by God's Spirit: the same Spirit now employed them as the 'spoilers' of 'the strong man's goods'.

'The doctrine of our regeneration, or new birth in Christ Jesus, though one of the most fundamental doctrines of our holy religion; though so plainly and often pressed on us in sacred writ . . . though it is the very hinge on which the salvation of each of us turns . . . yet it is so seldom considered, and so little experimentally understood by the generality of professors, that were we to judge of the truth of it by the experience of most who call themselves Christians, we should be apt to imagine they had 'not so much as heard' whether there be any such thing as regeneration or not.'

GEORGE WHITEFIELD,
Sermon on Regeneration, 1737

'The end of your meeting is not that you may think yourselves more holy than your neighbours, much less to form a sect or party, or to promote a schism or sedition in the Church or State. No: such thoughts, I trust, are far from you; for they are earthly, sensual, devilish. The only end which I hope you all propose by your assembling yourselves together, is the renewing of your depraved natures, and promoting the hidden life of Jesus Christ in your souls.'

GEORGE WHITEFIELD,
A Letter to the Religious Societies', 1739

'May God open my mouth wide when I come to Wales . . . I am glad to hear brother Rowland is with you. Go on in the strength of our dear Lord, and you shall see lightning fall from heaven.'

GEORGE WHITEFIELD
to Howel Harris, 1741

9

'Such Near Union'

Great responsibility lay upon Rowland for the progress of the revival in 1739. Harris was to be increasingly drawn into the work in England, his visits to London, Bristol, and Gloucester taking him away for a total of some ten weeks. Support from Howel Davies and William Williams in the burden of preaching was to come later. Davies was only settled in his first curacy in August of that year, and William Williams did not take orders until 1740.

There was another reason for the multiplying calls upon Rowland during 1739. On August 20 Bishop Nicholas Clagett licensed Rowland's brother, John, to the 'augmented cure' of Blaenpennal within the parish of Llanddewibrefi.[1] If the effect of this was to put another chapel at Rowland's disposal, it would also mean extra demands on his time. However, it does not seem to have curtailed his ever-increasing preaching activities in the counties of South Wales, frequently in Carmarthenshire, at least occasionally elsewhere, as in Glamorganshire and Breconshire during August.[2]

From Rowland's sermons of this period, it is clear that he viewed the revival as a work of reformation. Neither the exalted experiences nor the astonishing success which God granted under his ministry were allowed to modify his presentation of 'the whole counsel of God'. Thus in setting out the implications of conversion, he emphasised that it was Christ-centred not man-centred, its implications were for life not merely for a day, and its subjects were not to expect exemption or release from troubles and difficulties. In turn, these convictions led to the provision of nurture for young Christians in the religious societies which he and Harris established early in the revival.

Both Rowland and Harris knew that the revival was of God. Their

[1] *Itinerary* of Howell Harris, I. 24–26; xix. 123; xxxvi. 25.
[2] MS i. 211; xxix. 99.

unction and authority came solely and entirely from the Holy Spirit. There were times, however, when His powerful influences were absent, and they were cast afresh upon God in prayer for His return. At Llangeitho on March 1, 1739, Harris 'had some humblings in soul and sweet influences'. Two days later he records the over-riding consideration for all the Methodists: 'I am willing to go to Cardiganshire, and to live in a desert or anywhere so as I may enjoy God.'[1] No physical discomfort should be spared for the sake of the enjoyment of God's presence. It was important, therefore, that those whose hearts had been touched by God's Spirit should stay close to one another in lively fellowship, learning to evaluate and regulate their experiences by God's Word.

At Ystrad-ffin on August 4, 1739, Rowland warned believers, 'that they must expect persecution if they give themselves to Christ'. The following day was a Sunday, and Rowland's text at the mid-day service was Psalm 34:19, 'Many are the afflictions of the righteous, but the Lord delivers him out of them all.' Again Rowland gave timely instruction to the people, saying that 'the Lord could save the godly from unbelief and hardness of heart', and that 'the Christian lives as a stranger here, having his eye on another country'.[2] On the way to their next appointment at Ystrad-ffin on the 23rd of that month, Harris was conscious of a constraint to 'go about the societies, to root and establish them in God's truth'. Rowland preached a solemn, rousing sermon on Ezekiel 33:11, demonstrating man's inescapable responsibility for sin. Afterwards, Harris was 'inciting to societies and Welsh schools'.

At Llangeitho three days later, Harris profited more from hearing 'Mr. Rowland exhorting sweetly in the society' than he did from the preceding sermon on Matthew 5:20.[3] A pattern of indifference under Rowland's sermon, and blessing in the more private occasion with the society which followed, was Harris's experience yet again at Ystrad-ffin on October 27, 1739: 'When Mr. Rowland had done, I was so under the power of a dry, churlish, ill-natured spirit. . . . When Mr. Rowland went to examine young communicants, had some holy trembling and fear and sweet influence in me.' Under Rowland's heart-searching sermon the next day on Malachi 3:18, exposing the dangers of hypocrisy, Harris had some tender mo-

[1] HH Diary 41; cf. xxix. 96–7.
[2] HH Diary 46; cf. xxvi. 7–8.
[3] HH Diary 48; cf. xxix. 97, 98; HVP 14, 15.

ments, and a longing 'to be ever under the Word'.[1]

An objective, biblical assessment of the reality and progress of a work of grace in the soul was essential. This comes to the fore in a sermon preached by Rowland at Abergorlech, Carmarthenshire, on September 28, 1739. The text was 2 Peter 1:10, 'Give diligence to make your calling and election sure; for if ye do these things, ye shall never fall.'

'Those who show such diligence are called different things. Heaven calls them "pearls"; earth, that is, the man of the world, calls them fools. Others call them hypocrites; understandably, because so many who pretend a zeal for God's glory are guilty of hypocrisy. But not all are thus. God has some who are faithful. It is possible to make sure their calling and election, if they add to faith, virtue etc. (vv. 5–7). The godly seek Christ in every duty, secretly at first, then publicly. Others are satisfied with an outward reformation without asking whether they are genuinely affected. "Add to virtue, knowledge." There must be an experimental knowledge of Christ and of grace in everyone who is going to heaven. "Add to knowledge, temperance." Here there must be balance, without aspiring too high or sinking too low; avoiding presumption on the one hand and despair on the other. "Add to temperance, patience." From the mighty and the wise of the world there will be persecution, and there is need for patience. "To patience, godliness." It is not enough to show kindness and generosity, heaven demands godliness, etc. Doctrine: a man may be sure of his standing.'[2]

It was by such close biblical exposition and application that spiritual vigour, stability and persistence were to be nurtured in the converts.

Providentially, in March, 1739, contact was made with George Whitefield, by Harris in person, and with Rowland indirectly through his colleague. Whitefield was to provide the Welsh leaders with a shining example of fearless Gospel preaching, and with wise counsel for keeping God's people together. On March 4 Harris had received a cordial letter from Whitefield,[3] making their meeting three days later a matter of keen anticipation. Seeing Harris as a man 'full of faith and the Holy Ghost', Whitefield had wanted 'to catch some of his fire'. In retrospect, Harris was to say of the meeting, 'When the Lord sent brother Whitefield to Wales about two years ago, the first

---

[1] HH Diary 50; cf. xxix. 100–101.
[2] NLW Addit. MS 368A, Pocket book of Thomas William (1717–1765), for whom see DWB.
[3] HH Diary 41.

question he asked me was this, "Do you know that your sins are forgiven?" The question rather surprised me, having never heard it asked before.' There followed a 'conversation relating what God had done for us', says Harris, adding, 'Had my soul filled with heaven.' Whitefield, for his part, wrote in his *Journal*, 'We took an account of the several Societies, and agreed on such measures as seemed most conducive to promote the common interest of our Lord.' Further, they found themselves in agreement about the doctrine of election, and considered the best way of supplying an urgent need for Welsh Bibles. Whitefield supplied Harris 'with a horse and money for Bristol', and asked him 'to go to London'.[1]

Whitefield's links with Wales were to be particularly close and cordial. Gloucester, his birthplace, where his mother kept the Bell Inn, was on one of the chief coach and mail routes between London and South Wales. As an undergraduate at Oxford University, he received financial support from Sir John Philipps, Welsh benefactor of the S.P.C.K. and brother-in-law of Griffith Jones. There, also, he was converted, at about the same time as Rowland and Harris, and in a manner with which they could both identify:

'After having undergone innumerable buffetings of Satan, and many months' inexpressible trials by night and day under the spirit of bondage, God was pleased at length to remove the heavy load, to enable me to lay hold on His dear Son by a living faith, and, by giving me the Spirit of adoption to seal me, as I humbly hope, even to the day of everlasting redemption. But oh! with what joy – joy unspeakable – even joy that was full of, and big with glory, was my soul filled, when the weight of sin went off, and an abiding sense of the pardoning love of God, and a full assurance of faith broke in upon my disconsolate soul! Surely it was the day of my espousals, a day to be had in everlasting remembrance.'

Whitefield returned to Gloucester for his ordination in 1736 at the unusually early age of 21. Soon after this his preaching was owned of God at Bristol and London: 'The Word, through the mighty power of God, was sharper than a two-edged sword. The doctrine of the New Birth and Justification by Faith in Jesus Christ (though I was not so clear in it as afterwards) made its way like lightning into the

[1] *George Whitefield's Journals*, 1960, p. 230; *Bathafarn*, ix. 31; xvi. 30–35; Moravian Archives, London, Box A/3 'original Letters John and Charles Wesley 1735–1774, Letter William Seward to James Hutton dated March 10, 1739, from Bristol'; HH, 43, n; xxiv. 7–9; xlv. 17, ff., 52.

hearers' consciences. The arrows of conviction stuck fast, and my whole time between one lecture and another, except what was spent in necessary refreshment, was wholly occupied in talking with people under religious concern.'[1]

Whitefield had been a 'Methodist' at Oxford, along with John and Charles Wesley and others, but their association as such in 'The Holy Club' had been on the basis of a severe legalism, for they were trying to establish a righteousness of their own before God. With White-field's conversion and fruitful preaching, another kind of 'Method-ism' was emerging, to which the Wesleys were strangers. This was the evangelical Methodism of the Great Awakening, based on the message of regeneration by God's Spirit, and an experimental realisation of personal faith in Christ for salvation. It was this which brought Whitefield into such close affinity with the Welsh brethren in 1739.

Two other factors ensured for Wales a strong and lasting place in Whitefield's affections, one being theological and the other personal: the Welsh Methodist leaders to a man were solidly Calvinist in their doctrinal position, and Whitefield's wife was to be Mrs Elizabeth James, a widow who lived in Abergavenny. He had been in Griffith Jones' company a few days before his first meeting with Harris, but a meeting with Rowland was still more than three years away. However, Whitefield later forged closer bonds with Rowland. Their status as ordained clergymen, together with their sustained doctrinal orthodoxy and anointed preaching would have been contributory factors in cementing their friendship.

A letter from Whitefield as he was ready to depart for America in August 1739 fits well with an assumption that it was a reply to an epistle from Rowland:

'Reverend and dear Sir,
Your kind letter gave me much satisfaction. It breathed the language of one who is a Boanerges in the Church of God. Excess of business prevented my answering it sooner. As I am now retired from a public life, I trust I shall have time to try my heart and search out my spirit. . . . I hope I shall always carry you, and others of my dear friends in Wales, upon my heart, whenever I go in and out before the Lord. It would rejoice my soul to hear from you when abroad. . . .

[1] For Whitefield, see DAL; Eifion Evans, 'George Whitefield in Wales', in The Evangelical Library *Bulletin*, No. 45, Autumn 1970, pp. 1–7; *George Whitefield's Journals*, 1960, pp. 58, n. 69, 81.

Brother Harris, I find, has come off triumphantly. The hour of suffering is not yet come. God prepare us all for it! I expect to suffer for my blessed Master's name sake. . . . I know you not in person. Perhaps I may never see your face in the flesh. However, I shall see you in heaven. . . .'

Rowland certainly did write later in the year, to which Whitefield replied from Savannah on February 4, 1740:

'My reverend and dear Brother,
   I received your kind letter just on my arrival at this place. My Journal, which I suppose you will have read ere this reaches Wales, can best inform you what God has done for my own and other people's souls. Even here He is pleased to be with, and assist us. . . . I rejoice to hear that the Lord Jesus is so publicly confessed among your countrymen. If the Lord is pleased to send me, I shall gladly take a tour into Wales. . . . Experience of God's work upon our own souls is the best qualification to preach it effectually to others. . . . I expect to suffer in the flesh for what hath been done already: But what have we to do with the consequences of performing our duty? Leave them to God.'

From America in November, 1739, Whitefield had written to Harris, 'The people of Wales are much upon my heart', a sentiment he echoed a year later with as much fervency, 'O Wales, thou art dear to my soul!', with the added greeting, 'My love to all the brethren.'[1]

Rowland was doubtless included in those greetings and warm expressions of concern, but for a time he remained to Whitefield a shadowy figure. The reason was Rowland's own temperament: retiring rather than exuberant, studious rather than sociable. Even after their meeting, that reserved disposition caused some embarrassment to Rowland. Writing to Whitefield on February 2, 1743, Rowland confessed, 'It is much, as yet, for wise ends, with-held from me, to use that freedom I would, even with those to whom my soul is most nearly and dearly united. This is my trial and burden, and is, I know, an offence to many of my brethren whom I love in the Lord. This is the reason I am so little familiar with you, dear friend, with whom I have such near union.'[2] In time, however, the bond between the two leaders became strong, lasting, and productive.

   Consultation with Whitefield in the spring of 1739 gave the Welsh leaders confidence and encouragement. A common awareness of

[1] GWL i. 60, 149, 87, 220.   [2] HH, 129–30.

being fellow-workers in a mighty movement of God's Spirit in the land strengthened their resolution to faithfulness and persistence. There was also mutual concern over the societies which had already been set up by them, independently of one another. Whitefield's mind had been exercised about the matter as early as 1737, when he had preached on Ecclesiastes 4:9–12, 'Two are better than one . . . if they fall, the one will lift up his fellow.' It had been published in the same year under the title 'The Nature and Necessity of Society in General, and of Religious Society in particular'.

In 1739 Whitefield's mind was again sufficiently alerted to the need for spiritual guidelines in the matter of soul nurture to produce a pamphlet on the subject. It was written during his voyage to America in the autumn, and therefore only appeared in print in 1740, but the principles it advocated would have been formulated soon enough in 1739 to have been shared with his new-found Welsh brethren. The resulting *Letter to the Religious Societies* was a powerful document, and was immediately translated into Welsh. It echoed the emphasis of the Moravian, Peter Boehler's rules, drawn up in 1738 on confessing faults to one another and on prayer. Of the objects and advantages of such societies, Whitefield had this to say:

'The only end which I hope you all propose by your assembling yourselves together, is the renewing of your depraved natures, and promoting the hidden life of Jesus Christ in your souls. . . . None but those who have experienced it, can tell the unspeakable advantage of such a union and communion of souls. I know not a better means in the world to keep hypocrisy out from amongst you. Pharisees and unbelievers will pray, read, and sing Psalms; but none, save an Israelite indeed, will endure to have his heart searched out.'[1]

Regulating principles similar to these were gradually developing among the Welsh Methodists, too, and the finding of such correspondence of thought and purpose between them would have greatly heartened the Welsh leaders.

The fact that the Anglican Church made no provision for such close dealings in spiritual matters made the need all the more urgent. Harris had noted in his diary for March 18, 1737, three things lacking in the parish churches, one of them being 'The right to meet together as a society to consult together with regard to matters of salvation and self-examination.'[2] John Wesley was later to make the

[1] TGW i. 95, 317, 318, 319.　　　[2] BCM, 105.

same point: 'Look east, west, north and south, name what parish you please: is Christian fellowship there? Rather, are not the bulk of the parishioners a mere rope of sand? What Christian connection is there between them? What intercourse in spiritual things? What watching over each other's souls?'[1] If that was the need, they considered the 'experience meeting' or 'society' to be the best way of meeting it.

Both Rowland and Harris may have heard of the benefit of such societies from Griffith Jones. They knew that the Nonconformists, too, had at their disposal a church meeting for informal discussion and fellowship. This fact was brought to Harris's notice in a petition from some of his converts, dated April 5, 1737:

'We have been moved to throw ourselves at your feet to crave leave to meet together to read, converse about our souls, discover our observations on self-examination to ground the ignorant in the principles of our religion. . . . The granting of this will secure thousands of the ignorant sort from Dissenters who personally know many that leave the Church on account of this privilege the Dissenters have of conversing, etc. about sermons heard, meeting in houses, and they knowing no other occasion to leave the Church but that.'[2]

A 'Register of the Members' of a Breconshire society early in 1738 lists men and women separately, and states that 'every one is aged above ten years'. Another document of that year in Harris's possession gives the questions to be asked of the members 'to try them as to their state', together with the answers that would be considered right and satisfactory:

'1. How shall we appear and be known as wholly surrendered people to God's will? By being able to love our enemies and do good to them that hate us. By finding ourselves content or less troubled than before our conversion about the affairs of the world. By not neglecting to give a part at least of every day to a definite service of God. By finding that the zeal of our love to Christ curbs our love to all else. 2. What are the marks of a true child of God? Like a natural child, the spiritual child is also conscious of being born from darkness into light; it cries for food, and grows little by little.'[3]

Meanwhile, Harris had been giving the matter some thought, and by the summer of 1738, he had produced several 'articles' for the

---

[1] Quoted in A Skevington Wood, *The Burning Heart*, 1967, p. 189.
[2] HH Diary 24, quoted in HMGC i. 163.
[3] M. H. Jones, *The Trevecka Letters*, p. 228.

societies in Welsh.[1] As time went on the questions were more fully thought out and published.

Before the end of 1739 a sermon translated into Welsh appeared 'from a Churchman's collection' which was 'published on behalf of the author'. As the sermon was later attributed to Rowland it is necessary to examine it in some detail. The phrase 'from a Churchman's collection' is ambiguous in that it could mean that the sermon was taken from his own collection of sermons, or from his collection of the sermons of others. The claim that it was 'published on behalf of the author' clearly implies that 'the author' was alive. As to his authorship of the work, however, the phrase does not define either its nature (whether he was the original author or its translator) or its extent (that he was using the material of others as well as his own).

The only name to appear on the title page was that of the printer. The text of the sermon was 1 Peter 2:2, 'As newborn babes, desire the sincere milk of the Word, that ye may grow thereby', and it bore the title *Y Llaeth Ysbrydol* (The Spiritual Milk). Subsequently it appeared among Rowland's Welsh sermons, one of the five to appear in print in 1772, and as one of his *Eight Sermons* which appeared in 1774 (translated back into English!). Its inclusion with Rowland's sermons in 1772 is misleading since it gives the impression that it was as much Rowland's work as the other sermons which accompanied it. Rowland's involvement with its appearance in print is traceable only because of these later editions. The earlier anonymity of its authorship may have been due to Rowland's reticence.

The original sermon was preached by Henry Smith of London (1550?–1591), and appeared in several editions of his works from 1592 onwards. In the 1772 edition, Thomas Davies the publisher merely says of the sermon, 'It was printed in 1739, and is presently corrected of many printing errors. Many who heard it preached have gone to the world of spirits; we, of this present age, are about to go over.' Little is known of this Davies apart from his connection with the publishing of Rowland's sermons in the 1770's. In suggesting that the sermon was preached by Rowland, his statement must be taken as an assumption rather than as an assertion. Rowland was

---

[1] iv. 35; MS i. 121, 130; *Itinerary* of Howell Harris, i. 20. In a letter to Mrs Samuel Rogers of Abergavenny, dated April 28, 1739, Harris lists some questions which 'may be of use to ask our souls', possibly those mentioned in the text, translated into English. They are found in MS i. 169.

still alive in the seventies, and therefore in a position to prevent or disown any publication under his name that was not connected with him in some way or other. The sermon's later appearance in print may therefore be taken as being by his permission or approval. This consideration establishes his profound indebtedness to Puritan authors, and that from an early period of his ministry.

Rowland's translation follows the text closely, though not exactly, and some portions of the original text are omitted. The concluding four paragraphs of application are new. His purpose in making the sermon available in a Welsh translation was to encourage Bible reading among the society members. Clearly, he regarded it as a tract for the times, a homily which was timely and useful in the Welsh situation of 1739. In the 'Preface' Rowland considers the godless state of the land to be a fulfilment of Paul's prophecy of the 'perilous times' of 'the last days', when men would be 'lovers of pleasure more than lovers of God' (2 Timothy 3:1, 4). Particular concern is expressed at the scepticism and negligence shown by many towards God's Word:

'Some go so far as to make a satire of the Holy Scripture, others employ all their reason to oppose and refute God's truth. But their folly is no more than an attempt at devising means to quench the light of the sun from shining . . . they shall know that heaven and earth shall pass away before God's Word fails. And yet, as such obstinate fools confuse and disturb the minds of the insecure and fickle, corrupting many, and grieving weak Christians, it is necessary for God's messengers, ministers of the Gospel, to stand in the breach and oppose these enemies of the cross of Christ.'

In contrast to the spirit of the age, therefore, the Word of Truth speaks of life, assurance, and comfort from God in Christ:

'The tried witness of the godly in these things is no idle fancy, when they affirm that God's Word converts the soul, and is sweeter to them than honey, more precious than gold, and more desirable than their necessary food. As you do not allow the derision and prattle of fools to divert you from nourishing your body, neither should you allow the folly of evil men, nor your business, nor your own worldly lusts to devalue God's Word, which is the soul's food.'

The sermon is therefore prayerfully offered in order to encourage and constrain the reader to apply himself diligently to the spiritual milk and honey of God's Word.[1] Though not Rowland's original

[1] *Eight Sermons*, 'Sermon V'; The sermon is included in volume one of the 1866 (Nichol's Series) two-volume edition of *The Works of Henry Smith*, pp. 485–500.

work, its appearance shows him to have been aware of the importance of a literature catering for the distinctive soul culture of the Welsh Methodist societies. It also identified his theology as being firmly rooted in the Bible and cast in the mould of a lively and disciplined Puritanism.

Welsh Methodism also publicly identified itself with Whitefield's theology in 1739. After his meeting with Harris in March, Whitefield reported, 'My sermon on the New Birth and on the Marks of the New Birth are to be translated into Welsh', and they duly appeared before the end of the year.[1] These steps taken together gave a clear indication of the way in which Welsh Methodism was emerging and developing. God's presence was manifested in extraordinary power in the preaching of Rowland and the labours of Harris. In the providence of God, they were able to benefit from the printed works of Jonathan Edwards and from consultation with Whitefield. They openly aligned themselves with Whitefield's preaching and doctrine. Rowland and Harris also recognised the task of shepherding God's flock as their responsibility. The consolidation of the Awakening was to be a matter of spiritual oversight. Reformation is as much the Spirit's activity among saints as is the work of regeneration among sinners.

[1] Moravian Church Archives Box A/3, 'Letter of William Seward to James Hutton', March 14, 1739, Postscript by George Whitefield. See further; *George Whitefield's Journals*, p. 86; TGW i. 82, 294; DAL i. 124.

'*I trust we are of the same seed, and shall at last stand before the same throne for ever; and who knows but we shall first be tied to the same stake, and ascend up in the same chariot. Let us not then quarrel, though we can't see alike.*'

HOWEL HARRIS
to John Wesley, 1742

O Thou who camest from above
The pure celestial fire to impart,
Kindle a flame of sacred love
On the mean altar of my heart!

There let it for Thy glory burn
With inextinguishable blaze,
And trembling to its source return
In humble prayer and fervent praise.

CHARLES WESLEY

10

'Simple, Broken, Burning Souls'

Gradually, Rowland was being drawn into a position of prominence and leadership. The sense of God's presence under his preaching, and the evidences of God's power in changed lives were characteristics which spread abroad his fame. William Seward's 1740 *Journal* speaks of 'that famous Boanerges in the work of the Gospel, the Reverend Mr. Rowland of Llangeitho in Cardiganshire, where he has seven hundred communicants, and opens his mouth boldly, to make known the mystery of the Gospel'.[1] 'Amazing is the power that goes with Brother Rowland. I believe there is not such a congregation in the nation as he has to my knowledge of simple, broken, burning souls', writes Harris in 1741.[2] Rowland's 'people' were reflecting something of Rowland's characteristics. Such God-given success, however, was not without its responsibilities and its difficulties.

Rowland sought to meet those responsibilities by his sustained, solid preaching and by providing a close, nurturing fellowship for the converts. For him, the Bible was indeed 'the sword of the Spirit'. Man's first need is the knowledge of the truth. Physical and emotional manifestations, which were in evidence on occasions, were not made the index of authenticity or success. Nor were such experiences allowed primacy or prominence in the matter of conversion and edification. On the contrary, men and women were nurtured by sermons which were biblical and practical, reasoned and thorough. There was first instruction for the mind and then warmth for the heart. Complementary to this insistence on instruction was Rowland's careful provision for young Christians. Evidence of this early concern for the fruits of his labours comes from one who had known him personally, and writing in 1835, affirmed that Rowland

[1] Quoted in Morris Davies, *Deuddeg Pregeth*, 1876, tud. 12, n.
[2] MS ii. 155.

was the first to establish private societies.[1] In these ways the saints were edified.

Rowland's preaching had a penetrating quality, exposition being mixed with application. This is evident in his sermon on 2 Peter 1:10, preached at Abergorlech on September 28, 1739:

'Christ calls men, 1. In their youth, and if so, the power of corruption is weakened, Rom. 6:14; spiritual things are sweet to the soul, 2 Cor. 5:14, and godliness is their vocation. Those whom Christ calls press on, and they can never utterly fall away. 2. Christ calls in times of Gospel opportunity, Lk. 19:1–10. Zachaeus unashamedly came to where Christ was. Christ made no delay in calling him, he was not long kept in bondage, and this became evident in the four-fold restitution he made. Christ dwells in those who are called by the Gospel: "Today is salvation come to this house." 3. Christ calls in affliction. Here it is necessary to avoid presumption. The repentant thief reproved his friend, and spoke highly of Christ. He acknowledged that Christ suffered unjustly, and on Christ's calling him, he was given faith. He cried to the Lord, "Remember me when you come into your kingdom", cast himself on the Mediator, and rested on Christ's word, "Today shalt thou be with me in paradise." 4. Christ calls by the threats of the law, as in Acts 16:29.

'The marks of those who are called: 1. recognise the folly of sin; 2. repent of it; 3. sorrow for despising godliness; 4. coming to Christ as the repentant thief did. Let each one examine himself by these marks.

'Application: 1. how sad that so few are sure of their calling and standing in Christ; 2. men should be bolder with Christ in this matter; 3. many, such as Paul and others, have had this assurance in Christ of their interest in Him. Make it your special concern to seek your minister about this matter.'[2]

There was an in-built safeguard and discipline in such preaching. Men were being taught explicitly, as well as implicitly, that they should not rest on impressions and feelings, whether of sorrow for sin or exuberance of joy, however painful or exalted. The work of grace had to reach the hidden depths of the soul if a real and permanent change was to be wrought. For this reason the means of grace had to be carefully used.

Rowland's high view of Gospel privileges emerges in the conclud-

[1] i. 56. This was the Anglican clergyman, Thomas Richards (1754–1837). During a certain period of his life, he was able to visit Llangeitho frequently to hear Rowland preach. For the last 37 years of his ministry he was vicar of Darowen, near Machynlleth. See DWB.
[2] NLW Addit. MS 368A.

ing directions he added to his translation of Henry Smith's sermon on 1 Peter 2:2.

'I shall conclude . . . with a few directions suited to your state, as being desirous of a blessing on the Word of God, that you may grow thereby. First, be sure in the morning to look up to the Lord, and to direct a private, serious prayer to Him for your preservation in the spiritual conflict in which you are going to engage. Secondly, separate yourselves from the company of the profane. . . . It is grievous to see some men, while they approach God's house, burdening their memories and disturbing their hearts with fruitless or silly talk. These, when they come under the Word, can reap no advantage from it, for no vessel can contain more than what will fill it. Thirdly, when you are assembled together before God, follow the example of Zachaeus, who . . . was loath to return home disappointed; so, because a sight of the crowd would not content him, he ran and climbed a sycamore tree. . . . Most men think themselves very safe and good Christians if they are found within the walls of the church, though they never meet Jesus there, or have any thought of meeting Him; but probably fall asleep there or spend the greater part of the time in staring and yawning. After this they return home as merry and joyful, as if they had gotten their errand, and had seen the Lord Jesus Christ. . . . Finally, after you have received the good seed from the mouth of ministers, abstain from the society of lukewarm formalists, lest they dampen by their lifeless example the sacred flame which hath been kindled in your breasts. . . . And when you return to your respective houses, call your families together, and implore God's blessing on what you have heard.'[1]

Genuine spiritual impressions affected the inner man, whereas hypocrites were satisfied with an external show. Preaching at Ystrad-ffin on October 28, 1739, Rowland's text was Malachi 3:18, 'Then shall ye return, and discern between the righteous and the wicked, between him that serveth God, and him that serveth him not.' From the text Rowland drew the doctrine, 'Here there is very little difference between the godly and the ungodly, Eccl. 9:1–3', and 'There is a day coming when there will be a difference, Mt. 25:32.' The real difference is at present invisible: 'The ungodly are filthy inside, but the Christian is clean, Ps. 45:13. . . . The godly deal honestly with God from the heart as well as with their tongues, but the ungodly love God with their tongues, while they love the world with their hearts.'[2] Parallel counsel for young Christians, and that in

---

[1] *Eight Sermons*, 151–3.   [2] Diary No. 50.

a more permanent form, was provided in 1740 by a Welsh translation of Whitefield's sermon on 2 Corinthians 2:11, with the title 'Satan's Devices', exposing the opposite dangers of presumption and despair.[1]

The emerging Methodist movement also had to contend with opposition from Church authorities. By the end of August, 1739, the Bishop of St David's reported that he had received copies of 'the Bishop of London's excellent Pastoral Letter', and these he duly disseminated throughout his diocese. The full title of the tract was, *A Pastoral Letter by way of Caution, against Lukewarmness on the One Hand and Enthusiasm on the Other*. Of its fifty-five pages, thirty-six denounced Whitefield's 'enthusiasm', and the rest dealt with 'lukewarmness'. There were nine charges levelled against Whitefield, and, by implication, against the Methodists:

'1. A claim to extraordinary communications with God, and more than ordinary assurances of a special presence with them.
2. Talking in the language of those who have a special and immediate mission from God.
3. Professing to think and act under the immediate guidance of a Divine inspiration.
4. Speaking of their preaching and expounding, and the effects of them, as the sole work of a Divine power.
5. Boasting of sudden and surprising effects as wrought by the Holy Ghost, in consequence of their preaching.
6. Claiming the spirit of prophecy.
7. Speaking of themselves in the language, and under the character, of apostles of Christ, and even of Christ himself.
8. Professing to plant and propagate a new Gospel [the doctrine of regeneration], as unknown to the generality of ministers and people, in a Christian country.
9. Endeavouring to justify their own extraordinary methods of teaching, by casting unworthy reflections upon the parochial clergy, as deficient in the discharge of their duty, and not instructing their people in the true doctrines of Christianity.'

The *Letter* conveys the sense of outrage which the authorities felt towards the Methodists. They were clearly alarmed at what they took to be spiritual anarchy and fanatical excess. The document was widely circulated and more editions were called for before the year's

---

[1] It was translated by 'a churchman, E.W.', and 'printed at Shrewsbury by R. Lathrop, for Lewis Williams'. The sermon is in *The Works of the Reverend George Whitefield* . . . vol. vi. 1772, pp. 241–55. See also TGW, i. 294.

end. Whitefield immediately recognised its threat to the Methodist movement, and within two weeks had written his reply to it. While defending the immediacy of God's dealings with the soul in preaching, he denied all pretence to any super-spirituality or extraordinary inspiration. As to his doctrine, he affirmed its harmony with Scripture and the Church of England's Thirty-nine Articles, while his activities were in keeping with the Church's liturgical practices. The *Letter*'s impact within the Welsh-speaking diocese of St David's would have been minimal until its appearance in Welsh the following year. This last move stung the Welsh Methodists into action, so that Whitefield's reply in Welsh transla-tion had also been printed by the late autumn of 1740.[1]

The alignment of Methodist forces in Wales and England was beginning to take shape. In terms of leadership, Rowland and Harris in Wales had their counterpart in England in Whitefield and the Wesleys. The latter, too, had occasion to visit Wales, although their influence was neither as deep nor as extensive as that of Whitefield.

John Wesley was born in 1703, in the same year as Jonathan Edwards, Charles was born four years later. They were nurtured in the High Churchmanship of their parents at Epworth Rectory, Lincolnshire, and transferred its legalistic piety to the 'Holy Club' at Oxford, which Charles founded and John later led. In 1735 they went as missionaries to the Indians in Georgia under the auspices of The Society for the Propagation of the Gospel, returning to England three years later. First Charles, and then three days later, on May 24, 1738, John came to an assurance of salvation.[2]

Like Whitefield, John Wesley travelled and preached extensively throughout his lifetime with extraordinary zeal and unflagging

[1] Mary Clement (Ed.), *Correspondence and Minutes of the S.P.C.K. Relating to Wales 1699–1740*, 1952, p. 190; TGW i. 291–3; DAL i. 390–1; William Rowlands, *Llyfryddiaeth y Cymry*, 1869, tt. 382, 283.

[2] Nehemiah Curnock (Ed.), *The Journals of John Wesley*, vol. i, 1938, pp. 423, 422, 418, 472, 475–6; see also A. Skevington Wood, *The Inextinguishable Blaze*, 1960, Chapter VII, 'The Conversion of the Wes-leys'. Several influences combined to bring the Wesley brothers to Christ. The reasoned, disciplined, late Puritanism of their mother, the futility of human efforts at salvation, the piety of a Moravian Christian in the person of Peter Boehler, and the writings of Martin Luther: all these played their secret part under God. See John A. Newtown, *Susanna Wesley and the Puritan Tradition in Methodism*, 1968, pp. 150, ff; Robert C. Monk, *John Wesley; His Puritan Heritage*, 1966, pp. 22, ff.; Clifford W. Towlson, *Moravian and Methodist*, 1957, pp. 47, ff.

energy. In all, he set foot on Welsh soil forty-six times, although some of those occasions were for the purpose of visiting and returning from Ireland. Although Charles married a Welsh lady, he was esteemed by the Welsh Methodists more for the rich evangelical theology of his hymns than for his contribution to the cause of the Gospel in Wales.[1]

John Wesley's first tour in Wales was in response to 'a pressing invitation from Harris', whom he had met in Bristol in June, 1739. It lasted from Monday to Saturday, October 15–20, of that year, and was confined to the south-east corner of Wales. Afterwards he observed: 'Most of the inhabitants are indeed ripe for the Gospel.' A later visit confirmed this, and he wrote to James Hutton on April 12, 1740, 'I am just come from Wales where there is indeed a great awakening. . . . There is such a simplicity among the Welsh who are waiting for salvation, as I have not found anywhere in England.'[2]

Rowland first met John Wesley at Bristol shortly after this, on May 8, 1740. By this time Wesley's rejection of the doctrine of election was already a matter of public knowledge. Yet Rowland's attitude towards him was meek enough for Wesley to enter in his *Journal*: 'I was greatly refreshed by conversing with several who were indeed as little children, not artful, not wise in their own eyes, not doting on controversy and "strife of words", but truly "determined to know nothing save Jesus Christ and Him crucified".' On Rowland's return to Wales he defended his new-found friend's reputation in discussion with a fellow-Calvinist. The incident was reported to Howel Harris by Thomas James, one of the leading Methodist laymen in Breconshire: 'Mr. Rowland has been at Bristol. He came to Chapel Saturday the 10th of May, having set out Friday morning from Bristol, and came to Brecon that night, where there was a little debate between Mr. Lewis and he about Mr. Wesley.'

In spite of their acknowledged doctrinal differences they preached together at Machen, near Newport, on October 16, 1741, Wesley in English and Rowland in Welsh. Rowland had joined Harris at Abergavenny for their journey. They were both concerned about union with Wesley, and Rowland agreed with Harris's sentiments

---

[1] Frederick C. Gill, *Charles Wesley, The First Methodist*, 1964, p. 71, and Chapter 8, 'The Gwynnes of Garth'.
[2] A. H. Williams, *Welsh Wesleyan Methodism*, 1935, p. 17; *John Wesley's Journal*, ii. 292, ff.; *Bathafarn*, ix. 32; Moravian Church Archives, Box A3, 'Original Letters, John and Charles Wesley, 1735–1774'.

and prayer that God would bring them 'all together in the Truth'. Once more Wesley was impressed with Rowland's graciousness: 'Evil surmisings presently vanished away, and our hearts were knit together in love. . . . The spirit of peace and love was in the midst of us.'[1]

Details of the occasion emerge in both Wesley's *Journal* and Harris's diary. Although he could not follow the Welsh sermon, Wesley noted that Rowland's text was Matthew 28:5, 'Fear not ye, for I know that ye seek Jesus, which was crucified.' The service started at three and finished at six, Wesley's sermon following the prayers and lasting until 4.30, the remaining time being taken up by Rowland's sermon. In Harris's estimate, Rowland 'had great power indeed', and he found the message edifying:

'I see 'tis God's will to free us from fear, not from filial fear etc., but from that fear that is confusion in the mind. Why? Because it brings dishonour on His almighty power; many doubt God's power; others, His faithfulness to save them; but whatever God has promised, He will perform. Have you had no promise from God? My soul answered, "yes!" Are you trading with God, and has the union between you and sin been broken? Are you married to Christ? Is there no acquaintance between you and God? Do you converse with God? Do you know His loveliness, worth, etc? If not, your hope is in vain. Were you ever in straits and broken in heart? On whom do you think God looks? is it on those that are great, fair, laughing under the Word, etc.? No! but on the broken, etc.'[2]

Doctrinal discussions followed later that day. Wesley recorded that when someone tried to introduce the controversial issue of free will, 'This Howel Harris and Mr. Rowland strongly withstood; but finding it profited nothing, Mr. Rowland soon withdrew.' Harris remained to calm the dispute and later prayed, 'Is not dear Brother Wesley Thy dear child? O bring him from all errors and make him right in all.' Both he and Rowland were firm in their conviction that they should not separate from other Christians over this particular

[1] *John Wesley's Journal*, ii. 508; viii. 165; Letter of Thomas James to Howel Harris, endorsed, 'May 40', Congregational Library, London, MS II. a. 17, vol. ii. No. 124. Thomas James was the chief leader of the Breconshire societies (see HMGC i. 213–14). The 'Mr. Lewis', referred to in the letter as 'settled at Talach-ddu and Llan-ddew', was the Rev. Thomas Lewis, Calvinist adviser of Harris, and often hounded by the ecclesiastical authorities for his evangelical zeal (see BCM, 130, f.); *Bathafarn*, x. 42.
[2] *Bathafarn*, x. 43; Diary 80.

issue.

Despite this initial measure of concord, Wesleyan influence on Wales in the eighteenth century was not to be significant. Welsh Methodism developed along distinctly Calvinistic rather than Arminian lines. When Wesley visited South Wales in 1763 and 1767 he spoke disparagingly of the work of William Williams and Howel Davies. Although he passed close to Llangeitho in July 1764, August 1768 and August 1769 no mention is made of Rowland in his *Journal*.[1] Christian charity on the part of Rowland and other leaders in Wales, however, together with the eirenic efforts of Harris, enabled them to maintain fraternal relations with the Wesleys. On occasions the various branches of Methodism would at least be able to co-operate, if not unite.

Rowland's involvement with the English leaders of Methodism was considerably less than that of Harris. The reasons for this are not hard to find. Rowland's commitment was to Llangeitho as the scene of his parochial responsibilities, and to Wales on account of a distinct preference for the Welsh language. Harris, on the other hand, was free to move around. He was less retiring, and more ambitious for recognition from his peers, than Rowland. Shortly after Harris's first meeting with Whitefield at Cardiff he travelled eagerly to London. The journey was to have far-reaching implications for him and for the Great Awakening in Wales. It was to be the first of many visits (twenty-four in all), some lasting for days, others for months. Arriving on April 25, 1739, he preached in English to Whitefield's congregations, and in Welsh to his own countrymen in the capital. Primarily, however, the purpose of the visit was to observe God's power at work amongst his English brethren, and to seek their counsel. The journey had given him a first-hand acquaintance with the religious societies established in England. For his next visit, in May 1740, there was a different reason: he was in London to help Charles Wesley while his brother John was busy in Bristol. With the emergence of the Wesley's Arminian convictions, all Harris's subsequent visits were for the purpose of serving the Calvinistic Methodism which centred on Whitefield and the Tabernacle which he erected.[2]

With Harris away from Wales for greater or lesser periods of time,

[1] See *John Wesley's Journal*, v. 26–8, 89, 229, 280, 332.
[2] John Thickens, *Howel Harris yn Llundain*, 1935, 'Y Drydedd Bennod'; HVL, passim.

the burden of leadership fell predominantly on Rowland. It was he, more than any other, who provided the necessary stabilising influence and cohesion which the developing Methodism in Wales demanded. On occasions Harris felt the dilemma as to which was the right sphere for his labours:

'18 July 1741. London. . . . Almost persuaded it is His will I should stay here, 1. Because Wales is so well supplied; 2. As none is here; 3. As they so earnestly desire my stay here; 4. Having all my necessities supplied; 5. Some inward answers in my spirit to stay. Great earnestness for Wales. Crying – hast Thou not sent me to call them? O raise some or other to go about there. . . . 17 August . . . Had a letter from Wales to tell me of the poor dear lambs. O that I was with them! Was drawn between two; which should I, stay here or go to Wales now, drawn by love to both?'[1]

If the two loyalties, Wales and London, caused Harris some painful heart-searching, they also evidently created difficulties for his Welsh brethren. The letter to which Harris referred was from one of the leading laymen, Thomas Price of Watford:

'My dear brother, the Lord has called you and gave you a talent useful for the ignorant Welshmen, and He has owned you an instrument in his hand to do much good. To God alone be all the glory, as is most due. But now you have left us in one sense like fatherless children and you have gone to another country, and you know that we are but weak and dull. Therefore, inasmuch as the Lord has called you amongst us, I think you ought to stay where the Lord has most work for you to do. O remember the poor lambs that want to be fed daily with the sincere milk of the Word.'[2]

That this was no idle sentiment is borne out by Rowland's reproof of a year later:

'Don't you hear all the brethren in Wales crying out loudly, "Help! help! help! help! Brother Harris, thou bold champion, where art thou? What, in London now, now in the day of battle? What, has not London champions enough to fight for her? Where are the great Wesleys, Cennick, etc? Must poor Wales afford an assistance to England? Oh, poor Wales! it is thy ingratitude altogether that has been the cause of all this. Good Lord, pity poor Wales! Send our dear brother among us with Thy power, and in the fulness of Thy blessing, and let the devil tremble before him!"'[3]

This danger of neglect in the matter of oversight for the societies

[1] *Bathafarn*, x. 22, 28. [2] MS ii. 103–04.
[3] MR, 34–5.

posed by Harris's absences was a serious one. It created a deficiency which neither the ministerial nor the lay leaders could adequately supply, however gifted or laborious. Considerable numbers owned Harris as their spiritual father, and it took great wisdom and constant care on the part of Rowland and the others to maintain their spiritual growth.

There was another aspect to Harris's London visits which created problems as time went on. While in the capital, Harris was inevitably caught up in the religious controversies which were eagerly debated there, but carried less significance in Wales. Nor was Harris always reliable in doctrinal discernment. Over those issues which were in dispute in England, Harris was repeatedly out of step with his Welsh brethren, and Rowland's proverbial orthodoxy proved a correcting influence on many occasions.

One of the Welshmen that Harris became familiar with in London was the printer, John Lewis. The desirability of having a public platform for disseminating news and views of the Great Awakening was recognised as early as February 1739. At that time, William Seward suggested to Whitefield 'to have a religious Newspaper set on foot to be called "The Christian's Weekly Journal", and insert therein an account of conversions and other affairs relating to the progress of the Gospel, which may be a great means of strengthening our brethren in different parts of the world as well as of this kingdom.' When Seward wrote those words he anticipated that James Hutton would be the printer, but it was not to be. The first issue appeared on September 20, 1740, under the title *The Christ-ian's Amusement*, and the printer was John Lewis.

Although Lewis was a Calvinist, he promised in an early issue, 'This paper . . . will contain nothing but what is good to the use of edifying in love, promoting peace and charity, as much as possible, avoiding all disputes and contentions about words.' Financially, however, he sustained great personal loss through the venture, partly on account of fading support from Methodists of Arminian per-suasions. Its title was changed three times, successively, to *The Weekly History*, *An Account of the Progress of the Gospel*, and *The Christian History*. Under the third of these titles it ceased publication in 1745.[1] The venture had counterparts in both Scotland (*The*

[1] Moravian Church Archives, Box A/3, Folder 4, Letter of William Seward to James Hutton, February 22, 1739; CH 1980, 22; ii. 79; HMGC i. 407–09; MS ii. 24, 31, 39–40; STL i. 176, n. 3. For John Lewis, see DWB.

Glasgow Weekly History) and America (Thomas Prince's *The Christian History*). They all served a useful purpose, reporting the wonderful spread of the Gospel and propagating in popular form the Awakening's revolutionary message. Rowland was a subscriber, but its sales in Wales were restricted because so many of the society members could not read English.

Rowland was not altogether alone in his efforts at establishing and teaching the converts of Methodism. The Griffith Jones Charity Schools were also providing useful training and instruction in the things of God. In 1740 three 'Letters to a Friend' were published under the title *Welch Piety*. They were an attempt to publicise the good work done by the schools, claiming for the students: 'Very few of these could say so much as the Lord's Prayer when they first came to school, and many of them could, in six or eight weeks' time, not only read tolerably, but repeat by heart all the Church Catechism in their native Welsh language, and make pretty good answers to plain and familiar questions concerning all the necessary points of faith and practice in a system of divinity.'[1] Thus the work of revival and education went hand-in-hand, Methodist societies and Charity Schools being in some places almost synonymous.

All-in-all, the later months of 1740 indicated the need for closer consultation between those involved in the revival. Such evident tokens of the Holy Spirit's outpouring called for a concerted effort. 'The acceptable year of the Lord' was a time 'to build the old wastes, to raise up the former desolations, and to repair the waste cities' (Isaiah 61:1–4). Early in September, Rowland and Harris set themselves the task of meeting that need.

[1] W. Moses Williams, *Selections From The Welch Piety*, 1938, p. 21.

'Tis nought to hear of doctrine, though clear to the mind,
'Tis heaven's power only, no less, that I must find;
Base error and true teaching, to me are both the same
While I beneath sin's burden still grovel in my shame.

'How much I need God's power! for this a world I'd give,
For Satan's full of knowledge; this only, makes none live;
Without the Word that quickens, and in it heaven's power
I'll pine away and perish, though kneeling by the hour.

'No sooner had he spoken, a force from heaven's store
Came like a gushing river to flood his soul with more
Than he before had dreamt of, or understood, or knew,
That now he felt within him, and realised was true.'

WILLIAM WILLIAMS
in *Theomemphus*, 1764

'About Uniting in All Good'

During the summer months of 1740 the two leaders, Rowland and Harris, worked closely together. Their ministry of God's Word was with unusual power, and they were greatly exercised about two matters of supreme importance. One matter, which was constantly in their minds, was that of making provision for the societies under their care. The other was arranging a meeting of ministers, Dissenters included, for the purpose of collaboration in the work of the Gospel. On the latter issue, Rowland had reservations about the wisdom of seeking a united front, in the face of known Anglican prejudice towards Dissenters.

The two leaders met on July 4, 1740, and the next day, a Sunday, they 'had sweet conference together' at Ystrad-ffin. Rowland preached and administered the sacrament, an unforgettable experience for at least one person in the congregation. Later, Harris discoursed at another place with unusual power. His voice could hardly be heard above the sound of crying out, and afterwards he charged those who made a Gospel profession 'about meeting together often'. He spoke for some three hours, feeling 'God most amazingly present'.[1]

With such extraordinary success attending their labours, both leaders were at full stretch. The frequent and pressing calls on Rowland's time may have been the reason why another curate, Benjamin Morgan, was licensed to serve 'Nantcwnlle and the chapel of Betws (Leucu) within the parish of Llanddewibrefi' on August 4, 1740. In the subscriber's list of a book published in 1740, Rowland is identified as 'Rev. Mr. Rowland curate of Llangeitho'. It does not follow from this that Rowland had been dispossessed of his Nantcwnlle curacy, and neither Rowland nor Harris refers to any

[1] MS i. 482; xxviii. 120.

such move. Morgan's appointment must therefore be taken as a reflection of the brothers' need rather than of any displeasure on the part of the Bishop. With Morgan's departure in September 1743, Daniel and John found themselves back in the familiar pattern of sharing the load. The 1745 Deanery Returns record that John served Llanddewi and Llanbadarn Odwyn, while Daniel served Nant-cwnlle and Llangeitho, the latter place having 'sermons frequently besides on Sundays'! John's licence to serve the two places mentioned does not appear in the episcopal records until August 7, 1749.[1]

On August 14, 1740, Harris was again in Carmarthenshire 'settling four societies and putting them in Christian discipline'. He recognised the need to set that discipline on a firm foundation and prayed, 'Lord, if it be Thy will, if all the ministers that are sent of Thee should meet together, to strengthen and edify each other, let Thy love bring that about too, Lord'. Back in Ystrad-ffin with Rowland on the last day of the month, the need for consultation with other ministers was agreed upon, Harris being entrusted with the arrangements: 'Discover [that is, disclose] Thou to me all as are Thine and faithful to Thee among the Baptists and Dissenters, and make me love them dearly, with Brother Rowland. ' Such fraternisation with Dissenters was fraught with the possibility of misunderstanding, and Rowland's anticipation of possible censure by the Bishop was construed by Harris as fear. On the way to Llangeitho on September 22, 1740, therefore, Harris was 'much refreshed in hearing Brother Rowland saying how he has been freed from fear and to give himself wholly to Christ, body and soul'. The following day, Rowland's company was sweet to Harris, 'The Lord made us to be of one mind and one heart agreeing together.'[2] Fellowship in the Gospel over-ruled the prejudice of party spirit.

At Llangeitho on the 24th September, the crowds were enormous,

---

[1] NLW Church in Wales SD/BR/4p. 264, 265, 330–1; SD/BR/11; SD/P/2770; NLW MS 9145F; *Journal of the Welsh Bibliographical Society*, vol. x. p. 18, Rhestr tanysgrifwyr yr ail argraffiad o *Drych y Prif Oesoedd* gan Theophilus Evans.

[2] xxviii. 120; CMHO, 17; MS i. 482, 486; xxix. 120. The antipathy between Anglicanism and Dissent is repeatedly noted in Harris's diaries, cf. CMHO, 67, 'Brother Rowland did not receive Dissenters to him that would come, for fear of disturbance' (April 22, 1742); and CMHO, 72, 'I have been helped, five years ago, to declare against the bigotry in our Church against Dissenters' (May 29, 1742).

and when Harris spoke in English and Welsh to the five or six thousand present, 'many cried out "What must I do to be saved?" and fainted away'. Such physical prostrations, accompanying severe conviction of sin, had been common at Llangeitho from the early days of Rowland's ministry. They were not confined to Llangeitho, or even to Wales, during the Great Awakening. Nor were they regarded as the sure evidence or index of a genuine work of grace, but as occasional consequences of the Spirit's power, to be evaluated subsequently in the light of changed lives and a sustained, consistent profession.

Another day was spent by Harris at Llangeitho, the leaders' thoughts still at one, and Harris longing for Rowland and Whitefield to 'be brought into full liberty and all of us united in one, the Methodists and all'. That night, says Harris, 'it was set on my heart home to plead that God would either turn the Dissenters to the power of godliness or bring them to us, and let us have the full power of godliness in us'. The next day, matters of assurance and opening the whole heart in the societies were on his mind, and in this context he 'showed to them how the Lord leads Brother Rowland on from step to step, charging them not to rest without the full abiding assurance and the clean heart'. As he travelled again toward Ystrad-ffin, he asked God 'to join heart and hand together such as Thou wilt fit, such as will have Thy glory at heart. . . . For our society of ministers. . . . O! dear Jesus, come in Thy Spirit of love among us, that all may be swallowed up in a concern for Thy glory'.

On Sunday September 28, Rowland's text at Ystrad-ffin was 1 John 2:1, 'My little children, these things write I unto you, that ye sin not. And if any man sin, we have an advocate with the Father, Jesus Christ the righteous'. An unusually long entry in Harris's diary bears witness to a powerful message. Registering his response at the time, Harris pours out words at white heat: the words 'take me' are repeated fifteen times; 'Jesus is mine' three times, one after another; and after the sacrament of the Lord's Supper, 'a voice was in my soul suddenly, "I AM MADE TO SIT IN HEAVENLY PLACES".' Here are Harris's notes of the sermon, written excitedly as best as he could:

'1. That God would have his little children to be without sin. 2. That while we are little we may excel of improving [that is, we may excel at being sensitive to] sin. 3. That then we are to go to Christ's intercession, trust [apply] to ourselves [that] we can't fall. 4. That

God the Father gave the Son. First, it was God alone that had the property over [ownership of] us and so could give us to Christ, Jn. 17.7, "Thine they were and Thou gavest them to me". Secondly, he alone could fit to Christ a body able to bear the great burden of sin, Heb. 12:2; Isa. 53:6. Thirdly, it was God who was able to reward Christ for this. Christ says, "I will save them and do Thy will", and so He was made a reproach and a curse. All our sins were taken from us to be laid on Him, but it is the application of His death to us by name that changes us. The sins of Ephraim and Judah are not found (Hosea 13:12; Jer. 50:20). God is just and will not be paid twice for the same crime. Christ paid for them, and therefore thou art clean, all gone! Believers, God's justice found your sins on Christ and so you are acquitted. He showed a parallel, as if a man [we] had murdered a man. The dogs followed us by the smell of the blood, but while the man was almost taken, another came by and took his cloak of blood. Then the dogs bound to him, and the first man was acquitted. He died for all [sins], past and to come. He cleanses from all sin. Christ took our sins on Him and gave us His righteousness. Thou art as righteous in Christ's righteousness before God, as Christ; and He in thy sins was sinful as you. Objection; here is liberty to sin. No! the children of the covenant cannot, will not, and dare not sin! Sin you, if you can: you can't! . . . I speak not to your hearts but to your ears, it is God that says within you, "I pardon you for my own Name's sake." He pardons all that thou hast done and shalt do.'

Even powerful preaching and exalted experiences were not allowed to deflect the leaders away from their purpose of gathering and feeding young believers. Thus, the Harris account continues, 'Then was led to set the congregation in Bands and to desire the leaders to come to Mr. Rowland. Showed the order of the English societies. Then put to them about the Trefeca Welsh School, and about keeping a man to translate into Welsh, and to keep the Printer in work still: to keep the box in each society; about true Gospel discipline.' Such an undertaking demanded a measure of grace which was not theirs to command, and this explains Harris's confession before the end of that memorable day: 'I feel my soul knit to my dear Brother Rowland. I hope God will perfect His strength and wisdom in our weaknesses. We are young striplings.'[1]

For the meeting with Dissenting ministers which would soon be upon them, both Rowland and Harris would need in double measure that heavenly aid mentioned by Harris. The experimental nature of Methodist piety, the particular emphasis of their doctrine, and their strong ecclesiastical affiliation to the Church of England were to

[1] MS i. 487, 488, 489; xxix. 121–2; Diary 63.

bring about unacceptable tensions in the relationship between them.

For that meeting on October 1 and 2, 1740, Rowland and Harris chose Defynnog. About eight ministers of all denominations were present, among them John Oulton the Baptist minister of Leominster, and Edmund Jones, the Independent minister from Pontypool. A further eight or more 'laymen teachers' made up the full complement. Its purpose was to explore common ground for working together in the Awakening. The gathering was representative of a substantial number,[1] and for Rowland and Harris the prospects of co-ordinating their efforts was a great incentive.

There was much to unite them. Their faith was biblical rather than philosophical. Regeneration and justification were in the forefront of their preaching. There was a shared concern for the evangelism of their countrymen and the nurture of their converts. Both Dissenters and Anglicans alike were orthodox in their doctrine. They were equally concerned about the practical godliness of professed believers. For early preaching opportunities both Rowland and Harris had often been indebted to the Dissenters who invited them to their localities.

The vision for such a conference had undoubtedly come from Harris: 'I told them of the first motive in me to it was in hearing of associates in Scotland and America, etc., to meet to unite, to love and strengthen each other's hands.' Harris was referring to the 'Associate Presbytery' in Scotland, and the contemporary attempt by the Erskine brothers, Ebenezer and Ralph, to bring the Church of Scotland more into line with Scripture and the principles of the Reformation. The element of gathering together those with true reforming principles seemed commendable. He felt that a similarly united base for reform in Wales appeared appropriate and desirable. Harris's nervous record of the meeting, however, betrays the tensions which surfaced. He was in turn 'dejected' and 'had sweetness'; there was 'tenderness' and 'dryness'. Agreement between them was stated formally rather than joyfully: 'We proposed Rules for the (that is, this) Society – that we should open our whole heart to each other. Then settled a fast next Tuesday for four great ends, 1. of

---

[1] They included the Baptists, Morgan Harris of Blaenau Gwent; James Roberts of Ross; Miles Harry of Pontypool; and the Congregationalists, James Davies of Merthyr; Henry Davies of Neath; Rees Davies of Abergavenny; David Williams of Cardiff; and Lewis Rees of Llanbryn-mair. See MTU, 28.

humbling for all sins of the nation and professors, etc; 2. to be saved from all errors; 3. for faithful ministers; 4. for my persecution [that is, public opposition to his preaching].'

The achievements were minimal. For his part, Rowland would have found little in them to compensate for the danger of being branded a separatist and a turncoat. It is hard to escape the impression that the exercise was staged mainly to provide Harris with a platform to present his own blueprint for the Great Awakening in Wales. 'I was much helped to deliver my charge to them of Christ's little lambs, they promising to see the Welsh School and the Societies, and to promote universal love, and the sale of books, and about uniting in all good.'[1]

Nevertheless, for both Rowland and Harris, the outcome must have been a bitter disappointment, if not a major disaster. Their hopes of a new initiative in the work were shattered, and more seriously, the existing harmony, tenuous though it had been, between Anglicans and Nonconformists in the Welsh work, was soon in ruins. In January of 1742 Harris wrote in his diary, 'God must do the whole work, else it won't be done. We can't unite ourselves to each other, nor edify each other. This we had trial of in our last Society at Glyn [Defynnog], which soon broke.'[2] From Defynnog, Dissenters and Methodists went their separate ways.

There were several reasons for this failure. If Harris had exceptional organising abilities, he also had an overbearing manner, as Whitefield was to find some months later.[3] At Defynnog the Dissenters, who were older in years and maturer in spiritual judgment, would have been sorely tried by his dogmatism, inexperience, and impatience. On the issue of Church Order there was considerable divergence. The Dissenters could hardly be expected to dismantle their own simple structures for the sake of Methodist scruples about the strength of Anglicanism. In any case, on this point

[1] CMHO, 18, 50–1; M. H. Jones, *The Trevecka Letters*, p. 263–6. For 'The Associate Presbytery', see J. H. S. Burleigh, *A Church History of Scotland*, 1961, pp. 278–82; and David Boorman, 'Ebenezer Erskine and Secession' in *Diversities of Gifts*, 1980 Westminster Conference Papers. cf. also DAL ii. 86–90 for Whitefield's attitude towards the 'Associate Presbytery'.

[2] xxvi. 183.

[3] 'The Lord keep you and me, my dear brother, from a hot, rash, positive, overbearing temper. This I think is the predominant failing in my dear brother Harris.' Whitefield to Harris, October 28, 1741, in *Proceedings of the Wesley Historical Society*, vol. x (1916), p. 24.

of ecclesiastical identity the Methodists had a blind spot which they were unwilling or unable to recognise. They maintained that they were a part of the parish system of the Church of England, but already their societies were functioning as separate fellowships, and their laymen, like Harris, were involved in irregular practices.

Doctrinal differences, too, were already emerging. The Dissenters affirmed that 'many are gone to heaven who obtained not a full assurance thereof here, but none without being in Christ. . . . There is a weak faith, a strong faith, and a full assurance of faith'. Harris was adamant that assurance was of the essence of saving faith: 'We can't pass from death to life, from being children of wrath to be made children of God, from being blind to come to see . . . unknown to us; the work of the devil can't be destroyed by the Son of God in us and we not know it, no, it is impossible.'[1] Here, Harris was at variance with his own experience. 'Gave an account of myself', he recorded on August 2, 1740, 'how at first filled with assurance, and lost it by Mr. Dalton [one of Griffith Jones's congregation] calling it Satan's work till I met Mr. Whitefield, and he agreed to all'.[2] When his assurance was restored he began to teach that it was inseparable from saving faith. Writing to John Wesley in 1741, he complained of Jeremy Taylor's book, *Holy Living*, because it regarded assurance as presumption. His letter continued:

'When any would ask, "How is it with your soul?", my cry was like the rest of such as I conversed with, "I am up and down; I have great cause to doubt". And so I passed for a humble Christian, till the Lord sent Brother Whitefield about 2½ years ago and the first question he asked me was, "Do you know that your sins are forgiven you?" and the question astonished me, having never heard the like before. I could not say they were, being in great bondage under the law. . . . Then I began to groan for liberty, using one means after another to bring me out of myself to Christ. . . . A word that Brother Whitefield said was of great use to me and conveyed much light to my soul. Talking once in company he said, "As yet he is only working for life and not from life." There came such a conviction to show the difference between a man under the law and under grace, the first doing all good in order to have life, and the other doing good out of gratitude because he had life.'[3]

[1] MS ii. 11; 6–7. For this debate see Eifion Evans, 'Adding to the Church in the teaching of the Welsh Calvinistic Methodists', in *Adding to the Church*, The 1973 Westminster Conference Report, pp. 61–3.
[2] xxix. 11.
[3] MS ii. 145–6.

Clearly, Harris regarded the lack of assurance as proof that an individual was still 'under the law' and without a saving relationship to Christ, quoting Romans 8:9 and Galatians 4:24, 29 in support of his view.[1] At Defynnog, Harris alienated the Dissenters by his unyielding position on this issue.

The subject also became a cause of dissension between Harris and Rowland. It came to a head between them in the spring of 1742. 'There arose a dispute that held to midnight about our knowing our interest in Christ, between me and Brother Rowland. . . . What I was afraid of in him was his feeding hypocrites; and what he feared in me was my overthrowing weak ones.' A week later Harris wrote: 'had still on me a conviction that Brother Rowland is wrong, and I can't agree when he is dabbling so much with saying we may be in Christ and not know it.' Another week passed before he wrote to Whitefield, 'I believe the doctrine of assurance is what is needed. It would be to God's glory and the present good of the Church. If you should be called of the Lord to write a discourse upon it, we should translate it into Welsh. Indeed it is much wanting.'[2] There does not seem to have been any response from Whitefield to this request, but other works bearing on the issue were translated into Welsh for publication: Ralph Erskine's *Law-Death, Gospel-Life* which appeared in 1743 with some of Rowland's hymns appended, and *The Assurance of Faith* which was translated by William Williams in 1759.[3] Their appearance was an indication that the position held by

---

[1] HVP, 52.

[2] CMHO, 64; xxxiv. 79; MS ii. 242.

[3] HMGC i. 414. For the former, see *The Sermons and Other Practical Works of the Late Reverend Ralph Erskine*, vol. ii. 1865, pp. 9–102; and for the latter, see *The Whole Works of the Rev. Ebenezer Erskine*, vol. i. 1826, pp. 192–256. Ralph Erskine states, 'When their comfort is always up and down with their frame: if their frame be up, their comfort is up; if their frame be down, their comfort is down; if their frame be gone, their comfort is gone, their joy is withered; herein the legal spirit discovers itself. . . . It is a legal temper in the believer, when his assurance is lost by his challenges. It may be, the man attained some sweet measure of assurance, but behold sin prevails, conscience challenges him, and hereupon he razes all; this is an evidence of a legal temper, contrary to that gospel-spirit which we may see acting in David, Psalm 65:3' (p. 78). Ebenezer Erskine high-lights one aspect of the problem: 'When we speak of the assurance of faith, it is not to be so understood, as if every one that has faith were perfectly free of *doubting*. This, I apprehend, is what scares many at this doctrine of the assurance of faith. They think that if there be an assurance in the essence of faith, then it

Rowland and Williams prevailed among the Welsh Methodists.

Rowland's position emphasised the experimental nature of assurance as being the work of the Spirit. The Spirit confirmed the Scripture in the believer, strengthened the principle of faith in him to work by love, and witnessed to his adoption. His position is reflected in the relevant questions to be asked of those admitted to the 'general' and 'private' societies. These were included in the 1742 document *Sail, Dibenion, a Rheolau'r Societies neu'r Cyfarfodydd Neilltuol a ddechreuasant ymgynull yn ddiweddar yng Nghymru* (The Basis, Purposes and Rules of the Societies or Private Meetings which have lately started coming together in Wales). This document will be considered in greater detail later. For the present it is enough to note that the questions to be asked in the 'general society' included these: 'If you have not yet received the witness of the Spirit to bear witness with your spirit that you are a child of God, do you find that you are always seeking God with all your heart, and seeking Him alone? Do you find that you have no peace or rest, in all that has been wrought in you so far, until you prove Christ in you, until you know that you believe?' The first questions to be asked in the 'private society' were:

'Do you know that you believe? 1 John 5:10, 13; that you are in the faith? 2 Cor. 13:5; and that your sins are forgiven? Ps. 32:5; and that Christ died for you in particular? Gal. 2:20; and now lives in you by His Spirit? 2 Cor. 13:5; and that God has loved you with an everlasting love? Jer. 31:3. Does God's Spirit always bear witness with your spirit, that you are a child of God? Rom. 8:16.'

From these questions it is clear that the Welsh Methodists were being taught that assurance was the Christian's birthright, and were encouraged to seek God's face in that awareness. By implication, however, not every believer possessed that assurance.

This understanding of assurance remained as the accepted teaching of the Welsh Methodists. Only a little verbal modification is found in Williams' *The Experience Meeting (Drws y Society Profiad)* which appeared in 1777. The first questions to be asked of 'members of longer standing' echo those of 1742:

would follow, that every true believer behoved always to have such assurance as to be free of *doubting*; which lies cross to the experience of the generation of the righteous. But this objection goes on a palpable mistake, as if faith and a believer were one and the same thing' (p. 211).

'As to the clarity of their witness – how did they first receive their witness? And have they lost any of it since they first received it? What was the effect wrought in them by this witness? Has this witness been repeated by the Holy Spirit, or have they never received it since? And do they now believe that their sins are forgiven; and that Christ has died for them in particular; that God has loved them with an everlasting love? And does the Holy Spirit bear witness with their spirit that they are children of God? Do they possess these things? Or do they only have feelings of hope engendered by the enjoyment and pleasure they get from hearing the Word, and from various other religious exercises when they are met together with the saints, but which they then lose when they are by themselves? And further, when great tempests of unbelief beat upon them, where do they turn – to this old experience, or to Christ Himself, to seek for new light and a new experience, as well as for wisdom and strength?'[1]

Assurance, being experimental in its nature, was capable of ebb and flow, a greater and a lesser measure. All real assurance is given by the Spirit, traceable to His activity in the mind, heart, and life of the believer.

The questions also high-light another feature in the emerging Welsh Methodism which the Dissenters found disturbing. Some Dissenters were never happy about the experimental emphasis in the matter of 'opening the heart', while for the Methodists this was the surest way of determining authentic Christian experience and nurturing Christian growth. Harris complained of the Dissenters in 1742, 'I see all thirst after the Tree of Knowledge and not after the Tree of Life.' This was echoed in 1746: 'We emphasise faith in the heart rather than light in the head. . . . They do not search the heart.' And to Whitefield, Harris reported of some of them, 'They come to have no real spiritual discipline at all, for all their examination in receiving a church member in, is to examine the orthodoxy of their principles, and about the morality of their lives, of a common change, which many hypocrites have tasted more . . . being strong and bitter enemies to assurance, and to opening the heart.'[2] This was not to disparage orthodoxy or a reasoned presentation of the Gospel message: Rowland's sermons show ample evidence of both. Neither was it a claim that a 'believing frame' could be infallibly known or determined. It was, rather, an insistence that saving grace affected

[1] Morris Davies, *Deuddeg Pregeth*, tt. 322, 323; William Williams, *The Experience Meeting*, 1973, pp. 39–40.
[2] xxvi. 102; TM i. 334; STL i. 12, 13. cf. R. T. Jenkins, *Yng Nghysgod Trefeca*, 1968, tt. 22–30.

every aspect of human personality, providing evidences of change which could be both monitored and nurtured, however imperfectly[1].

The Dissenters also registered misgivings and opposition to the disorderly manifestations often accompanying the preaching of the Methodists. One of their number, Evan Davies, towards the end of 1740, objected to Harris about the effects of Rowland's ministry. While Davies 'much condemned it, [saying] that God was a God of order', Harris defended Rowland by saying 'it arose from a sight of their misery'.[2] For the Methodists, the revival's manifestations were no more disorderly than Isaiah's cry in the temple, or Peter's falling down, at the sight of the divine majesty and holiness (Isaiah 6:5; Luke 5:8).

At Defynnog in October 1740 two spiritual lifestyles, one old and the other new, were in tension around the same Gospel message. In the outcome the two went their own separate ways as 'the Dissenting Way' and 'the Methodist Way'. Once again the new wine could not be contained in the old bottles.

[1] cf. Jonathan Edwards' remarks in *Some Thoughts Concerning the Present Revival of Religion in New England*: 'Was there ever an age wherein strength and penetration of reason, extent of learning, exactness of distinction, correctness of style, and clearness of expression did so abound? And yet, was there ever an age wherein there has been so little sense of the evil of sin, so little love to God, heavenly-mindedness and holiness of life, among the professors of the true religion? Our people do not so much need to have their heads stored, as to have their hearts touched; and they stand in the greatest need of that sort of preaching which has the greatest tendency to do this'. *The Works of Jonathan Edwards*, vol. 1, 1834, p.391.
[2] HVP, 40.

'We stand in continual need of the Spirit of God to wound and heal us, to cast us down and lift us up, to show us our misery and help us destroy sin; to work grace and to act with grace when wrought in us; and to make, and keep us nothing in our own eyes; nothing less than Almighty power can do this well. But a sight of forgiving love, and a justifying Jesus, can make us leave all our idols and love Him with all our hearts and souls.'

HOWEL HARRIS
in 1740

'Of all the means of grace, I know of none more profitable than the special fellowship meetings, called private societies, to correct, to direct, to edify and to encourage weak members who are ever ready to stray aside. . . . First of all they are so, because they are means of keeping up this same warmth and liveliness that was ours at the beginning.'

WILLIAM WILLIAMS
The Experience Meeting

12

'Fire From Heaven'

In spite of the disappointment of the Defynnog gathering of ministers at the beginning of October 1740, Rowland was busier than ever in travelling and preaching. He was in the mid-Wales county of Radnor on the 7th of that month, preaching with 'much authority' on James 1:6-7, 'Let him ask in faith, nothing wavering.' 'He showed', says Harris, 'that doubt will destroy us unless we destroy it. My soul was fed sweet in a mysterious manner, so I can feel but not explain to others.' The sermon strengthened him for his ordeal the next day when he appeared before a Court at Presteigne, in the same county, facing a charge of riotous assembly.[1]

Neither Harris nor Rowland was a stranger to persecution. At Builth, Breconshire, in February 1739, Harris was silenced by constables sent from the Magistrate.[2] In June 1739, he had been arrested at Pontypool, and was acquitted at the trial which followed at Monmouth in August.[3] Further north, at Machynlleth, Montgomeryshire, in February 1740, he 'very narrowly' escaped serious injury at the hands of a furious mob.[4] Understandably, Harris was ever afterwards reluctant to venture into North Wales.

Even parts of the south were hazardous. William Seward was one of Whitefield's travelling companions in the early years. He died in October 1740, from injuries received as a result of mob violence while Harris was preaching at Hay, on the Welsh border.[5] Harris

[1] *Transactions of the Radnorshire Society*, vol. xx. pp. 68-9.
[2] xxiv. 33. cf. Harris's letter shortly afterwards, 'I hope a great work will go on in this country, but it will cost some battles with Satan first.' (MS i. 148.)
[3] MS i. 188, 189, 192, 209, 218.
[4] MS i. 289.
[5] DAL i. 583-4; MS ii. 35; xxxviii. 18; lviii. 12, ff. Portions of Seward's Diary are located at the University College of Wales Library, Bangor and at Chetham's Library, Manchester. Some family papers are included among The Bute Documents at the Cardiff Public Library.

heard of his death from Rowland on Sunday, October 26. They were together at Ystrad-ffin again, and Rowland's sermon was on Simeon's receiving the child Jesus in the temple, Luke 2:28–30. The obvious parallel between Seward and Simeon in their readiness for glory after 'seeing' God's salvation in Christ made the text an appropriate choice for the occasion. A comparison between Harris's notes of Rowland's preaching at the time, and the published sermon of Ebenezer Erskine on the same text shows a great measure of correspondence between them. It is clear that Rowland was relying heavily on Erskine's material. This bore the title, 'Christ in the believer's arms', and had been in print for two years in *A Collection of Sermons on Several Subjects, preached by Ebenezer and Ralph Erskine*. At Ystrad-ffin that day, 'all cried out aloud' under Rowland's preaching, and Harris later felt a necessity 'to join Brother Rowland in publishing these Glad Tidings over the world' as well as to 'the poor scattered lambs that come through persecution here.'[1]

When Harris ventured north again during November he consulted 'about bringing a Methodist' to the Bala area, and as a result Rowland followed him before the end of the year. Rowland visited Llanuwchllyn, at the other end of the lake from Bala. As was his custom, he first asked the incumbent and wardens for permission to preach in the church, and this was granted.

'It seems that the old clergyman cared for none of these things. Apparently, it mattered not to him who preached or what they preached. Mr. Rowland and he began to talk about the second birth, but the old clergyman acknowledged that he knew nothing of this subject. "What", said Rowland, "art thou a master of Israel, and knowest not these things?" It happened that Mr. Lloyd, the incumbent of nearby Llangower, was at Llanuwchllyn at the time of Rowland's visit. When he understood that permission had been given to Rowland to preach in the parish church, he bitterly railed on the careless old clergyman, and proceeded to the church, compelling the old man to go with him. By the time they reached the church the service had started. It is said that Rowland at the time was reading the chapter of curses in Deuteronomy, the 28th., and that Lloyd of Llangower became extremely agitated, asking among other things, "Is Stephen, Glan-llyn (a landowner who, it is thought, lived nearby)

[1] HH Diary No. 63A. The sermon is in Ebenezer Erskine's *Whole Works*, vol. i. 1826, pp. 138–65. The sections which Rowland used are on pp. 138, 139, 143–4 of this edition.

accursed?" "Yes", replied Rowland, "if he is an ungodly man." This was reckoned to provide reason for still greater disturbance, and between the Llangower clergyman, and an old woman who rang the church bell as energetically as she could, the service was hindered. To the great dismay of several who had earnestly longed to sit under his ministry, Rowland was obliged to go away this time without preaching.'[1]

Nevertheless, his journey in North Wales left a lasting impression. His sermon on 'the clean heart' was fervently repeated to Harris the following January when he visited the Bala area. This time Harris was violently opposed, and he felt deep remorse later at what he considered to be his cowardice in the course of his heavenly duty.[2] It was a heavenly duty because it was sustained by 'fire from heaven', as Rowland pointed out in his sermon on Romans 8:28, 'We know that all things work together for good to them that love God'. In it he speaks 'a word to the ungodly':

'O sinners! What do you mean by persecuting the people of God? if you purpose to smother, or cool that spark of fire which the Lord has kindled in their hearts, your purpose will never succeed. It may be blown into a flame, but it cannot be extinguished. It is fire from heaven; and the more the rain descends on it, the more it will blaze. You take the best course to keep them in God's ways. The heat of the sun will sooner strip the pilgrim of his vest, than the frost and snow. Let them alone: the Spirit of God in them is more than a match for hell and all its black battalions. These stars shine brightest when the night is darkest. . . . Suffer not the sun to fade your flowers, but to ripen your fruits.'[3]

It was such confidence in God that enabled Rowland to triumph over adversities. The 'fire from heaven' was inextinguishable, and it was spreading.

At Ystrad-ffin on November 11, 1740, Harris heard of Rowland's 'great power and success' in Carmarthenshire and Llangeitho, 'many falling as dead' at the latter place. Having been with Rowland in the chapel, Harris had reason to comment, 'Rowland is more persecuted or spoken against than me; saw that he is more faithful, but resolving to bear a part of his cross.' The next day he 'was most dreadfully

---

[1] MC i. 613.
[2] i. 18; MS i. 437. Harris heard about the sermon from Jenkin Morgan, at the time one of Griffith Jones' Charity School masters and later a Dissenting minister, for whom see HMGC i. 212.
[3] *Eight Sermons*, pp. 87, 96.

terrible, especially to such as opposed Mr. Daniel Rowland, a faithful minister owned of God'. Harris's withering reproof was probably directed against some of the Dissenters who were critical of the powerful manifestations which attended his ministry at that time. However, those who had the best opportunity to prove the value of Rowland's ministry found strong reasons for attending it faithfully, as Harris reported when visiting Llangeitho on December 15: 'Here many Dissenters leave the meeting to come to Mr. Rowland's communion.'[1] Those who joined Rowland's congregation did so in the face of considerable prejudice and opposition. In the spring of 1741 some Dissenters in West Wales were calling Rowland 'a madman', and assurance 'the doctrine of the devil'. Harris vigorously defended Rowland's character in the face of 'aspersions spread of him', and 'spoke of how the Lord owns him'.[2] The distance between Methodist and Dissenter was gradually widening.

To restore and realise the vision which had been so cruelly laid aside at Defynnog in October 1740 was not easy. Yet there were strong incentives to it. There were still some Dissenters sympathetic to Methodism, and in any case, Methodism was still growing under the blessing of God. More workers and more societies were being raised by God month after month. What was needed was a different base on which to build the distinctive Welsh Methodism which was emerging. Between them Rowland and Harris agreed that the next organising body should be different from the Defynnog grouping. It would consist only of those who acknowledged the revival to be of God, and considered its lively preaching and experimental soul culture to be biblical.

Harris's organising abilities were already activated. He could count over fifty societies in South Wales in November 1740. A month later he was already formulating rules for them. The local societies were to meet twice a week, and hold a fast day once a month before the Sacrament. In addition, the ministerial and lay leaders were to meet once every two months at specified locations in turn. Until this time there had been great variation in the quality of their membership and in the regularity of their arrangements. The Cardiganshire societies under Rowland, for instance, had 'the most power [that is, life], though not so good order'. Their welfare was

[1] MS i. 491, 493. [2] xxix. 126.

very much on Harris's heart: 'Lord, it is Thy work. Thou hast carried it on until now. O, go on with it!' Uncertainty crept into Harris's organising efforts, too: 'I hope this is not numbering the people, but for better regulating everything, that we may know and overlook [supervise] all, and how to propagate books printed around them all immediately.'[1]

Perhaps no more poignant reason could be given for pressing on with the plans for organised oversight of the societies than the letter of a Carmarthenshire exhorter (or recognised society leader), William John. After Harris's last visit in the area a number of families had begun family worship in the home, and another area nearby was also experiencing 'some reformation':

'I further acquaint you about the societies that are set up at Carmarthen and Llanlluan chapel, hearing that they are very zealous in edifying one another, keeping [meeting] twice a week. But with us it is very cold and very slow to come, for we keep twice a week and there are many gathering Sunday evening. But at other times we are only about three or four. Some persons that I hoped of them to be members are persuaded to the contrary by some worldly people and, as I suppose, by the minister saying it is but a hot zeal and an unnecessary work, and that it would be better to everyone in private to read at home than to come to the society, and instead of reading, the time is spent in telling stories and slandering their neighbours. Some take a great business to scoff but we are not in the least manner moved nor slackened, thanks be to God. . . . I had a sharp temptation of the world in these days which was in an unjust manner. For my landlord had set upon me [demanding money for which there was neither debt incurred nor value received] for the sum of about twelve pounds. I had received nothing for them, only they take them by violence, because I was a Presbyterian in their opinion. But I was not moved against them in the least.'[2]

Already, to belong to the society involved a willingness to be 'made a gazingstock both by reproaches and afflictions'. What the apostle said of the Hebrew Christians could also be said of them: 'ye . . . took joyfully the spoiling of your goods, knowing in yourselves that ye have in heaven a better and an enduring substance' (Hebrews 10:33–34).

In the light of these considerations, the meetings which took place on Friday and Saturday, February 13 and 14, 1741, at Llandovery in

---

[1] *Bathafarn*, iv. 58; xxiv. 57–8.   [2] MS ii. 21–2.

Carmarthenshire were extremely important. They laid down the basic framework of Welsh Methodism at an early stage in its development, and determined its character, identity, and practices for the rest of the century. The vigour of its life might flow and ebb, the distinctives of its doctrinal emphases might display a measure of fluidity, but the course of eighteenth-century Welsh Methodism was charted conclusively at these meetings.

Altogether there were some thirty persons present, two Anglican and two Dissenting ministers, and the rest were lay teachers. Rowland probably served as Moderator, as on so many future occasions, and many of the laymen had still to be 'examined' before they were officially admitted to the work. On the Friday night, after prayer, agreement was reached 'in principles' and on specific matters. A worthy conduct before the world was emphasised and it was decided to meet in future every two months 'going heart and hand after Christ'. Grief was expressed over those who had already 'gone off from the Defynnog Society' to the Dissenters because of false statements issued against Rowland and Harris. There was the recognition of the need to make provision for Welsh schools. Unity prevailed on the leaders' Calvinist stance in the Arminian-Calvinist issue between Wesley and Whitefield. This issue of divisions within Methodism will be discussed in the next chapter.

The following day the company travelled the ten miles to Ystrad-ffin to hear Rowland and Harris expounding God's Word. The size of the congregation was put by Harris as a thousand people. Appropriately, Rowland's theme was 'the danger of not being faithful to the end'. Harris 'yielded to the cutting' (that is, the reproof) he personally felt in the light of his cowardice at Bala when Rowland said, 'that it is the last works Christ rewards and not the first'. Rowland proceeded to show '1. that it is faith and not doubt that purifies us. 2. that we must some time or other renounce all and fall to God from self. 3. that it is by believing and not doubting that we obey and glorify God.' Harris's soul was fed and he had an overwhelming sense of God's love. When it came to Harris's turn to preach, he returned to the theme of assurance. 'Nothing goes to heaven but what comes from there, so the seed that comes from there will go there. Showed that all the saints had a witness . . . and that all doubt for a time, but don't abide in it. It is a mark of the hypocrite to be easy without testimony.'

Resuming their business meeting, there was harmony in doctrine ('established in the truth'), and in being open to each other about their experiences ('our need here was to be as little children'). One person dissented from their policy that the Methodists should attend the parish churches in spite of the fact that 'a carnal man' was officiating, on the grounds that the liturgy was pure. The main achievement of the conference was a set of rules for the purpose of managing their affairs and exercising efficient oversight over the entire Methodist movement in Wales. These were copied by hand and circulated to all society leaders. A Llangeitho copy, with hymns by Rowland, Howel Davies and others added to it, has been preserved. They were originally written in Welsh:

'1. The commandment of our Saviour through Paul is that we do not forsake "the assembling of ourselves together" (Heb. 10:25), lest we become hardened through the deceitfulness of sin.

2. It was the practice of His disciples to meet privately.

3. In every age He has confirmed that this is His will by granting His presence in such private gatherings. We, therefore, in submission to Him, on His command, following the footsteps of His flock, and on His promise to be with us when two or three are present, to strengthen each other's hands, to exhort each other to love, to enlighten one another and watch over one another, have agreed to meet every two months in agreement with the following rules:

a. that we are to open our whole heart to one another in simplicity like little children; and that we do not hide any of the evil which we see within, in accordance with James's command (James 5:16); that we may pray for one another; and of the good that is in us [that is, the good work wrought by God], after the example of David (Psalm 66:16), in order to strengthen love towards each other and to know our hearts better, the wiles of Satan and the work and growth of grace.

b. that we, according to the advice of our Saviour (Matt. 18:25), should watch over one another's tempers and behaviour, and with gentleness reprove one another. We should confess any suspicions that lurk in our minds lest love should grow cold; if the suspicions are true and confessed by the guilty party [he is to be reproved, and on repentance, restored].

c. that we shall allow ourselves to be examined by one another as to our motives, purpose, and principles in all things, regarding our souls, bodies, talents, knowledge, memory, understanding, times, wealth, strength, opportunities to do and receive good, as not our own but as God's gracious gifts in Christ to each one. And because we are so prone to keep things to ourselves, there should be a willingness to be examined by each other to ensure that every talent is laid out for God in Christ according to the rule of His Word.

d. since we trust we are led by God's Spirit, the Lord has made us of one mind in respect to doctrine; for free grace; weak and strong faith; election; perseverance in the state of grace; dominion over sin; absolute perfection in Christ, in parts in ourselves and allowing of progress in degrees.

e. as there is but one body in Christ, so opinion is not the entrance into our midst, but whoever is able to give us satisfaction that he savingly knows Christ, and is a genuine believer, we extend to him the right hand of fellowship.

f. that we take God's Word as our rule in everything; keep one day each month for prayer and fasting, for 1. the Society; 2. for the present divisions in God's Church. 3. for faithful ministers and an increase in their number. 4. for the general success of the Gospel. 5. for the sins of this kingdom and of the whole world. 6. for the supervision of the societies, the members of this conference, for godly schools, and to help advance every cause.'

In conclusion Harris entered in his diary, 'I hope the Lord made us simple, and all our concern is for God's glory.'

Returning to Ystrad-ffin the following day, a Sunday, Harris was convicted in chapel when he heard Rowland preaching from Isaiah 53. Rowland 'spoke hard on unfruitfulness', says Harris, for whom the sermon was without unction. Monday, February 16, was a better day for Harris. He 'discoursed to about 5 or 6,000 or more, the greatest crowd I ever saw in Wales', and had his faith established in reading Griffith Jones' sermon on the Covenant of Grace. News of further success made his heart joyful and submissive: 'I heard Brother Howel Davies in a particular manner being assisted most amazingly, the people crying out wondrously. Brother Rowland is owned more than any, and the Lord gave me to rejoice and to be willing I should become nothing so as others be exalted.'

The meetings at Llandovery had been a watershed. Before it there had been uncertainty about the way ahead. Hopes of embracing a wide circle of friends had not been realised, and a sense of disappointment at the resulting disagreements and tensions had followed. For a time it looked as if the Methodists' attempts at concerted effort in spreading the Gospel and safeguarding its fruit in Wales would flounder completely on the rock of suspicion and misunderstanding. In contrast, those present at Llandovery had shared a common understanding of what God was doing in the land. They had felt real union with one another. They had agreed on the most effective measures for achieving their objectives of preaching and regulating the spiritual life of the societies under their care. Furthermore, recent reports had confirmed that the success of the

Gospel was undeniable. However exaggerated Harris's estimates of numbers attending the public meetings may have been, a thirst for God was evident among many. Harris had every reason for optimism in his concluding remarks on the occasion: 'The Lord is opening a way for His Gospel farther, I hope.'[1]

The implementing of the decisions of the February 1741 Llandovery meetings went smoothly enough. Harris, appropriately, was entrusted with the task of initiating regular meetings of the societies in the different areas. He did so with evident relish, emphasising the importance of love, simplicity and openness towards one another. The agreed rules were presented and the policy of staying within Anglicanism 'till they would turn us out' was insisted upon. By June it was even possible for him to designate different persons to particular areas of responsibility, covering all of the South Wales societies.[2]

All this gave the societies security, identity, and independence. Locally, there was the guarantee of close and regular supervision along clearly defined principles of nurture and instruction. Corporately, the societies were linked together along clearly defined and distinctively Methodist lines. Far from being divisive, the doctrinal statement embodied in the rules gave cohesion and stability. Its experimental emphasis went a long way towards safeguarding warmth of fellowship and mutual caring and growth. However, this identifiable network of groups of people, dotted across the land and meeting for religious purposes, understandably gave an impression of a schism from the Established Church. It was a suspicion which the Methodist leaders were at pains to dispel from the minds of their allies and their foes, Dissenters and Anglicans alike.

While Methodists maintained a separate identity, they could still claim to be, in the main, Anglicans. Although they met together apart from the usual church services, they were careful to avoid clashing with the times of those services. For the two sacraments they still attended their parish churches. They sincerely subscribed to the Thirty-nine Articles, used the Anglican Prayer Book, and were irreproachably loyal to the civil authorities from the lowest to the highest in the land. Yet entrance into their midst was neither open

[1] HH Diary No. 69; M. H. Jones, *The Trevecka Letters*, pp. 245, 250–51; MTU, 35; HVP 51; William Williams, *The Experience Meeting*, 1973, p. 15; CMHO, 21, 24–5; xxxvi. 69–71; HMGC i. 149, 169–70.
[2] CMHO, 19–22, 31.

nor desirable to all and sundry. To the vast majority of their fellow-countrymen, Methodism was an extreme organisation made up of religious fanatics whose insistence on new birth and obedience was totally unacceptable. For society members, on the other hand, this was a God-given reality of belonging together to a common Lord on the basis of a common salvation and for the common purpose of edification and service. In their esteem it was the rightful expression of their high calling in Christ Jesus. Their submission to mutually agreed rules within the fellowship was both a discipline and a delight. Submission to abuse from the outer world was more than compensated by what God was doing in their hearts.

'I find I love you as much as ever, and pray God, if it is His blessed will, that we may all be united together. . . . Though I hold particular election, yet I offer Jesus freely to every individual soul. You may carry sanctification to what degrees you will, only I cannot agree that the in-being of sin is to be destroyed in this life. . . . May all disputings cease, and each of us talk of nothing but Jesus and Him crucified. This is my resolution.'

GEORGE WHITEFIELD
to John Wesley, October 1741

'He had a heart susceptible of the most generous and the most tender friendship. . . . This, of all others, was the distinguishing part of his character. How few have we known of so kind a temper, of such large and flowing affections!'

JOHN WESLEY
of George Whitefield, 1770

Many were the erring teachers,
Some to left and some to right;
But heaven's counsel kept in balance
Honest Rowland's Scripture light;
And whoever deviated
From pure paths of grace divine,
He exposed their serious error
Until all returned to line.

WILLIAM WILLIAMS
of Rowland

13

'The Glory of Free Grace'

In 1739 the most prominent ministers involved in the Revival in Wales were all Calvinists. They included Rowland, Harris, Griffith Jones, and others, Dissenters and Anglicans. Preaching at Ystrad-ffin on August 23, 1739, from Ezekiel 33:11, 'As I live, saith the Lord God, I have no pleasure in the death of the wicked; but that the wicked turn from his way and live: turn ye, turn ye from your evil ways; for why will ye die, O house of Israel?', Rowland's theme was repentance. In the sermon he emphasised that repentance was a response to God's initiative: 'Think not with the Arminians that you can be a devil today and a saint tomorrow; you cannot repent when you choose. Therefore the time is NOW, because it is God's gift.'[1]

The following month, however, Harris felt that the country was overrun 'with Arminianism and Darkness', and later was convinced 'that the Arminian doctrine is of the devil though it may be dressed up in fine colours, setting one foot on the Rock but the other on the sand'.[2] He had come to that position by listening to the sound preaching of men like Rowland, Griffith Jones, Thomas Jones of Cwm-iou, and Thomas Lewis of Merthyr Cynnog, and by reading 'the good old orthodox Reformers and Puritans' whose works he held 'in great esteem'.[3]

[1] HH Diary No. 48; HRS, 245; HVP, 14; xxix. 97.
[2] xxvi. 11, 13, cf. Harris's diary entry for the next day, October 27 (Diary No. 50): 'exposing the danger of Arminianism. Six things for us to see: 1. the necessity of believing before striving; 2. of working from and not for life; 3. of coming poor, wounded, lost, vile, sinners, blind, labouring, hungering, and not the reverse, to Christ; 4. of receiving the truth in the love of it; 5. that Christ comes by believing and not by working in; 6. how through Christ we hate sin, how faith in the promises (Deut. 30:5; Jer. 24:7; Ezek. 36:24, 26, 28; Lk. 11:18) subdues Satan's temptations.'
[3] STL i. 166. For a discussion of Harris's doctrinal pilgrimage and indebtedness to the Puritans see Eifion Evans, *Howel Harris*, 1974, pp. 15–18.

According to Harris, a 'long discourse' between Griffith Jones and himself in September 1739 had been about 'particular and universal redemption, he [Jones] saying that God has given a certain number to His Son of elect, but has reprobated none; that meritoriously we are justified by the righteousness of Christ, instrumentally by faith, and declaratively by good works'.[1] Back in November 1737 Harris had 'heard the doctrine of free grace being pressed home warmly, clearly and powerfully' by Thomas Lewis.[2] As for Thomas Jones, he wrote to Whitefield after the latter's visit to his parish in April 1739: 'The New Covenant is all of grace, the beginning, growth, and ending; He is the Alpha and Omega; it is all of grace, so this jealous God will have all the glory of man's salvation to be ascribed to his free grace in the face of Jesus Christ.'[3] Such were the convictions held unitedly by the leaders of the Revival in Wales regarding the sovereignty and freeness of God's grace in salvation.

Others in Wales, among both Dissenters and Anglicans, held the opposite position. In England the division was also found among the Methodists themselves. Simply stated the issue turned around the source of saving faith; was the individual sinner able to initiate and maintain faith, or not? If not, by whom and in whom was faith initiated, and on what principles, and with what effect? How certain could the individual be of its continuance to the end of his life? Theologically stated, the controversy concerns the nature and power of God's grace in saving sinners. Historically, it has found expression in the works of the sixteenth-century theologians, John Calvin and Jacobus Arminius.

Rowland followed Calvin in his understanding of grace, as did Jonathan Edwards in America, Whitefield in England, Griffith Jones and Harris in Wales. John and Charles Wesley took the opposite position, generally following Arminius. In spite of this they were able to work together for a time, so that Whitefield was able to call on John to take over at Bristol in April 1739 when he left the area. The distinctive doctrines which Whitefield held in common with Calvin and Rowland were to him Scriptural, precious and related, so that he was able to write in November 1739:

[1] HVP, 20.
[2] BCM, 143. Merthyr Cynnog is a rural parish 15 miles west of Trefeca.
[3] MS i. 166. Cwm-iou is some 15 miles east of Trefeca over the Black Mountains.

'This, however, is my comfort, "Jesus Christ the same yesterday, today, and for ever. He saw me from all eternity; He gave me being; He called me in time; He has freely justified me through faith in His blood; He has in part sanctified me by His Spirit; He will preserve me underneath His everlasting arms till time shall be no more. Oh the blessedness of these evangelical truths! These are indeed Gospel; they are glad tidings of great joy to all that have ears to hear. These bring the creature out of himself. These make him hang upon the promises, and cause his obedience to flow from the principle of love. They are meat indeed, and drink indeed to my soul. . . . I bless God, His Spirit has convinced me of our eternal election by the Father through the Son; of our free justification through faith in His blood; of our sanctification as the consequence of that, and of our final perseverance and glorification as the result of all. These I am persuaded God has joined together; these neither men nor devils shall ever be able to put asunder."'

Writing to John Wesley on August 25, 1740, Whitefield identifies the source of his convictions on the matter:

'Perhaps the doctrines of election and final perseverance hath been used, (and what doctrine has not), but notwithstanding, it is children's bread, and ought not . . . to be with-held from them, supposing it is always mentioned with proper cautions against the abuse. Dear and honoured Sir, I write not this to enter into disputation. I hope at this time I feel something of the meekness and gentleness of Christ. I cannot bear the thoughts of opposing you: but how can I avoid it, if you go about (as your brother Charles once said) to drive John Calvin out of Bristol? Alas, I never read anything that Calvin wrote; my doctrines I had from Christ and his apostles; I was taught them of God.'[1]

Having responded to Whitefield's invitation to preach in his absence at Bristol in April 1739, Wesley acknowledged a prior arrangement to which he had been party. 'Our dear brethren,' he says, 'before I left London, and our brother Whitefield here, and our brother Chapman since, had conjured me to enter into no disputes, least of all concerning Predestination, because this people was so prejudiced for it. The same was my own inclination.' Before the end of the month, however, Wesley had preached against this very doctrine. He later decided to print the sermon, and it was in print before May 14.[2]

Wesley's pamphlet of thirty-five pages bore the title *Free Grace*, taking as his text for the sermon, Romans 8:32, 'He that spared not

[1] GWL i. 98, 129, 205.
[2] Griffith T. Roberts, *Dadleuon Methodistiaeth Gynnar*, 1970, tt. 75, 78.

his own Son, but delivered him up for us all, how shall he not with him also freely give us all things?' There is little attempt at exposition of the Scripture passage, and 'the horrible decree of predestination' against which it is aimed is represented as making preaching vain and destroying all incentive to godly living.

Wesley took this step deliberately. Whitefield had pleaded with him 'to enter into no disputes – least of all concerning predestination' and repeatedly expressed his grief at the damaging controversy that would follow if he did. Three things combined to bring Wesley to a decision in favour of brushing this appeal aside; he had received some letters which inferred that he was a false teacher; he cast lots (to which he was prone) and the outcome was 'Preach and Print'; and finally there was the seemingly powerful impression the sermon created when it was preached.[1] Whitefield meanwhile went to America, and his reply was not published until early in 1741, and even then with considerable reluctance. It carefully answers Wesley's objections to the doctrines of grace, and ends with this vigorous appeal:

'Dear Sir, for Jesus Christ's sake, consider how you dishonour God by denying election. You plainly make salvation depend not on God's free grace, but on man's free will; and if thus, it is more than probable Jesus Christ would not have had the satisfaction of seeing the fruit of his death in the eternal salvation of one soul. Our preaching would then be in vain, and all invitations for people to believe in Him would also be in vain. But, blessed be God, our Lord knew for whom He died. There was an eternal compact between the Father and the Son. A certain number was then given Him, as the purchase and reward of His obedience and death. For these He prayed, John 17, and not for the world. For these, and these only, He is now interceding, and with their salvation He will be fully satisfied.'[2]

On his return from America in March, 1741, the separation between Whitefield and the Wesleys was public knowledge.

These events affected the Welsh Methodists profoundly. As ever, Harris was the one most directly involved, but Rowland and the others also felt the shock-waves of the controversy. Wesley's sermon had not been long off the press before Harris wrote to Wesley a frank reminder of his responsibilities:

[1] *John Wesley's Journal*, vol. ii. pp. 184–5; cf. DAL i, Chapter 8; *George Whitefield's Journals*, pp. 564, ff.
[2] *George Whitefield's Journals*, p. 587.

'The night you left London, you turned a brother out of the society, and charged all to beware of him, purely because he held the doctrine of election. My dear brother, do not act in the stiff, uncharitable spirit which you condemn in others. If you exclude him from the society and from the fraternity of the Methodists for such a cause, you must exclude brother Whitefield, brother Seward, and myself. I hope I shall contend with my last breath and blood, that it is owing to special, distinguishing, and irresistible grace, that those that are saved are saved. O that you would not touch on this subject till God enlighten you! My dear brother, being a public person, you grieve God's people by your opposition to electing love; and many poor souls believe your doctrine simply because you hold it. All this arises from the prejudices of your education, your books, your companions, and the remains of your carnal reason.'[1]

Harris was speaking for others as well as for himself. It was inevitable that the Calvinistic Methodists should see Wesley's doctrinal aberration in terms of a departure from the simplicity which is in Christ and the plain meaning of Scripture.

There was another aspect to Wesley's doctrinal position which troubled his fellow-Methodists, in Wales as in England, namely, his teaching on perfection. By this term Wesley taught that through the imparting of perfect love by God, the Christian's 'heart-sin' may be eradicated, and true love, for God and man, energised. The loose terminology he used gave rise to a great deal of confusion, suspicion, and accusation. Early in 1741 Harris received this enquiry from a London bookseller and friend of Whitefield's, Samuel Mason:

'This comes by the desire of many friends who have heard with grief that you countenance the Mr. Wesleys' in their strange, rash, hot, unwarrantable manner of speaking upon perfection. . . . I am sorry to hear any of the societies are infected with the artifices of Satan; and particularly that you and Mr. Rowland could give any countenance to it. . . . But it may be the reports we have had concerning your defection from the truth are without foundation . . . let me entreat you therefore to satisfy me, and many other of your friends in town . . . and I entreat you be simple and open and free. . . . When you write in answer to this, use no ambiguous words, but words that may convey a clear idea, and as Scriptural as may be, and words used in divinity whose sense is known; for I observe when people advance new doctrines, they also advance new and strange

[1] Luke Tyerman, *The Life and Times of the Rev. John Wesley*, vol. i. 1878, p. 315.

words and phrases, whose sense and determinate idea is known to none but themselves.'[1]

Harris's answer is lost, but his opposition, and that of Rowland, to the Wesley brothers' position was communicated to Charles Wesley in a long letter of twenty-six closely written pages sent in February 1741. Writing three months later to Griffith Jones, Harris defends Rowland's position: 'With respect to the charge of his holding sinless perfection, when I read to him my letter to Mr. Wesley against *his* perfection, he was the most earnest in persuading me to send, and even to publish it.'[2]

Now that Methodism had been fractured there was an inevitable polarisation of forces. Nevertheless, as has already been indicated, in October, 1741, Rowland was sufficiently confident of the Calvinism of the Welsh Methodists, leaders and societies alike, to invite John Wesley to visit Wales. Harris's judgment however, differed: 'I did not agree to that till Brother Whitefield and some of us should meet first, and so I believe he is not come.'[3] In the event, Wesley did come, and was respectfully received by both Rowland and Harris. By the end of November, however, Whitefield was concerned at the sustained partisanship of the Wesley brothers.[4] Wesley's relationship with Rowland was never close, and after the formation of a joint association between Welsh and English Calvinistic Methodists in 1743 Wesley was even further distanced from him. It was Harris, through his periodic visits in England, who mainly kept in touch with Wesley, and from time to time actively sought co-operation with him in the work of the Gospel.[5]

The Calvinism of the Welsh Methodists was not a sterile disputation about words. It produced hearty evangelistic endeavour, vigorous striving for conformity to God's law, and intense personal devotion to the Saviour. Something of this is conveyed in Rowland's

---

[1] MS ii. 17, 18, 19. For a lucid appraisal of Wesley's position on 'Perfectionism' see J. I. Packer, *Keep in Step With the Spirit*, 1984, pp. 132–145.
[2] MS ii. 24–28; Hugh J. Hughes, *Life of Howell Harris*, 1892, p. 176. See also MS ii. 86, and for Harris's letter to John Wesley, 140–142.
[3] MS ii. 147.
[4] *Bathafarn*, x. 43; *Proceedings of the Wesley Historical Society*, vol. x (1916), p. 24, Letter of George Whitefield to Howel Harris from Bristol, which should be dated November 28, 1741.
[5] See A. H. Williams, *Welsh Wesleyan Methodism*, 1935, pp. 23–8.

sermon on 'Free Grace Indeed', based on Luke 23:42–3, 'And he said unto Jesus, Lord, remember me when Thou comest into Thy kingdom. And Jesus said unto him, Verily, I say unto thee, Today thou shalt be with me in paradise.' The sermon begins with a sentence which sets the theme: 'In this passage the glory of Free Grace shines unrivalled.' It is supported by an appeal to the example of Jacob and Esau, Malachi 1:2–3, Romans 9:11, 21. 'By saving one thief, and leaving the other to receive the due reward of his deeds, is signified to us that the election prevailed', says Rowland.

'God's judgments are very secret and unsearchable. It is our duty to honour and reverence them, rather than to dispute about them. . . . The Almighty loves to display His sovereignty, and to act freely without control. . . . We choose to be at liberty ourselves to do as we please; but we would confine the Lord to do as we like, and limit His dealings with the children of men within the bounds of our narrow conception. We would lay Righteousness itself to our crooked line and find fault, if it doth not agree with our scanty measurement. . . . Down, therefore, in the dust let us bow before Him, and acknowledge our acquiescence in His sovereign will.'

In Rowland's view, these deep truths were for the eye of faith to admire, rather than for the skill of reason to judge.

They were also practical truths, keeping the sinner from the Scylla of presumption and the Charybdis of despair:

'The next instruction, that may be gathered from the distinguishing favour shown to one of the thieves . . . is this: we may learn from the mercy reached to the one, and with-held from the other, that the safest way to heaven is between hope and fear. Fear is the cable which lays hold on hope, and hope is the anchor which keeps fear firm. Fear makes thee cowardly and faint-hearted, when thou considerest what thou art; how little good is in thee, how unworthy thou art of any blessing, yea, even to breathe in God's air; but hope makes thee bold and enterprising, by showing thee how good the Lord is; how infinite He is in His mercy, and matchless in His love.'[1]

Rowland held to these convictions throughout his lifetime. He did so with firmness, but also with charity towards those who differed from him. These qualities proved effective in safeguarding Welsh Methodism from both disunity and censoriousness over this issue. Without them, Wesley's future visits in Wales might have proved disruptive or even divisive.

---

[1] *Eight Sermons*, pp. 47, 54, 55–6.

Another separation, however, took place within the wider Methodist ranks in 1740, namely, between the Moravians and the Methodists. When Harris first went to London he stayed with James Hutton the Moravian bookseller and Whitefield's publisher. Soon Harris was attending their society at Fetter Lane, as did Whitefield and the Wesleys. This first-hand acquaintance with the Moravians left a lasting impression on Harris, although he disowned some of their excesses. These focused particularly on an over-emphasis on the physical aspect of Christ's sufferings, on what amounted to a denial of the means of grace before conversion, and on confusion about the place of good works after it. In turn, Wesley's position on perfection caused the Moravians grave misgivings, and his exclusion from their pulpit was the occasion of a parting of the ways in July 1740.

For the Welsh leaders the break was not serious. Few Moravians laboured in Wales, and those who did were, in the main, confined to the English-speaking areas, such as Pembrokeshire. Further, Moravianism made very little impact upon Wales before the 1760's, by which time Calvinistic Methodism had firmly established its teaching and ethos among the new generation of Christians in the land. The most prominent of the Moravians to labour in Wales were, from 1744, John Gambold (a Pembrokeshire man), and John Cennick (who toured Wales in 1753). In October 1743, before he joined the Moravians, John Gambold stayed at Rowland's house and was able to give Harris his assessment of the Welsh Awakening's progress. Much later, in 1772, Rowland could pay a cordial visit to the Moravians at Haverfordwest, although he strenuously withstood what seemed to be their Antinomianism.[1]

The Welsh Methodism of 1740 was kept identifiably one, and doctrinally Calvinistic, by the lively zeal and clear teaching of its leaders. In its essence and character it was simply New Testament

[1] John Thickens, *Howel Harris yn Llundain*, tt. 89, 90; iv. 2; *Bathafarn*, ix. 35; Luke Tyerman, *op. cit.* i. 305–311; Clifford Towlson, *Moravian and Methodist*, 1957, Chapter 5; STL i. 108, f.; R. T. Jenkins, 'The Moravian Brethren in North Wales', in *Y Cymmrodor*, vol. xlv, p. 40, n. 1; Gomer M. Roberts, 'Y Morafiaid yn Neheudir Cymru', in *The National Library of Wales Journal*, vol. xx. No. 3, Summer 1978, tt. 273, ymlaen; Moravian Archives, London, Archives Book p. 45, 'John Cennick's Journals, 1748–1753'. For John Cennick's theology see Vernon Williams Couillard, 'The Theology of John Cennick', in the *Transactions of the Moravian Historical Society*, vol. xvi. Part III (1957).

Christianity. In its expression it was emerging in a mould which bore unmistakable resemblance to the teaching and piety of Augustine and Calvin. Yet it had its own distinctives: a fervent spirituality and a lively proclamation, discipline and freedom, devotion and practice, being woven together and held in tension within the prevailing Anglicanism of the time. Even in this early period, however, that same tension produced in some an objection which was both unexpected and sad, in others, a reaction which was quite predictable.

'When the Gospel comes, and is faithfully preached, then the harvest begins, the day of grace commences. . . . How dreadful will be our lot if we neglect our harvest! We are guilty of the greatest sin; and we shall suffer the greatest loss, and we shall have to endure the greatest misery, and that an eternal misery. You had better suffer the loss of everything than the loss of your salvation. Whatever interferes with your harvest, with the eternal interest of your souls, you should lay aside, as you do when engaged in your earthly harvest. . . . So you should by all means do with respect to the harvest of the soul. It should engage your principal attention; especially as there is no second harvest; so that you cannot repair your loss by another. If you neglect and fail to secure this, you are undone for ever.'

GRIFFITH JONES
preaching on Matthew 9:37

'Never will your name be wanting
While men's alphabets abound;
Still your schools, and still your writings
Sound your praise and fame around.
Your memorial rather lingers,
Not on gravestone, wood, or wall,
But by heavenly impression
Carved on hearts that God did call.'

WILLIAM WILLIAMS
Elegy to Griffith Jones

14

'A Father in Israel'

In terms of losing friends, the least expected, and for a time the most serious setback for the Welsh Methodists, was the withdrawal of Griffith Jones' support. Both Rowland and Harris owed him a great deal, and were dependent on him for wise counsel. All of them were committed to the Established Church, and to the Calvinistic aspect of its teaching. They had shown extraordinary zeal in spreading the Gospel among their countrymen, and had faced a measure of opposition for doing so. From the spring of 1740, however, Jones became increasingly critical of Rowland and Harris. Matters worsened to a crisis in May 1741, and several years passed before the estrangement ended.

Ever since their first meeting at Defynnog in 1737, Rowland and Harris had known a closer association with each other than with Griffith Jones. They were both in their twenties, while Jones, in his fifties, was more of an elder statesman than a crusading colleague. In his earlier years he had itinerated for the sake of preaching the Gospel. Later, however, his vision of literacy evangelism fully occupied his time.

His early evangelistic fervour had found recognition and support, first from Sir John Philipps, an active member of the Society for the Promotion of Christian Knowledge, and later from Madam Bridget Bevan, wife of the Member of Parliament for Carmarthen. Sir John had contributed to Whitefield's support at Oxford for a time and regularly provided funds for religious education and literature. His links with Jones were very close: his sister was Griffith Jones' wife, and the living of Llanddowror had been given to Jones by Sir John 'entirely upon the account of his learning and piety, without solicitation'. Madam Bevan's house at Bath provided both Jones and Whitefield with contacts and opportunities for evangelism among the titled people of their day. Madam Bevan herself was no mean debater, the Countess of Huntingdon's biographer mentioning the Earl of Chesterfield as one who crossed swords with her: 'Having studied the Deistical writers of the age, she was enabled to give all her eminent ability and clearness to the discussion of the topics he was fond of introducing. She easily and solidly refuted his plausible objections to revealed religion.' Her home was at Laugharne, and Howel Harris could say of her: 'She gives up herself entirely to doing good, distributes Welsh Bibles about, has several charity schools on her own foundation. . . . It was a taste of heaven to be with her; she made me a present of a very fine pocket Testament.'[1] These powerful patrons had protected Jones' zealous activities, and in time he had settled down within the limits agreed by episcopal authority.

At first, Jones recognised in Rowland and Harris the same zeal that he had felt so strongly himself. Rowland's position as an Anglican clergyman provided similar opportunities and imposed limitations, as did his own, while Harris for the time being could usefully serve the charity schools. The constraints which Rowland and Harris felt, however, could not be contained within these limitations, and they were sufficiently compelling to fortify them against Jones' censure. For an emerging Welsh Methodism, therefore, the association between Rowland and Harris was crucial. Without it the influence of Griffith Jones might have channelled the Awakening into a more regular ecclesiastical movement, but it would have been a far less effective power in the life of the nation.

Griffith Jones' misgivings originated with Harris's itinerant preaching. Jones felt strongly that Harris should temper his zeal with wisdom and refrain from his evangelistic travels in order that he might seek ordination at the hands of a bishop. This Harris would not do. On March 6, 1740, he heard that Mr Griffith Jones and Mrs Bevan 'are very angry with me because I am not ordained'. When he next visited Llanddowror, Jones was amiable enough on hearing Harris give an account of his travels, and even suggested to him, 'When some term offends, use another; if they won't hear "born again", preach the same thing as "repentance".' On the next occasion of their meeting, however, Jones 'lashed the young men that mount up chairs to exhort', a clear indication of his disapproval of some Methodist practices.

[1] For Sir John Philipps and Bridget Bevan see DWB; *George Whitefield's Journals*, p. 67; GWL i. 13, 14; (A. C. H. Seymour), *The Life and Times of Selina, Countess of Huntingdon*, vol. i, 1844, pp. 454, 455; MS i. 87.

1. *Wales, showing location of places mentioned in the text*

2. 'Old Llanddewibrefi from the Tregaron Road', from a water colour of 1836 by John Parker at the National Library of Wales

3. *Pantybeudy, birthplace of Daniel Rowland. See p. 29*

4. *Caerllugest, birthplace of Elinor Davies, who became Rowland's wife. See p. 30*

5. *Daniel Rowland as a young clergyman, from* The Gospel Magazine, *July 1778*

6. *Duke Street Chapel, Westminster, London, where Rowland was ordained deacon in 1734. From* The Journal of the Historical Society of the Presbyterian Church of Wales, *Vol. xxxv, p. 81. See p. 30*

7. *Ystrad-ffin Chapel in the Towy Valley, Carmarthenshire, a favourite preaching location in Rowland's early ministry. From* Y Tadau Methodistaidd, *Vol. i.400.* *See pp. 41–2*

8. *Defynnog Church, where Rowland and Harris first met in 1737. From* Y Tadau Methodistaidd, *Vol. i.101.* *See p. 51*

9. Howel Harris, layman and organiser, Rowland's fellow-worker for many years

10. Griffith Jones of Llanddowror, forerunner of the Awakening, pioneer in Christian education, Rowland's spiritual father and early counsellor. From Transactions of the Carmarthenshire Antiquarian Society, Vol. xxiv (1933), Frontispiece

11. *Contemporary drawing of William Williams of Pantycelyn,
hymn-writer, Rowland's colleague and closest friend.*
From Y Tadau Methodistaidd, *Vol. i.141*

12. *Pantycelyn, near Llandovery in Carmarthenshire, the home of
William Williams*

In August of the same year another issue highlighted their differences. This time it was doctrinal, Jones 'speaking favourably of Archbishop Tillotson', and challenging Harris to declare his opinion of Whitefield's statement that Tillotson 'was no better than Mahomet'. 'I said', writes Harris, 'I would prove that whatever would fall short of the inward real change in the Gospel is nothing better than the Koran, though we may have the terms of Christianity.' The disunity between them was becoming more and more apparent, and in the November of 1740 Harris was praying, 'O unite all thy faithful ones, (feeling grief for the division between Brother Daniel Rowland and Griffith Jones.)'[1]

After the Llandovery meeting of February 1741 matters worsened rapidly. Harris was in Pembrokeshire in the month following, hearing that Griffith Jones had been preaching there. Amongst other things, Harris reported Jones as saying, 'That we should not speak our experiences'. This last statement seemed to cut at the very root of Methodism, and Harris must have been filled with dismay on hearing again the next day of Jones' opposition to 'opening our hearts to each other, the good or the bad'. Worse was to come, for when Harris reached Llanddowror he found that 'they here fell on dear Brother Rowland', even a housemaid deriding him. Harris, too, had his share of derision on account of his 'irregularity in going about . . . twitting me with not labouring, that it was now dear times' [that is, by holding meetings during working hours he was keeping people from earning their wages].[2]

A spate of letters from Jones to Madam Bevan which appeared in the Spring of 1741 were highly critical of Methodism and its leaders. 'Our new itinerant preachers are exceedingly erroneous, harsh, conceited and disorderly; and have, as I am informed, no appearance of that soberness and humility in their temper, discourse or doctrine, that become true godliness.' In another letter they were charged with being 'very defective in common sense, common manners, and veracity or common honesty'. On a more personal note, Rowland and Harris were said to 'make no great conscience of speaking the truth' and were guilty of 'enthusiastical and incredible fooleries', in spite of being personally reproved by Jones. At the time Howel Davies was serving as curate under Jones, but even he was 'tinged with a little dotage', and had a 'sly prevaricating temper'! In

[1] MS i. 479, 480, 481, 483, 430.
[2] HVP 52, 53, 54-5.

addition, Rowland was charged with blatantly ignoring the rules which regulated the payment of schoolmasters in Jones' Charity Schools. This public dissociation from the Methodists on the part of Jones would, he felt, serve a useful purpose: 'to convince all people, who know of it, that I am in no degree a favourer of their rude enthusiasm, which is so void of common civilities and moral conversation etc., that none, who is acquainted with the spirit of the Gospel, can approve of'.[1]

Some of the information about Rowland and Harris evidently reached Griffith Jones only by hearsay. He did not attend the meetings of the Methodist leaders, and therefore was not present at the February Llandovery meeting to counsel or modify their policy. Advancing age had perhaps made him more cautious in his dealings with the ecclesiastical authorities, and added to his awareness of the dangers of a zeal without knowledge. His strictures regarding lay preaching, 'opening the heart', and a careless attitude to their daily walk before men were both timely and salutary. Some of his other allegations against the Methodists are less convincing, and probably stemmed from too much attention to the rumour and slander of trouble-makers.

Meanwhile, opposition to the Methodists was becoming more marked and more vocal, and Jones was clearly unhappy about the future usefulness of his Schools. He was widely regarded as a supporter of the Methodists, if not their originator. Indeed, a pamphlet issued in 1750 went so far as to charge Jones with having 'put the windmill' into Whitefield's head, and sent him 'a-Don Quixoting up and down the world.'!'[2] As things stood in May 1741 the Rector of Llanddowror was deeply implicated in Methodism. Hitherto his zeal for the Gospel had found a twin expression in an educational and evangelistic crusade. Now, regrettably, there had to be a choice between two types of evangelism. Griffith Jones held on to his Schools, disowned the Methodists, and gradually distanced himself from the Great Awakening. As a result, Welsh Methodism lost its respected figurehead and senior statesman. Today he is

---

[1] xxxv. 54, 55.
[2] *A Letter to the Revd. Mr. George Whitefield*, p. 6. See also W. Moses Williams, 'The Friends of Griffith Jones' in *Y Cymmrodor*, vol. xlvi (1939), p. 3; Thomas Kelly , *Griffith Jones, Llanddowror*, 1950, p. 34; TGW ii. 221–2; and Eifion Evans, 'Early Methodist Apologetic', in CH 1979, pp. 33–42.

remembered as an 'educational reformer', a 'pioneer in adult education', rather than as a pioneer preacher of the Great Awakening.

While at Llanddowror early in May 1741, Harris found himself 'set upon' by Jones, and 'called reviler, a railer, proud and haughty'. Nevertheless, he parted from his old adviser in 'great love.' The main purpose of his visit, however, had been to defend Rowland, for he felt that Satan was 'busy carrying tales' against him to Jones. The attempt at reconciliation failed, and Harris wrote to Jones on the 15th of the month:

'It is the concern of the Lord's cause that makes me write to you, not cunningly and artfully, but in simplicity, in the spirit of our common Lord, and from the abundance of the heart. On hearing Mr. Rowland about four years ago, experiencing myself the power of the Word under him, seeing the visible sign of power in him, and the ardent effects of his ministry in the calling of some within my own knowledge, I was persuaded of the Lord's being with him in a more than ordinary manner. That these persons were called effectually appeared from their brokenness of spirit, humility, love and watchfulness, as well as from what they said of the work of grace in themselves, with their simplicity of mind, and growing acquaintance with the evil and plague of their own hearts. Such were the signs of conversion under his ministry in hundreds from time to time, which I saw. It was not difficult to read a broken heart and a humble spirit in their streaming eyes. Some have applied to me, crying "What shall we do for an interest in the Saviour?" And on asking when they came to be thus concerned about the state of their souls, have owned that it was not until they heard Mr. Rowland in such a place. Many, when they are thus awakened, complain that they hear of nothing elsewhere but duties, not food for faith, no discoursing on the stratagems of the devil and his way in keeping them from Christ, of the mystery and difficulty of believing and of denying their own righteousness, their own wisdom, and their own sufficiency. They never hear elsewhere of the various workings of unbelief, how it keeps the soul from Christ, and of their utter helplessness and blindness; that they, notwithstanding all their reading and studying, are but natural men; that until the Spirit opens their eyes they cannot see the holiness and purity of God and their own impurity, the excellency of Christ and the various workings of sin and grace, of faith and unbelief.'

Having spoken of the authenticity of the effects of Rowland's preaching, Harris turns next to defend his friend's attainments and industry:

'When the difference is shown between light in the head, (that comes from second causes, and affects neither the will nor the affections), and that which comes from the Spirit of God through His own Word; and when cautions are given against reading unsound authors, an outcry is made that human learning is wholly laid aside, whereas it appears from a sermon of Mr. Rowland now in print that no one is more for reading the Bible than he is. He also reads all the old experienced authors he finds. I know he gathers and gives as much time as possible to reading. But having three congregations of between two and three thousand to look after [Llangeitho, Nant-cwnlle and Llanddewibrefi], and being called out to preach almost every week, and to build up hearers in a more private manner [in the societies], he cannot have much time for reading. But if you were to hear him and witness the effects of his preaching, I believe that all your prejudice would fall to the ground, and that your soul would be united to his in divine love. I am persuaded that you are both sent by the same Lord; and if severe persecutions should come, you would be two of the first called to the flames together, to ascend to the same place, to praise that distinguishing eternal love to all eternity, that called you from so many thousands and made you to differ. And shall anything now divide you? I feel there is nothing nearer my heart than union between all the faithful labourers of Christ, and that their hands may be strengthened to the utmost.'

This impassioned plea, that nothing should be allowed to separate God's servants, was typical of Harris. He fervently believed that those, who had experienced the same divine operations on their soul and served the same eternal kingdom, belonged together in spite of their differences. The malice of some and the misunderstanding of others accounted for a great deal of opposition to his own ministry:

'But I find many that I once thought would come on, resting; some on their duties, some on their works, prayers, tears, and feelings, who never had the deadly wound to see that they must be damned unless covered with Christ's righteousness, and His nature wrought in them. Others rest in convictions, without any life, divine love, fellowship with God and Christ, and without growth in knowledge of themselves and of our dear Lord. Others fall back to the world, to love it as much as ever; others to their old sins and to a careless, lazy, carnal spirit, keeping up the old form of godliness. These are the most ready to oppose. They, in a most artful manner, not willing to be searched and cut to the heart, take away perhaps a word, or half a sentence, not fully explained, and carry it to others that may be the children of God, which may stagger them. It is true an unguarded expression may be spoken from the vehemence of our soul. I believe that when you look a little calmly you will find that all aspersions against Rowland come from such a spirit. As to what has been reported of some expressions used by him in preaching, I am persuaded they are false. It is true that when he has been informed that they were mistaken by his hearers, or not explained in the sense which he intended, he has had the humility to correct what was not clearly stated. I find that there are some people who make it all their business to gather and set all in the blackest light, in order to divide you. There are but few faithful ministers, especially in this dark benighted church, and shall they be divided?'

Objections to some of the powerful manifestations of the revival are next dealt with. As the Awakening progressed, and indeed later intensified, these were to provide critics with matter for accusation and ridicule, and would draw from the Methodists some of their most valuable treatises. Harris's early attempt at apologetic is therefore significant:

'As to "crying out", some I have seen and spoken to. They were so penetrated by the Word that they could not help crying out, some on seeing that they were lost, and others on seeing that they had pierced the Son of God by their sins; whom if you had seen you would have had no scruple about, but have blessed God on their account. There is, it must be confessed, much of the evil spirit and hypocrisy in the crying out of some. I publicly objected to it, and Rowland thanked me. Their singing together on the way has much simplicity in it. The heart being thus kept heavenward, trifling thoughts as well as idle talking are prevented. When my heart is warmed by love, I cannot help singing, even if I am hoarse. Their speaking to or embracing each other in love, I am sure, was also in great simplicity. I find such love in my own spirit towards you, that if I were near you I could not help embracing you in the love of God, which others may construe into imprudence.'

Rowland's high regard for Griffith Jones is reaffirmed next with the utmost confidence. To some it may appear strange that no reference is made to Jones' instrumentality in Rowland's conversion. It may be that Harris is merely showing respect for Rowland's reticence in talking about his own experiences. In any case, the point at issue is more concerned with a right ministry of God's Word than the validity of a person's salvation:

'I have been informed that it has been told you that Rowland does not speak well of you, which I am sure is not correct. Such is his opinion of you that when any wish to be admitted to communion, if he finds that they have been under your examination, [Llanddowror, the scene of Jones' labours, was about thirty miles south of Llangeitho] his usual way is to raise his hand and say, "If you have been there, I have nothing to say after him". I have always heard him speak of you with great esteem. As to your books, I never speak to him much about them; but his selling and encouraging the sale of them is sufficient proof of his approbation.'

One paragraph remains of this illuminating letter. It gives a clear insight not only into Rowland's doctrinal position, but also into the Welsh Awakening's most cherished citadel, namely, an experimental Christianity:

'As to his holding that there is no true faith without full assurance, I have heard him say that doubting is like a city through which all saints pass, but none can be satisfied until God sends the Comforter, the Spirit of adoption, to bear witness with their spirit that they are born of Him. Then they drink the water of life, sup with Christ, and He with them. Their eyes being spiritually enlightened, they understand what full and complete satisfaction the Son of God has made to divine justice for all who believe. This they are enabled to apply to their own hearts having the testimony of the blood and of the water also, or the "washing of regeneration and renewing of the Holy Ghost" which is known to be of God by comparing it with the Word.'

When Harris wrote that letter 'he had great power to plead' in prayer for both brethren. The actual writing of it cost him a night's sleep.[1]

In spite of its courtesy and reasonableness, however, the letter failed to achieve its objective. Two lay teachers were discouraged by Jones when they visited him shortly afterwards, Herbert Jenkins on the 17th May and Richard Tibbott in July. To Jenkins he complained of the irregular activities of unordained, itinerant preachers, of unguarded expressions used by the Methodists, and their pride. 'Now there are signs of more persecution than ever', Jenkins writes to Harris, 'the clouds begin to gather. It may be the great rain of persecution is now beginning to drop. The Lord help us to be faithful, and to aim only in all things at the glory of God.' To Herbert Jenkins, Jones' emphasis on church order and Scripture literacy was unacceptably strong. 'I asked Mr Jones what to do to the little Societies. "Desire them", says he, "to learn my Catechism, and so to examine it one to the other, and pray, and sing Psalms, and no more." That indeed is good, but an experimental knowledge of Jesus Christ in the heart is better.' With Tibbott, usually an honest, discerning reporter, Jones questioned whether there was any grace at

[1] Hugh J. Hughes, *Life of Howell Harris*, 1892, pp. 172–6; xxiv. 111, 113.

all in Rowland and Harris. On hearing this Tibbott was 'cast down', and it made him doubt all that he had ever experienced.[1] In November 1741, Harris heard 'how the old saint, Mr. Griffith Jones, is led away to be against us by carnal ministers'. It was also reported that Jones was 'blaming Brother Rowland for calling ministers carnal ministers', terminology which Jones himself had used of some of his colleagues in the earlier years of his ministry!2

While in some measure Jones and the Methodists went their separate ways from this time, the Gospel which they believed in common was stronger than their differences. Jones knew better than to rest content with educating people in Christian principles, and the Methodists did not emphasise an experimental Christianity at the expense of 'head knowledge' but through it and along with it. At one of Jones' churches in May 1742, Harris heard him preach on the Prodigal Son and he comments, 'he was affected deep himself in showing Christ's love'. No Methodist could have asked – or experienced – more. The same day Harris was noting again in his diary, 'Setting up catechisms on Sunday.' It was not merely a Harrisian whim, but from the end of 1743 it was Welsh Methodist policy. In 1747 the resolution was confirmed and extended: 'That the brethren should do all they can to stir up the people to a more diligent reading and searching of the Scriptures, and to inform themselves in all the practical principles of the Christian religion in order to set up catechising in our families and societies. . . . They should use all the help they can come at, the Rev. Griffith Jones' Exposition on the Church's Catechism, and the [Westminster] Assembly's Catechism, etc. until such time as the brethren shall draw up a catechism.' Even in 1745 relationships were still strained, Jones being 'offended with the screamings and crying out under the Word', and Harris thinking that in Jones' esteem of the catechism he had raised it 'too high, that the use of it is not universal but subservient to preaching'.3

From this point on, Jones' influence on Methodism was a

---

[1] i. 66 and footnote; MS ii. 74, 75.
2 CMHO, 43, 44; HVP, 64; See NLW Ottley Papers No. 100, Griffith Jones' letter to the Bishop, dated July 11, 1715, 'The next sort (worse or as bad as any) are the carnal, covetous, profane and voluptuous, whose lives give the lie to their doctrine.'
3 HVP, 72, 94, 115; xxiv. 117; xlviii. 74; l. 49; cf. STL i. 138; HMGC ii. 479.

corrective one from without rather than a determinative one within. Leadership and initiative passed to Rowland, often to be resented and on occasions even challenged by Harris, but otherwise generally acknowledged as strong and responsible. Given Rowland's personal indebtedness to Jones, and his sustained admiration of his ministry, the prophetic voice which issued from Llanddowror continued to make its impact on the development of Welsh Methodism.

It did so particularly in two areas. One was Jones' strenuous insistence on the authority of God's Word over individual experience. Harris got this message in May 1741, when Jones explained 'the spirit of error' in his sermon. '1. When we lean on our own experience before the Word; and 2. on our own understanding to read and apply the Word above the judgment of others: 3. When we set up little things or even great truths any further than they affect us.' On another occasion 'valuable Mr. Griffith Jones' drew from the parable of Dives and Lazarus (Lk. 16:31) the doctrine 'that the testimony of the Scriptures is the only means, and if any will not receive this, no other shall be given'.[1] Experiences were not an end in themselves and were to be tested as well as regulated by God's Word. This was a salutary lesson for the Methodists at a time when dramatic spiritual experiences were commonplace, and the danger of counterfeit manifestations was correspondingly high.

Jones' other main contribution to Welsh Methodism was his insistence on the centrality of God's Son in the believer's salvation. In March 1740 he preached some ten sermons on 2 Samuel 23:5: 'He hath made with me an everlasting covenant, ordered in all things, and sure; for this is all my salvation, and all my desire.' Harris heard at least two of them, and told Mrs James of Abergavenny, 'Sure your soul is starved for want of being here.' In summary, Jones had shown, 'the riches of this covenant; that all that belongs to our salvation is in Christ – grace, increase of grace, faith, love, repentance, pardon, assurance. He was led much to speak of the goodness of the Lord in choosing His children and in suffering them to be buffeted, trampled upon by Satan and the world.'[2]

Covenant theology ranked high in Jones' esteem. His 600 page *Hyfforddiad i Wybodaeth Iachusol o Egwyddorion a Dyledswyddau Crefydd* (Instruction in a Saving Knowledge of the Principles and Practices of Religion), is an extended exposition of the Church

[1] HVP, 63, 81.   [2] HVP, 24, 32; MS i. 300.

catechism. The first part appeared in 1743, and its subtitle demonstrates the covenantal framework of his theology:

'setting out man's fall by sin, and his recovery by Christ; the excellency, privileges, and conditions of the Covenant of grace; the great advantages, the superlative comforts, and religious duties which stem from those privileges; together with the obligations, nature and marks of self-denial, the faith and the obedience which are included in the Covenant's Conditions.'

In all, five parts appeared, the subsequent parts dealing with the Apostles' Creed (also issued in 1743), The Ten Commandments, The Lord's Prayer, and the Sacraments (in 1746). Doctrinally, Rowland and Jones stood on exactly the same ground. Even so, Jones' extensive treatment was invaluable, both to the leaders and in the societies. It held before the Methodists the priority of graces over gifts, and the subordination of the Spirit's manifestations to the realisation of the Son's glory. If in his public stance Jones did not allow himself to be aligned with the Methodists, his influence, and even perhaps his sympathies, remained very much with them.

'Oh! sanctified adversity carries the richest pearl in its mouth: it makes sin odious to us, and the return of the Saviour's presence doubly sweet! By it we are made meet for the Master's use. Shall we not kiss the rod which scares away our sins, and whips our corruptions to death? God separates thee by afflictions from thy idols, that they may not be as fuel to inflame thy corruptions, or as thieves to steal thy heart from Him. If thou hast been taught of God to distrust thine own heart, to be vile in thine own eyes, and to take no idolatrous delight in creature comforts, thou hast received ten thousand better answer to thy prayers than if thou hadst been lifted up by joyful frames, or hadst obtained thy fond wish in every prayer. The lowly graces of the Spirit thrive best under crosses.'

DANIEL ROWLAND

'Opposition is coming from without. God greatly strengthens me within. . . . I only fear the removal of the cross.'

GEORGE WHITEFIELD
in 1739

15

Persecution: 'No Gold Without Fire'

With the loss of Griffith Jones' support in 1741, the Welsh Methodists were even more vulnerable than before. Rowland and Harris were still comparatively inexperienced, and entirely without reputation in the world. They could no longer count on Griffith Jones and Madam Bevan to defend them before the Bishop. Ominous clouds were gathering around Rowland as the year progressed, and it was not long before the storm broke. Opposition from the Established Church found expression in the imposition of ecclesiastical sanctions and in public denunciation, verbal and written. Before the end of 1741, Rowland was attacked in print.

The first blow fell at Ystrad-ffin. On September 30, 1740, Harris had heard 'that the great men intend to do all they can to remove Brother Rowland from the chapel'. Two weeks after the new year opened the threat had crystallised sufficiently for Harris to enter in his diary that Rowland was 'likely to be turned out of Ystrad-ffin'. The entry continues, 'I had faith to see that God can't be hindered in His work. He'll carry it on still in His own place and ways against opposition.' That night Rowland and Harris spent together at Ystrad-ffin. The following day was a Sunday, and Rowland had 'uncommon power' in preaching. Harris's comment was, 'I never heard such earnest calling to Christ. Sure there must be some great things to follow here.' He also heard 'how the great men rise against Christ's message, threatening to hinder Brother Rowland where he had a call to go next week'.[1]

Whoever the 'great men' were, they succeeded, and the Bishop licensed a John Jones to serve at Ystrad-ffin from August 2, 1741.[2] The chapel had served well as a Methodist centre in North Carmarthenshire, drawing numbers of people from a wide area. Its

[1] XXXIV. 37; XXVI. 68, 69.
[2] NLW Church in Wales, SD/BR/11.

very isolation and previous neglect had been advantageous in securing for it a measure of immunity from the attention of the ecclesiastical authorities. Rowland's regular ministry had attracted crowds of people. The small building could hardly have accommodated them all, but the surrounding fields supplied the need, and hospitable believers who lived nearly provided a base for a Methodist society. Furthermore, the chapel at Ystrad-ffin had also been used by Griffith Jones in 1740–41, forty-four scholars attending his school there.[1] With the departure of Rowland, however, both Methodist and educational influences at Ystrad-ffin were terminated.

The parish vicar and his magistrate brother were both hostile to Methodism, and Rowland would have preached at Ystrad-ffin on the permission, or even at the request of the patron of the chapel, John Campbell. It is unlikely that this would have been suddenly withdrawn if, as appears to be the case, Campbell had come under Gospel influences. The explanation must lie in the Bishop's intervention. Between them the ecclesiastical authorities imposed on Campbell a change that proved in time to be detrimental to both Methodism and Anglicanism. A report to the Bishop in 1755 says of the place, 'No chapels but one belonging to John Campbell Esq., wherein though not ruinated, no divine service is now performed.' By 1812 the chapel was in 'such a decayed state that it must be rebuilt from the foundation'.[2]

As for the Methodists at Ystrad-ffin, in 1742 Harris was reproving the society members 'for despising the means they had there (Brother Rowland having been here a long time), reading their hearts as rejoicing in being rid of him, and liking their present carnal preaching'. By 1744 their tone had changed, and reports of the society there speak of nine or ten members, 'some sweet souls', against whom 'the enemy is full of malice'.[3] In a sermon on

---

[1] HVP, 235; J. E. Lloyd, *A History of Carmarthenshire*, vol. ii. 1939, p. 196, n.

[2] In 1812 the inhabitants wished the chapel to be re-sited at a more convenient location, and this Lord Cawdor, the new landowner, was willing to do, 'provided his future right to the nomination to the chapel will not be affected.' The same document notes that the chapel 'was endowed by the Lord of the Manor (in which the chapel lies) who has time immemorially exercised the right of nominating the curate'. See xlviii. 59–60; xxvii. 108; STL i. 83; NLW Church in Wales, SD/QA/61; Dyfed Record Office, Carmarthen, Cawdor MS 2/74.

[3] CMHO, 73; xxvii. 15; liii. 21; liv. 24.

Romans 8:28, Rowland quotes Psalm 66:11–12, 'we went through fire and water; and thou hast brought us to a wealthy place', adding later, 'There can be no gold or silver without being first purified with fire.'[1] Such was the experience of the Ystrad-ffin Methodists.

Shortly after his expulsion from the chapel, Rowland wrote to Mrs James of Abergavenny, who was not yet married to Whitefield. She was one of those who travelled great distances to Ystrad-ffin to hear him, in her case over 40 miles:

Dear Sister,
I am heartily sorry I could not send sooner to you; excess of business prevented me. I trust you will pardon me. I cannot but thank you for what good, under God, I received by your relating your experience. I hope the Lord enables you to go on more and more; yea, I really trust you are daily fed with the spiritual manna, which comes down from heaven, and that you have, in a wonderful measure, experienced that the Lord is good.
When I had the pleasure of your company, I could not have room in myself to blame you, all the time seeing you more zealous than me and eyeing more of the glory of God. However I could not persuade myself about your holding out. I was suspicious of some secret sin, but when I would think of free grace, and the everlasting love of Christ, I could do nothing less than check myself for such a suspicion. I trust, my dear, dear sister, that this will not offend you. I open my heart. I love you dearly in Christ Jesus. I hope your prayers are for me who am less than the least of the ministers of Christ. My soul is united to you; may the Lord increase this love more and more.
I am suffered to be no more at Ystrad-ffin. I preached them my farewell sermon from Acts 20:32. It reached their hearts. I believe such crying out was not heard in any funeral in the memory of man. May the Lord hear their cry and send them an able and powerful minister, who will dispense them the word of truth as it is in Jesus. Now I am to settle at Llanddewibrefi, which is a large church as will contain several thousands of people. Several of my communicants at Ystrad-ffin will join there at the next month's end at Abergwesyn.
As for the cause of your soul, I hope it is safe, yea, in your own sight; if not, if you see yourself sick, Jesus is a physician; if filthy, a soap; if comfortless, a balm; if condemned by the Law, Christ is an Advocate with the Father. Therefore, throw yourself wholly upon Him, come life or death. Be often at the throne of grace, and pray

[1] *Eight Sermons*, pp. 83, 85.

think often, yea pray think of him who is your very humble and obedient servant, and unworthy brother,
Daniel Rowland.[1]

The letter speaks of close spiritual dealings in the society, and outlines the alternative arrangements for attending Rowland's preaching. Abergwesyn lies to the north of Ystrad-ffin, and would have provided a convenient meeting point for Methodists travelling to Llanddewi from the more easterly parts of mid-Wales. Alternatively, Llanddewi was directly accessible on horseback, lying nine miles across rough, secluded, hilly country to the west of Ystrad-ffin. Either way, the bigger building at Llanddewi was more suitable for growing needs, and young believers had much to gain from fellowship with others.

Hardly a month had passed before another alarming event occurred. On Harris's third visit to London he read a London-based periodical 'painting us out in terrible colours'. It had one positive effect, because after reading it he 'could now write with life to Brother Rowland, which before I could not'.[2] The date was September 14, 1741, and he had read the issue of *The New Weekly Miscellany* which appeared on Saturday, August 29. This attacked the English Methodist leaders, as 'several actors, who are ordained as clergymen in the Church of England; and who, by their education, are qualified to do the greater mischief, and Daniel Rowland is in the Diocese of St. David's, where the people follow him as if they were really mad; and of this perhaps you may have a farther account at another time. . . . Among the laymen, Howel Harris is a precious tool, and spares no pains either in England or Wales.'

The issue of three weeks later reported that,

'on Friday, September 4th, in the afternoon, Howel Harris began his performance at the New Booth (Whitefield's newly-erected Tabernacle) with these very words, "Look down, O Lord, upon Thy dear son, and open his mouth that he may speak to the people." This, in the highest sense is perfect blasphemy. However, it plainly shows that false Christs, and false prophets, do daily arise.'

The same paper had been heaping abuse on Whitefield ever since

[1] Cardiff Public Library, MS 2. 282. See xxxvi. 28–9. The recipient became Whitefield's wife shortly afterwards, and in a letter to Harris in October 1746 she poignantly states 'our dear Lord makes the remembrance of the times going to Ystrad-ffin, and the meetings at your house, sweet to me now'. STL i. 205–06. For Whitefield's marriage, see DAL ii, Chapter 6.
[2] *Bathafarn*, x. 33, 36.

1737, and later, the Wesleys, too, were singled out for attack.[1]

When the storm of words broke on Rowland in the London Press, it followed much the same pattern as when it had raged against Whitefield. This at least served to identify them, and the same labels – 'Enthusiasts' and 'Methodists' – were again used. The attack on Rowland was the more significant because of the remoteness from London of his sphere of labour, and the fact that his success was sufficiently widespread to merit such extensive and detailed attention.

The issue of *The New Weekly Miscellany* for Saturday, October 31, 1741, carried a lengthy, front-page attack on Rowland. The anonymous correspondent wrote on September 26 from Aberystwyth, and acknowledges that while he has 'been cautious not to insert anything' which was dubious, he 'may be misinformed in some particulars', and asks for Rowland's correction in these matters. In the body of the article Rowland is said to serve the 'curacies of Nantcwnlle, Llangeitho, and Betws' (Leucu, a chapel attached to the parish of Llanddewibrefi). This suggests either that he was not completely familiar with Rowland's affairs, or that his letter had been written some time previously, for Benjamin Morgan had been licensed by the Bishop to the curacy at Betws only a month before the date of his writing. It also casts doubts on the reliability of his information about certain people in his neighbourhood who were thought to have been driven to despair by Rowland. The writer seems to have been an educated landowner or clergyman, familiar enough with the *New Weekly Miscellany* to know of its relish for anti-Methodist invective, and who had connections with the Aberystwyth area.

Typically, the criticisms of Rowland and his followers are threefold, and lie in the areas of personal integrity, theological polarity, and ecclesiastical identity. Rowland's integrity is questioned because 'scarce any can be so griping and greedy as he is. . . . His visible salary is £20 a year, and yet, by a very moderate computation, he makes upwards of £250.' The article continues:

'Every person that is accepted to be of his congregation enters his name in a book, which is called "The Book of Life", and for this he

---

[1] TGW i. 91, 217, 278; Luke Tyerman, *The Life of the Rev. John Wesley*, vol. i, pp. 250, 326, 359; DAL, i. 136; Eifion Evans, 'Early Methodist Apologetic', in CH 1979, pp. 33, ff.

pays a shilling. Now admit of but 400 that enter their names every year, this brings in £20 ready money. He makes his boast that there are 1600 who have entered their names in "The Book of Life"; admit these should communicate but six times a year (though the greater number of them communicate much oftener) and each communicant to pay but two pence every time, this brings in £80 a year. At Christmas these people meet to make him a free contribution, from whom . . . he receives a shilling a-piece; this makes £80. For the like contribution the 25th of June, £80. . . . For preaching about the country; for serving his curacies, and in private presents . . . in all £291.'

Doubtless, the societies had a register of members, and contributions were made to various causes, including Whitefield's Orphan House in Georgia, but evidently these things exposed the Methodists to allegations which were quite unfounded.

Rowland is charged with being an imitator of Whitefield from motives of financial gain and public applause:

'No sooner had it come to his knowledge, that Mr. Whitefield, by extempore preaching, and by holding unlawful assemblies, and disorderly meetings, had gained much applause, and more money, but without any regard to decency and order, he rambles about the country, holding forth to weak and ignorant people, tumultuously assembled in private houses, public tippling-houses, barns, fields, etc., and without any regard to his solemn promise of conformity to the Liturgy of the Church of England, omits its prayers to give more room to his own extempore effusions, which he judges to be more devout and edifying . . . out of the many arts and methods he has made use of, so effectually to engage their attention . . . there is none he appears more assiduous in, than in vilifying and reviling his brethren the neighbouring clergy . . . that they are a set of lazy, indolent, greedy, carnally-minded and lukewarm people, and regardless of the souls committed to their charge.'

This was an echo of the complaints made against Griffith Jones a generation previously, and the Methodists' answer would have been along the same lines. Gospel urgency, the serious plight of men in sin, and the necessity for personal dealings with God, demanded close, plain, honest dealings. 'Whether it is right in the sight of God to hearken unto you more than unto God, judge ye. For we cannot but speak the things which we have seen and heard' (Acts 4:19–20).

Further charges follow: 'Private assemblies, which are called religious societies, and which he [Rowland] has instituted in several of the neighbouring parishes, when they are at too great a distance to return home at night, men and women lie promiscuously together in a barn or hayloft. . . . There are abundance puffed up with spiritual pride, and boast of themselves, that they are in a sinless state, and sure of salvation; they despise all the world, except such as are of their own fraternity, and peremptorily affirm, that all who join not with them are in a state of damnation.'

Christian assurance was certainly a hallmark of Methodism, and the leaders stood by this as being the heritage of every believer through the sufficiency and finality of Christ's atonement. Sinlessness and pride they unequivocally and repeatedly denounced, but they insisted on that personal godliness which recognises the constraints of God's holiness on God's people.

Furthermore, in the matter of doctrine, Rowland is charged with following Whitefield:

'In his first setting out, he professes himself an Arminian, but upon hearing that Mr. Whitefield affirmed Predestination, Election and Reprobation . . . he strenuously maintained these, and whatever other doctrines, right or wrong, he heard come from Mr. Whitefield. When Archbishop Tillotson began to be run down, he immediately took it in hand, and exclaimed against him, as one that understood Christianity no better than Mahomet; his works were not to be endured; they were Arminianism; they belonged to the Covenant of Works, and the like stuff. The Author of *The Whole Duty of Man*, and his Works, underwent the same fate and treatment. . . . When he heard that Mr. Whitefield, upon his return from Georgia, condemned Mr. Wesley's doctrine of sinless perfection, etc., like a true weathercock he wheels about, and now preaches down what he before preached up.'

Contrary to the writer's belief, Rowland had come to a settled doctrinal position independently of Whitefield. Significantly, however, the writer recognises that the two held certain doctrines in common: God's eternal election, regeneration by the Holy Spirit, and personal assurance of salvation.

Without question, in great crowds, moved by strong emotions there were some excesses which could be condemned. The Methodist leaders were themselves aware of that fact. They saw the danger of spurious emotionalism to which religious fervour is prone. It was in this area of discriminating between true Christian experience and emotional excess that, first, Jonathan Edwards in America, and later, William Williams in Wales, were to make their invaluable contributions. They recognised on the one hand that outward, physical manifestations were not infallible signs of genuine spiritual experience, and on the other hand that the soul's affections were nevertheless worked upon by the Holy Spirit in varying degress in true and vital dealing with God. Such insights were at a formative stage when Rowland was held responsible for all disorder in 1741. In this same critical account there is this caricature of a Methodist congregation:

'While one is praying, another is laughing; some howl and beat their hands together; others are weeping and groaning; and others are grovelling on the ground in a swoon, making various kinds of antic postures; then they laugh out all at once, and continue laughing for about a quarter of an hour. . . . Some are so unruly that their friends are obliged to tie them up with ropes; some burn their clothes; some, before they recover from this disorder and despair, die in this miserable state.'[1]

It is agreed by all that under the preaching of Rowland and others there were remarkable instances of physical agony and ecstasy. More often than not it was time alone that would vindicate or condemn their authenticity. This was the very reason why the societies were so important, providing the leaders with a means of assessing spiritual life and growth.

[1] NLW Church in Wales, SD/BR/11; MS ii. 229–30; CMHO, 53, 58; xxx. 49, 50; STL i. 2, 11–14. Information about the Methodists was often second-hand, e.g. a letter from John Edwards, vicar of Llanbadarn Fawr near Aberystwyth from 1724–1761: 'These things I mention only as conjectures of my own, founded upon what information I could pick up among some favourers of our famous Mr. Daniel Rowland's notions, though at least no constant followers of his. Such, I think, there are not in either of my two parishes. . . . I now hear no more of Methodism than if the family was quite extinct. One of the holders forth, said to have spent too much of his time in following Mr. Daniel Rowland, and afterwards in the nocturnal meetings pretended to be held for mutual edification in Llansanffraid, Llanrhystud, Llanddeiniol, and your native parish, has condescended to work for his daily bread. . . . I would not willingly misrepresent any man or thing, and probably might in that of February last give you some intimation of practices I highly approve of in these people. Spending the Lord's Day in religious duties, reading God's words, family devotion, prayer, psalmody, and frequent communicating, which some say they are very observant of, will be readily allowed . . . to be valuable, commendable exercises.' The date of the letter was July 9, 1741, and the recipient is unknown. The parishes mentioned are in the surrounding area. NLW Cwrt Mawr MS; NLW 1626C, s.v. Llanbadarn Fawr.

Nor was Rowland alone in having to distinguish between true and false experiences at a time of revival. At about the same time, William Grimshaw witnessed similar scenes in the North of England:

'In this year [1742] our dear Lord was pleased to visit my parish (Haworth). A few souls were affected under the word, brought to see their lost estate by nature, and to experience peace through faith in the blood of Jesus. My church began to be crowded, insomuch that many were obliged to stand out of doors. Here, as in other places, it was amazing to hear and see what weeping, roaring, and agonies many people were seized with at the apprehension of their sinful state, and the wrath of God.'

In retrospect, Grimshaw noted that such physical effects were not invariably due to genuine conviction of sin or wrought by the Spirit of God: 'Soon after the devil observed such crying and distress of soul and agitation of body to affect people under the word, he also began to seize people under the word, with strange unnatural distortions, convulsions, hideous roarings; to bring, as we plainly saw, contempt and disgrace upon the true work of God.' They were also more frequent at the beginning of the revival than later, and the false among them were in time shown to be such by the absence of godly living. As Howel Harris would point out to Whitefield early in 1743, 'nature' could indeed be 'overcome' under the power of the Word, whether in abhorrence at the sight of sin's ugliness or in rapture at the sight of 'the unsearchable riches of Christ.'[1] Nevertheless, although the experimental aspect was prominent in the Great Awakening, it was not the touchstone of its life. The Word of God reigned without rival as the arbiter of truth and experience.

The presence of 'private assemblies' was a sore point to the ecclesiastical authorities, partly on account of the prominence they gave to laymen: 'so infectious is the itch of "exhorting", that no sooner one of them can scarce read, but he catches the distemper, and sets up for a public exhorter.' More serious, however, was the impression given of schism, since the societies enjoyed a separate life, apart from Anglican control. Even in the early days of the Awakening the Anglican Way and the Methodist Way were clearly distinguishable, although the latter protested otherwise. Methodists turned a blind eye to this anomaly and sought to distinguish their version of what the Church should be from that of schismatics.

[1] John Gillies, *Historical Collections*, 1845, p. 507; Frank Baker, *William Grimshaw 1708–1763*, 1963, pp. 63–4; STL i. 81.

Rowland was not allowed to remain ignorant of this public challenge. Whitefield wrote to Harris on December 28, 1741, 'As the Bishop hath sent the *Miscellany* to dear Brother Rowland, I think he is called to answer his Lordship'. Harris had hoped to enlist Whitefield's help, but in January 1742 Harris was at Llangeitho and 'was persuaded' and 'assisted' to answer it with Rowland. A few days later he wrote to Whitefield: 'The *Miscellany* is answered, and I believe sent up to be printed by Brother John Lewis; but I believe it calls for your perusal of it to correct it before it goes to the Press.' When two months had elapsed and it still had not appeared, Harris wrote to Whitefield: 'I wonder where Brother Rowland's answer to the *Miscellany* is from Brother John Lewis, unless you have thought best not to print it; if so Brother Lewis should send a word.'[1] Regrettably, the Welsh Methodists' response to the article does not appear to have been printed, and any manuscript copies of it seem to have been lost.

As public notice was now being taken of Rowland's Methodism, pressure was mounting on him to conform to the Anglicanism of his day. He was preaching at Llanddewibrefi in the closing months of 1741, but on December 20, when Harris had just left the place, he heard the disturbing news: 'that the Bishop has written to turn Brother Rowland from Llanddewibrefi'. For some time there had been the threat of sanctions on society members, 'they are likely to be turned out of the churches everywhere'. Now it seemed as if it might soon become a reality. Harris shared his fears with Whitefield at Abergavenny on Christmas Day, 1741, and urged him to attend the next meeting of the Welsh leaders. In January 1742 Harris 'had a strong cry from the lambs that are now scattered about this country, having no shepherd (being now turned away from Brother Rowland)'. With the help of Marmaduke Gwynne (Charles Wesley's father-in-law, and prominent landowner friend of Harris), Harris 'prevailed on' Herbert Lloyd, another landowner, who had interests in the Llanddewibrefi area, for support to Rowland's cause with the Bishop. However, on March 24 he was writing sadly to Whitefield's wife that the turning out of Rowland from Llanddewibrefi was now a fact.[2]

[1] CMHO, 53, 58; xxx. 49, 50; STL i. 2; MS ii. 229–30.
[2] iii. 13; xxvi. 75, 81; CMHO, 46, 51–2, 29, 47, 48, 56; MS ii. 207, 231; Bethan Phillips, *Peterwell*, 1983, Chapter 5, 'The Methodist Connection'. For Marmaduke Gwyne, see DWB under 'Gwynne family of Garth'; and lv. 56, ff.; 65, ff.; lvi. 7, 38.

A possible initiative still lay with Rowland's brother John. With five churches to serve between them, Llangeitho, Nantcwnlle, Llanddewibrefi, Llanbadarn Odwyn, and Blaenpennal, it was merely a matter of avoiding the Bishop's somewhat arbitrary technicalities. John Rowland was at least supportive of his brother's ministry, even if he was a stranger to his experience. A document rejecting the allegations made in the *Miscellany*, as 'idle tales . . . false reports and unjust accusations', is endorsed 'John Rowland, 1742', although its source and destination are unclear.[1] When the Bishop moved to Exeter in August 1742, parish affairs were once more quietly arranged by domestic agreement between the two brothers, so that in October, Daniel Rowland was again preaching in all five churches.[2]

The appearance of the *Miscellany* may also account for Griffith Jones' opposition to Rowland's preaching at Llanlluan in Carmarthenshire in November. When Harris heard this he was at first angry, but the Lord 'rectified' his heart: 'when it was in his power set, he was against Mr. Rowland coming to Llanlluan chapel, where was likely to be gathered many lambs, because it would be stirring up envy and uneasiness in congregations about there, and because it would be on a weekday he must come there, and they should lose their work'.[3] Jones had used Llanlluan as a preaching centre since 1736, when the chapel was rebuilt, and one of his first schools was established there. Rowland was also using the chapel before the end of 1740, and Howel Davies in January 1741.[4] When Davies eventually settled in Pembrokeshire it left Llanlluan open for Rowland. Richard Tibbott, one of the Methodist exhorters, heard him preaching there 'with much assistance' on Acts 12:11 in September 1741, and again in the society afterwards, which was greatly blessed and wrought 'some alteration' in Tibbott's spirit. Harris obviously considered this a strategic centre for Rowland, and he wrote in December to Philip Lloyd, who held the patronage of the chapel:

'I hope you'll not be offended at this freedom, though I am almost unacquainted with you, being I find the Lord has put to your heart to

---

[1] NLW CMA Trefeca 3181.
[2] For Nicholas Clagett, see *Dictionary of National Biography*; STL i. 55.
[3] CMHO, 43–4.
[4] Gomer M. Roberts, *Methodistiaeth Fy Mro*, 1938, pp. 12, 13; NLW Church in Wales, SD/Misc. B (List of Benefices and Revenues, Eighteenth Century), p. 4; HVP, 235; xxi. 72; xlix. 3–5; MS ii. 22.

open a door for the everlasting Gospel in the neighbourhood, and to admit to your chapel all as preaches it with power. I hope you'll not be prevailed upon to shut it against any minister of Jesus Christ. I believe you are persuaded Mr. Daniel Rowland is of that number. . . . The many hundred seals the Lord has set to his ministry loudly proclaim him to be sent of God. And as such he must expect to find his adversary the devil to shoot his arrows at him, and I fear that some have been to bring an evil report of him to prejudice your mind against him, but I hope as there are some in many of the neighbouring parishes to my knowledge that say they received no small benefit from his ministry, whose prayers I am sure you'll engage if you'll give him the use of the pulpit now and then.'[1]

This appeal carried the day and Rowland's use of Llanlluan was to continue for some time.

Persecution sometimes took a dangerous as well as a threatening aspect. Early in 1741 Harris at Bala in North Wales thought he would 'die Stephen's death' in the midst of a furious mob which surrounded the house where he was discoursing, broke the window, hit him on the face, and threw 'stones and dirt' at him. At Llanilar, ten miles north of Llangeitho, Rowland met with much the same treatment. Here the mob 'assaulted him so fiercely with stones, brickbats, and other missiles, that he was obliged to desist and escape for his life'. A few miles away, at Aberystwyth, 'a certain individual, who swore in a dreadful manner that he would shoot him immediately . . . aimed his gun at him and pulled the trigger, but it would not fire'. Edward Morgan, Rowland's biographer, records another instance of the danger which he faced:

'He was to preach in a very ungodly neighbourhood in the open air. The children of the wicked one . . . put a large quantity of powder under the ground where they knew the minister and people were to stand; then they covered it over so well that no one could discover it. A train of powder was laid underground for some distance; at the end of this a straw was placed, which appeared above the ground. Fire was to be applied . . . so as to blow up the preacher and the congregation! But very providentially some good man came to the spot long before the meeting was to take place. He discovered, in walking about, the straw, and had the curiosity to examine it . . . and at length traced it. . . . They at last found a man sleeping in a certain retired hole, and upon examining him, they discovered the whole of the dreadful scheme. . . . However the only punishment the trem-

[1] ii. 70; xxiv. 110, 111; MS ii. 185–6.

bling creature had was prayers and supplications to heaven for mercy and compassion to his poor immortal soul.'[1]

To Rowland and his colleagues it was 'given in the behalf of Christ, not only to believe on him, but also to suffer for his sake' (Philippians 1:29).

In the sermon on Romans 8:28, Rowland refers to an incident in the life of David, 1 Samuel 29, to illustrate the theme of triumph through trials. The application might have come from Rowland's own experience in 1741: 'See how circumstances concurred to make that act of his enemies which was contrived to complete his disgrace, and to hasten his entire ruin, work together for his good. O who would not trust the Lord! who ever followed his guidance, and was confounded?[2] Through the fire of persecution God was bringing forth the tried gold of His people's faith.

[1] William Williams, *Welsh Calvinistic Methodism*, 1872, pp. 45, 46, 50; MR, 102, 103–04.
[2] *Eight Sermons*, p. 89.

'I came accidentally to a place in Wales where Rowland was preaching to an immense congregation in the open air. Indeed I never witnessed such a scene before. Oh! the striking appearance of the preacher: his zeal, animation, and fervour were beyond description, and such effects descended on the congregation under him as never came within the sphere of observation before.'

E. BURN
of Birmingham, in Edward Morgan,
Ministerial Records, 1840, pp. 119–20

'Are you explaining away the great phenomena accompanying the revivals of the past in terms of the 20th century, and saying that the people at Llangeitho listening to Daniel Rowland were a sort of primitive people lacking education, and just emotionalists? The Apostle Paul reminds the elders of the church at Ephesus of how he preached "with tears". And Whitefield used to preach with tears. When have you and I last preached with tears? What do we know, to use the phrase of Whitefield, about preaching a "felt Christ"?'

D. MARTYN LLOYD-JONES

16

Rowland's Preaching

In the midst of these increasing pressures Rowland's ministry was becoming more widespread and more powerful. From one end of 1741 to the other Harris was reporting Rowland's 'amazing' success. His February comment referred to Rowland's labours in Carmarthenshire, 'The Lord has in an amazing manner owned Brother Rowland.' Visiting Llangeitho itself at the beginning of November, Harris witnessed 'fresh tokens of the Lord being with Brother Rowland in an amazing manner, I think there, not more, if as much, with any minister, at least in our country'. From time to time reports of Rowland's usefulness were conveyed to Harris by others, and the news often ministered to his own soul: 'Enlightened much from a brother repeating a sermon of dear Brother Rowland on "I will be thy death, O death" (Hosea 13:14)'.[1]

Such lasting impressions on the hearers argued an exceptional measure of unction on the preaching, even in the face of trying circumstances, as this letter describing Rowland's activities in mid-Wales, at the end of June 1741 shows:

'We have had that faithful minister and servant of Jesus Christ, the Rev. Mr. Daniel Rowland amongst us, and our poor hungry souls were fed by his ministry as with marrow and fatness. He makes the devil's kingdom shake wherever he comes. Our scribes and Pharisees concerted among themselves to deny him the use of their pulpits, after they had made a fair promise of admitting him to preach at Llanidloes, Trefeglwys and Carno. Mr. Rowland came to Llanidloes on the 30th . . . and went immediately to the minister and had about half an hour's private conference, on the conclusion of which he told him he could not grant him the use of his pulpit. . . . The parson of Trefeglwys had [informed] us some few days before that he should not preach in his churches because he had been credibly informed

[1] xxiv. 59; MS ii. 155, 156; xxvi. 73.

that he was a downright madman. Now by this time we had a large
suspicion that we should never have a church for him to preach in,
after troubling him to come so far [some fifty miles from Llangeitho].
However, we being willing to leave no stone unturned, one of our
friends went to Mr. Tilsley, vicar of Llandinam, and informed him
how the clergy of the adjacent parishes had served us . . . whereupon
he promised . . . he should preach at his chapel . . . [Rowland]
preached to us on Jn. 7:37 "In the last day, that great day of the feast,
Jesus stood and cried, saying, If any man thirst, let him come to me
and drink", where we had full and ample satisfaction for all our
former disappointments. God was with us of a truth, for he spoke
with such demonstration of the Spirit and power, that most that
heard him were melted into tears. Oh! the infinite goodness of our
God to his own heritage!'

Under such ministry, spiritual appetite became insatiable and people
willingly deprived themselves of sleep and comforts to receive more
'times of refreshing from the presence of the Lord'. It is not
surprising, therefore, that the letter continues:

'When he had done preaching he was very much for parting with us
and had some thoughts of going that night to Rhayader. However,
the earnest intreaties of Christ's little lambs did prevail with him to
suspend his journey till the morning, whereupon we appointed a
society at the Tyddyn at Mrs. Bowen's. He discoursed to us on Jn.
1:43, "The day following Jesus would go forth into Galilee, and
findeth Philip, and saith unto him, Follow me". Oh! we had a double
portion of the divine Presence, my heart leaped within me to think
how the Holy Ghost did shine. . . . The goodness of God to my soul
in these times is much better understood than expressed. . . . We held
a society . . . on the morrow morning. . . . Mr. Rowland discoursed
to us for about an hour out of a window of the aforesaid house. He
invited us so closely to embrace Jesus as held forth to us in the
Gospel, that one would have thought it impossible for the most
obdurate heart to resist. Yet I am thoroughly convinced that Paul can
but plant and Apollos but water, [and] that nothing short of God's
free grace is able to convert one soul. By this time there was such a
mystical union among us that we were at a loss how to part with each
other. The love of Jesus Christ so bound us together that it resembled
the cutting off of a right arm or plucking out of a right eye to part
both shepherd and flock. We asked him if he would stay an hour at
Edward Lucas's Llangurig . . . if we would come there. He consen-
ted, [and] accordingly we set out. Our way being through Llanidloes
they pelted us with stones as fast as they could. We proceeded to the
place above where we had another sweet banquet. There we took our
leave with this glorious minister of God's own making, and departed
everyone to his own place. But oh! how irksome it was to put hands

to the world after being as it were lifted on the wings of faith into the third heaven!'[1]

Another witness of these events wrote: 'Mr Rowland's preaching is so captivating to me that I am ready to say as the primitive Christians for the Apostle Paul, "Oh! that we should hear Paul preach once more before we die". And I say "Oh! that I should hear Mr. Rowland once more before I die". . . . One true preacher of Jesus Christ is worth a thousand worlds.'[2]

These honest statements of appreciation for Rowland reflect not only the hearers' views but also the preacher's character. Evidently Rowland was a man of great warmth and compassion, for whom personal convenience was always secondary to the spiritual welfare of others. At thirty years of age, his preaching activities away from Llangeitho involved costly and prolonged separation from his wife and young children (a son and perhaps two daughters). Yet, a large measure of self-denial on their part, together with Rowland's sensitivity to the Spirit's prompting, allowed him to be flexible and open in the face of unexpected developments. Furthermore, when thus presented with an unscheduled opportunity for preaching, a knowledge of Scripture which was kept fresh each day provided him with a relevant message. There was also a passionate concern for Christ's neglected people, and this constantly motivated his decisions. In this way he reflected a care for Christ's churches which, in spirit and intensity, if not in office, was as apostolic as Paul's.

A fortnight after this visit to mid-Wales, he was at Cwm-iou, Capel-y-ffin, Llanover, Blaina, and Llanhilleth in Gwent, preaching 'to the great benefit of several souls'. Throughout the summer of 1741 he was kept busy 'with much activity day and night'. In anticipation of meeting Rowland at Defynnog on October 20, Harris reflected and prayed:

'Dear Rowland, much owned of God everywhere. O what power is with him! Had in secret great earnestness to wrestle for him, crying,

---

[1] MS ii. 92–4; MTU, 39–40. Richard Jenkins, who wrote this, was a Methodist exhorter, and a fortnight later he was commanded to appear before the Bangor Diocesan Chancellor at Llanidloes parish church. He rejected the charge of schism, justified exhorting from Hebrews 3:13 ('exhort one another daily, while it is called today'), and refused to give up his Methodist activities. For Jenkins, see HMGC i. 273–4.
[2] MS ii. 97.

O Lord! let him mount on eagle's wings! Never leave him! Own him yet more and more! Give him all qualifications! Keep him from errors.'

In November Rowland was heading for a preaching tour in mid-Wales again. At Llanwrtyd on Saturday the 28th, he preached on Caleb from Joshua 15 'with great power, and sweetly opened the text'. On the following night the incumbent was persuaded to let Rowland preach in the church. The account continues:

'Monday morning he went to Radnorshire, and there was such power that there was hardly a dry cheek there. The devil was forced to quit the field. Monday after nightfall he came to Builth, where he was disturbed by the owner of the Red House. There he discoursed at Sarah Williams's, and there were three of them that came, one being the parson Phillips with a great paper in his hand. . . . The effect of it all was to strengthen Brother Rowland. Said he, "I know the word is of God. I am now much bolder than I have been this great while." Tuesday morning he went for Llwyn-y-berllan.'[1]

The strengthening which he needed was physical robustness as well as a sanctified determination. God graciously granted him both in abundant measure.

In Rowland's choice of texts there was both variety and discernment. The variety stemmed from a conviction that preaching should embrace 'the whole counsel of God' (Acts 20:27). The threatenings of the law (on Psalm 85:5 at Llanddewibrefi in December), the delights of union with Christ (on Solomon's Song 4:16 at the same place in November), and the blessings for children in the Covenant of Grace (on Mark. 10:16 at Llangeitho in July), illustrate something of the range of his subjects during 1741.[2]

Wisdom and prayer were necessary to discern God's message for each occasion, and how he should apply it with relevance to his congregation. Honest and close dealings with the text in exposition were followed by plain and close dealings with the people in application. An example will serve to illustrate these qualities in Rowland's preaching. On October 27, 1742, at Abergorlech the text was Revelation 22:17, 'The Spirit and the bride say, Come. And let him that heareth say, come. And let him that is athirst come. And whosoever will, let him take the water of life freely.' First, the

---

[1] MS ii. 113, 122, 120, 179; HVP, 69; *Bathafarn*, x. 44; Diary 80.
[2] xxvi. 81, 75; i. 65.

Scripture was expounded lucidly, then the Gospel invitation was offered with fervency:

'There are four things in these words, 1. invitations; 2. portrayal of those invited; 3. to what they are invited; 4. how they are invited.
1. The invitation. God's Spirit invites (a) by convictions. Nathan's parable to David, and applying "thou art the man" (2 Samuel 12:7). The Spirit draws under the Word, imprisons the conscience, and calls forth out of that prison; (b) by allurements to the timid, bringing them gradually under convictions, as in the case of the disciples.
2. It is the Bride, and not a prostitute or any woman, that invites. Invitation is extended to the one who hears, who may be without assurance that Christ loves him although in covenant with Him. Those invited are the thirsty, who are uneasy without Christ, and long for Christ, who have no pleasure in sin; the willing, eager to have the Water of Life, and desirous that sin should be killed.
3. To what they are invited: to the Fountain of Living Water. This water is indispensable, it washes; it brings life and nourishes it.
4. How it is received: freely. Doctrine: No one is fit to receive Christ except those who are thirsty and eager, (a) because no-one else will come and choose Christ, except those who will be nothing, and will take the cross; (b) because no-one else will see Christ as precious except these.'[1]

Rowland's preaching was a declaration of God's truth, regardless of the views and the status of members of the congregation. His sermons are nothing if not urgent: 'O conscience! conscience! conscience! awake from your deadly stupor, and ponder, intensely ponder, on the height and depth of redeeming love. . . . O for strength to speak to your consciences!' Urgent, yes, and humbling, too:

'Have we not been told, that the Lord Jesus has purchased an eternal kingdom for us? Is it not a truth, which we cannot gainsay, that He is willing to give it freely to us? And shall we be indifferent about it? Is it not worth our seeking after? O shame to us! that we should be more anxious to secure a passing shadow, or a fleeting phantom than we are to obtain and possess the most substantial realities. Blush, sinners, at your past folly, and turn to the Lord with your whole hearts. O run to Him without delay; if you cannot run, walk; if you cannot walk, creep towards Him.'[2]

The preacher's responsibility was to be faithful to God's Word; it was for God's Spirit to make it live in the sinner's experience.

[1] v. 60–1. [2] *Eight Sermons*, pp. 23, 35, 172.

Another occasion, this time at Llangeitho itself, illustrates Rowland's concern for saints as well as sinners. The text was James 1:12, 'Blessed is the man that endureth temptation, for when he is tried, he shall receive the crown of life, which the Lord hath promised to them that love him'; the theme was 'temptation', and the date was Saturday, October 31, 1741. 'He showed', says Harris, 'first, that God permits Satan to tempt God's children; Second, how does he tempt? He suits his temptations to our natures . . . with lust to the lustful, with the world to the worldling; Third, when does he tempt?' In answering the question Rowland used familiar analogies:

'He is a fisherman and knows where to draw his net; when under the Word, and especially when we come from under the Word. When one is newly come from the war, he throws his armour down, and goes to drink and rejoice, until the enemy comes on him and finds him unarmed. So when you have had victory over Satan, he'll come in again through levity or self.'

For illustrations and examples Rowland turned, as usual, to the Bible itself:

'Through what means does Satan work? Through relations, Job's wife; through God's children – Peter said to Christ – see how seemingly kind Satan was here to Christ – Christ said, "Get thee behind Me, Satan" – that word came from Satan on Peter's heart, not from the new part. Then see that you have all the weapons on.'

Relentlessly, Rowland pursues the full implications of the text, exposing the devil's strategies in the believer, and yet showing that these have God-imposed limits:

'Satan comes under pretence of godliness. Satan can preach amazingly, and quote Scripture, crying "It is written"; he preached through the serpent, and Eve held his sermon before God's doctrine. She saw God's doctrine hard in saying "you'll die", but Satan's doctrine sweet, saying "you shall not die but live if you eat, and shall be as gods". . . . Next, see Satan's subtlety in setting proper objects before your eyes to draw your heart after them when you are praying. If you would keep your house warm, keep your door shut. So if you would keep zeal burning in your heart, watch over your senses. It is vain to strive to cast Satan out when he is come in, watch before he comes in. . . . Satan will set anything so as he may but draw your heart from God. Satan has power, first, to set objects before us, secondly, to poison the fancies and to entice them to reason with him, and so to incline the will (for he can't force it); be sure, then, you fly from his baits to Christ's blood, nothing reasoning, else he'll work on your affections, and he'll entangle you in sin and unbelief. Fly then to Christ's blood immediately!'

With great vigour, Rowland proceeds to demonstrate how God's sovereign power and grace can turn temptation into triumph, since 'a blessing from God goes with all these temptations to sanctify them' to the believer:

'1. Satan's temptations make the soul pray more. . . . 2. Temptation when it does not turn into sin makes us run further from sin; Joseph was in the house with his mistress until she tempted him, then he ran away out of the house. 3. It makes a man to search and try and know himself more than ever. . . . To be ready always to take up arms in the light, and strength, and wisdom of God against all enemies, pleases God. . . . 4. . . . When we have been in Satan's school, we can speak of his strategy, we can pity and help the tempted.'

Finally, when there is failure, Rowland can still bring Gospel consolation to God's children:

'When you have fallen into sin there is a cry within you. The cry is not from you, or your nature, but the Spirit of God in you cries, and then God forgives and says, "Go and sin no more", and then you cry. At this point, says Harris, "vast power came and a great cry through the whole church for to have Satan down, crying 'Down with him!'. . . God break Satan under our feet! Amen. Amen.'

Harris's concluding remarks were spontaneous and sincere: 'Sure there is more of God here than anywhere in the nation, here is such simplicity and power.'[1]

The phrase 'simplicity and power' summarises two leading characteristics of Rowland's preaching. Simplicity stemmed from the fact that his preaching was a declaration of biblical truth rather than the airing of speculative ideas and human opinions. In this way the entire congregation was edified, a fact which Williams of Pantycelyn tries to portray in his elegy to Rowland:

> On their visit to Llangeitho
> If perchance that Daniel preached,
> Then the sun with heaven's brilliance
> Rose on all, each one was reached;
> Words like arrows found their targets,
> Sticking fast with power sublime
> In men's hearts, though heavy sleeping,
> Dying, even, 'till this time.

[1] Diary 80.

Christ Himself on Calv'ry's mountain,
Clearing books in heaven's store;
Paying all of sin's demerit,
Healing thus transgression's sore.
All who hear are now rejoicing,
All are full and satisfied;
On the heavenly manna feeding,
From the dawn 'till day has died.[1]

An Englishman who happened to visit Llangeitho on one occasion refers in similar terms to the effects of Rowland's preaching, even though he could not understand Welsh: 'I heard much of him, but it never could have entered into my heart to conceive of the mighty energy and power that accompanied his preaching. His words did fly like darts.' David Griffiths was another clergyman who had ample opportunity to assess Rowland's preaching, and he describes the way in which God's power manifested itself under it:

'This great preacher, in his public ministrations resembles the gradual swelling and bursting of the waves of the ocean, when the wind agitates the bosom of the deep. The overwhelming power of the mighty influences of the Spirit in his ministry came on gradually, in manner like a wave of the sea, increasing more and more. He commenced his address calmly, but as he advanced, both his matter and his manner increased in interest. . . . At length his eloquence attained its climax, and then his preaching, under divine influence, would most nobly break forth like the rising swell of the sea, and would overwhelm the great concourse of people in an astonishing manner. The intenseness of their feelings found relief in the same moment in a simultaneous burst of hallelujahs and ascriptions of praise to the most high God. The preacher would then pause for a short interval, until the people had enjoyed the feast. . . . He would then commence another paragraph of his sermon . . . his voice, his countenance, and his discourse gradually altering, and that in a wonderful manner as he was advancing; and when his evangelical and extraordinary eloquence arrived at its climax, it was most glorious, it went forth like the bursting of another wave. And the great mass of the people was again overpowered by their feeling, and again burst into loud Hosannahs to the Son of David.'

One more testimony to the power of Rowland's must suffice. It is that of the Baptist minister, Christmas Evans. 'There was such a vehement, invincible flame in his ministry as effectually dispelled and drove away the careless, worldly, dead spirit; and the people, so awakened, drew

[1] CYN i. 585, 586.

nigh, as it were in the bright cloud, to Christ, and to Moses and Elijah.Eternity and its amazing realities were rushing into their minds.'[1]

Rowland's sermons were not long, but they were certainly invigorating. Those who arrived at Llangeitho weary after travelling long distances found his sermons physically as well as spiritually refreshing. 'You never heard such a thing in your life', said one such pilgrim from North Wales on hearing Rowland preach.

'I was so tired I was fitter for bed than for chapel. But Rowland began to preach. The text was, "And in this mountain shall the Lord of hosts make unto all people a feast of fat things, a feast of wine on the lees, of fat things full of marrow, of wines on the lees well refined" (Isaiah 25:6). He began to tap the barrels of the Covenant of Grace, and to let out the wine well refined, and to give to the people to drink. It flowed over the chapel. I also drank, until I was as drunk as a fool. And there I was, and scores of others with me, thinking nothing of fatigue, shouting, and some of us jumping, for hours'.[2] If Rowland was the instrument, God's Spirit was the source of that 'vehement, invincible flame', which brought both light and warmth to the souls of men. It was, nevertheless, a flame that some sought to extinguish, and others sought to manipulate. For these reasons, and as early as 1741, the Methodists considered the definition of their position and their work to be a matter of prime importance. The Bishop's action in sending Rowland a copy of the *Miscellany* article could only be interpreted as a threat to the continuance of Methodism within Anglicanism, a signal of impending expulsion. It had now become a matter of grave urgency for the Welsh Methodists to set their house in order, and to declare their future identity and intentions.

When Rowland and Harris were together just before Christmas, 1741, they arranged to hold 'a Society of brethren preachers to settle the cause of God'. Two days later Harris shared with the prominent Methodist landowner, Marmaduke Gwynne, the vision of 'our meeting, all of us ministers, to consult about the state of the societies, our being likely to be turned out'.[3] If the year had witnessed unparalleled scenes of Gospel power, it closed under the threat of a curtailment of Gospel liberty.

[1] MR, 120, 123, 124, 128.
[2] Owen Thomas, *Cofiant y Parchedig John Jones, Talsarn*, cyf. ii (1874), tud. 804, quoted in JO 62–3.
[3] CMHO, 46–7.

'I did not know much about the plague of my heart, my misery by nature, my fall in the first Adam, and the Lord Jesus was but a little Saviour in my sight. . . . About this time [1744, at the age of 14] I joined a small company of godly people . . . who, when they examined me, received me lovingly, wondering at the Lord who had visited me as it were in the days of my infancy.'

IOAN THOMAS
Rhad Ras

'I was afraid the preachers would examine me very strictly, and that upon finding my experience so unsatisfactory, they would refuse to accept me; but they, to my great astonishment, were very kind to me. I was accepted, and had what I had longed for many years, and had often feared I should never obtain, a place in the house of God! As far as I can remember, this took place about the end of September 1793 [when he was 19 years old]. The small society at Hendre Howel was made up of very godly people; they were quiet, kind, brotherly, of a tender conscience and brokenness of heart. I found succour there, and splendid nourishment. I marvelled, and often thanked God that I had a place among God's people.'

JOHN ELIAS

17

Society Rules in 1742

By the beginning of 1742 Rowland and Harris were painfully aware of the possibility of imminent ecclesiastical sanctions. The Bishop of St David's, Nicholas Clagett, in whose Diocese the vast majority of their activities were conducted, had made his position clear. He had arranged the distribution of the Bishop of London's Pastoral Letter, with its attack upon Methodism as 'enthusiasm', and had recently drawn Rowland's attention to the *Miscellany* article, by way of personal warning. There was real need for wisdom in avoiding every appearance of ecclesiastical irregularity, doctrinal heresy, and fanatical excess.

There was widespread public unease about the existence and emphasis of the societies. They were seen by some as divisive and hypocritical. The honest sharing of experiences or 'opening the heart' was the special focus of attack. It was regarded by critics as being, at best a morbid introspection and unhealthy subjectivism, and at its worst, an excuse for meddling in the private affairs of others. The Methodists themselves on occasions had exceeded the boundaries of prudence as well as the guidelines of Scripture. It was not easy to hold authority and liberty together in biblical balance in a caring, disciplined fellowship of believers. They were increasingly aware of the difficulties implicit in that openness which they advocated as their ideal and practised as their norm. For them, however, there was ample and clear Scripture precedent, and the advantages far outweighed the dangers, provided that care was taken to insist upon the proper safeguards.

Griffith Jones' misgivings centred on the Methodists' seeming indifference to the attainments and activities of the laymen. Throughout the century there were echoes of this criticism, Methodist preachers being called 'bold, visionary rustics', and 'illiterate mechanics, much fitter to make a pulpit than to get into one'.[1] Jones was not being awkward. He was merely expressing his conviction that the office of teacher in the Church of God was a Scriptural one, subject to regular and disciplined order. Harris had no doubts that a lay ministry of 'exhorting' could be justified from Scripture, and he was fond of quoting the example of Apollos, doing so with great relish to the Bishop of St David's in 1739.[2] Both Rowland and Harris felt that the extent of the country's spiritual decline warranted the use of 'exhorters' to supply a deficiency which could only be viewed as grave and urgent. It was, therefore, necessary to provide a means of assessing the spiritual maturity, motives, and abilities for public ministry of such men.

With these issues in mind, a meeting was arranged for January 7, 1742, at Dugoedydd, a Methodist home not far from Ystrad-ffin. In time this gathering of leaders, ministerial and lay, came to be known as an 'Association', a name which persists to this day with the Welsh Calvinistic Methodists. The central purpose of this forthcoming Association, usually reckoned to be the first such of exclusively Methodist membership, was to be reaffirmed at many future meetings: 'In order as far as we can to remove stumbling blocks, [we are] to communicate in the parish churches, and to advise people to do so, in order to prevent our appearing like a sect; having before agreed not to call our Societies "Churches" but "Societies in the Established Church", and not to call the exhorters ministers.'[3]

There was common consent about the desirability of having Whitefield's presence for the occasion. Accordingly, his advice was sought, in case he found it impossible to attend. Deprived of Griffith Jones' support, Whitefield was the obvious alternative. His spiritual acumen in dealing with the societies had already been demonstrated in his *Letter* to them in 1739. This had been written originally with the societies in England in mind, but its wider usefulness had been recognised in the issue of a Welsh translation. Furthermore, in dealing with the ecclesiastical authorities he had considerable experience. To have Whitefield's counsel at this early stage in

---

[1] Quoted in Richard Green, *Anti-Methodist Publications Issued During the Eighteenth Century*, 1902, pp. 56, 100; see also Albert M. Lyles, *Methodism Mocked*, 1960, Chapter 4, 'Satire of the Methodist Preachers and Preaching'.
[2] HVP, 12. See further Eifion Evans, *Howel Harris, Evangelist*, 1974, pp. 13, f.   [3] CMHO, 18, 100; cf. M. H. Jones, *op. cit.*, pp. 261–5.

formulating policy would be an invaluable asset.

Bristol, however, was engaging Whitefield's attention, and so he wrote to the Welsh brethren instead. Having acknowledged the importance and urgency of a meeting, he sets out guidelines for regulating their duties:

'One great matter then is rightly to know to what particular part Jesus Christ has called each of you. For I take it for granted none of you will presume to run before you are called, or have evidences of your conversation [godly living]. Different persons have different gifts and graces. Some are called to awaken, others to establish and build up. Some have popular gifts fit for large auditories, others move best in a more contracted sphere, and may be exceedingly useful in the private societies. Those who are called out to act in a public manner I think ought to give themselves wholly to the work, and go out without purse or scrip. Their Master will bear their charges. Others, who can only visit privately, may mind their secular employment, and give their leisure time to the service of the Church.'

Whitefield saw the Welsh work of Rowland and Harris, and his own English work, as one Calvinistic Methodism. He therefore suggested that similar arrangements should prevail throughout, with mutual correspondence between the two countries:

'I wish also you could meet monthly: if not all together, yet in little bodies as you lie nearest to each other. I am now about to settle a monthly meeting in Bristol and London, where correspondents' letters are to be read, and prayer made accordingly. If you had monthly meetings, each exhorter or labourer might communicate his success; an abstract might be sent over to England; and we in return would send you an abstract of our affairs. Unity would thereby be promoted, love increased, and our hands strengthened, and we should be like an army with banners.'

Such closer links with England would become a reality in time through Whitefield himself presiding at Welsh Associations. For the present, the other major, delicate matter for discussion concerned the Methodist attitude to the Established Church. On this issue Whitefield had this to say:

'Some of you are ministers of the Church of England. But if you are faithful, I cannot think you will continue in it long. However, do not go out till you are cast out, and when cast out for Jesus Christ's sake, be not afraid to preach in the fields. And while you remain in, oh! let not the children of God starve for the want of the Sacrament, though they may belong to another parish. . . . If a brother or sister has a mind to communicate among the Dissenters, and has freedom to receive in the Church too, they ought to be left at liberty.'

This was 'Whitefield's plan' for the management of the work. It met with general approval, becoming the cornerstone of Calvinistic Methodism in England and Wales, and proved 'of wonderful advantage with the blessing of God'. Harris received this letter on January 5, 1742, and immediately replied to Whitefield, 'I entirely agree with your thoughts in the letter to the society.'[1]

Whitefield's letter was not the only one to come before the brethren. There was also a letter, dated October 2, 1741, from James William, the exhorter responsible for the societies in Rowland's area of south Cardiganshire and north Carmarthenshire. Like all area exhorters, William was answerable to Harris as 'General Superintendent', and to the Association, hence the letter. The letters were complementary, Whitefield's dealing with Methodist policy, William's with Methodist practice. William's letter highlights the issues which the Dugoedydd meeting was convened to resolve.

First among these was the need for spiritual nourishment in the societies. Their numbers were increasing, and their experiences were often elevated. Many of these society members would have been converted under Rowland's ministry, and his regular visits provided the means of their edification:

'Beloved Brethren, we have every reason to praise and bless God for His wonderful love in visiting so many souls on one day. . . . I think I can say that the Lord teaches us to know the Lord Jesus in a more enlightened and experimental manner. . . . At Talley [near Llandeilo, Carmarthenshire], some grow in a true acquaintance of their interest in Christ, others are pressing hard after Him. They grow in fruitfulness, and long to see the Lord's work go on in union with one another, so that by God's goodness prejudice cannot raise its head. . . . At Capel Gwynfil [strictly, the name of the old village, now Llangeitho, where there was a ruined chapel-of-ease bearing that name; the society met in a barn belonging to Meidrim farm nearby], there are about ninety, all except one or two increase amazingly more and more in the knowledge of God. Indeed, I believe that many of them "have the mind of Christ"', and His cause and interest is on their hearts. They never come together without meeting God, and most of them return home ravished by His love. It is hard for anyone to pray, or preach, or discourse without others entering

[1] CMHO, 52–4; cf. TGW i. 541–2; MS ii. 217.

into his spirit. I can humbly say that they have the anointing. Blessed be God! Brethren, sing His praise!'

This was most encouraging, but clearly it laid on the leaders the responsibility of providing for Christian growth in truth, grace, and love. To ensure a disciplined oversight, and to formulate biblical principles of spiritual acceptability and maturity were part of their task at Dugoedydd.

Problems of life were not only problems of growth, as in the case of Llangeitho with ninety society members showing evidences of God's grace in their lives. They were also problems of conflict. Not surprisingly, therefore, in the same report there is mention of 'the roar of the enemy and his instrument.' It adds, 'he is unsuccessful in his work. The Lord Jesus carries His work on, so that the devil never makes an onslaught against them without suffering loss.' Other difficulties were more tangible, in particular, the relationship between the Methodists and the Dissenters in some areas of Carmarthenshire:

'At Forest lately I find some whose souls follow wholeheartedly after Christ, but there are also some Dissenters, full of knowledge but void of experience, who are prone to raise unprofitable questions. . . . At Caio, they are taught in greater earnestness and union with each other, but the Dissenters leave us nearly everywhere. That enhances unity and eliminates empty disputes. . . . There is a society begun recently at Llanllwni. They are a mixed company of Dissenters and Methodists, and I find very little union there, but they are thinking of separating.[1]'

This was the other basic issue which had to be faced at Dugoedydd, the question of church affiliation and identity. The leaders were adamant that there was no cause to separate from Anglicanism. Provided that the societies were nurtured by lively preaching (from visiting exhorters and ministers), and had denominational freedom to partake of the Lord's Supper, they should achieve their aim of carefully avoiding all appearance of schism.

Rowland presided over the Dugoedydd meetings. Apart from Harris and William Williams there were two other Anglican ministers and some eighteen laymen present. Howel Davies was either unable or unwilling to attend, possibly because of the influence of Griffith Jones. When Harris heard that he would be absent, he accepted it as God's will, and 'was helped to rejoice in all crosses'.

[1] xxxix. 22, 23.

There was a considerable measure of unity, and their affairs were 'settled according to Mr. Whitefield's letter'. The place and work of each one was reviewed, and assent was given to the rules. 'We sat up to near 12', says Harris, 'praying and consulting; and I hope our Lord directed us, and did set His fear before our eyes.' Reporting the outcome to Whitefield afterwards, Harris could say with joy, 'Everyone agreed with your thoughts, we had much union, sweetness, concord and brotherly love together.'[1]

Following the Dugoedydd meetings Rowland and Harris made their way to Llangeitho for the next day, a Sunday, January 10, 1742. In the afternoon service at Nantcwnlle, as well as in the morning service at Llangeitho, Rowland preached on Deuteronomy 7:22, 'The Lord thy God will put out those nations before thee by little and little.' Both sermons were borrowed extensively from two sermons on the same text by Ralph Erskine, preached originally on July 3, 1727, and issued afterwards in pamphlet form under the title *The Gradual Conquest; or Heaven Won by Little and Little.*[2] It is difficult to determine how much of Erskine's sermons were used on this occasion, as Harris's notes could never be a complete record. There is, however, sufficient correspondence between the notes Harris made at the time and the printed sermons of Erskine to establish that Rowland was following the Scotsman closely both in presentation and matter. It is impossible to determine whether Rowland's preaching that day also contained original material, either by way of exposition or application or both. Harris's comments later referred to other matters. He complained that the Llangeitho crowds were 'losing some heat', at the same time praying 'for all as shall be inclined to join with us', and 'for a blessing on the rules of the Society'.[3]

Shortly it was time for another Association meeting, held on February 11, 1742, at Llwyn-y-berllan some three miles from Dugoedydd, and the home of one of the exhorters. After prayer all the exhorters were examined and approved, except one. Occasionally, when suitability for public ministry was evidently lacking, an

---

[1] CMHO, 55–6; xxvi. 102–04; xxvii. 93–7; HMGC i. 171–3; STL i. 1.
[2] The sermons are numbered CXX–CXXI in volume 5 of the 1865 edition of Ralph Erskine's *Sermons and Other Practical Works*. The material Rowland used is found on pp. 395–8 (at Llangeitho), and pp. 406–08, 412–14 (at Nantcwnlle).
[3] Diary 84; cf. xxx. 49–50.

exhorter would either withdraw his services or be asked to refrain from the work. An instance of this is found in the case of John Jones, some of whose hymns William Williams later included in one of his selections. Jones graciously wrote to the brethren:

'By seeing that all of my brethren did accord in their testimony that my call to exhort publicly was not clear, and some words that Mr. Rowland had to speak did come to me. . . . I had some power to resign myself to the glory of God. Then I had more liberty to give over exhorting. . . . When I manifested my condition to some of my brethren, they informed me that they thought that my work, to the best of their light, was translating some books from the English to the Welsh.'[1]

In this way the brethren had liberty to open their hearts to one another. Most of the time, however, was spent 'in making rules', which were agreed upon and the decision was taken to publish them.[2]

When the rules appeared later that year they bore the title *Sail, Dibenion, a Rheolau'r Societies neu'r Cyfarfodydd Neilltuol a ddechreuasant ymgynull yn ddiweddar yng Nghymru* (The Basis, Purposes, and Rules of the Societies or Private Meetings which have lately started coming together in Wales). Four hymns were appended, the one by Rowland used the familiar pilgrim imagery for the Christian life, and the one by Harris was on 'brotherly love and Christian Unity'. This work remained the standard code of practice for the societies until the appearance in 1777 of William Williams' *Drws y Society Profiad* (The Experience Meeting).[3] In it the Methodists succeeded in presenting a warm pastoral theology with convincing scriptural argument. Its theme was the ministry of believers to one another in their need, a ministry of mutual trust, honesty, encouragement and exhortation. The verses quoted on the title-page were all taken from the Book of Proverbs; two of them spoke of 'counsellors' (in Welsh, 'exhorters'), the third mentioned the advantage of close dealing, 'iron sharpens iron' (Proverbs 15:22; 24:6; 27:17).

[1] WW ii. 58, 59.
[2] CMHO, 61–2; xxvi. 106–107; HMGC i. 173.
[3] *Sail* . . . appears in full in Morris Davies, *op. cit.*, tt. 315–332; *Drws* . . . is in CYN ii. 479–533, and in GWP ii. 181–242. The latter has been translated into English as *The Experience Meeting*, 1973. See also HMGC i. 176–8; WW ii. 235–9.

While the authors are said on the title-page to be 'of the Church of England', the preface refers to 'a few ministers' who have had it 'laid on their hearts to agree to the following Rules'. There is very little else to identify the authorship, except that in requesting prayer on their behalf, they acknowledge that they are few, and full of corruption, but for the sake of the societies have forsaken all, to seek nothing other than to be faithful to their spiritual children. With that solemn responsibility in mind they have met as often as possible, watching over one another's souls, seeking how best to be laid out in their Master's vineyard and how to be better informed about the welfare of Christ's flock. Even with such scanty evidence the general public would have easily identified Rowland as the chief instigator and composer of the work. Three of the four hymns were by exhorters, and their contribution, particularly that of Harris, would also have been widely recognised.

The identity of the document's destination was clearly stated: 'To all who have been made willing to deny themselves, take up their cross, and follow the Lamb, and especially to the Societies within the Church of England.' They were scattered, persecuted, and disciplined. There was a variety of ages, spiritual experience, and social standing represented among them, but they had one thing in common: 'through Christ alone have we been saved. Let us show our love to Him, for redeeming and delivering us freely by His life and death, by sincerely obeying all the commandments, loving the Law as that Rule of our new life in Christ, which we renounce as a covenant by which we come to God to obtain life.' There is careful avoidance of any suggestion of separation from the Church of England, and a specific warning against a sectarian spirit.

Reasons are given why it was thought necessary to go into print. For the societies, guidance is given as to how best to edify one another; for the world it was necessary to demonstrate the scriptural validity of private societies, the irreproachable nature of their activities, and the nature of their discipline for the sake of interested enquirers.

Some favourite Methodist passages were used to establish a scriptural basis for their existence – Malachi 3:16, Hebrews 3:13 and 10:25. Their purpose, too, usually finds scriptural support:

'to provoke to love and good works, Heb. 10; 24; to prevent hardness of heart and backsliding, 1 Cor. 3:1–3; to be more aware of Satan's wiles, the heart's deceitfulness, the work and progress of grace in the soul, 2 Cor. 11:14; 1 Pet. 3:8; to enlighten in the Word of God, and build one another up in the faith; to forestall strife and lovelessness, 1 Tim. 6:4; to watch over and bear one another's burdens, Gal. 6:2; to relate what God has done in our souls for the glory of God, as David did, Ps. 66:16; to strengthen each other against the flesh, the world, and the devil, with prayer and the sharing of lessons learnt since the last meeting.'

'Opening the heart' was encouraged, and it might involve confession (Prov. 28:13), admonition (Matt. 18:15–17), and mutual soul examination (2 Cor. 13:5).

So much for the 'Rules'. They followed closely the Rules drawn up at the Llandovery meeting a year previously, using much the same scriptures and phraseology. Some of the earlier material is found in the final section of the 1742 work under the title 'Questions by which to prove ourselves'. These were in two parts; questions asked of those in the 'general' or 'public' society, and questions asked of those in the 'private society'. Admission to the latter was restricted to those who had assurance of salvation and gave some evidence of growth in grace.

The underlying issue raised by the questions was an important one: the nature of genuine Christian experience. Here the Welsh Methodists were facing an urgent task. It was necessary for them to chart for their own people a course within the heightened spiritual experiences of revival which would both safeguard and advance God's work in their individual souls and in their corporate gatherings. All in all, they were aiming at a manual of Christian self-appraisal and mutual encouragement. The Welsh Methodists sought to meet the need by setting questions that would search the heart, and yet at the same time would edify the fellowship.

They first set out the character of the 'general' society. Entrance to this was open to those who could answer 'yes' to the following questions:

'1. Have you been convinced by God's Spirit to see yourself . . . the chief of sinners?
2. Have you been awakened by grace to see that you can never know God savingly, nor yourself, except your mind is enlightened by a supernatural operation of the Holy Spirit?
3. Have you been taught by the Lord to know that sin has poisoned your whole nature . . . and that you are unable to rescue yourself from this condition?
4. Do you believe and prove that it is through the imputation of Christ's righteousness alone that we are justified, and that it is

received by faith, and that the Holy Spirit alone can work that faith in us?

5. Do you find that the Holy Spirit has made your affections willing to part, for Christ's sake, with all that was before precious and pleasurable to you?

6. Have you secretly counted the cost. . . ?

7. If as yet you have not received the testimony of the Spirit to witness with your spirit that you are a child of God, is it your desire at all times to seek God with all your heart, seeking nothing but Him?

8. Are you uneasy . . . until you prove that Christ is in you . . . and your heart has been broken . . . truly to hate every sin; until you have received the Spirit of adoption crying Abba, Father, within you?

9. Do you believe and assent to the fundamental truths; the Trinity, election, original sin, justification by faith, perseverance in the state of grace, etc.?

10. Is it Christ's love which constrains you to join us?'

Throughout the work, scriptural support for each question is supplied. The privacy of shared experiences is emphasised: 'that you tell no outsider what we share together in the simplicity of our hearts (since repeating such experiences to the ungodly is like casting pearls before swine)'. While such sharing was encouraged it was important for the general public to know something of the nature of these otherwise private gatherings, and the Rules were printed with this in mind. Further, there was no parallel with the Confessional of Roman Catholicism, as here each believer was participating on an equal footing of mutual priesthood. The purpose of the meeting was also quite different: the Methodists met to encourage one another in their conflict with sin rather than to obtain forgiveness. Nothing would have been further from their minds than the concept of a priestly power of remission and the imposition of meritorious penances. Methodism was nothing if not direct in dealing with God alone for salvation.

Pressing on to maturity was implicit in the Christian life. For the sake of progress, therefore, a fellowship meeting of closer dealing with God, the 'private society', was provided for by the 1742 rules. Its hallmark was, unashamedly, assurance of salvation, and this difference between the two forms of 'society' meeting owed a great deal to Rowland's teaching on the subject. The questions now centred on a clearer acquaintance with the things of God. 'Whoever has been for some time in the "general society", and whose conversation is fitting, is to be received into the "private society" when he can answer the following questions' [affirmatively]:

'1. Do you know that you believe? . . . Does God's Spirit at all times bear witness with your spirit that you are a child of God?

2. Do you find in your heart a greater sympathy with those who are tempted?

3. Do you experience more spiritual light within, revealing more and more of God's holiness and the spirituality of His Law?

4. Is your conscience more sensitive in reproving the first beginnings of sin in the mind? . . .

5. What lessons has the Lord taught you since we last met?

6. Are you more amazed at God's distinguishing love towards you? . . .

7. Are you more rooted and grounded in love?'

If the Methodists erred, it was on the side of strictness rather than leniency. Their concern was to protect, not merely individual believers and vulnerable societies, but also the whole Methodist witness in Wales. Consequently, there was an emphasis on practical as well as experimental Christianity. The 'Rules' insisted on a conscious effort to maintain the unity of God's people and the vigorous pursuit of personal holiness. The questions were written against the background of deadness and hypocrisy which prevailed in Welsh religious circles, the head-knowledge of the Dissenters, the self-righteous morality of Anglicanism. The Methodists were aiming at lively spirituality, as well as strict orthodoxy and morality. The solidarity and proliferation of the societies to the end of the century was a measure of their success.

In him were a thousand virtues
More than in the ones who scorned,
And repeated faults and failures,
For much grace his life adorned;
Levity and foolish jesting,
Empty words, he aye eschewed;
And the work of his Lord Jesus,
Night and morning, he extolled.

Farewell, Harris, now ambition
To be chief no more's your love;
Yours now the true promotion,
Praising God in heaven above.
We are also hasting hither
On our pilgrimage below,
With but little time between us
And redemption's final blow.

WILLIAM WILLIAMS
Elegy to Howel Harris, 1773

18

Tensions and Triumphs

With the setting up of the first clearly Methodist Association at the beginning of 1742, the Revival's seventh year promised well. Storms were never far away, but with such widespread success and so many achievements, it seemed as if there could be no end to the manifestation of God's glory; so many lives had been changed, and so many societies had been formed. There was now a regulated order, with more workers and new doors of opportunity. The Spirit's power was still very much in evidence upon the preaching of Rowland. Harris's zeal was unabated. In many a community in South Wales there was an awareness that God was visiting the land, and an expectancy for yet more. All seemed set for 1742 to be another 'acceptable year of the Lord'. But the progress of the work very nearly floundered on the frailty of its instruments.

Certainly there was physical frailty. At the year's beginning, William Williams had smallpox.[1] There was also on occasions the frailty of inexperience and excessive zeal, as Griffith Jones complained of in his curate, Howel Davies.[2] By far the most serious, however, was the frailty of human nature in the most prominent leaders, Rowland and Harris. Hence the prayer of Harris towards the end of 1741: 'Begging for Brother Rowland, that he may be cleared from everything as may darken his ministry.'[3] No indication is given of what lay behind the prayer. Shortly afterwards, others are prayed for with the same vehemence:

'Prayed for dear, dear Rowland, set him free from all chains, slavish fear, darkness, rashness, imprudencies and everything that may keep him from honouring Thee. Set Brother Howel Davies, too, free from all hindrances, so Brother Jenkins and Williams, and all of all sects. Bless dear, dear Mr. Griffith Jones, set him free from his reasonings.'

[1] WW i. 51.   [2] xxxv. 54.   [3] CMHO, 51.

Within a month Harris was praying again for Rowland: 'O Lord, destroy his lightness and unbelief, and make him to shine in grace.'[1]

Nor was Harris himself exempt from faults, for which in turn he was reproved by his brethren. As recently as January 5, 1742, Harris had apologised to Whitefield for blameworthy conduct, adding, 'spare me not though bitter it may be to the flesh, and I know you'll pray that the Spirit of God may breathe with all your reproofs on my soul to the destruction of the flesh'.[2] Rowland is referring to the same heart-rebellion when he writes in a letter in September 1742, 'Oh! when shall I see myself delivered from this body of corruption?' To Harris in October he writes, 'I wish I could skip and leap over all the mountains of pleasures and laziness, hard-heartedness, unbelief, etc., and rest upon the breast of the Beloved and never-never-enough-praised Jesus!'[3] If there were times when 'the flesh' in all its ugliness marred their lives and their witness, the Welsh Methodists were aware of its presence within, and they grieved much over its offensiveness to God. Sadly, in 1742 it caused much friction between Rowland and Harris.

On Saturday, February 13, that year, Rowland was preaching at Llangeitho. His text was Revelation 3:18, 'I counsel thee to buy of me gold tried in the fire, that thou mayest be rich; and white raiment, that thou mayest be clothed, and that the shame of thy nakedness do not appear; and anoint thine eyes with eyesalve, that thou mayest see.' 'He had a vast and uncommon power, lifting up his voice like a trumpet, and calling them out of Satan's chains', says Harris, adding, 'he had a great sight of their danger and great love to them and great earnestness with them.'

Rowland began by reminding his congregation that it was when the Apostle John had been banished that God granted him a revelation. From this Rowland drew encouragement and warning; 'When we are despised by all then God values us, and when the world admires us we are mean before God.' Then he dealt with the nature of the Gospel call:

'God's advising does not imply a power in men, for God's hand and Word go together. He exhorts to come, and draws too. As we call our

[1] HVP, 69; CMHO, 51, 59; xxx. 50; HVL, 8.
[2] MS ii. 200.
[3] *Glasgow Weekly History*, No. 45, p. 2. There is a copy of this issue in The Mitchell Library, Glasgow; *Account of the Progress of the Gospel*, vol. II. No. 1, p. 4.

beasts we draw them too in the halter [rope]. . . . By "buying" is meant receiving or exchanging: in the Gospel to give our misery for His happiness. He showed, 1. that a true church may become lukewarm; 2. but they shall not rest long so, God will come to awaken them; 3. that some please God in accepting of His white robe of Christ's righteousness imputed. He showed that we are naked till we put on Christ. 1. This is God's will, your sanctification (1 Thess. 4:3). If we sin we shall not enjoy God's presence, and that is the heaviest judgment of all. The saint had rather lose 10,000 worlds than be without the enjoyment of Christ. . . . [Here are] the causes of our lukewarmness: complaints and murmurings and all spiritual distempers, and it is because we go out of Christ's righteousness. When we are out of His love we are full of sin. All things harden the wicked for hell and ripen the godly for heaven. When the distemper is in thy soul, thou art angry even with the stones of the way, and with thine own feet under thee, and this is when God hides His face. But when He returns again all crosses and pain vanish. This is food for you that are spiritual, but nothing to you that are all flesh. But we are sent to preach and to feed not the flesh but the spirit. When once thou doubtest of God's love to thee, thou art all wounded. Thou canst not bear to be touched, but art full of peevishness and tired of God and His Word and ways. 2. God's love inclines saints to desire this vesture of holiness. 3. That others may have benefit from your holiness etc. In vain do you boast of faith, love and grace; if you have no fruits you are dead; the saint can't help living according to the Gospel. 4. By reason of our state and danger we should put on the Lord Jesus. 5. If you will put on Christ you will be exposed to many dangers etc. but all that falls to me is in love. Here [in the text] we see that many of the saints are very poor of grace; yet though thou hast such advantages and yet grow not so much, yet Christ loves thee. . . . Because thou art so poor, come to Christ. Do not say "I am sinful and therefore depart from me!" That is Satan's doctrine.'

In dealing with the sovereignty and freeness of God's grace in Christ, Rowland was setting out the very heart of the Gospel, and doing so in a 'lively' way as one who had a profound experience of the truth he proclaimed.

Rowland's text on Sunday was John 3:8, 'The wind bloweth where it listeth, and thou hearest the sound thereof, but canst not tell whence it cometh, and whither it goeth; so is every one that is born of the Spirit.' He dealt with what was to him a familiar theme, the thundering of God's holy Law against the sinner, bringing conviction and alarm, a necessary 'Law work' in bringing a sinner to salvation in Christ:

'[Some] say they have not been enough underneath law work, but if thou seest thyself quite lost without Christ, the Law has done with thee, for that is the office of the Law, to lead thee to Christ. . . . The wind blows sovereignly, we can't command it to come or go. The wind goes through little chinks, so the wind of the Spirit blows through thy whole soul. If thou seest thy sins and loathest thy heart, and in truth dost long for a new heart, then this gale came over thee, and God has begun a work and He will carry the work on. God's eyes, hands, arms, feet and breath are all for our salvation. Here we see that out of Christ flows all our salvation. The wind blows secretly, but it leaves an effect on us.'

Harris's notes of the sermon are rounded off with an unusual comment about Rowland: 'He was dry in preaching', and he adds, 'many sweet lessons were taught, but nothing is effectual till the Spirit comes.'

At the sacrament which followed the congregation was restless and noisy, a fault which roused Harris to administer a severe public rebuke shortly afterwards:

'Had great power indeed to cut and tear and thunder for their behaviour at the ordinance, convincing them home [that is, plainly] for their looking about and talking, declaring it was plain that they were tired of God's work, saying in their hearts, when shall we go away? Nay, some went out. Did a stranger come in he would think he had gone to a Market House and not to God's House. Next time the door must be locked to keep you in. Is this growing in grace? . . . Once you would have warmed one that would come among you, now you would cool anyone in looking at you. . . . How many do I know now that are so thankful and fruitful and watchful, that hear a powerful sermon only once in three months, what determination they have! What good use they have made of them! But you hear so much, till it is common, so that instead of growing more and more simple and humble and meek, you rather carp. Where is your fruit?'[1]

A measure of disorder was inevitable in a great congregation gathered under extraordinary spiritual impressions. On this occasion, however, Harris detected an element of disrespect and resistance to God's Word. With typical candour and force he lost no time in pouring out his soul's abhorrence of such irreverent behaviour. Rightly so, if it was deserved, but was Harris being totally objective in his judgment? First, Rowland's preaching, then Rowland's congregation, had been lacking, in Harris's estimation. Did Llangeitho that week-end seem a total disaster, or did some of the blame lie with Harris himself? It was at least important to resolve the areas

[1] Diary 85; xxvi. 108; xxx. 52.

of dissatisfaction or disagreement that lay behind Harris's misgivings with those around him in the opening months of 1742.

It did not take long for the tension between Harris and Rowland to surface publicly. The March Association was held again in Carmarthenshire on the 18th. In preparation for the meeting at Llwyn-y-berllan, the two leaders met the previous night at Talley. Evidently it was an opportunity for the society to meet with them. Harris wrote in his diary:

'In discoursing Brother Rowland and I differed and disputed about the Covenant, about God's making a Covenant; with man he said: and I, with His Son as man's Head. But it arose so high, I was to blame chiefly in contradicting him publicly; and then he said (when I said of one's seeing one's nature all over against God's nature, contrary) what is experience to us, to the Law etc., we have the surer word of prophecy. I was then struck dumb. . . . I felt no love, but selfishly could not pity the lambs; but somewhat in me would be pleased to divide from him without any consideration of the consequences to others, but rather I felt my soul humbled under a sense of my darkness and ignorance, willing he should go about and I should be laid aside.'[1]

Since Harris does not specify the passage which was under discussion at the time, it is difficult to identify the area of misunderstanding. In the counsels of eternity, the Father entered into covenant with Christ as His people's federal head, in terms of Isaiah 42:6 and Galatians 3:16–17. In time, also, he enters into personal covenant with those who by faith are joined to Christ, as indicated by Jeremiah 32:40 and Hebrews 8:10. At the time Rowland seems to have reproved Harris for basing his theology on the subjective criterion of human experience rather than on the objective teaching of God's Word. Harris was quick to recognise the gravity of this charge, and it was this which silenced him.

For all that, the next day Harris 'rejoiced in that God gives the power I had to Brother Rowland'. At the business meeting, however, prayer was only tolerable, 'not near God', and although they 'settled some to overlook the societies everywhere, and read the letters' there was friction. Harris was reproved for writing his journal and losing time; Rowland for 'not being willing to go according to the Rules of the Society'. There was a further doctrinal dispute 'that held to midnight about our knowing our interest in Christ between me and

[1] HH Diary 86; xxvi. 109–112; CMHO, 62–66; HMGC i. 173.

Brother Rowland, and being dry and not in love I became stiff, and that stirred the same spirit in him again, and then we could not understand each other'.

Worse was to follow. This time the disagreement was such that it put the whole future of the work in Wales in jeopardy. Here is Harris's account again:

'I laid out the case when we could apply the comfort of perseverance to any but: 1. such as are on the Rock; 2. such as heard the Voice; 3. such as are living branches in the Vine. It arose to a great dispute; some were for me and some were for him and some confounded. I was dry, but no anger, but divided, and said I could not join in society with him, nor invite him to us because we could not build up the same people.'

Before retiring for the night they prayed together and some of the wounds were healed. The next day there were extraordinary scenes of reconciliation:

'Some little sense on me that it was my duty to go to Brother Rowland and tell him I loved him. Self would hinder and it was a hard battle, but from his principles though I did not feel the freedom of love yet (O how good it is to obey when we don't feel) I was helped to break slavish shame and to go and fall on his neck and then (O ever to be remembered!) what we could not do by reasoning was done by praying. My heart went as it were to millions of pieces and burst out to a flood of tears . . . there was a general weeping among us . . . with brokenness of heart and utterance while with many tears I publicly owned my pride and self to God. For Brother Rowland especially, that the face of the Lord may ever shine on him. . . . Then we sang together on our knees, Brother Rowland continuing to weep, all broken to pieces. We rose and rejoiced in the victory together. . . . We agreed in love now what we could not before, that when a man is effectually called, he knows he has something, but does not know it is justification or faith by name, until he hears it explained. So now we agreed with Brother Rowland.'

Both Rowland and Harris were to blame. The differences could and should have been resolved between themselves in private. As it was, others became involved. One effect of the affair was to put pressure on the society members to take sides with their favourite leader. Another detrimental effect was doctrinal polarisation. Even though it began with a misunderstanding over one particular issue, it gradually affected other related teachings, suspicions, emphases, and personalities.

Sadly, in spite of the seemingly united note on which the

Association of March 18, 1742, ended, the tensions continued to simmer underneath the surface. They were also causing widespread concern. 'The rumour of my disagreeing with Rowland already has cankered and done evil', says Harris on March 24, but he still clung to the conviction that Rowland was wrong on the matter of assurance.[1] On April 14, Harris felt his union with Rowland incomplete, '1. because he is not clear about assurance; 2. can't admit mixed communions; 3. does not walk close enough.'[2] At an Association on the 22nd of the month Harris felt 'no life or liberty or love or sweetness among the brethen, and I was the cause of it. . . . Hearing Brother Rowland and another discourse I had nothing affecting my devilish heart.'[3] Afterwards, Thomas Price, a prominent exhorter wrote to Harris expressing concern at his conduct towards Rowland:

'Since I left you I was grieved much concerning your conduct toward Mr. Rowland, as I believe you are thoroughly satisfied that he is a dear child of God, and that the Lord owns his ministry in a very particular manner. And such a word to drop out of your mouth as to say that you received no more good by his last sermon at Trefeca than if there had been a ballad read, had almost made me tremble. Whence does this language proceed but from the old creature? . . . Another thing which appears to me as an error in you – your spirit is a little too imperious.'

In reply Harris regretted his faults, and pleaded his lack of bitterness, his love and simplicity, at the time. He also argued that Rowland was not free of blame in some of the expressions he had used about assurance.[4]

In May, on another visit to Llangeitho, Harris found himself still at odds with Rowland and his congregation. During the sermon, when Rowland was applying the message 'others were melted, but I could not stir myself up', 'I was dry and could not draw near to God.' Rowland's text was 1 Corinthians 7:35, 'This I speak . . . that you may attend upon the Lord without distraction', and the sermon sought to expose the danger of indifference:

'God is a sea, the ordinances are the pipes, lukewarmness and wandering thoughts are like stones that interrupt the channel. You shiver with cold, when God is a fire. You are hungering with famine and Christ is all food. You are thirsty and He is water to refresh you. Come up, then, nearer to God and don't stand off. Lukewarmness is

---

[1] xxxiv. 79.   [2] CMHO, 66.   [3] HH Diary 89.
[4] STL i. 10, 15–16.

a wound, and wandering thoughts are like the vermin that blow on it to make it stink. You begin with hearing and praying with God, but soon you go from God. Wandering from God. 1. takes us from duty; 2. from the benefits of His ordinances; 3. from the comforts of them. Much profit and sweetness flows to the true worshipper in God's House. Song of Solomon 2:3. When the sun comes to shine on us, wandering thoughts are like clouds coming between the sun and us, so we fail to find love and light flowing from God. . . . Though you can't keep vain thoughts from tempting or coming to the mind, you may keep them from nesting and coming to the door of the will. Many salute each other when they meet on the way, but friends know not how to part . . . you crack the nut but never eat the kernel. Why do you starve at Christ's door? You seek Christ in the earth or in men, but it is in His Spirit He is to be found. Are you under a curse, like the Sodomites who could not find Lot's door? . . . 4. These evil thoughts grieve the Spirit. He dwells not in Babel (a heart full of confusion), but in Salem, a city of peace. 5. They offend God. When the king speaks you should hear; when you are under the Word, listen. God there reads His will. Why does God's Spirit so soon leave you? Because you are entertaining His enemies at His Table. Give your soul to Christ that you may have victory over your sinful thoughts and not they over you. For this power is in grace to overcome all these: they can't stand before the Wind.'[1]

That same evening Harris discoursed to 'a vast crowd' on Galatians 5:25, 'If we live in the Spirit, let us also walk in the Spirit.' The meeting lasted three hours, and he was surprised that there was 'no crying out, though it was usual here'. Wrongly, Harris tended to regard physical manifestations as an index of the Spirit's power. Their absence under his ministry, and in contrast the 'meltings' under that of Rowland, compounded his misery.

In June 1742 there was an Association at Trefeca, which Rowland refused to attend on account of his misgivings about Harris.[2] During the summer months Whitefield was expressing great sorrow at the news from Harris of a 'narrow spirit' which prevailed among some of the brethren in Wales. He responded to the report, as always, with intercession ('I laid upon my face this day, and for some time pleaded with groans unutterable'), and encouragement ('dividing times generally precede settling times').[3]

Whitefield's comment was both wise and prophetic, as events proved. Rowland had been to North Wales before August, and was

[1] Diary 90.   [2] xxxv. 20–21.
[3] GWL i. 393, 398, 426.

twice in Montgomeryshire before the end of the summer.[1] During his July visit to the county, he told one of the mid-Wales exhorters, James Beaumont, what the Lord was doing at Llangeitho: 'Sometimes they will be, it may be near a hundred at a time, down on the ground crying out; some crying "Bless Jesus for me", others crying in the agonies of their souls for Jesus to deliver them.' William Evans, Beaumont's exhorter friend, having just returned from a Llangeitho visit, had confirmed this with the comment: 'The work of the Lord goes on gloriously in those parts.' Rowland and Beaumont had been discussing Whitefield's revival experiences in Scotland. There, too, deep convictions had produced physical prostration, and careful investigation had satisfied several godly ministers that the work was not spurious.[2] Rowland and Whitefield successes in the summer of 1742 demonstrated that the Awakening's power was far from spent.

This could not fail to leave its mark on Harris. On the first day of August he was back once more in Rowland's territory, listening to a sermon of his on 1 John 2:2, 'And He is the propitiation for our sins, and not for ours only, but for the sins of the whole world.' Rowland dealt searchingly with the real character of saving faith, saying that the Apostle John 'here was preaching to the heart, calling them to see God's love':

'We see here God's children are of great repute with God. He trusts His grace and Son with them, but won't trust anything to the ungodly. True ministers must preach so that all the people may know where they are going and be most sure of either heaven or hell. None will admire God's love but such as saw their misery. When we are convinced in the understanding only there is not haste in the soul, or striving, but promises and delays. But grace goes about the work immediately and won't rest. We see here also God's children at times do admire their happiness, not in their sanctification, but in their justification. . . . The inside of God's people is the best in all ages. . . . It is not our grace and holiness God praises in the Song of Solomon, but our imputed righteousness: the best part of the saint is inside. . . . Righteousness imputed is like the sun; thereon God looks – hence is sure foundation of a witness; but sanctification is like the moon, changeable, and so the witness arising hence is uncertain.'

At this point Rowland was touching Harris's favourite theme,

[1] xxx. 57; MTU, 49.
[2] *Account of the Progress of the Gospel*, 1743, vol. ii. No. 1, p. 34. The original is in the Memorial Hall Library, Farringdon Road, London. Part of the letter is in TM i. 247. It was received by Harris in London on August 28. (HRS, 11.)

assurance. Not surprisingly, therefore, Harris 'had great strength in hearing him say how Christ did justify us before we knew where or what we are', because it echoed Harris's own experience. When Rowland went on to apply the message, Harris records that 'there came a great outcry, indeed, so that one could hardly hear':

'Art thou come like Christ, though not equal to Christ? Is the mind of Christ in thee? Where is Christ, is He in thy heart? . . . Where is thy grace? Dost thou in thy heart say "I am damned"? Thou art now nearer than ever to heaven. Dost thou feel that thou canst not wait too? If so, thou art now at the foot of the way, and Christ cries "Come to Me, I am the way! Climb up, I am the ladder." There is life in Christ: breathe! Is he a blind soul? then says Christ, "I'll give him sight"; Is he lame and weak? "I'll make him run, I'll give him feet and make him shoes!"'

Both leaders knew that the smile of God's face upon them, and the power of God's Spirit in their midst, would resolve their difficulties. God graciously granted them just such another visitation, so that when Harris left Llangeitho the next day, he 'parted in deep love with Brother Rowland'.[1]

[1] Diary 92; xxvii. 18.

'We are about soul's work, eternity work, and God's work. There is no jesting with God.'

HOWELL HARRIS
in September 1742

'In the third chapter of Hebrews we are bidden to "exhort one another daily, while it is called 'Today'; lest any of you be hardened through the deceitfulness of sin", which shows that the Holy Spirit means us, first, to gather ourselves together, and then to exhort each other lest we depart from the living God.'

WILLIAM WILLIAMS
in *The Experience Meeting*

19

Letters to London

The autumn of 1742 was a busy time for Rowland. Records of his activities are, however, scarce, as Harris was in London from mid-August to mid-November. On the other hand, the very fact that Harris was in London may account for the preservation of some Rowland letters written during this period, as each one had a London destination.

The letters brought news of Rowland's ministry. Their main purpose, however, was to discharge the responsibility he felt for members of his congregation who, for some reason or other, were in the capital city. For this reason, they provide an insight into Rowland's pastoral concern. A warmth of sympathetic fellow-feeling and homeliness, coupled with strong exhortation and incentive to godliness, is still conveyed by them. They distil and epitomize, in letter form, the close dealing so typical of early Welsh Methodist culture.

The first of these letters, dated September 6, 1742, is addressed to 'Mr W.G. (one of the members of his congregation in Lambeth)'. It confirms the impression that Rowland at this period was extremely busy and his ministry was being greatly blessed:

My dearly Beloved,
 I know I can be justly reproved by you for my negligence in writing; 'twas not want of love, but excess of business prevented my doing it. I hope you all thrive in the Lord, and that you still press forward toward the mark. I thought of coming to London myself vastly [that is, definitely] this year, but it seems the Lord does not call me as yet, but He only knows how soon He may.
 Religion flourishes now in our parts. Thousands flock to the Word, and while under the Word great part of them are under such agonies as is enough to melt the hardest heart. Some made it their business to chide them, and now they themselves are overcome by the power of God. They cannot but cry out, 'What

shall I do!', etc. You would all wonder at what we daily see and hear. As for my part I can say I never had such power as I have now every day, (may the good Lord continue it!) mostly to preach. Whole multitudes are under concern. Many of them that were enemies to my doctrine, and way of preaching, do now (blessed be God!) experimentally understand what He enables me to deliver them from the pulpit. Some confess that they went from home on Sundays with an intent to go to another place of worship, but were, they know not how, carried to Llangeitho.

Oh! that you would help me to praise the Lord! The more the Lord blesses my poor endeavours, the more sinful and ungrateful I am! Oh, when shall I see myself delivered from this body of corruption? Good Lord, hasten that time! Methinks your very souls cry out Amen! Amen! So says your brother and fellow-traveller.

Oh, what shall I say to strengthen your hands and to drive you on in the ways of God. Shall I say that God loves you? Nay, that Christ died for you? What! does the Blessed Saviour now plead for you at the Throne of Grace? Does His tender heart now bleed for you? Can you sin by being light and carnal? No, no, my dear flock, you can't do it; you can't do less than pray to Him day and night. His love constrains you to be holy. Pray keep under a powerful preaching. Let some sound preacher water the seed that has been sown in your hearts. Give my tender respect to dear, dear brother Harris, and pray remember to pray for your poor, weak brother,

Daniel Rowland.[1]

One of the early traditions preserved in John Hughes's monumental three-volume work on Welsh Calvinistic Methodism, *Methodistiaeth Cymru*, published in 1856, relates to Rowland's visits to Lambeth. 'There is a strong tradition which has survived to this day', he says, 'that Harris and Rowland occasionally preached in Welsh at Lambeth'. This is certainly true of Harris: he preached in Welsh to his countrymen at Lambeth as early as May 3, 1739.[2] There was, thus, a Welsh-speaking congregation at Lambeth, and Rowland's preference for his native tongue, especially in the early years of his ministry, has already been established. A visit to London by him for this limited purpose would not have been widely known or publicised.

Such letters, bearing news of the Revival's progress, were widely

---

[1] *Glasgow Weekly History*, 1742, No. 45, pp. 1–2.
[2] Cyfrol iii, tud. 435; cf. John Thickens, *Howel Harris yn Llundain*, tud. 114.

circulated and read among Methodist circles. Sooner or later they reached Harris, and he promptly wrote to Rowland:

'I had the good Providence of seeing your line to some of your flock here, which was greatly blessed to my soul indeed, and made my heart and many others, I believe, in a flame of love and praise. I sent a copy of it to Brother Whitefield. . . . How it would revive my soul to have but a line from you! As you go so much about, and are so favoured by our dear Lord, why should not we be favoured with a letter of your success and journeys to read on our Letter Day. It would, I believe, revive many a soul here, and cause many prayers to be sent up for you. . . . It is natural for one part of God's family to rejoice on hearing of the other part.'

The reference to a 'Letter Day' needs some explanation. Once a month at Whitefield's 'Tabernacle' in London, accounts of the Awakening's progress, in England, Scotland, America and Wales, would be shared. Harris explained its purpose to Howel Davies in a letter of October 15, 1742: 'We have a day once a month to read letters from ministers and others of all sects and persuasions all over the world that correspond with us, and great is the power that is amongst us those days.' That same day, he also wrote to Whitefield: 'On our Letter Day last Monday the Lord was indeed powerfully there, like a flame of fire, filling us with zeal and love.' Rowland's letter, however, had evidently arrived too late for sharing on that occasion, as he continues: 'I have since heard most glorious news from Wales of the success attending Brother Rowland and many others. They are wounded by scores and flock under the Word by thousands.'[1]

This fuelling of prayer and ministry of encouragement was very much in the leaders' minds when they set up their Methodist Newspaper. It was a conviction shared by Jonathan Edwards across the Atlantic. He argues in similar vein to Harris in *Some Thoughts Concerning the Present Revival of Religion in New England*, published in 1743: 'One thing more I would mention, which, if God should still carry on this work, would tend much to promote it, and that is, that a history should be published once a month, or once a fortnight, of its progress. . . . It has been found by experience, that the tidings of remarkable effects of the power and grace of God in any place, tend greatly to awaken and engage the minds of persons in other places.'[2]

[1] NLW CMA Trefeca Letters 697, 695; STL i. 55.
[2] *The Works of Jonathan Edwards*, vol. i. 1834, p. 429.

When Rowland responded to Harris, it was with amazing news, as the letter, dated October 20, 1742, shows:

My dear brother,

I bless you for your letters. They were like a shower of rain to a dry land. Indeed the Lord gave you the tongue of the learned. But oh! O what am I? A painted hypocrite, a miserable sinner! I know all the to's and fro's, up's and down's that are in religion; but the blessed liberty that remains for the children of God is still hidden from me. I believe you pray for me. God grant you may prevail! . . . O blessed time, when all prisoners of hope shall be released, and enter into the rest of their dear IM-MANUEL! I don't doubt but your soul joins with me to say, Amen! Amen!

I have been now of late in Montgomeryshire. I had great power there to convince and to build. Persecution increases; some of the brethren are excommunicated. I hope you will consult with the brethren in London, and send us what is best to do. Afterwards at Brecon in several churches and houses I preached with uncommon power. I heard since that I am put into the Court for discoursing at an alehouse there. Your sentiments about this, too, would be very serviceable. Brother Williams is put in, too, for not living in the parish where he officiates, etc.

The last week I have been in Carmarthenshire and Glamorgan, and brave opportunities indeed they were; whole congregations were under concern, and such crying out that my voice could not be heard. Some persons of quality did entertain me with uncommon respect. O what am I, that my ears and eyes should hear and see such things! O help me to bless the God of heaven! I hope His Kingdom begins to come. O Satan, be packing! Fly, fly with trembling lest the God of Israel come at thee! O Lord chastise him! Amen! Lord, down with him! Let his kingdom shatter, and let him be trampled under the feet of Thy children. How long shall he domineer over Thy little ones? My dear brother, up with your arms! Yield not an inch! That God whom you serve can, yea, and will, deliver us! In His might we shall win the field! . . . My poor flock increase daily. They would be heartily glad to see you.

Brother Williams was here last Sunday, and a sweet day it was. I love him more and more because of his simple, honest, plain way of dealing with the people. His parishioners are highly incensed against him. I trust we shall have him out before long. Methinks I hear you inquiring after Caernarfonshire. Benjamin Thomas is there. They come by thousands to hear. Brother Howel Davies promised to go there, what detains him I know not. I can't possibly go this winter, for want of one to supply my room at my churches. The next week I promised to be at Pembroke and the lower part of Carmarthen, shortly after at Cynwyl, etc. Dear brother, never fail to intercede for me, who am your loving friend, well-wisher and unworthy brother.

Daniel Rowland.[1]

When Rowland used the phrase 'prisoners of hope' he had himself in mind, along with others who were labouring under a sense of inward corruption. He was expressing his fervent desire for that liberty of the children of God which is experienced with some measure of assurance and joy even now, but which will be complete only at the 'day of redemption' (Romans 7:22–25; 8:19–21.)

An echo of these sentiments is found in a letter written by Rowland on the next day, October 21, 1742, 'To a lady, one of the pilgrims of Zion'[2]:

Dear, dear Sister,
    How do you do? Does your soul thrive in the Lord? Can you say that Christ is your beloved? Have you been upon the mount of Pisgah? Have you had a sight of the country that is flowing with milk and honey? Methinks you say, "Sometimes I can answer all your questions in the affirmative, but generally I walk in darkness, in the valley of unbelief, doubting my state, whether I am predestined to salvation or reprobation." Oh! my dear sister, is it so? May the Lord rebuke your unbelief! Down, down, down with that villain that has destroyed so many thousands of souls. Oh! That I could make it shake and shiver in you. Oh! that I could tell you a word that would strengthen you to set upon it with might and main, and not yield, till you be made, through the grace of God, more than a conqueror. This is the hearty desire of your poor brother.

Rowland was, of course, reminding his correspondent of that conflict with sin and unbelief which is the common lot of God's people. This work of sanctification also means that the believer is always thirsting after a closer walk with God. There are times when the subjective enjoyment of spiritual realities is greater or less than usual. One of Rowland's sayings was this: 'It is winter with the saints sometimes, when the tree has no leaves, yet the life is in it.'[3] Being 'a partaker of the divine nature', the believer 'earnestly presses towards the mark', desiring growth in grace and in the knowledge of Jesus Christ, and a greater passion for God's glory.

[1] *An Account of the . . . Progress of the Gospel*, 1743, vol. ii. No. 1, pp. 3–7; also in Morris Davies, *Deuddeg Pregeth . . .* , 1876, tud. 306–08 (with some variations).
[2] MR, 65–7; also in Morris Davies, *op. cit.*, 309–11.
[3] MS i. 492.

Rowland next dealt with the means of that sanctification.

> I hope there is no need of rebuking you for any negligence in hearing the Word. I trust you are often compelled to frequent sound and powerful preaching, even such as unravels sin, uncases the heart, and condemns self and human wisdom, and sets forth in godly simplicity Christ as your all. Such ministry is dreadful to doubts and unbelief; yea, under such, your little mustard seed will in a short time become a great cedar. May the Lord enable you to attend the same with diligence. Look often on your state by nature, the passion of the sweet and lovely Jesus, and the things of eternity; then, and not till then, you will see the necessity of running after sermons, and cleaving to the Lord.

Rowland consistently and passionately believed in the sufficiency of Scripture for salvation. As expositions of Scripture, sermons were the vehicle *par excellence* of teaching God's people. They were rendered effective and powerful by the Spirit's application to the soul, and His enabling in the arena of personal and public life. In Rowland's teaching, there is a finality about Scripture which is exclusive. All other claims to authority, whether on the part of Church Councils, or of individuals asserting an immediacy of 'prophetic' utterance, are both dangerous and superfluous.

Another conviction which Rowland considered salutary for all believers, was that of holding 'the things of eternity' constantly in focus. This was the daily companion of the Reformers and the Puritans, yielding the precious fruit of self denial and resolution. 'For when there is no promise of any eternal inheritance implanted in our hearts, we shall never be torn away from this world', says Calvin. 'But when we understand our inheritance to be in heaven, while we are strangers upon earth, then we put off that clinging to the life of this world to which we are too much devoted.'[1] Richard Baxter's *The Saints' Everlasting Rest* was written from the same considera-tion: 'It is not our comfort only, but our stability, our liveliness in all duties, our enduring tribulation, our honouring of God, the vigour of our love, thankfulness, and all our graces, yea the very being of our religion and Christianity itself, dependeth on the believing serious thoughts of our Rest.'[2] Heavenly-mindedness, for Rowland too, was a necessary and productive discipline in every believing soul.

Rowland's letter therefore proceeds with more exhortation:

[1] Commentary on Daniel 3:16–18.
[2] *The Saints' Everlasting Rest*, 'A Premonition'.

Perhaps now you are tainted by the example of the ungodly. Their ridiculing you may make you presently cold and lukewarm. Alas! alas! shall fools laugh you away from Christ! Only consider the enmity that is between them and God, and the endless torments they are to bear for ridiculing such as flee after Christ. This, this, I say, would cause you to turn your eyes from them, and stop your ears against them. You will say, 'Good Christians are not always in such a hurry as I command you to be in.' I answer, a great many professors are lukewarm, but who knows that they shall speed. It is good to be sure thereof. On, on, on, my dear Sister, you cannot come too soon to the gate of heaven. I am at a loss to find out words that may revive and quicken your soul. May the love of Christ be a burning spur in your soul, driving you towards the heavenly Canaan.

I saw your sister: she gives her love to you both, and to Mr. Willis and his wife. She hopes they may not fail to hear Mr. Whitefield when he comes there. Your mother is in health, and gives her love to you. I must tell you though, I am in a great hurry. We enjoy the presence of God almost every Sunday! Oh! help us to praise Him, He is altogether lovely. Blessed be His holy Name, says your poor unworthy brother,

D. Rowland.

P.S. give my love to Christian friends, particularly to such as are under my care. My kind regards to Mr. Harris, and you may show him this letter if you think fit. I thank you kindly for your love.

Having 'the presence of God almost every Sunday' made the autumn of 1742 a spiritual summer at Llangeitho!

This same theme occurs in the other letter of spiritual counsel by Rowland which has been preserved, addressed 'to two Welsh Sisters of his flock in London'. It appeared undated in *An Account of the ... Progress of the Gospel* amidst letters written in September 1743, during which period Harris was again in London.[1]

I hope these lines will find you in or near your Father's House, leaning upon your Beloved, refreshing yourselves with wholesome spiritual food; bewailing your former transgressions, yet rejoicing in the Lord for being effectually called. But methinks I hear my poor Sisters say, 'Blessed are such, but as for us, we are in the dark, not knowing what will become of us, full of fears and discomforts, sad, sad, sad!' O sad indeed! to hear such a cry in summer season! I pity you; may the great God lift up the light of His countenance upon you.

[1] *An Account of the ... Progress of the Gospel*, 1743, vol. iv. No. 2, pp. 13–16. This letter is also in Morris Davies, *op. cit.*, 313–14. Harris was in London from August 20 to September 28, 1743.

But where have you been all this while? What are you doing? Whom do you hear? What conscience do you make of secret prayer? Do you greedily run after the blessed ordinances? Do you join in public and private worship with other Sisters? The neglecting such means will dry up your spirit, and cause you to walk disconsolate and comfortless. You may answer, 'We have no time; we must mind our business here; 'tis not the same as in the country.' If you have no time to frequent ordinances, you had better leave your places than leave God; better that the body should perish than that the soul should starve. Away with such excuses, and run with all speed imaginable into the country, where, through God's mercy, you will have spiritual meals at your pleasure.

Do not the shouts and rejoicings of your sisters here in the country pierce and melt your hearts? Don't you hear them crying out, 'O my dear and lovely Jesus, hold Thy hand; I can bear no more!' Others saying, 'O Michael, the Archangel, sing thou glory, glory, glory to God the Father, I can't, being overcome with the love of my dear IMMANUEL!' Others crying, 'O ye cherubim and seraphim, treble your notes till we come to you!' These, and several others, have been the pathetic expressions from time to time of your Brethren. O that they may inflame your hearts also!

My dear Sisters, I love you dearly, and wish I could write something for your edification. I should be glad of a letter to know the state of your souls. Give my love and service to all friends in London, particularly to the members of the Society and their teachers, Brother Howel Harris, F. Pugh, etc. I remain (being very busy), your worthless Brother in the work of the ministry,

Daniel Rowland.

The same urgency that characterised Rowland's preaching is thus found in his letters. Spiritual counsel for the believer was a necessary ministry. As the work of God prospered in their hands, and the numbers attending their societies increased, the Methodists sought to provide, in the words of Rowland, 'something for their edification'.

Some of Rowland's sermons excel in edifying material, as in this on 'The Happiness of the Godly, or glad tidings to the mourners in Sion', from Romans 8:28, 'And we know that all things work together for good to them that love God, to them who are the called according to his purpose.':

'The efficiency of grace can never be so clearly seen as in the dark night of adversity, or under a violent struggle with the powers of hell. . . . The metal of a sword is judged to be well-tempered when iron cannot blunt its edge. So the grace of God, ingrafted in the heart, is such a plant as neither the tares of the field nor the thorns of the bracken can stifle or choke. . . . You are aware of the mark at which Satan and all his archers aim their shafts. . . . It is at your conscience void of offence, and your holy life and conversation, that all the mad and raging fury of earth and hell is levelled. "Now be strong in the grace of God which is in Christ Jesus". . . . Suffer not the sun to fade your flowers, but to ripen your fruits. Let your spark be kindled into a fervent flame, and let your grain of mustard seed grow into a wide-spreading tree. . . . Be tender to all. Forgive your enemies, pity the unconverted. Knowing the destruction and misery which are in their way, try to win them over to the Lord by your kind reproofs and gentle persuasions. Remember how long the Lord waited to be gracious unto many of you.'[1]

By means of such rich instruction in God's Word from Rowland the members of his congregation, whether in London or at Llangeitho, were established in the Faith. The joy of the Welsh Methodists had a solid, biblical foundation. In this way, too, their witness was made both consistent with their profession, and as extensive as their lives.

[1] *Eight Sermons*, pp. 94, ff.

'If thou wilt live a Christian life, leave unto thy God to care how the fishes shall come into the nets, and go thou and take upon thee the state wherein thou mayest labour.'

MARTIN LUTHER
on the miraculous draught of fishes, Lk. 5:1–11

'Saint Paul telleth us flatly, that we must be Jesus Christ his soldiers; as if he said, that God leaveth not his in idleness; nay we cannot have an angel's life in this world, but because we are mixed with the contemners of the Gospel . . . we must needs fight; and in the mean season God comforteth us, when he saith that Jesus Christ is our Captain. . . . If we will love God, we must not make our reckoning to live a quiet life, but that we shall be grieved and troubled; and moreover, we must overcome it patiently. . . . Seeing that Jesus Christ is our Captain, and we are under him, let us not fear one whit, though our enemies be full of a murdering spirit, and full of madness, malice, and treason, let them do the worse they can, we will go on boldly.'

JOHN CALVIN
Sermon on 2 Timothy 2:3

20

1743: 'A Critical Time in Wales'

During the summer of 1742 a number of factors brought Rowland and Harris into close harmony once more. One was the greater measure of success that God was giving upon the work, sweeping away suspicions and petty sensitivities in its wake. When Harris left for London in the middle of August, as already noted, to be away for three months, Rowland was left with virtual supreme control of the Welsh work. That time of working apart removed them from each other's irritations and misunderstandings.

A number of seeming setbacks provided a further unifying influence. The death of David Jenkins, a young clergyman, was one of these. He was a native of Llanddewibrefi, and had been ordained deacon in 1740 to serve as curate at nearby Cellan. From that time he had occasionally assisted Rowland, possibly supplying the churches in Rowland's absence. His brother Daniel was later to marry Ann, one of Rowland's daughters. News of the death of this young man, 'one of the sweetest of all the young Methodists, as many account in Wales', reached Harris on April 26, 1742. When Rowland heard the news he is reputed to have lamented, 'Behold, my right hand is cut off.' 'He shone for a brief while like a bright star, and the powers of heaven attended his ministry', says a later Welsh writer.[1] His death was a bitter blow, and the Methodists felt his loss with much grief.

Anglicanism seemed to be mounting a concerted attack upon Methodism within its Welsh borders. William Williams was serving as curate in a Breconshire parish, at that time within the jurisdiction of the diocese of St David's. Here he had to face fierce persecution, and on June 10, 1742, he had been called to appear before the ecclesiastical authorities. Outside the diocese of St David's, a complaint had been filed, also in June, against John Powell in

[1] STL i. 14; Robert Jones, *Drych yr Amseroedd*, Ail Argraffiaf (1814), tud. 74.

Monmouthshire for neglect of duty. The parishes he served were in the diocese of Llandaff in South-east Wales. The Montgomeryshire persecution, to which Rowland referred in his letter of October 1742 to Harris in London, was equally serious; this part of the country was under the jurisdiction of the Bishop of Bangor.[1]

Rowland's appeal for advice in that letter did not go unheeded. Whitefield, as one of the brethren that Harris would have consulted on the matter, responded quickly and positively. He wrote on November 19 to the Bishop of Bangor, setting out the facts and the possible consequences of the matter:

'My Lord, the whole of the matter seems to be this: In Wales they have little fellowship meetings, where some well-meaning people meet together, simply to tell what God has done for their souls. In some of those meetings, I believe, Mr. Cadman [who was threatened with excommunication, in those days involving serious social sanctions, as well as ecclesiastical censure] used to tell of his experience, and to invite his companions to come and be happy in Jesus Christ. He is therefore indicted as holding a conventicle, and this I find is the case of one, if not two more. Now, my Lord, these persons thus indicted, as far as I can judge, are loyal subjects to his Majesty, and true friends to, and attendants upon the Church of England service. You will see by these letters, [Whitefield enclosed personal statements from the accused] how unwilling they are to leave her: and yet, if all those acts, which were made against persons meeting together to plot against Church and State, were put in execution against them, what must they do? They must be obliged to declare themselves Dissenters. I assure your Lordship, it is a critical time in Wales. Hundreds, if not thousands, will go in a body from the Church, if such proceedings are countenanced.'

'A critical time in Wales' indeed! Even though Whitefield had 'a very favourable answer' from the Bishop,[2] the Welsh Methodists continued to meet considerable opposition. Cadman was hounded for three more years, and eventually turned to Independency. In 1742, therefore, it was imperative that Whitefield and the Calvinistic Methodism he represented in England should be actively involved in the affairs of the Welsh Methodists. This visible unity had been Whitefield's vision for some time. The circumstances had now ripened for its realisation.

---

[1] HRS, 30; iii. 103; xxxi. 3; STL i. 46, 53, 14, 49; NLW Church in Wales LL/CC/G.918 (a–d); MTU, 50; *Bathafarn*, xxiv. 36.
[2] GWL i. 463, 466; HMGC i. 274–5.

Writing to an anonymous correspondent on December 6, 1742, Whitefield speaks of plans for a 'General Meeting of all the ministers [of Methodist sympathies] in Wales on the 5th January next.'[1] When he wrote it, the Welsh brethren were experiencing another awakening season. 'God is returning to us again with fresh power', writes Harris on December 3. As he approached Llangeitho the next day, he 'heard such news of the power of God, some falling dead, others losing themselves'. Harris could hardly refrain himself as he reported the news to a friend in London: 'There is a general reviving everywhere, but such account as I never heard with Brother Rowland. The power that is with him is uncommon indeed. His voice is generally drowned by the cries of the people, and among his congregation when they meet themselves to pray, such is the power that falls on them, that some are taken up as dead. Most of the spiritual Dissenters about him come over to the Church' [that is, to the Church of England].[2]

On the following day at Llangeitho church, Harris heard Rowland preach on Isaiah 6:5, 'Woe is me, for I am a man of unclean lips, and I dwell in the midst of a people of unclean lips: for mine eyes have seen the King, the Lord of hosts.' It did him much good: 'I was quite melted away to love, and my heart burnt solidly indeed with true heat and love, feeling God there indeed. . . . Never did my eyes see or my ears hear what power is here! . . . I was made sweet to meet the dear lambs who were full of zeal and life and liberty, burning with coals from the altar of God, and my own soul now burning with fire and zeal, and rejoicing.' His account continues:

'On hearing him preaching: 1. on the evil of the sin of self-righteousness; 2. how a sight of Christ's faithfulness makes us see it; 3. how He does abide in the soul and is a real sight, not imaginary, as sure knowing God is in the soul as that we see the sun; 4. how he makes the soul trust in God's Word – bare Word – God having spoken it in the soul; 5. how when he sins, he does not go to "doing", but to Christ's blood directly; 6. how seeing God's pity to him, makes him pity others; 7. as the sight of God's justice and wrath reflects from him – wrath to others – a sight of His love makes us full of love to Him and to all His creatures; 8. gives a real victory over sin, and so as the present help gives power over the present difficulties – so fear not, thou shalt have greater strength against greater evil. But the hypocrite, having only light in the head and conscience stands, till

[1] Moravian Church Archives, Box A/3, Folder 14.
[2] *Account of the Progress of the Gospel*, 1743, vol. ii. p. 26; iii. 46.

the trial comes, he then falls; 9. this soul is not only for storming the devil but for starving him too.'[1]

'Present help gives power over present difficulties', 'greater strength against greater evil': the force of these truths must have brought fresh hope to both Rowland and Harris that day, sealed to them by the power of God's Spirit.

At Nantcwnlle, Rowland's text was Ezekiel 37:9, 'Thus saith the Lord God: Come from the four winds, O breath, and breathe upon these slain, that they may live.'

'He showed how we come alive. 1. they are bones; 2. we are now dead; 3. we should not give up any (or the church), though dead. He showed how when God comes in once He gives light to show it is He, and there is a sensing of Him thereafter, like liquor giving its taste to the vessel. He showed from Rev. 22, God saying to the Church "Come" and she saying "Come" etc. . . . He cautioned home against lukewarmness. The dead man loves doctrine; the new life is fed by fresh knowledge of Himself. When deadness comes on there is an outward appearance of it, now he is weak and can't withstand temptation, which he once opposed and overcame, and can't move on. The Breath of God cools (like the wind) the heat of God's wrath; it purges sin away, like the wind. It runs freely, it can't be drawn and compelled as we will, it blows gratis, for nothing, and nothing can withstand it. The first work the Spirit does is to convince. This cold north wind makes us to put on as much clothes of self-righteousness as we can till we come again to put them all off and put on Christ. This work of self-renouncing may be without knowing to us, but we shall not be long ere we shall know who covered us. 1. if God has taken away thy self-righteousness, He is going to give thee His Robe; 2. He comes to renew the soul; now the soul sees a wonder in all things; 3. He draws the soul after God; 4. He strengthens the soul after our own rags are taken away; 5. He works groanings and intercessions in us; 6. He seals the soul – more or less all have this. Give thy soul and body to Christ and the Spirit of sealing will come indeed.'[2]

With renewed faith in the power of their message under God's Spirit, the Welsh leaders were equipped to undertake the work again. This time they had the help of others of like mind.

The meeting arranged for January 5 took place near Caerphilly at Watford, the home of Thomas Price, a leading Methodist. Six clergymen and twelve 'public exhorters' were present. Whitefield

[1] xxix. 104–106.   [2] Diary 96.

was the only English clergyman. The Welsh clergymen were Rowland, Howel Davies, William Williams, John Powell and Thomas Lewis. The English laymen were John Cennick, Joseph Humphreys and Thomas Adams; their Welsh counterparts were Harris, Herbert Jenkins, James Beaumont, Thomas James, Morgan John Lewis, John Jones, Richard Tibbott, William Richard and Thomas Lewis. A picture with the title 'The First Association' is an imaginary attempt at depicting the scene of this meeting. It was painted in 1912 by Hugh Williams, and for the likeness of Rowland, Whitefield, Harris and William Williams he used eighteenth-century prints.

The 'Moderator' presiding over the meetings was Whitefield, and Rowland was given the task of preaching the following day. Spheres of labour were agreed upon for the Welsh brethren, and three main decisions were taken:

'That the brethren who had scruples about receiving the sacrament in the Church on account of the ungodliness of the ministers, and receiving with the Dissenters on account of their lukewarmness, should continue to receive in the Church, till the Lord should open a plain door for leaving her communion; That no exhorters should be reckoned one of us but what was tried and approved, and that no one should go beyond his prescribed limits without previous advice and consultation; That each private exhorter should bring an account of his respective societies and of those who would be admitted into fellowship to the next Association.'[1]

Agreement was also reached as to a regular joint meeting twice a year. So much of the groundwork had already been done in Wales that this Association meeting, although the best-known subsequently to posterity, was almost an anti-climax. Had it not been for the renewed measure of extraordinary blessing from God's hand the work at this time might have floundered on the friction between the two Welsh leaders, and the discouragements suffered at the hands of their persecutors. The meeting at Watford demonstrated the solidarity, fervency, and determination of Calvinistic Methodism. The policy of that Methodism was shown to be at once peaceable and uncompromising, responsible and disciplined, in keeping with its doctrinally orthodox, and experimentally directed, character. With relief as well as conviction, Harris could write to Griffith Jones

[1] xlviii. 30–1; CMHO, 89–94; HMGC i. 179–82.

afterwards, 'We are now so well regulated as to prevent, for the future, irregularities. . . . All are brought under discipline. . . . All should continue in the Established Church as before.'[1]

With this evidence of a stricter control over the lay preachers Griffith Jones mellowed in some measure towards the Methodists. Jones must also have been impressed with the fact that the Bishop of Bangor had written 'two very kind letters' to Whitefield about the Montgomeryshire affair, a fact that Harris eagerly reported to him in the same letter. Thus, contrary to the intention of enemies and even the expectation of friends, the work of God in Wales became more intense during 1743. Rowland's ministry was more powerful than ever and his journeys took him further afield. Harris was kept at full stretch implementing the Rules of the Association by consolidating the societies and co-ordinating the workers available to maximise their usefulness. God's hand was clearly upon the two younger clergymen, Howel Davies and William Williams, both of whom were clearly endued with gifts and power. Now just over 25 years of age, their sympathies were with Methodism, and they showed the promise under God of great usefulness. For more than a year there was phenomenal growth and success.

As far as Rowland was concerned, requests for his ministry came with greater frequency and urgency. His travels began in the middle of January with a tour in the mid-Wales county of Montgomeryshire. He preached to some 3,000 people at Llanllugan with such power that they were amazed at the sense of God's greatness.[2] At the end of the month Harris heard in Glamorganshire of the 'growth of Brother Rowland's soul, and power in his ministry'. Another report a few days later astonished him even more: 'Never have I heard from Cardiganshire of such outpourings of the Spirit there, such flames of love.'[3] It was no idle rumour. The evidences of God's Spirit at work were plain for all to see. Among the crowds that thronged to hear Rowland preach there were clear signs of conviction and restoration, there were rapturous expressions of praise and joy, and believers were proving more and more of God's establishing and sanctifying grace.

In the midst of this season of extraordinary divine activity Rowland wrote to Whitefield an account of the Llangeitho scenes. The letter is dated February 2, 1743, and speaks of people coming

[1] STL i. 73–4.   [2] MTU, 57–8.   [3] xxvii. 169, 107–108.

under fresh convictions, and of greater power in preaching. The numbers present were reckoned in hundreds, and the influences of the Spirit were general in extent, and in intensity like a flame running through the congregation. Rowland closes on an encouraging note: 'This is our condition generally every Sabbath! The convictions are now more deep and solid than formerly. I trust the exhorters move for the most part very gradual and proper, and every one is owned in his own place.'[1]

However impressive the crowds or the outward manifestations of grief or joy, Rowland was learning by experience not to attach too much importance to these. He was now more discerning and careful in his assessment of the reality of the work. Certainly, a deeper and more solid acting of the Spirit in individual experience was to be welcomed, but it was also to be safeguarded.

In this respect, Rowland was given much wisdom. When James Gough, an itinerant Quaker, visited Llangeitho about this time, February 1742, Rowland refused him permission to preach. Gough had been hindered from travelling to his destination by a heavy snowfall, and as it was Sunday, he had been persuaded to attend the service at Llangeitho:

'I then went to their market-town called Tregaron, and there had two meetings that day, the latter of which was large. Next day being first day (that is, Sunday), hearing of a priest called Daniel Rowland, whose parish worship-house was at Llangeitho, three miles beyond Llanddewibrefi, who was much flocked after by many people, even from other parishes, thither I went, accompanied by three friends. When we arrived we found the house full, and many at the outside, who seemed to listen to the preacher with attention, who was preaching in Welsh. I desired a young man to endeavour to get in to the parson, and acquaint him that an Englishman without wanted to speak to him, which I suppose he did. For when he had ended his sermon, the congregation broke up, and he came out one of the first. I went to meet him and told him, I had found my mind drawn in Christian love to visit him and his congregation, and therefore desired then the opportunity to deliver to him and them what was on my mind. After some enquiries he said it was not convenient then, as he had himself preached largely to the people. Finding myself clear of him, I got upon a pretty high tombstone, and the people generally drew near, being a very large multitude. The opportunity was greatly favoured. . . . When I had got a little way on the road, I was overtaken by one, who looked like a gentleman, on horseback, with his wife riding behind a man on another horse. He told me he had come out of Carmarthenshire, fourteen miles over the hills, to hear Daniel Rowland.'[1]

Eighteen years later when Gough returned to the area he found the Quakers at Llanddewibrefi with 'little signs left of that fervency toward God, which then seemed impressed on their minds.' His explanation was that 'the enemy had got entrance, and too much stole it away.' By that time Methodism was established to such an extent that in both numbers and appeal the Quakers were considerably diminished.

It may have been the snow which prevented Rowland from keeping another preaching appointment in Montgomeryshire on March 14; James William the Cardiganshire exhorter went instead.[2] Alternatively it may have been due to injuries he received while preaching near the Cardiganshire coast early in February, a fact Harris recorded in his diary: 'I heard how Brother Rowland and Brother [William] Williams had been beaten and abused much indeed.' He also wrote about it to Whitefield a few days later:

'I saw Brother Williams on his return from Brother Rowland. He informed me of the enemy's being let loose on them both, in discoursing near the seaside in part of Cardiganshire. There came a company of ruffians upon them, armed with guns and staves, and beat them unmercifully; but they escaped, through the care of the good Shepherd, without much hurt; only Brother Rowland had one wound on his head. They were set on by a gentleman of the neighbourhood.'[3]

The injury could not have been serious since Rowland was serving his own church at Llangeitho on the last Sunday of the month. Many hundreds took communion and Harris, who was present, tried to convey to Whitefield some of the unforgettable scenes he witnessed:

'I was last Sunday at the Ordinance with Brother Rowland where I saw, felt, and heard such things as I can't send on paper any idea of. The power that continues with him is uncommon. Such crying out and heart-breaking groans, silent weeping and holy joy and shouts of

[1] James Gough, *Memoir of the Life, Religious Experience, and Labours in the Gospel, of James Gough*, 3rd edn., 1830, pp. 81–2, 83; cf. John Wesley's *Journal*, iii. 397.
[2] Trefeca Letters 807, 826, Thomas Bowen to Harris, February 24 and March 25. For James William see HMGC i. 256.
[3] iii. 46; HH, 107.

rejoicing, I never saw. Their "Amens" and crying "Glory in the Highest" etc. would enflame your soul were you there. 'Tis very common when he preaches for scores to fall down by the power of the Word, pierced and wounded or overcome by the love of God, and sights of the beauty and excellency of Jesus, and lie on the ground, nature being overcome by the sights and enjoyments given to their heaven-born souls that it can't bear, the spirit almost bursting the house of clay to go to its native home. Some lie there for hours, some praising and admiring Jesus, free grace, distinguishing grace; others wanting words to utter. You might read the language of a heart running over with love in their heavenly looks, their eyes sparkling with the fire of love and joy and solid rest in God; others meeting when the Word etc. is over, to sing, and you might feel God there among them like a flame; others falling down one after another for a long time together, praying and interceding, and you might see and feel it is the prayer of faith, and that they are worshipping a God that they know, and love, and delight in, and that now no veil is between. Others lie wounded under a sense of their piercing Jesus, so that they can hardly bear it; others in triumph over all their enemies. Others mourning and wailing for the Comforter, and such love and simplicity that a spiritual eye must see and acknowledge that God is there. . . . His congregation consists, I believe, of above 2,000 whereof a great part are brought to glorious liberty and walk solidly in clear light in the continual enjoyment of God without a moment's darkness. Many others walk in solid faith, rejoicing in the hope and expectation of the clearer manifestation of God's glory and the glorious liberty of His children; all the rest are seeking and mourning; and as the Spirit purges them inwardly, and frames and unites them, they enter to order daily, and all the rest I believe will gradually come as the Spirit works on them.'[1]

Rowland might have felt physical weakness on account of the injuries he had received, but God's Spirit was enabling him to come to his congregation 'in the fulness of the blessing of the Gospel of Christ' (Romans 15:29).

Similar power attended Rowland's ministry in other parts at that time, as well as at Llangeitho. Harris followed Rowland to Pembrokeshire early in March 1743, and here again he could report vast crowds and extraordinary blessings attending the ministry of the Word:

'It would rejoice your heaven-born soul indeed to see the poor souls flocking by thousands to hear the delightful Gospel sound. And O! such power as generally attends the labours of brother Rowland, in

[1] STL i. 81–2.

particular, is indeed uncommon and almost incredible until one sees it himself. Their singing and praying is indeed full of God! . . . They fall almost as dead, by the power of the Word, and continue weeping for joy, having found the Messiah; sometimes mourning under a sense of their vileness, and some in the pangs of the new birth! . . . The power at the conclusion of his sermons was such that multitudes continued weeping and crying out for the Saviour, and could not possibly forbear.'[1]

The letter had begun on a triumphant note, 'The kingdom of our Lord is coming on everywhere with great power.' And so it seemed, for this fresh awakening was not confined to Rowland's ministry.

In February 1743, Harris had heard William Williams preaching at one of his Breconshire churches. The sermon on Luke 7:47 was delivered with great earnestness, showing 'the difference between Christ in the head and Christ in the heart', and Harris felt that 'the spirit of Rowland' had 'fallen on Brother Williams'. At the beginning of March, Harris was in Pembrokeshire, pleading with Howel Davies to join the Methodist ranks, and he estimated the numbers of people coming to hear God's Word at that time to be between 8,000 and 10,000. Under Davies's ministry again in June Harris experienced 'much of the power of God here to heal and to wound, to call to Christ and to build up'. The sermon was on 'the woman of Samaria' (John 4), a passage which Davies expounded 'most gloriously' as 'showing the necessity and advantages of strong faith':

'1. we have fellow-feeling with Christ in His sufferings; 2. we triumph over death and the fear of man; 3. we rejoice in tribulation; 4. we love the cross; 5. it enables us to be patient in all affliction; 6. and to walk with God. It is according to the measure and degree of your faith that you walk with God; 7. to do the will of God and suffer ills . . . we can't long for Christ's coming to Judgment or love His appearing; we can't strongly hate sin, nor conquer strong temptations, nor bear great afflictions without strong faith; we can't love much and bear much fruit and rejoice as He told us.'[2]

To Harris it was virtually a Llangeitho experience.

It was not without reason that Harris engaged in letter-writing more fervently and excitedly than ever during those early months of 1743. To Whitefield he spoke about powerful spiritual impressions in Glamorganshire, adding, 'many such instances of the outpouring

[1] HH 129.   [2] iii. 46; xxx. 100; Diary 100, s.v. June 5, 1743.

of the Spirit have we among us'. In May his correspondent was John Wesley: 'Blessed be God, our Saviour is getting the victory more gloriously among us in several places, especially in Pembroke, Cardigan and Carmarthenshire; many daily come to the glorious liberty, and walk in and with God in power, love, and light and sweetness.' Throughout this period of general revival, the work at Llangeitho was reckoned to be the measure of authenticity and power in all other places. One of the exhorters wrote to Harris about mid-Wales: 'There is a fire kindled . . . at Llanbister, of the same nature as at Llangeitho, and in as high a degree, in about eight or ten of the members of the society. Glory be to God. I was there lately, and my voice could hardly be heard by reason of their cries. Some, under deep convictions of their lost estate, said they were damned; others, for joy of the discovery of salvation by Jesus Christ, saying, "Glory, glory to God for Jesus Christ to all eternity!" This held with them for about four hours.'[1]

Such fresh advances took place in spite of much opposition and danger. Rowland and Williams were not the only ones to suffer at the hands of persecutors. Morgan Hughes, one of the exhorters, was imprisoned in Cardigan jail, ostensibly on a charge of vagrancy, but in reality it was on account of his Methodist activities. The month of March was a particularly testing one for the Methodists until his release was secured. They worked vigorously for this, consulting Whitefield, influential landowners, and attorneys. Rowland was advised to seek legal advice from a sympathetic magistrate. Harris and others spent a 'night in the suburbs of heaven' with Hughes 'in the place of his confinement' at Cardigan. Marmaduke Gwynne, particularly, proved a tower of strength in the affair, enlisting the help of his nephew John Lloyd of Peterwell (Lampeter), and telling Rowland 'to bring some witnesses with him to Cardigan Sessions, and to indict the persons who abused him'.[2]

Rowland, Harris and many other Methodists prepared to attend the trial and prayed much for the outcome. On March 27, 1743, Harris called at Llangeitho on the way to the Magistrates Court. There he heard a sermon from Rowland on Isaiah 32:2, 'And a man shall be as an hiding place from the wind, and a covert from the

[1] STL i. 79, 97; *Christian History*, vol. v, No. 3 (1744), pp. 38–9, undated letter from James Ingram to Harris.
[2] STL i. 83, 84, 87, 93; *Account of the Progress of the Gospel*, vol. ii. No. 3, p. 66; Trefeca Letters 817, 832, 833; HH, 54–5; xxx. 100–102.

tempest; as rivers of water in a dry place, as the shadow of a great rock in a weary land.' It was a timely reminder of God's protection of His people in the face of dangers:

'He showed of the new creature, how it has God for a house about him, and Christ for a Robe, and the Spirit dwelling in him. He showed how the new creature is made and fed by God's Breath. . . . Sin is like the devil's breath, and this wind may blow off for a little the cloak, and the wind too sometimes shakes the earth; but it can't move its foundation. . . . He showed how the justification is still safe; the house of sanctification may be shaken; and the new creature, let Satan tempt as he will, can't sin, can't yield; for our grace, faith, love, humility, etc., is God's Breath on our souls, and this, being born of, or proceeding from God, can't turn against God again, though the flesh yields. . . . Have filial fear in all places, but flee slavish fear. . . . Christ is the peace of the soul – He is the food – He is the Physician and protection of the soul.'

Fortified with a measure of assurance from that message, Rowland and Harris proceeded to Cardigan, Harris 'seeing the tenderness and wisdom of the Lord in managing us and our sufferings together'.[1] In Court the prosecutor was stopped, and Harris, responding in 'the Christian spirit', offered to drop counter charges, 'only let them pay the expenses'.[2]

As the year progressed, both Davies and Williams were in trouble with the Church authorities. The former was 'set in the Bishop's Court for receiving strangers' [granting communion to people from outside his own parish], and there was great concern lest he should be deprived of his curacy. With the outcome still uncertain, Harris wrote to him from London, suggesting a course of action, and adding, 'I know you are taught from the eternal Charter of Heaven not to be afraid of their menaces or to be dejected at the seeming insuperable difficulties that may set themselves before you. You know the work is the Lord's and 'tis He began it and sent us out and has stood by us and with us and in us and for us hitherto, and will do to the end, for His Name's sake.' For various reasons Davies was at the point of leaving Anglicanism at the time, and his fellow Methodists had much difficulty in persuading him otherwise.[3]

The charges against Williams had been simmering for a year. They included neglect of duties, omissions from the Prayer Book service,

[1] Diary 98. [2] xxx. 100–102.
[3]CH 1980, pp. 29, 30, n; STL i. 105.

and not residing in his parish. The charges were answered carefully by Williams, but he was refused ordination as priest in August 1743. For this 'full ordination' Williams had the statutory letters of approval from other clergymen, and the support of some of his own parishioners, but the grounds of his refusal were 'his being a Methodist, and going about to preach'. The Court's judgment was not finalised until January 1744, when Williams was deemed guilty of neglect, admonished, and ordered to pay costs.[1]

The prime mover in these affairs seems to have been the Diocesan Chancellor rather than the Bishop. The Chancellor would have been responsible for writing on the back of the list of ordinands in 1743 the names of known Methodists in the Diocese. Among them were Rowland, Harris, Davies, Williams ('assistant to Daniel Rowland at Llangeitho'), and Griffith Jones (derisively labelled 'the Methodist Pope', a name he would have strenuously disowned). Early in August of 1743 Harris became involved with the Bishop, sending him a letter in defence of Methodist doctrines and practices. During the same month the Chancellor 'preached extempore against the Methodists and Mr. Whitefield, so that the minds of many of the people were turned again'. As a result many society members were required to justify holding a society meeting in their homes. 'After their examination they [the Church authorities] owned they were well-meaning people, if they could but consult to keep Harris and Rowland in their own limits. And the Chancellor said he would seal a Process to take Brother Rowland next time.' In the light of this, Rowland felt it necessary to appeal personally to the Bishop of St David's, and when he did so on September 5, 1743, he was received with kindness and respect.[2] God used even the 'critical times' to serve the purposes of grace. 'The Lord reigneth, he is clothed with majesty: the Lord is clothed with strength, wherewith he hath girded himself; the world also is established, that it cannot be moved' (Psalm 93:1).

[1] xxxiii. 2–12; *Account of the Progress of the Gospel*, vol. IV. No. 1, p. 77; WW i. 58–66.
[2] *Account of the Progress of the Gospel*, vol. IV. No. 1. p. 78; STL i. 103; xxii. 94; xxxiv. 60; TM i. 250–2.

Then the great Association,
Born that time, and still alive,
Now for fifty years remembered,
Meeting to make God's work thrive.
Holding doctrine in sweet union,
Tying knots both firm and true
Which no prejudice, suspicion,
Ever can their pow'r undo.

WILLIAM WILLIAMS
Elegy to Daniel Rowland, 1791

2 I

Associations and Unity

As one Association followed another early in 1743 the leaders spoke of them in superlative terms such as 'most heavenly', 'our hearts beat together', and 'the Lord came powerfully among the brethren in singing and praying one after another'.[1] Rowland was present at both Associations held in Carmarthenshire – February 2 at Llanddeusant, March 1 at Glan-yr-afon-ddu – where 'proposals' were being aired for future decision. These included such matters as how often the leaders should meet, how many societies should be under their care, principles for determining an exhorter's fitness to the work, and practical details of supervision and administration in the societies. From the outset it was felt that no rule should be established which was excessively demanding or inappropriate ['higher than it ought, and that it answers the ends, too']. Throughout their discussions the work in England and Wales was thought of as one work, and people like Whitefield and Cennick were included in the arrangements.[2]

The Watford (Caerphilly) Association of April 6–7 was to have met a week earlier but was delayed at Rowland's request. This change of date excluded Howel Davies who was disappointed at missing the opportunity of meeting the English brethren, especially as he wished to urge Whitefield to visit the English-speaking parts of Pembrokeshire. However, in the event Rowland himself could not attend. Whitefield summarised the proceedings in this way: 'On Wednesday about noon I opened the Association with a close and solemn discourse upon walking with God. Indeed much of God was with us. The brethren and people felt much of the divine presence. Afterwards we betook ourselves to business: several matters of great importance were dispatched'. The chief of these were:

[1] HH, 130; STL i. 81; xxvii. 110.
[2] xlviii. 36–7; STL i. 77.

'That the Rev. Mr. Williams should leave his curacies and be an assistant to the Rev. Mr. Rowland.

'That Brother Howel Harris should be Superintendent over Wales and go to England when called.

'That an abstract of all the Monthly Associations should be brought to the General Association.

'That each Superintendent shall have a book wherein he shall write the names of each of their private exhorters, and the names of each member of the private societies, and divide them into married men, married women, single men, and single women, and likewise to bring the state of each society to the General Association.

'That each Association shall begin with prayer and end with prayer and exhortation.'

Harris concludes his record of the meetings with these sentiments: 'The whole Association was carried on with great unity and love. The brethren left each other praising and blessing God for what He has done, still expecting to see greater things than these.'[1]

To ensure the smooth working of these rules called for immense wisdom and patience. For these qualities the Welsh leaders leaned heavily on Whitefield. Occasionally one of the exhorters objected to the rules, as did John Richard in June 1743: 'He complained that our division of the people into married, single and widows, examining into the particular state of the souls was Popish, and putting down their names, unscriptural, and that appointing the Superintendents to particular districts was not right, and that he had a mind to go (let the brethren say what they would) where he thought the Lord should call him.' The task of replying to this letter was allotted to Whitefield, who duly approached the matter from Scriptural considerations:

'Does not Jesus Christ say a good Shepherd calleth all the sheep by their names? does not every parish keep a register book of their parishioners, and do not the Dissenters put down the names of all that come into fellowship with them? What is the Book of Numbers but a catalogue of the names of the children of Israel? As for enquiring into the particular state of every soul, we think it highly necessary: we take it the Church is like a Hospital, that Ministers are Physicians, and they are from time to time to come and enquire how it is with their patients. . . . The dividing them into classes as virgins, single men, married men, married women and widows, is only a prudential rule in order to make the account regular, and that a minister may know of what station in life his people are, and suit his

---

[1] Trefeca Letter 819, letter of James Ingram to Harris, dated March 14, 1743; xlii. 23; xlviii. 38–42; GWL ii. 13.

exhortations accordingly. We find the Apostle John writing to young men etc., and St. Paul mentions the widows. . . . You think we lay an insufferable yoke upon the brethren by assigning the Superintendents a particular district. . . . It is plain there were particular districts in the Apostles' time. They ordained elders in every city where they were obliged to keep and therefore we hear of Paul's calling together the elders of Ephesus and giving them a particular charge concerning their flock, over which the Holy Ghost had made them overseers. Without this there can never be any order in Church or State. . . . We think you mistake when you say the flesh does not like going; we think the contrary, nature does not like to be confined: settling inside work is not agreeable to the old man, though exceedingly useful to the old creature. Upon the whole, dear brother, we think you are mistaken at present, and judge us without a cause. We thank you for your cautions; we have turned them into prayers and our loving Saviour will answer us.'[1]

This reproof, administered in a loving spirit, eventually won the day, and John Richard responded with a gracious submission.

Considerable authority resided in the Association in the matter of personal movements. Men were asked to settle in new areas, or to undertake different skills: schoolmasters were placed, permission for marriage was granted or refused, one was sent to learn the trade of bookbinding. Recognition of a man's calling to be an exhorter was the result of careful scrutiny: 'After a close examination of Brother Edward Bufton about his knowledge of the Divinity of Jesus Christ, and of His bearing His people's sins away on the tree, and of the perseverance of the saints etc. by the revelation of the Holy Ghost, and of the misery of all mankind by nature; and having been satisfied of his grace and call to speak for the great God, we agreed that he should assist Brother Rowland as a private exhorter.' At the Llandrindod Association, May 27, 1743, it was agreed 'that Brother Watkin Watkins should qualify himself to be a scribe or amanuensis to Brother Rowland or Brother Davies'.[2]

Societies in a defined geographical area were grouped together for supervision by named ministers and exhorters. The latter were given responsibility for certain societies, and reported regularly to the area's monthly Association, which was presided over by its own 'Superintendent'. In addition to these monthly Associations, a 'General' or 'Quarterly' Association was also held, reviewing the

[1] xlviii. 47; xxvii. 150–2; cf. CMHO, 97, ff.; HMGC i. 242–4.
[2] xlviii. 43, 79, 46; xlix. 85, 24.

whole of the work every three months. Faithful attendance at Association meetings was required of all its members, ministers and exhorters. Only a valid reason was deemed to justify absence, and this was to be explained by letter.

In its management of Gospel affairs the Association was, in effect, acting as a superior ecclesiastical court. Its officers, ministerial and lay, were admitted on biblical principles of fitness and competence. Its purpose was the spreading of the Gospel in Wales, and its important corollary, the oversight of those people whom the Gospel message had effectively reached. The exalted experiences of reviving seasons were real enough, but they were also transitory. The leaders did not envisage, nor did they expect, that the ecstatic expressions of conviction and joy and praise would continue unabated. In contrast, the exercise of faith and love, self-denial and watchfulness was to be encouraged and nourished. Consequently, the societies were virtually Gospel churches, consisting as they did of people whose response to the Gospel was real, transforming and progressive.

Writing in the middle of April 1743 to William M'Culloch of Cambuslang, Scotland, Harris declares the policy and aims of the Welsh Methodists:

'Blessed be God, we move daily nearer towards an Evangelical order. As we are not turned out of communion in the National Church yet, and as we meet the Lord there, we think it would be running before the Lord now to separate ourselves. But such as labour among the lambs, and such as join themselves to us, are now brought under discipline and better order than we have been. Many thousands, I believe, will at the Last Day bless God for this last outpouring of the Spirit among us.'[1]

The statement was a true summary of the character of early Welsh Methodism: a vigorous spiritual life disciplined by a biblical nurture within existing ecclesiastical structures. Delicately and deliberately, Welsh Methodism maintained its identity within Anglicanism, accepting the tensions from within of coldness and hostility, and from without, of suspicion and scepticism. From time to time those tensions came close to breaking point, but for the whole of Rowland's lifetime they remained unresolved.

It was during the early formative months of the Association's existence that Welsh Methodism became aware of its identity. The

[1] Hugh J. Hughes, *op. cit.*, p. 223; Trefeca Letter 854.

regular, detailed, responsible nature of Association proceedings shows how much importance and priority the leaders gave to it. For them it was as basic to their work as preaching, and complemented it perfectly. Reviewing the achievements of the Association at the beginning of 1744, Harris wrote:

'Everything was settled so that hitherto the Lord visibly blesses and leads and unites us, and shows each his place, and gives us fellowship together, and gives His presence in our meetings, and comes as a Prophet among us and countenances our order. . . . We write nothing down here of our doctrine, because in a wonderful manner we are led in the same light, speaking the same things, agreeing in general with the Reformers and Puritans. Most of our business hitherto in our Monthly meetings being to examine the call of our private exhorters, having been satisfied as to the Superintendents in the Quarterly Association. It is wonderful what subordination the Lord works in our spirits to each other, so that we are enabled to go on in faith, our outward order following the inward. So far as we run before the Lord we have a cross from some quarter or another. We begin and end with prayer and opening our hearts together. It is amazing how such a body of proud, ignorant, and unfit creatures should be so taught, united and led in so great a work. Lord, this is Thy doing, glory to Thee alone!'[1]

Harris is speaking with great satisfaction. Within the space of two years, from the Llandovery meeting to the time of writing, the essential character of Welsh Methodism had been determined. Doctrinally, it had shown a return to biblical truth and was therefore unashamedly established on Reformation and Puritan principles. Practically and actively it was vigorous in its propagation of the Gospel, using an unadorned preaching as the vehicle of that work. Experimentally it looked for personal, fervent dealings with God, nurturing a piety that was both pure and practical. Its disciplined organisation was merely the handmaiden of its life.

Rowland's contribution to Methodism lay more in the area of its life than in that of its organisation. Even so, as Welsh ministerial head of the Association he had a major responsibility for the policies and decisions of the movement for some fifty years. That influence was implicit rather than explicit, more in the way of determining emphasis and direction rather than in implementing decisions. For the latter activity Harris was more inclined and more fitted. In his capacity as 'Moderator', Rowland's authority in all matters affecting

[1] xlviii. 69–70.

the Great Awakening in Wales was crucial.

Together with the recognition of a separate identity there was also the recognition of a practical need. Society meetings in private houses exposed the Methodists to misunderstanding and legal proceedings. The fact that some society meetings were labelled 'private' to define their more disciplined membership created suspicions of political or even immoral activities. But these were private, not in the sense of 'secretive' or 'treasonable', but for the sake of spiritual freedom and edification.

With regard to the legal position, the Toleration Act of 1689 had been intended as a concession to religious bodies outside the Church of England. It allowed people who acknowledged the truth of the Anglican Thirty-nine Articles to hold religious gatherings in places officially registered for that purpose. While the Methodists had no difficulty with regard to the Articles, their meetings were obviously at risk as they were held in unregistered buildings. In March 1743 there had been a nasty incident at Lampeter which illustrated the vulnerability of such meetings. 'When the members of the society were in unity together singing Psalms and praying to God, there came a Justice of the Peace and his servants to interrupt them. He that was then praying was taken prisoner, but by Divine Providence it is something assuaged, and the person aforementioned set free, but the magistrate follows the same threatening still.'[1] In a letter to Rowland in March 1743, Harris sets out their thinking on the matter. 'If we are robbed of this privilege of meeting privately to consult together about the affairs of our souls, while we give all proof of our being truly loyal and peaceable subjects . . . we are deprived of our rights as Britons and subjects of this Realm. . . . The power of the Magistrates in such cases is a discretionary power. . . . For the Law is the limit of their power'.[2]

As much for legal definition as for convenience, therefore, the Methodists began building 'society houses'. The historic Watford Association at the beginning of the year had held some of its meetings in the first of these, the so-called 'New Room', which had only just

[1] Trefeca Letter 3005; lii. 20; William Williams, *Welsh Calvinistic Methodism*, 1872, pp. 31–2; cf. xii. 112, 'About the year 1743 signs of Methodism begin to appear [in Lampeter]; we hear of a gathering being broken up, of persecution and imprisonment; of 38 members worshipping at Ty'nrheol, and of Daniel Rowland coming over from Llangeitho to preach on a Sunday afternoon.' (From George Eyre Evans, *History of Lampeter*, 1905, p. 86.) [2] STL i. 86.

been completed. The property's Deed defined it as being 'for a Society or Meeting House for and towards the public worship of God, or a Charity School for the Education of Children'. Shortly afterwards Harris mentions in a letter to the Tabernacle Society that 'one house is built in Glamorganshire; another will be, I believe soon, in Carmarthenshire, and some in other places'. Rowland was one of the signatories to the Carmarthenshire property Deeds (Cil-y-cwm), the purpose of which was stated to be 'for the exercise and performance of divine worship' and it was to be called 'Society House, School house or meeting house'. Those using the building for divine worship 'or to do other act or acts for teaching and propagating the Gospel' were to be appointed by the Trustees.[1] As time went on the Association was more and more involved in the oversight of building proposals and financial arrangements.

In many ways Association meetings marked out the Awakening's progress for the Methodist leaders. They were at once preaching occasions, business meetings, and times of fellowship. They were a constant means of keeping the leaders in touch with one another. While apart, they knew they would have to give an account of their labours, and this in itself disciplined their efforts and expectancy.

Whitefield was involved as often as possible, in response to many and earnest appeals. On each visit he combined his public preaching activities with private counsel, the exercise of what Harris called 'his amazing wisdom, wherein he is taught to manage the church'. Most of his visit to Wales in April 1743 was spent in this way. On the 14th his sermon at Carmarthen on Isaiah 54:5, 'Thy Maker is they husband', was blessed by God to the conversion of Peter Williams. At the time Williams was in his twentieth year and studying at the local Grammar School. Within three years he was widely accepted as another Methodist leader, although, like William Williams 'complete' Anglican orders were denied him on account of his Methodism. In later years his Commentary on the Bible would be almost a household possession in Wales, although when it first appeared it proved somewhat controversial.

The clergyman schoolmaster at Williams' school had warned his pupils to beware of Whitefield's oratory, and to be even more wary of his doctrine: 'I am told he preaches original sin, that man must be born again, and that we must be justified before God by faith,

[1] HMGC i. 196–200; xxvii. 1–5; 104–107; *Account of the Progress of the Gospel*, vol. ii. No. 3, p. 68, letter dated March 17, 1743.

without works' – teachings which he found repugnant. In spite of this, Peter Williams and three others from the school attended the meeting, as well as some magistrates 'and many thousands more'. Williams' record of his conversion is very simple:

'The dayspring from on high visited me. The time of my conversion was accomplished. All my sins in thought, word, and deed, were brought to my remembrance, as though a floodgate had been opened and the angry flood poured furiously upon me; so that my soul was overwhelmed with fear and confusion. Everything around me appeared strange and uncouth, nay, the neatest building was no more to me than a nauseous dunghill; I had no more any delight in heathen authors; I went to school, but could not collect my thoughts to study my lesson.'

'Jesus was with me', says Whitefield of that occasion, 'and I hope much good work was done'.[1] Much good work indeed, in the light of Williams' subsequent usefulness to his countrymen, but much good, too, in the immediate context as the crowds who attended him at each place found that Whitefield's preaching confirmed that of the Welsh Methodists.

A week later Whitefield was back at Carmarthen, preaching and guiding another Association meeting: 'I preached there twice', he says, 'to about ten thousand people, and dear Mr. Rowland preached after me. Yesterday we had another blessed Association, and have now settled all the counties in Wales.' According to Harris, Whitefield's two sermons were on 'Jacob's ladder' and 2 Corinthians 5:17; Rowland's sermon was on Hebrews 9:15, 'And for this cause He is the Mediator of the New Testament.' Listening to Rowland, Harris 'saw the excellency of the Gospel dispensation' and 'had great light and liberty and strength in hearing him showing with amazing authority and power indeed how God was a Sun, but once a year to be seen, and that only by the High Priest, and how He was but in one place' in Old Testament times. Rowland proceeded to show how the Gospel Day outshone the former dispensation, when

'neither the guilt nor the power of sin was fully taken away till death came. But now tis not so: every broken heart is God's temple and He dwells there and all may see Him in the face of Christ now by faith, and are freed from the guilt and power of sin. Now our Testator is dead, and all the legacies are ours, and we should demand them;

[1] CMHO, 83; xxvii. 105, n, 113; Gomer M. Roberts, *Bywyd a Gwaith Peter Williams*, 1943, tt. 15, 16; For Peter Williams, see DWB; GWL ii. 15; TGW ii. 58–9.

before, God gave a promise He would come and they lived in this hope, but now He is come, and we are under grace.'

Such a spirit of harmony and joy prevailed that shortly afterwards Whitefield could give a triumphant report of the Welsh scene: 'Thousands and tens of thousands flocked to hear the Word, and the souls of God's children were much refreshed. I have been also at two Associations in Wales. The work begins now to show itself. Many are taking root downward, and bearing fruit upward. Ere long I trust they will fill the land. . . . Our divisions in England have the worst aspect, while they are now united in Wales.'[1] The harmony and joy was a result of the leaders' diligence in preaching and organising.

During May, Rowland attended Associations in Carmarthenshire, at Gelli-glyd on May 1; Pontarddulais on the 19th, and Dugoedydd on the 25th. Harris felt the same strong bond of unity in June when he was with Rowland and Davies in Pembrokeshire: 'No tongue can express what bliss we felt together; my heart burned and rejoiced in God indeed in hearing of the brethren's success. I felt a true Gospel spirit, true love, true humility.' The next day, June 8, he heard Rowland preaching on 1 Corinthians 1:24, 'Unto them which are called . . . Christ the power of God, and the wisdom of God', and he 'felt a sense of God's love': 'on his showing how Christ has purchased a stock of grace to live upon as well as paid our debt; of His power by which the heavens and all the creation do stand; how the fountain of grace runs continually from Him to wash us, though Satan is continually defiling us, the fountain will at last prevail; and how, when grace is grown, everything sends us nearer and nearer to God'. The Association at Trefeca at the end of June proved something of a climax. Rowland preached on the privileges of believers, 'and how the Church is now a-reviving'. As he listened, Harris was aware of strong impressions: 'My soul was set free indeed and made to leap for joy within me so that I could not forbear laughing and crying, blessed be God! my heart did burn indeed.'[2]

So, too, did the hearts of others burn during the summer of 1743. From Montgomeryshire came news of another of Rowland's visits in mid-June:

'Mr. Rowland was with us this week and has great power in many places, especially Llanllugan, where he preached to about 3,000

[1] GWL ii. 17, 19; Diary 99, s.v. April 21, 1743.
[2] xlviii. 42, 44, 45; Diary 100, s.v. 8, June 29, 1743.

people, the greatest of all companies that was seen in our country. The fold was too little; he went on the middle of the field. There were a great many persecutors before he came, threatening after a violent manner, but when he began the power was so great that fear fell upon most, and silent weeping fell irresistibly upon them.'

Such was the impression made by Rowland that believers expressed 'a cry for some to come among them, especially Mr. Rowland'. Rowland made a positive response, preaching there again in 1744, one of his sermons being on Job 2:1 at Capel Betws.[1]

The leaders' journeys to the Associations provided preaching tours, taking in regular and new locations. On July 12, 1743, Rowland preached at Abergorlech 'to a very large congregation, and such was the light and power in preaching, and such were the cries of the people, and the presence of the Lord so filled the place, in the sermon and the sacrament (which he administers there once a month) that ... few were unaffected'. The following day at the Association he preached again. From Carmarthenshire he moved to Pembrokeshire, a week later, and preached at Twrgwyn, Association matters being dealt with thereafter.

With these regular appointments bringing Rowland and Harris together a great deal, the latter had ample opportunity to witness the fresh blessing of God upon the work. In a letter to Whitefield at the end of July 1743 he talks of 'power and union and harmony among the private societies', with the ministers bearing 'the flaming sword' and 'the lambs' being brought 'to the Gospel spirit and a close walk'. There were other encouraging signs: 'prejudice falls, and fresh doors are opening everywhere'; under Howel Davies's ministry 'the clouds dropped fatness', and similarly with Rowland. 'Their churches are twice and sometimes thrice filled with the communicants ... some full of joy from the discoveries of faith, and some ravished and overcome with love, and some awed by the sense of God's majesty, while others are bathed in tears.' Harris was preparing for another visit to London, but before leaving Wales he heard Rowland preaching once more, at Capel Ifan, near Llanelli, on August 7. Rowland showed from Galatians 2:20 – 'I am crucified with Christ' – 'how the soul sees itself void of all good in itself, and sees all for time and eternity in Christ':

[1] Trefeca Letter 895, Thomas Bowen to Harris, dated June 20, 1743; lii. 55–6; MTU, 78.

'2ndly. what sort of death this is; a painful death, a lingering death, a shameful death, but it brings joy at last. 3dly. what is this life he had, and what a mystery is a Christian, dead but yet living, weak but yet strong, sinful but yet pure, blind but yet seeing, falling but yet up. Negatively, it is not a natural or moral or legal life; positively, it is a holy, just, sweet, growing, and eternal life. Inference: is everyone who is void of this spiritual life under the curse? then what will become of you? O come out of the law and sin and self and the world, to Christ.'

Harris concluded his notes with the comment, 'He [Rowland] had very great power indeed to call, and my heart was drawn up with him to heaven to be earnest that God would come among us to Wales.'[1]

Two weeks later, Harris set out for London. There he met Selina, the Countess of Huntingdon, on August 26. She had been converted in 1739 and formed one of a circle of English nobility that attended Whitefield's ministry, and was later to give much support to Calvinistic Methodism in both England and Wales.[2] In September Harris heard from one of the Welsh exhorters that Rowland, Davies and Williams continued to preach with power, news which prompted him to write to Rowland in vivid terms: 'How does your warlike soul do? Methinks I see hell trembling, and the enemy flying before you. Go on, bold champion, and fight the Lord's battle!' Another letter from Harris urged one of the exhorters to 'intreat Brother Rowland and all as are called to exhort in public and private, and other solid judicious Christians to meet him, as likewise to settle places for him to preach'.[3] It was a fitting recognition of Rowland's authority and usefulness in the work in Wales.

[1] STL i. 98, 100; HVP 86, 88; Diary 102; cf. TM i. 252–3; HRS, 47; xxiv. 120.   [2] HRS, 50; DAL ii. 262, ff.
[3] STL 103; HH 130; MS ii. 338.

'When the honour and service of God are at stake there can be no excuse for timidity.'

JOHN CALVIN

'Men may not dislike religion at a distance, or so far as it consists of forms and ceremonies; but when it comes near home, and offers to lay its restraints on their lusts, to debar them of their beloved gratifications, and to strike at the root of their false peace, they beg it to be gone, and desire to have no fellowship with it. They would sooner lose Christ and the joys of heaven, than part with their idols, or be deprived of their earthly delights.'

DANIEL ROWLAND
Sermon on Matthew 2:8–9

22

Methodist Priorities

Expansion and consolidation were the twin objectives of the Welsh Methodists in 1743. Both the policies and the activities fostered by the Association reflected these strategic areas of concern. Preserving an Anglican identity occasionally shielded them from persecution on their preaching journeys, and gave them fresh opportunities in unused ecclesiastical buildings. Society members were provided for by regular ministry and supervision. Above all, the Breath of God was still blowing upon the land.

In the Providence of God, the Revival had begun in some of the remoter parts of South Wales. Gradually the work had spread throughout the various counties. The leaders could only regard the north as a vast mission field. Neither the difficulties of travel nor differences in the spoken Welsh could be regarded as diminishing in any way a clear responsibility to evangelise their fellow-countrymen. Early attempts at penetrating the north were daunting. In March 1742 Harris had written:

'Last week I saw some of our brethren come home from North Wales, where they escaped very narrowly with their lives. Some they sent from one prison to another, one they struck [as] dead, another they followed for many miles in order to execute their rage on him. They were sent there by Mr. Griffith Jones to teach Welsh Schools. The populace was stirred up by the magistrates and clergy. However, there are many sweet dear lambs there among these lions and tigers. I find my nature rebels much against going there.'[1]

Before the year was out Rowland had also ventured north. On one of these early journeys, a threat was made that if he opened his mouth to preach his bones would be ground so small as could be put in a bag. Nevertheless, Rowland went on to the Lleyn Peninsula, and the

[1] i. 24, 25–6; xxvi. 108; MS ii. 230.

church being refused at one place, he preached from steps near the churchyard gate. His text was Jeremiah 30:21, 'Who is this that engaged his heart to approach unto me? saith the Lord.' As he spoke of Christ's willingness to render the perfect obedience which God's holy Law required, there was a general commotion among the crowd; many burst into uncontrollable, loud weeping and praising of God.[1] In spite of fierce opposition from 'lions and tigers' to both their message and their methods, the Welsh Methodists could not be silenced.

At the end of July 1743, however, Harris felt that doors were about to open in North Wales, and Rowland was 'settled to go' some time in the summer. On this occasion Harris's zeal and optimism were misguided. A slanderous pamphlet, originating in Anglesey, had been recently published. In it the Methodists were portrayed as covetous, immoral Antinomians. Its caricature of Rowland depicted him as 'once a wicked priest of Cardiganshire' whose preaching brought him a fortune, and whose 'Book of Life' was worthy of imitation only for the purposes of illicit procuring of women. Far more serious and ominous was the letter of some North Wales clergymen to Griffith Jones, dated July 2, 1743, complaining of his schoolmasters:

'These South Wales enthusiastic itinerants pretend to be Church of England people, and come to Church; but at nights they creep into such houses as they are able to work to themselves a way to, and there delude ignorant men, and lead captive silly women and children, by despising the clergy, and accusing them of not preaching the truth of the Gospel; assuring their hearers that we are all dumb dogs, blind guides, false prophets, hirelings; that we lie in our pulpits. But that they, and none others, are the elect, the chosen of God, the predestinated, the regenerated; that they cannot sin in their regenerate state; that they only are the true ministers of Christ . . . and that they see the visible marks of damnation in the faces of such as will not become Methodists.'

Consequently, when Rowland undertook the arduous journey north at the end of September, he was to face considerable opposition.[2]

---

[1] TM i. 50; *Y Llenor*, cyf. xv. Gorffennaf, 1898, 'Gwaith Robert Jones, Rhoslan', tt. 56–7.

[2] HH Diary 101, s.v. July 27, 1743; *Cofiadur*, Rhif 46, tud. 21, n. 5; xxxvii. 29–30; HMGC i. 431–2; F. A. Cavenagh, *The Life and Work of Griffith Jones*, 1930, p. 45.

In Rowland's absence, Llangeitho was to have been supplied by John Gambold. The latter was a Pembrokeshire man, one of 'the Oxford Methodists' along with the Wesley brothers, but he had recently resigned his Anglican charge and was leaning towards Moravian beliefs. While staying 'at Mr. Rowland's' house, he wrote to Harris on October 3, 1743 about his journey through Wales, 'I have had matter of great joy in seeing such large Awakenings in different counties, and seeing too the sincere desire and taste for spiritual things which is so manifest in the souls.' But he had also had 'a few thoughts' about the work, which he proceeds to mention. He considers the difficulties encountered to be due chiefly to the fact that there were too few workers. Public ministry needed to be supplemented more than it was by private counsel.

'1. Tender hearted upright poor people take the reproofs and terrors to themselves in ignorance and humility, and so become discouraged, while the hypocrites, to whom such words were due, put them off from them and are untouched. 2. Many, by such large casuistical treating of things, get a form of knowledge in the head, especially the acute reasoning people of this country, which fatally hides from them, and covers, the emptiness and deadness of their hearts; (and by the way, the eagerness about theological niceties, and the measuring all grace and improvement by the readiness and skill in speaking of divine things upon several occasions, is an evil that wants to be remedied in Wales). 3. By hearing severity so quickly and constantly added after mildness in all public discourses, the people are generally very apt to confound the Law and the Gospel in their own ideas and apprehensions, and more yet in their spirit and temper; and this bondage of mind, and secret resting on their own works in some view or other, is equally plain and painful to see in very many of them.'

Gambold did not stay as long as anticipated at Llangeitho, Rowland's journey being cut short by persecution, as Gambold reported to an anonymous friend:

'When I wrote last to you, I was going to Cardiganshire to serve Mr. Rowland's churches. . . . When I got to Mr. Rowland's, I found he was returned from North Wales sooner than he had purposed, not being suffered by the severity of the Opposer to open his mouth there. I preached only at one of his churches, and there was led, (as I found afterwards) to say some things which tended to reconcile the audience to me, who before were much prejudiced. Mr. Rowland was very hearty and kind, and next morning, he going to the conference of the chief labourers in Carmarthenshire, I wrote a letter by him to Mr. Howel Harris. . . . With regard to the present work

[237]

among the souls, I make but a poor figure, and they don't see that I can do much good. For it is expected that one should be a ready orator, active and zealous, severe and searching (for the souls are afraid to be healed and comforted), and where this fails, they apprehend nothing that can be useful. Besides, neither you nor I can be very welcome to them as belonging to the Moravian Brethren, who are here despised for not being more stirring in England, and also suspected of errors. The not preaching the Law first, the not praying more in meetings, but above all the not holding the doctrine of Reprobation, must needs be very offensive here, and appear as great errors. . . . My heart is frequently sighing . . . that after the seed time of awakening (which has indeed been very large and glorious, and the instruments used therein are choice men, greatly assisted and blessed by the Lord for the purpose), there might follow a time when the sheaves shall be bound up together, brought in order, and taken care of.'[1]

In the letter, Gambold was touching on matters at issue between Moravian and Methodist. The Welsh Methodists, certainly, insisted on a Calvinistic frame of reference for their theology, and on the Law's role in both convicting sinners and controlling saints; on both counts the Moravians differed. They were agreed, however, on the need for order and care to build up the societies. This aspect of the work was being actively promoted by the Welsh Associations.

Meanwhile, North Wales continued to draw the Methodists, even though it was penetrated for the Gospel only by arduous and costly forays. When Rowland returned there in August 1744, William Williams accompanied him. On this occasion they had 'wonderful liberty and power, and no interruption'.[2] In the work of the Gospel, Rowland was a man of perseverance as well as power.

By the ecclesiastical authorities, however, Rowland was seen in a very different light! In 1745 they were making closer scrutiny of Methodist activities in North Wales. They issued a questionnaire asking for details of Methodists in each parish, an exercise repeated in different dioceses at various intervals. The first of these, at St Asaph, spoke of Methodism as 'that religious frenzy', and of Methodists as those 'who assemble before day from house to house

---

[1] STL i. 110; Moravian Church Archives, Box A/3, Folder 10, 'Letters of John Gambold', letter dated October 13, 1743; cf. Trefeca Letter 1022, Harris to Whitefield, October 31, 1743, 'Brother Gambold was down and preached in one of Brother Rowland's churches, but was not received by the people at all. I believe stillness will not take here.'
[2] Trefeca Letter 1224, quoted in WW i. 72, 73.

to pray and sing Psalms'. They were from 'the lower ranks' of society; their 'principles are so wild and uncertain' as to be indefinable, their meetings clandestine enough to 'encourage strangers to propagate their enthusiastical notions to the prejudice of the churches'. Later reports, from Bangor as well as St Asaph, supply information about their 'teachers', naming Harris and some other laymen. Rowland, Howel Davies, and Peter Williams were also included under that heading, with the added description, 'half-starved curates from the Diocese of St. David's', and collectively referred to as 'enthusiastical quacks'! By 1747 there were signs that the Lord was blessing Methodist persistence. As a result, one Association item records the leaders' decision: 'After reading a letter from Anglesey about taking the souls in North Wales under our care, we agreed that Brother Harris go there now immediately, and exhort them to abide in the Church of England, and settle them in private societies; and we agreed that some brethren from South Wales shall be there continually to succeed each other.'[1]

Earlier, in October 1743 the Association had to resolve another issue. The Welsh brethren faced dissatisfaction about the Established Church from within their own ranks. Both Harris and Whitefield were known to oppose all moves to separate from Anglicanism. At the Glanyrafon-ddu (Carmarthenshire) Association on October 5, 'Brother Morgan John Lewis opened his convictions about leaving the Established Church.' He did so on the grounds 'that its foundations are Jewish, its Canons unscriptural, its ministers God's enemies, and its worship intermixed with much Popish superstition'. He was also convinced 'that we should now leave it . . . that now we are a Church, and should separate'. While in response 'all the brethren agreed against this motion', Harris was the prime mover. Lewis had been converted under Harris's ministry about 1738, and the issue of separation still troubled him in 1744, when at the May Association he 'agreed by way of forebearance till the Lord should thrust us out or bring in a Reformation'. The final blow to Lewis's Anglican affiliation was apparently the refusal of his parish church to invite Rowland for a preaching occasion. Lewis's society at New Inn, near Pontypool, had difficulties in finding a regular ministry of the Word and the administration of the Lord's Supper. On Rowland's

[1] l. 86, 49; xlii. 45; xxxi. 30–5; xxxvi. 3–4; xv. 104–109, 149–51; William Griffith, *Methodistiaeth Fore Môn*, 1955, tt. 57–9.

advice they ordained Lewis as minister in 1756 and became an independent church.[1]

Lewis was not the only one to be troubled by this issue. Five Glamorganshire exhorters approached the Association in March 1745 with a complaint of too much bondage to the Established Church. They had sought the views of the leaders on the matter for two years, but as no positive response had been forthcoming they told the leaders, 'too many of the prejudices of your upbringing cling to you'. They owned themselves to have been converted and called to exhort in the Gospel through the ministry of the Methodists. Now they sought ordination, basing their appeal on Acts 6:6, and 'the splendid results which followed'. 'Therefore', they argued, 'we pray you to do what they did. By so doing you cannot offend any man who takes God's Word as the guiding rule of his life; then we may expect the same effects, increasing our number, and strengthening such as are already called'. In conclusion they made this appeal: 'We could leave you quietly, and so be ordained, and have congregations under our supervision. No, brethren, we are willing to labour together with you, as we have up to the present, and to be governed by you as hitherto, but "in the Lord", and according to His Word'.

Harris saw this as stemming from pride and compared it to the Israelites wanting a king. He also pointed out that ordination 'can't keep carnal men from taking the work in hand', and 'when Apollos did preach, he was not charged for going about unordained, but for want of better light to know Christ'. Eventually the exhorters submitted to the Association's policy, although some rumblings continued for a time.[2] The tensions were especially acute when the Methodist's itinerant preaching was threatened. This was the vanguard of the work, the most sensitive and vulnerable nerve of its activity network. Harris reacted strongly in April 1745, for instance, when the vicar of Talgarth became 'very bitter against Brother Rowland, threatening him with a citation if he would come again [to the parish]'. Later in that year, when Harris visited Llangeitho on October 26, he recorded in his diary, 'Finding how all things are shaken, he about leaving the Church or being turned out. I see none but God can keep him in, both sides being of a mind. I cried for the poor Church.'[3] But that particular storm of ecclesiastical censure

[1] CMHO, 98, 99; xlviii. 78; HMGC i. 230–31, 388.
[2] CMHO, 103–05; HMGC i. 189.
[3] CMHO, 110; HVP, 118.

passed, too, and Rowland was constrained to remain within Anglicanism.

The Methodists' ultimate response was to reaffirm that the societies were not to be looked on as churches, nor were exhorters to be as ordained ministers, preaching and administering the sacraments, but merely 'exhorters'. Methodists were not to be thought of 'as a sect, but a people in the Church, called to reform till either . . . heard, or turned out; and that whoever is called to labour as a reformer must have strong love to bear much'.[1] This was far from satisfactory. It left many questions unanswered: the nature of a Gospel church, its doctrinal distinctives, the character and authority of its officers, the nurture and discipline of its life. Few Methodists, however, were ripe for a discussion of these matters of faith, order, and unity. For the time being, their common Methodist heritage, young and vulnerable though it might be, held them together. On the issue of ecclesiastical identity there was more to unite than to divide them.

Satisfactory arrangements for regular ministry and sacramental occasions were therefore a priority. On his return from London in October 1743 Harris considered Rowland's preaching to be 'closer, with more power than ever'. He also noted to a correspondent that 'Mr. Rowland has three places to administer the Sacrament', in addition of course to his own parish. The three were in Carmarthenshire: Abergorlech, Capel Ifan, and Llanlluan. As to the means of grace, the important thing for Rowland was life: 'If God is alive, a living God, then we must offer a living sacrifice. . . . See that you are in God's service full of zeal and life, do it with all thy strength. . . . Keep in the Gospel Way, for you are living stones': this from a sermon on Hosea 1:10, 'Ye are the sons of the living God', one of several sermons from the Minor Prophet during this period.[2]

On November 1, 1743, Rowland's sermon at the Llanddeusant Association was on Hosea 2:19–20, 'I will betroth thee unto me for ever.' 'He showed', wrote Harris, 'how God marries Himself to His children in righteousness and judgment, viz. He'll work such will, such truth, such love and faithfulness, that it will be just in Him to give all to them.' These graces, however, are not in perfection in the

---

[1] CMHO, 114–15, 126.
[2] xxviii. 158; STL i. 111; Diary 103, s.v. October 9, 1743, the first sermon on Hosea 1:10. Other sermons on Hosea 1:12 (October 9); 2:14 (October 18 and 19); 2:19–20 (November 1); 1:11 (December 28); and 2:14 (February 23, 1744).

believer at present. 'There is nothing in heaven but what is, in part, wrought in the believer here. If truth, faithfulness, light, and grace are in God, so are they in the believer. I expect nothing new in heaven, only a perfection of all graces.' On this side of glory the believer has these graces in measure only, at times more than at others, and in each believer some measure of all graces. Since believers are so precious to God, He 'makes His ministers to spend even to their death for this Bride'.[1] This last sentiment reveals the nature and extent of the motivation which spurred on the Methodists during that period of tempestuous opportunity.

It also reflects Rowland's concern to establish new believers in the faith. Following Christ stemmed from God's sovereign grace, but it issued in self-denial and persistence. This was the burden of a sermon he preached at the end of the same month on Ephesians 6:10: 'Finally, my brethren, be strong in the Lord, and in the power of His might.' 'He declared', says Harris, 'he was persuaded that glorious times are coming on the church, but that the world would go worse and worse; and many will arise from among us speaking perverse things.' Then Rowland addressed himself to the question, 'Why does every Christian need much strength?'

'1. Because he fights against strong enemies. You must sacrifice your Isaacs. Isaac was willing to die, but such is not sin, for sin cries, "let me live a little and I will hide myself, and none shall see me". But children! you must kill sin, and that now! 2. Because they have great work and a great war. . . . The King is obliged to provide men, arms, etc. . . . All the care is on Christ's shoulder. . . . If Satan has carried the day, renew the battle again and seek help, and you shall have an army with Christ at the head of it, for you are fighting for the Lamb and for God's glory! Christ's name is written on you, and if you fall, God's name and ark is fallen! Don't say, "God elected me"; true, but God has elected us to fight and conquer sin! He elected us first to holiness, then to glorification. Don't say, "Christ will conquer"; true, but you must see that God conquers in us. Christians should fight manfully because Christ is their Captain. The eagle tries the young ones when born; so does God try us, and if we conquer little temptations, you shall overcome greater. Doctrine: The strength of the Christian is in God, 'tis God fights, but 'tis in us and by His grace in us.'

At this point in the sermon Harris was so much impressed with the reality and sufficiency of Christ's grace that his soul was drawn 'up to

[1] Diary 104, s.v. November 1, 1743.

God, crying deliberately, "O Father",' and made willing to leave all for God's presence. Rowland's application was full of encouragement:

'Why does God give this strength to the Christian? 1. Because God purposed it; 2. Because He loves him. God saw you from eternity and conceived you in eternity; every soul is God's stage where God will act either His grace or His anger on them; 3. Because He looks on you as the purchase of Christ's blood, and so you are precious, not because of anything in you; 4. Because of Christ in heaven. Christ came here, and married a spouse and begat children, but He and His spouse and children were taken prisoner; but He broke the prison, and is now gone home and will come to set you free, or else He'll burn the prison, which is the devil, the world and the flesh. . . . Inference: how vain is it to hinder God's saints! No castle so strong as the Christian, though they may be blocked up with enemies, and though your comforts may be robbed; yet there is a river runs sweetly through your soul, and it can't be stopped or poisoned. . . . Go on courageously, then, for none can rob you of your salvation.'[1]

With such lively preaching Rowland sought to fulfil his responsibility to God's people of encouraging them to 'Keep in the Gospel Way'.

At the close of 1743 Harris was writing excitedly to Whitefield:

'I have been obliged to discourse out of doors for above this fortnight twice or thrice a day, so that you may imagine, nature is pretty well worn out. But I could not avoid it, and almost all my strength has been supernatural, the congregations I believe by a moderate computation being from five hundred to three or four or six thousand. The two last Sundays, perhaps I heard two of the loudest trumpets in the nation, Brother Rowland and Brother Davies. The light, divine wisdom, and power to wound and heal, and to reveal the Lord Jesus Christ was such, that words can give no true idea of. . . . The outpouring of the Blessed Spirit is now so plentiful and common, that I think it was our deliberate observation that not one sent by Him opens his mouth without some remarkable showers. He comes either as a Spirit of wisdom to enlighten the soul, to teach and build up, and set out the works of light and darkness, or else a Spirit of tenderness and love, sweetly melting the souls like the dew, and watering the graces; or as the Spirit of hot burning zeal, setting their hearts in a flame, so that their eyes sparkle with fire, love, and joy; or also such a Spirit of uncommon power that the heavens seem to be rent, and hell to tremble; and often in all these and various other

---

[1] HH Diary 105, s.v. November 29. The sermon was preached at Abergorlech.

manners at the same opportunity. And to see and hear of the particular effects, and the news of some awakened, and some set free, is our continual entertainment. And the work seems to be but beginning too; we only want labourers; churches are opened, cries for ministers and curates daily; and prejudices so abated that a dog hardly barks.'

No less significant was the effect of fresh reviving on the societies:

'The lambs are coming in great multitudes to liberty, and 'tis a glorious sight indeed to see them! 'Tis not like that first love, or of first believing, attended with strong self, heats, and evil surmisings; but it being with most of them after long and manifold trials from all quarters, after sore combats with unbelief and corruption; and after a deep acquaintance with their own hearts and the wiles of Satan, the graces harmonize in them. Great views of the Lamb not only feed faith, love, zeal, etc. but produce also sympathy and tenderness, much brokenness of spirit, and humility. These, with the filial fear, mixed with their joy and confidence in God, makes most melodious music together indeed. The power of their Amens, and the joyous cries of their souls, I am persuaded, reach heaven, when the spirit and voice of the minister is raised up. This you must conceive from experience. And this is not at some times, but it grows thus more and more daily.'[1]

The letter closed on an unmistakable note of glorious triumph: 'All things go on in such a manner that I must assure you the Lord Jesus is in the field. Therefore, my dear brother, take fresh courage, redouble your valour, and follow your blows, for indeed Satan flies, and his kingdom falls to the ground! A war is begun afresh, and I believe the Lord will not put His sword into the sheath till He has avenged the blood of His Son upon him.'

For the Welsh Methodists the new year of 1744 began with another Association at Watford. Rowland was prevented from attending, 'the road being so hard, my horse so slow, and myself fatigued'. Writing to explain his absence he added these sentiments: 'I long to be among you, for I know God is with you. Surely, Satan's teeth water at you, and the wicked world cannot but persecute you! But, dear companions, keep your file! make no division! and you will see great things. Heaven is coming down apace!'[2] It was a fitting word for an extraordinary season.

[1] CH. 1980, pp. 32–33.
[2] *Christian History*, vol. v. No. 3, p. 10; HH, 132–3; Morris Davies, *Deuddeg Pregeth*, 314–15.

'A legal spirit in a Christian may be compared to his shirt, being the first thing he puts on, and the last he puts off.'

DANIEL ROWLAND

'When you consider the devil's diligence and subtlety to entice and lead your thoughts secretly away from God and eternal things, to earthly and perishable things; and you know that not only is fervent prayer to God an excellent remedy for this, but also among many other things it is necessary to fix in your memory and thoughts the Scriptures (which are in God's hands the sword of the Spirit against the wiles of the devil); to help you in this, I have written for you some hymns, composed as near as possible to the sound and language of the Scriptures, so that in song they might come more easily to mind and be more effective in working on your affections.'

WILLIAM WILLIAMS
Preface to Alleluja, 1744

23

Writing, Singing, and Praying

In addition to providing for the societies by preaching and oversight, the Methodists also fostered the publication of Christian literature. During the Dugoedydd Association of May 25, 1743, a decision was taken to publish a Welsh translation of Ralph Erskine's four sermons on Galatians 2:19, 'I through the law, am dead to the law, that I might live unto God', which bore the title *Law-death, Gospel-life: or the Death of Legal Righteousness, the Life of Gospel Holiness.* 'We thought it would be of universal use to all the lambs with us,' wrote Harris, 'as it is very sound and sweet and heart-searching, and would be received by all.' The sermons had originally been preached in 1724 and now the book was translated into Welsh by John Morgan, appearing with 1743 as the date of printing and with six of Rowland's hymns appended to it.[1]

The Methodist leaders evidently felt that its availability in Welsh would meet a very real need in their situation. Its main thesis or 'doctrine' was this: 'That to be dead to the law, in the point of justification, is necessary, in order to our living to God, in the point of sanctification.' The law is dealt with in the sense of a principle on which God deals with sinners ('a covenant of works'): in this sense, the believer is dead to it, but unbelievers are still 'living' under it and (vainly) looking to it for salvation. 'In the law, as a covenant of works, there are three things; 1. the precept of obedience; 2. the promise of life; and 3. the threatening or penalty of death.' Consequently, the man that is dead to the law has 'no expectation from the law, or from his obedience thereto'. On the principle of

[1] CH 1980, p. 28; HMGC i. 412–14; *The Sermons and Other Practical Works of the late Rev. Ralph Erskine*, vol. ii. 1865, pp. 9–102. The Welsh title was *Traethawd am Farw i'r Ddeddf, a Byw i Dduw*. See also David Boorman, 'Ebenezer Erskine and Secession' in *Diversities of Gifts*, 1980 Westminster Conference Papers.

merit through obedience to the law there is no acquittal for sinners, only conviction, threat, and condemnation; in a word, death. So the sinner, under a sense of failure, guilt, and danger, turns away from the law as a vindicating agent, and this turning away from it to another principle is in itself a being dead to the law. By contrast, living to God is the result of a spiritual life-giving operation of God's Spirit. He works faith, obedience, love.

The use of the law is now seen in quite a different light. 'The commands of the law, in the hand of Christ, have lost their old covenant-form, and are full of love. The command of the law of works is "Do, and live"; but in the hand of Christ, it is "Live, and do".' Similarly for the promises of the law: before, the reward was to be earned, and it was to be 'a reward of debt'; 'but the law, in the hand of Christ, promises a reward of grace to gospel-obedience'; and also 'the threatenings of the law, in the hand of Christ, have lost their old covenant-form, quality and nature and are now turned to threatenings out of love.' The law cannot hold the sentence of eternal death over the believer, any more than 'a living wife needs to fear the threatenings of her dead husband'.

It follows then that 'the law can neither justify nor sanctify a sinner; it cannot justify him, for he must be dead to it in point of justification; it cannot sanctify him, for he never lives to God, until he be dead to the law'. For this reason the believer must beware of a legal spirit which brings him to bondage by turning his gaze away from Christ to his own works and achievements, or lack of them, as 'when the joy of sanctification is greater than the joy of justification'. Living to God is a holy life, and 'grace is the spring from which the living water does flow'. To live that life, 'Cry, cry mightily to the Lord, that he would kill your self-confidence: cry for the Spirit of life, to quicken you, that you may live to God.' In this way Erskine dealt with issues affecting the believer's assurance and godliness.

These two areas of discussion were also of fundamental relevance to the Welsh societies, and the book's appearance in Welsh for their sakes was most timely. The society reports to the Associations give a detailed assessment of the spiritual state of each member. Frequently a person's experience is measured in relation to the law. This indicates the profound extent to which the Welsh Methodist mind was being exercised on the use of the law and the nature of Gospel liberty. Examples like the following, are taken at random from reports sent in September 1743 and early 1744. They show that a spirit of conviction and grief for sin was wrought on many by the preaching of those days:

'Llanddeusant Society comes on and keeps close with God in life and experience. Some who were under examination are left on trial for some time; I don't see it right to receive any immediately except their experience be very clear.

'There seems a sweet Revival amongst the members of Groeswen and Aberthaw Society, where are a few that enjoy full liberty; the rest believe it to be obtainable and are pressing on.

'John Henry, under the Law; had no testimony of his justification, but seeking Christ earnestly;

'John Griffith, hath comfort sometimes, but no sure testimony;

'James Williams and John David, both under the Law, seeking and waiting at Christ's feet;

'Llanegwad Society: most of them walk close with God, pressing forward, struggling with many temptations, but find strength to overcome; others who are under the Law are more lukewarm, etc.

'Llanbryn-mair [Four men] It is quite dark with these regarding their justification, but their souls thirst after God, so that they have no true rest, but long to enjoy it.

'Llandinam [Two women] These are justified and walk in love and zeal. [Six other women] Under the Law, and often with many doubts.'[1]

The societies thus catered for a variety of religious experiences, and a differing measure of assurance and growth in grace. Erskine's work was useful to distinguish between justification and sanctification, and to show their inseparable connection. According to Erskine, the use of the law to the Christian is held to be 'not formally, as a covenant; but materially, as a rule of life . . . an active directory for his walk.' By this 'rule of life' he comes to rate Christ's righteousness highly and it drives him to seek more sanctifying grace from God, living in humility and filial fear.[2]

More translations from the Erskines' works followed, issued seemingly from personal conviction rather than by corporate decision of the Association:

In 1745, two separate collections from *Gospel Sonnets*; one collection, "The Mystery of the Saint's Life, State, and Frame" being translated by Daniel Rowland, the other by an anonymous translator;

[1] lii. 10, 17, 19; MTU 74, 75.
[2] *The Sermons . . . of . . . Ralph Erskine*, vol. ii, 1865, p. 64.

In 1759, Ebenezer Erskine's sermon on Hebrews 10:22 bearing the title "The assurance of faith opened and applied" was translated by William Williams, with a hymn by Rowland at the end. A second edition was issued the following year;

In 1764, two sermons by Ebenezer Erskine appeared separately, the translator being anonymous in each case: One was of "The believer exalted in imputed righteousness", on Psalm 89:16; the other: "Christ in the believer's arms', on Luke 2:28. Printed with this is a sermon on Psalm 74:20, "Faith's plea upon Christ's Covenant"; and more of the *Gospel Sonnets*.

Although neither of the Erskine brothers was a major theologian, or even a major figure in Church History, they were both remarkable men. They were involved in a secession movement from the national Church of Scotland, and for a while corresponded with Whitefield. James Hervey 'highly prized' Ralph Erskine's *Gospel Sonnets*, and paid as high a tribute to Ebenezer Erskine's sermons: 'Were I to read, with a single view to the edification of my heart in true faith, solid comfort, and evangelical holiness, I would have recourse to Mr. Erskine.' During this early period of the Awakening, their works were together the single greatest literary influence on the Welsh Methodists.[1]

There was much in their respective situations to attract the Welsh Methodists to the Erskines. The latter had been involved in an attempt to bring back the Church of Scotland to a purer faith and more Scriptural church practices. The controversy centred initially on the right of a congregation to call the minister of its own choosing. Its scope widened to more basic, doctrinal issues concerning the relations of law and grace under the Gospel. The Erskines and ten others favoured the teaching of a seventeenth-century book, *The Marrow of Modern Divinity by* Edward Fisher, while the Church authorities denounced its teaching as Antinomian, that is, as leading

---

[1] *ibid.* vol. vii. p. xxv; *The Whole Works of the Rev. Ebenezer Erskine*, vol. i. 1826, p. xxxiii. For the Erskines' relationship to Whitefield, see DAL ii. 83–92. The translated Sonnets are respectively from Pt. III, Section ii (vol. vii, 172, ff.); Pt. VI, Chapter ii (vii. 261, ff.); and Pt. VI, Chapter v, Section i (vii. 300, ff.); HMGC ii. 427; David Williams, *Cofiant J. R. Jones*, Ramoth, 1913, Pennod xxxvi. The Welsh titles of these works are respectively: *Traethawd am Farw i'r Ddeddf, a Byw i Dduw*; *Dychymyg ym mha un y gosodir allan Ddirgelwch Bywyd, Stat, a Thymer y Saint*; *Sinai a Seion*; *Sicrwydd Ffydd*; *Derchafiad y Credadyn mewn Cyfianwder Cyfrifol*; *Crist ym Mreichiau'r Credadyn*; *Dadl Ffydd ar Air a Chyfamod Duw*; *Odl ar Waith a Dadl y Nefoedd*.

to lawlessness and licence. One of the twelve, Thomas Boston, had republished the book in 1726, adding extensive notes in its defence. The book was in the form of a dialogue and asserted the spirituality of the law, convicting men of sin. For the Christian it was important to receive the law, not at the hands of Moses, 'but only at the hands of Christ', the sinner coming to Christ for Gospel-righteousness, rather than coming to God with law-righteousness. Subsequent obedience to the law for the believer then becomes 'the middle path' between legalism and Antinomianism.[1] The controversy lasted from 1731 to 1740, and included a secession on the part of the Erskines and the formation of 'The Associate Presbytery'.

While the Welsh Methodists could identify themselves with the Erskines' biblical convictions, they avoided any appearance of having a separate ecclesiastical identity. They did so strongly and repeatedly: 'We discoursed on several heads of divinity and agreed that we are not, and should not call ourselves, a Church or Sect, but Societies called in the Established Church till turned out; and that such as discourse are not, nor should they be, called ministers but exhorters': this in April 1744. This did not prevent them from profiting immensely from *The Marrow*, the Erskines' theological favourite. Early in 1742 Harris was reading that book with 'much light to see that in the Covenant of works we go to the command first, and on keeping or breaking that have hopes or fears, but under grace we go first to Christ'; and again, 'light, sweetness, and power came in, in seeing that Christ is made my Righteousness to free me from the Law. Sweetly fed indeed, and then seeing yet more clear that my salvation is all of grace, my soul cried O! grace, grace, grace, grace, free grace! I can sing of nothing but grace and talk of nothing but grace!'[2] These phrases are familiar in Welsh Methodist usage, occurring with a regularity that is impressive.

The strength and appeal of the Erskines' theology lay more in its searching application than in its originality. With its unashamedly Calvinistic and Covenantal framework it was Christ-centred, warm, and practical. That it appealed to the Welsh Methodists is therefore no surprise. They read, borrowed, translated, used, and commended the Erskine brothers' work with great relish. A copy of Ebenezer

---

[1] See J. H. S. Burleigh, *A Church History of Scotland*, 1961, pp. 280, 282, 288, 323; Ernest F. Kevan, *The Grace of Law*, 1976, pp. 65, 186–7, 248; cf. Thomas Boston, *Human Nature in Its Fourfold State*, 1964, pp. 25–30.

[2] xlviii. 76; Diary 84, s.v. January 7 and 9, 1744.

Erskine's *Sermons and Discourses*, published in 1761 has Howel Davies's signature with the date 'July 1761' on it; later it passed into the hands of Rowland's son, Nathaniel. Some of William Williams' hymns are free translations from Ralph Erskine's *Gospel Sonnets*. In 1764, four years after the second edition of Williams' translation of *The Assurance of Faith* appeared, he bemoaned the fact that 300 copies were still unsold, since they were

'the best books printed in Welsh for these times, when some regard believing as feeling pleasant and happy breezes in God's service, so that when they have lost these, nothing remains but to seek them again or else suffer under the power of unbelief; and others who would assert that faith is a bare belief of the words of the Bible, and make of it a dry, dead, sterile, insipid, impotent thing, differing only slightly, if at all, from the devil's believing. Hymenaeus, Philetus, and Alexander the coppersmith, brought forth in Scotland, now try and settle in Wales, seeking to draw people away from that experimental faith, which is the mother of all good fruit and virtuous living, to the vain talk and disputable questions of those who undermine faith rather than edify it.'

Although his first Welsh translation did not appear until 1759, the usefulness of its English edition had been appreciated by the Methodists for many years. The reason for this was that it set out clearly the nature of Gospel dealings (Christ offered freely, wholly, particularly or individually, and earnestly), and the degrees of faith ('there is faith, then the assurance of faith, and then the full assurance of faith'). So highly were the Erskine brothers esteemed, that in Williams' elegy to Griffith Jones', after his death in 1761, they are located by Williams in heaven together with Vicar Rhys Prichard, James Hervey and Isaac Watts.

> He [Griffith Jones] is seated with Rhys Prichard,
> I suspect, 'midst heaven's throng;
> With good Ralph and Ebenezer,
> Hervey, Watts, there they belong;
> He could choose his anthem's story,
> This the theme that first came forth:
> Saving grace, so deep, amazing,
> That's the song of endless worth.

Their influence on Rowland was next in importance only to that of Griffith Jones.

The hymns by Rowland bound with the translation of Ralph

Erskine's *Law-Death, Gospel-Life* were on the theme of communion with God. The title of the first is 'A longing to remain in God's presence'. The following verses are translated from the hymn which bears the title 'A hymn of invitation to praise God for His free love, and for His gracious Spirit's enabling to believe in Christ.'

> Come! Praise the King of Heaven above,
> His grace to me is sealed!
> He gave His Son, no greater gift;
> I know whom I have trusted.
>
> I doubted long His loving grace,
> Religion I rejected;
> Illumination now has come:
> I know whom I have trusted.
>
> Through Christ I'm justified by faith,
> To this the Spirit's witnessed;
> Henceforth who dares condemn my soul?
> I know whom I have trusted.
>
> I see by faith that now I live,
> God's earnest has been granted;
> Th'inheritance will duly come;
> I know whom I have trusted.
>
> He who began this blessed work
> Its progress also charted,
> Till Canaan's rest is mine for aye;
> I know whom I have trusted.[1]

In 1744 William Williams issued his first collection of hymns, *Alleluja*. Another collection, 'mostly by the Reverend Daniel Rowland' appeared in the same year, and the same title, *Hymnau Duwiol* (Godly Hymns) was used the following year and described as 'from the Collection of a Churchman'. This was issued by John Morgan from a Carmarthen Press, the 'Churchman' being Griffith Jones. From the same Press, and in the same year, appeared *Rhai Hymnau Duwiol* (Some Godly Hymns) 'by the Reverend Mr. Daniel Rowland, Minister of the Church of England'.[2] In this work there is a greater variety in the metres used, a reflection of Rowland's greater

---

[1] The complete hymn in Welsh is in D. J. Odwyn Jones, *Daniel Rowland Llangeitho*, 1938, tt. 186–8.
[2] See HMGC i. 424; cf. WW ii. 29, 33, 52.

confidence in writing hymns, and also possibly reflecting a widening acquaintance with contemporary English hymn-writers, such as Isaac Watts, John and Charles Wesley and John Cennick. Rowland was the first Welsh Hymn-writer to use the metre 8.3.3.6, with the rhyme sequence a.b.b.a.[1] The only hymn of Rowland's included in the current edition of the Welsh Methodist Hymn Book uses this metre, and was first published in the 1744 work *Hymnau Duwiol Yw Canu Mewn Cymdeithasau Crefyddol* (Godly Hymns for Singing in Religious Societies). Here are some of its verses in translation:[2]

> When shall I, O Lord, come yonder
> To my place,
> See Thy face,
> Live with Jesus ever?
>
> When shall I, from sin and tempting
> Be set free
> From them flee,
> In Thine arm reclining.
>
> When Thy Kingdom comes with power,
> Then I'll hide,
> And abide
> In Thy love's safe shelter.
>
> Widely open, then, heaven's portal
> That we may
> Fully say
> Ours is life eternal!

Prominent elements in the hymns are the Christian's conflict with sin while on his earthly pilgrimage, and a passionate longing for his heavenly home. Throughout, however, there is the strong assurance of triumph in Christ. The finality and sufficiency of redemption in Christ is shown to be the ground of the believer's confidence and thankfulness. In turn this explains the many hymns extolling the condescension of His coming to earth, and the glory of His exaltation. Rowland's hymns, as well as Erskine's sermons, were 'sound, and sweet, and heart-searching', too.

[1] WW ii. 106.
[2] D. J. Odwyn Jones, *op. cit.*, tt. 200–202; cf. John Thickens, *Emynau a'u Hawduriaid* [1945], tt. 43–6.

The same fervency which characterises Rowland's hymns also permeates his recommendation of a Welsh translation of John Bunyan's *Holy War* in 1744.

'If you read this, you shall hear tell of a war, with which the wars of this world were mere games in comparison. The stadium is the soul of every man. There is no neutrality in this battle; all the world fights, either for God against Satan, or for Satan against God. My brethren, whom are you for? O distinguishing mercy, that you are in a world where by grace you may choose your side! In eternity you must stand to your colours; but here you may flee from the militant tent of Satan, and be accepted by Christ's scouts. The Gospel drum beats for volunteers. May God make you 'willing in the day of His power'! I know you wish to be on the safest side. Och! if you are for Satan, you are sure of damnation. God's curse is on him, and on all who are for him. Men! God's cannon is levelled at you. . . . I would not for all the world leave you in the place where God's bullets fly! Flee! flee from the wrath that is to come!'[1]

In Rowland there was no lukewarmness or double-mindedness. What was said of Calvin could with equal validity be said of Rowland: he was 'a bow always strung'.[2] With might and main he was for Christ and His Kingdom. His published works as well as his sermons make it clear that he expected every Methodist to be the same.

If Rowland's warning about the battle for 'Man-soul' went unheeded by most, not so the talk of another kind of war which gathered momentum during the latter half of 1744. It created a great national stir in 1745, with an abortive attempt to restore the Monarchy to the Stuarts. The 'rebellion' was defeated, but it was seen as an expression of French interference and Popish aspirations. Loyalist, Dissenter and Methodist had found common cause in supporting George II. In England, Philip Doddridge encouraged the raising of troops in his congregation and neighbourhood, while the Nonconformists as a whole held days of 'humiliation and prayer'. Public suspicion of Methodist allegiance was common. 'Every Sunday', says Charles Wesley, 'damnation is pronounced against us, for we are papists, Jesuits, seducers, and bringers in of the Pretender.' For this reason his brother, John, was inclined to present a 'Humble Address to the King from the Methodist Societies' affirming loyalty

[1] Morris Davies, *Deuddeg Pregeth*, tt. 305–06.
[2] G. E. Duffield (ed.), *John Calvin*, 1966, p. 76.

and support, but he was dissuaded from it by Charles on the ground that it might imply a Methodist existence independent of the Established Church. Instead Wesley wrote *A Word in Season*, warning that the rebellion's success would restore Papal power, and viewing the rebellion's cause as 'the prevalence of ungodliness'.[1]

In Wales support for 'the Pretender' was organised around certain landowners, notably Sir Watcyn Williams Wynn in the north. After ten years of Methodism many of the common people had come to recognise their obligations to the civil authority under God. Whatever may have been their inclinations before, now they were solidly loyal. Writing to Whitefield in November 1745, Harris could say, 'We have all everywhere great freedom in heart to wrestle for our lawful King George, and also for this poor sinful nation, which by all signs seems ripe for destruction; notwithstanding, there are many stirred up to take arms.' William Williams echoed his sentiments:

'Here are some fears by reason of the rebellion in the north, but it would fill your soul with love to God to see how fervent the poor despised Methodists pray for King George the Second and the present Government. We had a society last week to fast and pray . . . we have very many here and in Cardiganshire that are willing to wear arms as soon as called for; certainly this disproves their disloyalty as was accused by some.'

Pembrokeshire, too, had its quota of men ready to demonstrate their patriotism. Howel Davies had a list of 1,500 between the age of 17 and 40, Rowland a list of 500, and this proved convincing evidence to many of 'their character in respect of their loyalty to the present Establishment'. The occasion presented the Methodist Association with an opportunity to acquaint their people with the errors of Romanism, and more especially, to call them to prayer.[2]

Rowland was a man of prayer as well as an eminent preacher of the Gospel. It was his habit to seek God's face with a prolonged season of prayer and intercession before taking a service. Llanbadarn Odwyn church was situated on a hill overlooking Rowland's home. From this vantage point the congregation could see him setting out

[1] John Stoughton, *History of Religion in England*, vol. vi, 1901, p. 16; J. Wesley Bready, *England Before and After Wesley* (1939), p. 205, quoting from J. H. Overton, *The Evangelical Revival in the Eighteenth Century*, p. 176, f.; Frederick C. Gill, *Charles Wesley the First Methodist*, p. 116: *John Wesley's Journal*, iii. 215, n. 3.
[2] STL i. 179; xx. 133; xvi. 115; l. 45.

for their service. On one occasion the crowd lost sight of him in a cluster of trees on the way up the hill. As the time for the service passed, some went to find the cause of his being delayed. They found him on his knees and as they approached he greeted them with the comment, 'Dear brethren, I have had a sweet opportunity in that place.' The service which followed was attended 'with amazing power and effect'. In his public ministry he would usually pray before the sermon or ask someone to pray for him. At one rather lifeless Association he asked a godly old man to do so. In his prayer he cried for the divine influences: 'Lord Jesus, your servants have been winnowing here yesterday and today in vain, but there has not been the slightest breeze. The Wind, gracious Lord! for the Wind is in your hand now and always.'[1]

This emphasis on prayer permeated the thinking of the Welsh Methodists. From early days, Harris was 'filled with zeal' to press on the other leaders 'to lay aside days for prayer' for the success of the Gospel. In the mid-forties the call to prayer became more insistent and urgent, and it was joined with a time of fasting. Initially such days were 'about various things', later the focus was more specific, on account of 'the war' in the autumn of 1744, in 1745 'on account of the division in England and the lukewarmness and other sins in England and Wales', for an impending law-suit in 1748.[2] This burden for prayer received fresh impetus from Scotland in 1745 and America in 1747. The Scottish proposals for a union in prayer were sent to Harris by James Erskine and they were duly brought to the Association in March 1745:

'As a proposal was sent from Scotland to keep one day in every three months, beginning Nov. 1st, a day of prayers for two years, and to meet every Sunday morning on account of the late work in England, Scotland, Wales, and America, both to praise God for it and intercede and pray for its furtherance, and to be humbled for the sins that attended it, we agreed to it; to keep the first of May next . . . and every Sunday morning with as many as we can have, and also in private to give it a place in our hearts and time as much as we can every Saturday night, and to recommend it to others, too.'

Jonathan Edwards caught the vision and wrote in 1747 *An Humble*

[1] JO, 68; *Traethodydd*, 1850, p. 284.
[2] MS i. 417 (February 5, 1740); xlix. 22 (June 26, 1744), 86 (October 23, 1744), 90 (March 2, 1745); li. 28 (October 26, 1748).

Attempt to Promote Explicit Agreement and Visible Union of God's People in Extraordinary Prayer, for the Revival of Religion and the Advancement of Christ's Kingdom Upon Earth.[1] While he intended it should continue for seven years from November 1746, he expressed his fervent hope that there would not be an end 'of extraordinary united prayer among God's people for the effusion of the blessed Spirit'.

When God's people set themselves to pray there is certain to be strong opposition from the kingdom of darkness. A message which Rowland preached in April 1744 was both timely and prophetic in this respect. It was based on Jeremiah 8:7, 'My people know not the judgment of the Lord':

'God like a father is a long time threatening and preparing the rod before He strikes, to see if we will own our faults; seven days He compassed Jericho before He destroyed it. . . . God has permitted a time of sin and of repentance, too: see then that this be improved. God has decreed a time of judgment also. Doctrine: that it is the duty of the faithful to know and understand God's time and judgment, and the sign of the times. . . . A sign that judgment is near is when sin is gone over the bounds of shame and conscience, so as to boast of it.'[2]

This was a salutary reminder to the Welsh Methodists of God's mercies and judgments. In the light of the storm that was to break over them, they would need both the 'sound and sweet and heart-searching' comforts of God's Word and the support of disciplined prayer.

[1] Trefeca Letter 1312, Harris to James Erskine, April 12, 1745; l. 27–8; Harold P. Simonson, *Jonathan Edwards*, 1974, pp. 150–1; Jonathan Edwards, *Works*, ii. 278–312. See also Derek Swann, 'Jonathan Edwards and the 1744 Concert for Prayer', in *Foundations*, Issue No. 3, November 1979, pp. 10–21.
[2] HH Diary 109, s.v. April 17, 1744. The sermon was preached at Abergorlech.

'I am now taught to remember how necessary and desirable it is to be favoured with the gracious breathings of the good Spirit, to move our affections towards the things of God. If our duties and prayers do not, through Christ, prevail for the stirring up of these kindly gales, our profession will come to a shipwreck, or we shall hardly be able to set out for, much less to arrive at, the desired haven.'

GRIFFITH JONES OF LLANDDOWROR

24

'A strong Pillar in the Church of God'

Ten years after the beginnings of revival in eighteenth-century Wales there was still extraordinary life and vigour in Gospel preaching. The leaders in 1746 were having to caution their people 'that nature should not mingle in the present revival of rejoicing the Lord has been pleased to visit His lambs with in most places'. They were also adamant about attributing the origin and sustenance of the work to God, speaking of it as 'this late revival that He has begun, and that in so eminent a manner', and again, of 'His continuing to carry it on against all opposition even still'.[1]

With such evidence of the Lord's good hand on the work, the conscious policy of the leaders had been clearly determined. It had a dual aspect, inward and outward, providing spiritual vitality and preserving ecclesiastical order. For this purpose the Association meeting under Rowland's guidance on October 18, 1744 had concluded,

'After a long discourse about the state of the societies and of the danger of lukewarmness and necessity of divine fire and life, agreed that all the brethren should stir up the people to hear where there is life, and to receive affectionately every lively messenger. Agreed that as there is a general negligence about bearing fruit to the Lord, and much carelessness in the walk of some, that all should stir the people up zealously to a strict walk and to bear fruit.'[2]

No revival perpetuates itself. Every work of God is sustained by the Holy Spirit's activity, whether during the steady planting and watering season of usual Gospel labours, or at a time when He causes 'a nation to be born at once'. Especially during the latter, the manifestations of the flesh, together with the tares sown by 'the

[1] l. 48, 31.   [2] xlix. 85.

enemy' of God's Kingdom, yield 'a mixed work', demanding vigilance and diligence. It was for this reason that the Welsh Methodists issued such solemn exhortations.

The Welsh Methodists' greatest trial, however, was not avoided, in spite of determined effort on the part of Rowland and others. Before this episode is examined in a later chapter, it is important to show that it took place against the backcloth of sustained and unusual blessing. In spite of the controversy which was to rage amongst the leaders, they insisted on meeting, as far as was humanly possible, their obligation to God and to the work He had committed into their hands.

One such obligation involved clergymen such as Rowland and Davies in supplying disused or neglected chapels once a month. While this was demanding in terms of time and energy, it provided a regular ministry of the Word and Sacrament for believers where this was lacking, while at the same time preserving Anglican usage and order. However, there were threats from the authorities in 1744 to deprive the Methodists of the use of two such chapels, Capel Ifan and Abergorlech, both in Carmarthenshire, and both strategic centres. The Association petitioned the Bishop about the latter, and for the time being their use was uninterrupted.[1] A fresh opportunity opened in 1747, and the Association minutes recorded that 'Brother Rowland agreed to go once a month from August 4th. next for a year and administer the Ordinance at Capel Illtyd [near Defynnog] from the 10th of March to the 10th of September, and the other 6 months to come as often as he can, and propose to be then assisted by Brother John Powell or Brother Thomas Lewis if they will come.'[2]

For Rowland the year 1745 began with another Association, this time at Watford. Harris believed that Rowland had unusual liberty, indeed, an influence which he had never before witnessed, and he was compelled to honour his ministerial brother. Preaching on the text Nehemiah 13:29 Rowland applied his message to all conditions of men: 'If you are a backslider, read Hebrews; if devotional, read the Psalms; if you are prone to be rebellious, read Joshua and Judges, but if you would accomplish great things, read Nehemiah.' There was still power in the preaching and liveliness in the work of God. 'Such a sermon I never before heard as Brother Rowland preached there', says Harris to Whitefield afterwards, 'and so much of the

[1] xlix. 6, 26. *The Carmarthenshire Antiquary*, vol. ii. p. 28.
[2] l. 53.

powerful working of the Holy Spirit I think has never been known among us.' Of the work in general he could say: 'the believers mostly are strong and full of Divine life and warmth, they indeed adorn the Gospel. The weak grow up daily, and much of the real liberty of faith and teachings and comforts of the Holy Ghost are indeed among them. Many are daily called and old professors awakened.'

More good news followed: 'There is much of the Divine fire kindled where lukewarmness had prevailed, and they meet at 5 in the morning, and in some places are kept up all night in prayer and praise. This revival the Lord did by means of (seemingly) a very mean, unlikely instrument, an exhorter that had been a cobbler.' In another comment Harris gives an insight into the amazingly sustained nature of the work in Wales: 'it is not for a while [that is, spasmodically] thus, but it has more or less continued these several years.'[1]

A highly significant letter was sent by the Montgomeryshire exhorter, Richard Tibbott, to the Association in October 1745. It dealt with the need for maintaining the unity of Methodism, and suggested how this would best be achieved:

'(a) we should spend less time with matters that are purely external, and concentrate on the chief principles of religion; examining ourselves of our experience, certainty, and settled use of them. Having travelled such distances to our Associations, we should be prepared to curtail our sleep and mealtimes in order to edify one another spiritually; (b) I tend to think that it would be profitable for us to set out our principles and print them, so that there shall be no misunderstanding or misrepresentation. This would also help us to understand one another and would make for greater unity. Further, it would be an advantage to leave a testimony of the Truth of the Gospel for future generations; (c) I believe, should Providence open the way, that we should set up a school to instruct those who exhort.'[2]

This was a far-sighted and timely letter. Hitherto the Methodists, in their Rules and in their practice, affirmed adherence to the Anglican Thirty-nine Articles. In spite of Tibbott's appeal, this was to serve their doctrinal purpose until 1823 when the Methodists produced their own *Confession of Faith*. Tibbott's idea of a 'school of the prophets' found partial realisation in 1749, and later fulfilment in the Countess of Huntingdon's College at Trefeca in 1768.

[1] TM i. 283; STL i. 159–60.   [2] TM i. 215.

Daniel Rowland

Meanwhile, for Rowland each successive year seemed busier than the one before, and 1745 was no exception. He travelled extensively in South Wales, and in the North it was being said that 'Rowland the Methodist makes a rare hand of his Gospel harvest'. A request came from London for his ministry, and he spent some time in Bristol. In 1746 he had an estimated 3,000 communicants at Llangeitho. This was also the year in which he became acquainted with the Countess of Huntingdon, and managed another visit to Bristol.[1] On August 2, 1749, there was a joint conference at Bristol of the leaders of English and Welsh Methodism. Among those who attended were Whitefield, the two Wesleys, the Countess of Huntingdon, Rowland and Harris. Doctrinal differences, however, were too great, and it proved a vain attempt to join the forces of Calvinistic and Arminian Methodism.[2]

In spite of all this travelling, however, reading and preaching remained Rowland's priorities. One reproof administered by Rowland to Harris was his neglect of reading, especially the Bible. 'Brother Rowland owned he did depend much on the old Puritans, and I on my feelings', wrote Harris, and yet he acknowledged of Rowland that 'in his pulpit he is a second Paul', and even as 'a father of the Association'. Perhaps the most astute comment on Rowland came at the end of 1745 from William Williams: 'a strong pillar in the Church of God, a means to keep the Welsh Methodists from many errors'.[3]

Wise perception and sound grasp of biblical principles were needed to discern and regulate the work. It was easy for the leaders to mistake excitement for power, and equally it was easy for others to regard profound conviction of sin as emotional excess. A relative of Rowland's who visited Llangeitho in 1746, and availed himself of the opportunity to hear him preach, displays a total lack of discernment in these matters:

'I own I heard a pretty good discourse (as far as I could hear), delivered to a very large congregation. While he was performing divine service, the people seemed to behave quietly and somewhat

[1] HVP 111; xxxi. 25; Trefeca Letter 1935; HVL, 74; HH, 154; William Griffith, *Methodistiaeth Fore Môn*, 1955, tud. 50; *Evangelical Magazine*, 1814, p. 418; CH 1980, p. 36; xxxvi. 31; xxii. 105.
[2] vii. 31–4; xii. 57; Wesley Historical Society *Proceedings*, vol. v. p. 108; A. H. Williams, *Welsh Wesleyan Methodism*, 1935, p. 28.
[3] Diary 123 (June 28, 1746); 122 (April 10, 1746); STL i. 164; Diary 123 (June 27, 1746); xx. 134.

devoutly, but as they began to sing, I could hear a voice louder than all the rest crying out, "*Rhowch foliant*" (extol Him), and by-and-by another holloing "*Rhowch glod*" (give praise). By this conduct (being yet a mere prelude in comparison of what ensued), I concluded that these two persons might be seized with a fit of the lunacy or frenzy. But as soon as this solemn part of the service was over, Mr. Rowland made a long extempore prayer before his sermon, which prayer it seemed worked so upon most part of the audience, that some cried out in one corner, "*Rhowch glod*"; others in different parts of the church bawled out as loud as possibly they could, "*Bendigedig, rhowch foliant*" (Hosannah! give praise), and so on, that there was such a noise and confusion through the whole church that I had much ado, though I stood near the minister, to make sense of anything he said. His preaching again flung almost the whole society into the greatest agitation and confusion possible. Some cried, others laughed; the women pulled one another by the caps, embraced each other, capered like where there was any room, but the perfectionists continued as before their huzzas. By this time poor me began to be uneasy too, to see (I am sorry to say it) so much madness, so much irreverence in the house of God. . . . I am sorry I had no time to speak to Mr. Rowland upon this subject.'[1]

As an interpretation of events, the account lacks credibility because of its superficiality. There is no attempt to determine, even less to understand, the meaning of the outcries. The report is completely devoid of such concepts as awe at the majesty and holiness of God, the agonies wrought by deep conviction of sin, raptures of mind at the contemplation of Christ's love, invigorating views of Scripture promises, and the delights of God's forgiveness. It is the absence of such a theological framework which makes the critic's case far from convincing.

It was, of course, important to avoid making the physical manifestations an index of spiritual reality or power. This was so especially as similar scenes might have been witnessed in any number of places in South Wales in 1746. Harris bears witness to this in a letter to Whitefield in August: 'they continue under the ministry of Mr. Rowland, Mr. Davies, and Mr. Williams to be higher and higher to Mount Sion. Their united Hosannahs and Alleluias drown the ministers' voices in many places . . . there is a general revival, and our Saviour rides in triumph.'[2] However, it was important for the leaders to be aware of the realities, as well as the dangers, of the Spirit's powerful manifestations.

[1] i. 54.   [2] STL i. 195.

Unmistakable evidences of those realities were occurring almost daily. God was still owning Rowland's preaching in a mighty way, but there was no departure from the familiar pattern of a regular ministry of God's Word. The comments in Harris's diary are usually an index of the profit he continued to derive from the message preached. It was the message itself, rather than any spectacular effect it might have on their congregations, which provided the Methodists with zeal and vision to persevere in its propagation.

'April 20, 1747. Went to Groeswen to hear Brother Rowland. Had such love to dear Brother Rowland as I never had before.
August 9, 1748. Trefeca. This evening Mr. Rowland came here and preached on Rev. 11:16–17. Was made thankful for Brother Rowland in particular. He showed how the exercise of praise is the most heavenly part of worship, and that none but saints can do right; and they only when in God's presence and in some glory. Other graces they act when at a distance: patience, prayer, repentance, faith, etc. These only suit us in the world, but praise abides for ever. He raised the saints very high. They can't be damned. There is so much of God in them, and if they were to be cast into hell, they would quench the flames! When he mentioned the blood of Christ, was made thankful in heart for hearing of it.
Feb. 1, 1749. Errwd. Heard Mr. Rowland, preaching on Moses saved in the basket. Felt a oneness with him.'[1]

While the Welsh leaders were privileged to witness some of the most glorious works of God in the land, they were enabled in surprising measure to preserve the resulting spiritual harvest as well.

One means of safeguarding the fruit of the Revival adopted by them through their Association was to insist that the society members gave themselves to study. The usefulness of a catechism for this purpose was quickly recognised, and successive Association meetings decided that the societies avail themselves of this form of instruction. In 1747 the following resolution was agreed upon, and it remained the policy of the Association for some time:

'That the brethren should do all they can to stir up the people to a more diligent reading and searching of the Scriptures, and to inform themselves in all the practical principles of the Christian Religion, in order to set up catechising in our families and societies; and in order to help them that they should use all the help they can get from the

[1] Gomer M. Roberts, *Bywyd a Gwaith Peter Williams*, 1943, tud. 25; xxxix. 64; xli. 33.

Rev. Mr. Griffith Jones's Church Catechism, and the Assembly's Catechism, etc. till such time as the brethren shall draw up a Catechism.'[1]

The success of this decision depended on the literacy of individual members, and the skill of their teachers. For the former, Griffith Jones' Charity Schools proved invaluable. For the latter it was necessary to make special provision.

At the Builth Association in February 1749, therefore, it was 'agreed that as the brethren stand in need of improvement for their places and work, that till some more effective means be found, that such . . . should go . . . either two days in the week or a week in the month, to improve themselves in grammar, divinity, logic, philosophy, and all knowledge necessary to make them more useful'. For this purpose a centre was established for each county in South Wales, and ministers were appointed as instructors. Harris, too, on occasions shared his insights with them, 'keeping them from discouragement, showing how learning is like stairs going gradually up. If one looks at the top at once and strives to jump up, he'll never go, but if he looks at the first step, and so to the next, it will be easy'.[2] In the midst of so much consolidation, if the Welsh Methodists were to endure the storm which was soon to break upon them, they needed a wise counsellor and reliable leader. In Rowland they had both.

[1] l. 49. [2] li. 28; iv. 136–7.

'We must expect that the great enemy of this work will especially try his utmost with us. . . . Humility and self-diffidence and an entire dependence on our Lord Jesus Christ will be our best defence. Let us therefore maintain the strictest watch against spiritual pride, or being lifted up with extraordinary experience and comforts, and the high favours of heaven that any of us may have received. We had need, after such favours, in a special manner to keep a strict and jealous eye upon our own hearts.'

JONATHAN EDWARDS

Some brought Anti-trinitarian
Heresy, both dark and strange;
Holding God without the Persons,
First, Third, Second, yet no change;
Daniel then stood firm and solid,
Like a pillar, straight and strong;
Publicly withstanding falsehood,
Showing clearly what was wrong.

WILLIAM WILLIAMS
Elegy to Daniel Rowland

13. *Howel Davies, friend of Rowland and Whitefield, who laboured chiefly in Pembrokeshire. From* The Journal of the Historical Society of the Presbyterian Church of Wales, *Vol. vii, Frontispiece*

14. *A reputed portrait of Peter Williams, converted under Whitefield, itinerant preacher and Bible commentator. From* The Gospel Magazine, *1777. See pp. 229–330*

15. *Llwyn-y-berllan, in Carmarthenshire, location of the second Welsh 'Association', 1742, from an oil painting of 1896 by S. M. Broad in Calvinistic Methodist Archives, National Library of Wales. See p. 180*

16. *Watford, the mansion near Caerphilly where the first joint Welsh-English 'Association' was held in 1743. From Y Tadau Methodistaidd, Vol. i.194.* *See p. 213*

17. 'The First Association', at Watford in 1743, an imaginary painting showing from left to right John Cennick, Joseph Humphreys, John Powell, William Williams, George Whitefield (Moderator), Daniel Rowland, and Howel Harris. See p. 213

The New Weekly Miscellany.

By RICHARD HOOKER, of Doctors-Commons, L.L.B.

SATURDAY, October 31, 1741.

— — — — Facies non omnibus una,
Nec diversa tamen, quales decet esse sororum. Ovid.
Sed vetitum est adeò sceleri nihil. Ovid.

Mr Hooker,

MONG the many *Enthusiasts*, who call themselves *Methodists*, lately sprung up in several Parts of this Kingdom, one *Daniel Rowlands*, Curate of *Nantgwnlle* in the County of *Cardigan*, is not the least remarkable.

No sooner had it come to his Knowledge, that Mr *Whitefield*, by *extempore* Preaching, and by Holding unlawful Assemblies, and disorderly Meetings, had gain'd much Applause, and more Money, but without any Regard to Decency and Order, he rambles about the Country, Holding-forth to weak and ignorant People, tumultuously assembled, in private Houses, publick Tipling-Houses, Barns, Fields, &c. and without any Regard to his solemn Promise of Conformity to the *Liturgy* of the *Church of England*, omits his Prayers to give Room to his own *extempore* Effusions, which he judges to be more Devout and Edifying; and, in short, in Imitation of Mr *Whitefield*, sets up as some uncommon Reformer of the Age. But what should one talk of Promise, Decency, and Order to one, who makes such Gain of Godliness, and who is so weak, as to pride himself upon the empty Commendations of a giddy Multitude?

But as he has rais'd himself to a Degree of Esteem not inconsiderable among his ignorant Countrymen, methinks it would not be unacceptable to mention some, out of the many Arts and Methods he has made use of, to effectually engage their Attention. Among these, there is none he appears more assiduous in, than in Vilifying and Reviling his Brethren the neighbouring *Clergy*; dumb and greedy Dogs being the best Language he gives them; and a common Topick of his publick Harangues to the Populace is, that *they are a Set of lazy, indolent, greedy, carnally-minded and lukewarm People, and regardless of the Souls committed to their Charge.* When he has thus dress'd them in the most odious Colours, he expresses his Astonishment at the Figure they make; and out of his tender Concern for Religion, zealously prays, that *God would be pleas'd either to take them out of the World, or, at least, to remove them from whence they are.* Now as nothing strikes in more with the Prejudices, and approves itself more to the corrupt Inclinations of Mankind than this; so it serves not only to lessen Mens Esteem for, and to beget in their Minds a mean Opinion of the *Clergy*, but also naturally fixes Men's Eyes on himself, and sets him out as being the only zealous, disinterested, careful, and faithful Messenger *God Almighty* has. And that no Doubt of this might remain on their Minds, he publickly stiles himself a *Saint*, frequently taking Occasion to say, *This Saint that speaks to you.*

Another Method, that gains Attention, and which, by weak Minds, may be esteemed to carry the Face of an extraordinary Sanctity, is his Singing of *Psalms* or *Hymns* on the Road, when he is from home: As several loose and idle People always accompany him, these join in the *Chorus*; and that they may appear the more solemn, when they pass through a Village they cry out, *Who will follow Christ? Who will follow Christ?* In a late Ramble of his into *Pembrokeshire*, he had a white Flag carried before him, while his Companions were Singing of *Psalms* behind him; and by the Bye, as he is strongly suspected to have to do with more Women than his own Wife; so he seems not averse

to grant his Followers the like Indulgence; for when they are at too great a Distance to return home at Night, Men and Women lie promiscuously together in a Barn or Hayloft: And if any unbecoming Familiarity should happen in the Dark (and one can scarce avoid thinking some such Familiarity should not happen among People, that so affectionately kiss and embrace each other) yet it is no Sin in them.

Again, in his publick Discourses, when he finds the Audience don't groan and howl, he turns his Back upon them, telling them, they must unavoidably be damn'd, for that he sees no Signs of Repentance near them; and let them beware, left *God* should do, as he did, and turn his Back on them likewise; then follows an hideous Outcry.

Again, the private Assemblies, which are call'd religious Societies, and which he has instituted in several of the neighbouring Parishes, as they seem to have a View to further Religion, have likewise been very serviceable to promote his Interest: These Societies are held in the Night-time, and when they pray at them, they put out the Candles, and pray in the Dark. And further, he has prescribed his Followers a monthly Fast; and that they may appear indeed unto Men to fast, he takes them with him at Twelve o'Clock at Night into the Church, where they continue 'till Twelve the following Night.

In his first Setting out, he profess'd himself an *Arminian*, but upon hearing that Mr *Whitefield* affirm'd *Predestination, Election, and Reprobation,* he drop'd his old Friend, and strenuously maintained these, and whatever other Doctrines, right or wrong, he found Mr *Whitefield* affirm'd. When *Archbishop Tillotson* began to be run down, he immediately took it in Hand, and exclaimed against him, as one that *understood Christianity no better than Mahomet*; his Works were not to be endured; they were *Arminianism*; they belong'd to the Covenant of Works; and the like Stuff. The *Author of the Whole Duty of Man*, and his Works, underwent the same Fate and Treatment.

Upon Mr *Whitefield's* Going to *Georgia*, Mr *Wesley* was lifted to: His Doctrines of *sinless Perfection in this Life,* and that *whatever had not an Assurance of his Salvation, were in a State of Damnation*, our *Enthusiast* became a strenuous Asserter of. But when he heard, that Mr *Whitefield*, upon his Return from *Georgia,* condemn'd Mr *Wesley's* Doctrines of *Sinless Perfection*, &c. like a vile Weathercock, he wheels about, and now preaches down what he before preach'd up. But that I may not detain you from what is of greater Moment, I shall pass by several odd Expressions he has made use of in his *extempore* Harangues; such as, That *Christ will send a Horse from his own Coach to carry the Penitent to Heaven*; That *he is but a Dog to bait Christ's Sheep*; And that *Sinners, when they pray, ought to say, Our Father, which art in Hell, hallowed be thy Name,* &c. I shall pass by, I say, numberless such as these, in order to set before you some of the dismal Consequences of this Man's Proceedings. And here, the more immediate ones are Despair on the one Side, and Presumption on the other. When he tells his Hearers, that whoever has not a full *Assurance of his Salvation, is in a State of Damnation,* and that *they must live without Sin,* 'tis natural for People to imagine, that as 'tis impossible for them ever to arrive at such a State, so they may as well leave off all Thoughts of Doing what lies in their Power towards Attaining it, and to indulge Despair; and the great Number of Persons that now are, and from Time to Time have

been in Despair in this Neighbourhood, too manifestly testifies this. On the other Hand, those are Abundance puss'd up with spiritual Pride, boast of themselves, that they are in a *sinless State* and *sure of Salvation*; they despise all the Worship except such as are of their own Fraternity; peremptorily affirm, that *all that join with them, are in a State of Damnation.* What induces much to this, are the catechetical Questions put to each of them by their Teacher; particularly, *How long can you live without Sinning? Can you live a Day? Can you live a Week?* So that, when that, from the Nature of the Question, which imply they can live some Time without Sinning; and what from his Approbation of several Answers they respectively make, such an Hour, a Day, a Week, &c. they are led to fancy, they may live without Sinning as long as they please. While in Church, they cry aloud, at the End of every Petition in our Great Reformer's *extempore* Effusions; when they come out, they fall down in the Church-yard and work up their Bodies into violent Agitations, sometimes laughing, sometimes weeping; as esteem themselves perfect laugh and rejoice with them, saying, *So the primitive Christians us'd to do.* I shall next observe to you, how the aforemention'd Societies are manag'd: You must know then, they are held in the Night-time, and he set Number of Overseers appointed over them, under Pretence of keeping them in order: Members pray and exhort alternately, as they inwardly moved thereto; but it sometimes happens, that 'tis not in the Power of either of them (as they say) to pray or to exhort; this they attribute to the Absence of the Spirit, or because the Sins of some that are present; and that may not remain long in Suspence, a discerning Power is communicated to one or other of them to point out the sinful Person, whom immediately they turn out. When the Spirit thus deserts them they have no Power to pray, until he is pacify'd the Expulsion of the sinful Person. And so effectious is the Itch of Exhorting, that no so one of them can scarce read, but he catches Distemper, and sets up for a publick Exhorter. Some of them boast they can tell, whose Prayers are accepted, and whose not; and by Privilege this pretended Gift, interrupt others, and compel them to desist, because they know their Prayers are not accepted. 'Tis a Rule in these Societies that each Member should, every Time they meet, lay something in the Overseers Hands (it is pretended) towards charitable Uses; and to encourage People to come in, it was industriously spread about, that Mr *Whitefield* had promised pay the Debts of all such, as will become Methodists, provided the Society to which the independent Person is a Member, makes up to him such a ticular Sum first. Several indigent People by this Means been deluded to contribute the Remainder they had, and are now about the Country a Begging. At these Societies the Women pray as well as the Men, and both of them cry out in their Prayers, *There is Christ; there is he; Don't you see him? Oh! I wish I catch him, and embrace him!* At other Times while one is a praying, another is laughing; howl and beat their Hands together; others weeping and groaning; and others are grovelling on the Ground in a Swoon, making various Fits of antick Postures; then they laugh out at once, and continue laughing for about a Quarter of an Hour; then Men and Women jump to another, and promiscuously embrace, hug, kiss each other; one Woman's Husband is another Man's Wife; and they call this *Rece—*

Price TWO-PENCE.

19. *George Whitefield preaching at Lurgan, Northern Ireland, in 1751. From a gouache on paper by William Miller at the Ulster Museum. See pp. 286–7*

20. *The Countess of Huntingdon's College at Trefeca. From Y Tadau Methodistaidd, Vol. i.87. See p. 336*

21. *Nathaniel Rowland, one of Daniel's sons, and friend of the Countess of Huntingdon. From* The Gospel Magazine, *1799. See pp. 330–31*

22. *David Jones, whose powerful ministry at Llangan in Glamorganshire from 1767 to 1810 helped establish Calvinistic Methodism in the county. From* The Evangelical Magazine, *1807. See pp. 328–30*

23. *Thomas Charles, 'of Bala', second-generation Welsh Methodist converted under Rowland's ministry. From an oil painting in Calvinistic Methodist Archives, National Library of Wales. See pp. 331–3*

24. *Thomas Jones, 'of Denbigh', influenced by Rowland's preaching in North Wales, Methodist leader and writer. From National Library of Wales Castell Gorfod Collection. See pp. 338–9*

EIGHT
SERMONS
ON
PRACTICAL SUBJECTS,
PREACHED AT THE
New Church in Langeitho,
SOUTH WALES;

BY THE

Rev. Mr. DANIEL ROWLAND:

AND NOW

Attempted to be Translated from the
Original British.

Si Christum discis, nihil est si cætera nescis;
Si Christum nescis, nihil est si cætera discis.

THE SECOND EDITION.

LONDON:

PRINTED for the EDITOR; (THOMAS DAVIES, near
Haverfordwest, South Wales) by THOMAS PARKER,
Jewin-Street; and Sold by Mr. WATTS, Bookseller,
Mr. JONES, No. 8, Eyre-Street, Cold Bath Fields,
at the TABERNACLE HOUSE, Upper Moorfields; and
in most Towns in England and WALES.

(PRICE TWO SHILLINGS.)

25. Title-page of Rowland's
Three Sermons in Welsh,
describing him as 'Chaplain to the
Duke of Leinster'.
See pp. 336, 345

26. Title-page of Rowland's
Eight Sermons (1778), the first
edition of which had appeared

TAIR
PREGETH,
Ar y TESTUNAU canlynol:

I. Luc xv. 5. Ac wedi iddo ei chael, efe a'i
dyd hi ar ei Yfgwyddau ei hun yn llawen.

II. Ioan v. 6, &c. Yr Iefu pan welodd hwn yn
gorwedd, a gwybod ei fod effelly yn hir o am
fer bellach, a ddywedodd wrtho, A fynnu di
dy wneuthur yn iach?

III. Salm lxv. 5. Attebi i ni trwy Beibau
ofnadwy yn dy Gyfiawnder.

A bregethwyd yn ddiweddar
Gan y Parchedig DANIEL ROWLAND,
Gweinidog yr Efengyl yn Llangeitho,
A Chaplain i'r Duke o Leinfter.

Gloria mea Chriftus.

CAERFYRDDIN,
ARGRAFFWYD GAN I. ROSS, TROS THO'. DAVIES
O SIR BENFRO. 1775.
[PRIS CHWE-CHEINIOG.]

25

The Disruption

Keeping the work from floundering on the rocks of counterfeit experiences, conflicting personalities, and doctrinal deviation had never been easy. The difficulties were, of course, compounded by criticism and opposition from without. Pride and ambition, working within in subtle and hidden ways, also threaten the unity of God's people and the progress of God's work. Evidence of this danger, undetected at the time, had surfaced as early as 1743. By his own confession, in that year Harris was increasingly absorbed with the subject of the divine nature of Christ. A tract called *A Sling and a Stone* affected him profoundly: 'I now was brought to see more and more wonders of His infinite Incarnation, Life, Blood, Death, and Resurrection.' He was now convinced that 'every truth, when revealed by the Spirit, is practical, and will have its proper influence on the soul by humbling the sinner and exalting the Saviour'. He spoke of the impression this made on his soul: 'It increased my faith, and my love became more habitual, my joy more solid, my resignation more entire, my spirit more smooth and quiet, and more bowels of compassion and mercy towards poor sinners. . . . What I saw and understand in other Scriptures before, I came now to see a much greater depth and more glory in them.'[1]

So far so good; problems arose, however, when Harris began to make such understanding and experiences the measure of maturity, or even the test of spiritual life in others. At this point he failed also to allow for the deep mysteries of the faith, and sadly confused things which differ. By giving almost exclusive prominence to one aspect of the truth he departed from the balance of 'the whole counsel of God', and this ultimately proved his near-undoing. During the rest of the 'forties, episodes of doctrinal lapses, and

[1] *A Brief Account of the Life of Howell Harris*, 1791, pp. 59, 60.

personality clashes with his fellow-workers, became increasingly frequent and serious.

Rowland was widely regarded as the only one who could effectively neutralise Harris's aberrations. Thomas James, one of the Glamorganshire exhorters, wrote to the Association in October 1744:

'Persecution seems to be much abated, but we still need to watch and pray. His [Satan's] next attempt will be perhaps under the mask of religion. Therefore we need to give heed to Brother Rowland's observation, "Keep close to the work", and take to us the whole armour of God. We have great cause to fear the wolf in sheep's clothing; the cloven foot of heresies will be very apt to attempt to tread upon the sacred ground of God's vineyard, the little foxes may creep in unawares; but this will avail him nothing, Jesus reigns. . . . The societies are in a flame in some places, and others are growing gradually in the Lord. Some that have been deadish begin to recover their strength; some are now walking in thick darkness, but groaning for the Sun of Righteousness to arise after a tedious night of desertion. Some few there are endeavouring to reconcile Christ and self, Christ and the world, and not knowing which to choose; but I hope they will choose the better part, and leave all and follow Him fully. Indeed there are many can experimentally rejoice in God their Saviour, and have no confidence in the flesh, daily thirsting after the full enjoyment of God.'[1]

The Association of October 1744 proved decisive for Welsh Methodism. Differences between Rowland and Harris had not been as public or alarming before. Given Harris's intransigence in doctrine and temperament, division could hardly be avoided.

The Association had started with a sermon by Rowland on Matthew 16:23, 'Get thee behind me, Satan.' In it Rowland sounded a note of warning about 'pride in gifts and pride in graces':

'The danger of pride of gifts: 1. they are not given for our own use, but for the use of others. . . . 2. where there are many gifts there is but little grace; the growth of these generally hinders the growth of the other; 3. you are not anything better in God's sight for all your gifts, any more than if you had none of them. God only looks on faith; 4. Gifts are only given on condition, and may be taken away and often are, but grace is never taken away; 5. gifts expose us much to temptations, as Joseph's coat.'

Rowland then dwelt on 'the nature and danger of pride of grace and

[1] liii. 50–1.

how God is against all pride, and nothing done in pride will prosper'. Whatever removes our trust from Christ, even though it is our grace, amounts to unbelief.

During the Association meetings temperamental and doctrinal differences between Rowland and Harris widened. This open disagreement between them caused much concern. Richard Tibbott was distressed and disgusted enough to write afterwards to the leaders in the strongest terms:

'What was particularly blameworthy in our Association was the carnal attitude and superficial spirit, the idle, fruitless words, and the trivial talk, which gave rise to argument and dissension, and resulted in our neglecting that work for which we had met, and which was far more necessary and important. We therefore wasted our time, and instead of strengthening each others' arms, we weakened and discouraged each other with controversy, especially when Mr. Rowland and Mr. Harris disagreed, the chief pillars of our fellowship.'

Rowland was further censured by Tibbott for a past instance of levity, one word of Rowland's on that particular occasion causing much offence. Rowland and Harris together were blamed for the way they had behaved towards each other, 'one in giving, the other in receiving admonition'.[1] As events were to prove, both leaders had still a great deal to learn in the school of grace.

Harris was finding confirmation for his doctrinal emphasis, significantly so, during his time in London at the end of 1744. With the free flow of movement between Moravian and Methodist in London at the time, Harris was caught up in the ferment of ideas and doctrines which jostled for primacy and influence. On December 3 he went to hear some Moravian letters being read. They were 'about experience of the Blood of Christ, how that is all', and Harris 'saw them gone before me far in faith and strength and the divine life'. John Cennick also added to his dissatisfaction: 'Many expressions I could not agree with, but as he exalted Christ, my soul loved him.' In retrospect he referred to this London experience as 'the glory of our Saviour breaking forth among the people, and many rising out of the law to see the glory of God in the face of Jesus Christ; the completeness of the Atonement, with the mystery and glory of His precious Blood'.[2] When he returned to Wales on December 30,

[1] MTU, 85–91; cf. HH Diary 113, s.v. October 2, 1744.
[2] HVL, 60; *A Brief Account*, pp. 60, 62.

1744, Harris was not quite the same man. There was a greater dogmatism, an impatience, a censoriousness which before had erupted on occasions but now became his more settled frame.

With the passing of time, Harris found himself becoming more and more isolated from his brethren on this issue. In January 1745 he was reading *A Sling and a Stone* once more, with much the same effect. Throughout the year he used expressions like 'the Blood of God' quite indiscriminately. 'As my spirit increased more and more in beholding the glory of that God-man . . . I began to find great and strong opposition to my preaching his Godhead and death, etc. Especially in Wales this opposition gained ground, and began to be openly opposed.'[1] This was hardly surprising. The looseness of Harris's expressions implied a confusion, rather than a trinity of Persons in the Godhead, and combined with an uncompromising manner, this created friction in the areas of public teaching and private relationships.

At the same time, tendencies that had been latent in Harris gradually emerged in a public way. He charged Rowland with levity and legalism, unscriptural expressions relating to Christ's person and death, impatience with the reproof of others, an uncharitable judgment of the spiritual state of some and defence of error in others; and errors of judgment in personal relationships.

Writing in 1750, Harris said of the division which had taken place among the Welsh Methodists, 'This separation began four years ago in Mr. Rowland at Bristol, and working underhand ever since.' In the *Brief Account* of his life, Harris traces developments as he saw them:

'About the year 1746, I saw another spirit of sifting creeping into the work, which was yet different from that which had been before, viz. the spirit of levity, pride, foolish-jesting, unwatchfulness, and carnal rejoicing. . . . The year following, the enmity grew stronger against the preaching of God's humiliation and death. . . . Towards the end of the year 1749, I went to London, and in January 1750, I parted with my friends and Brethren there, imploring them to attend to the Lord only, and to preach his Godhead and death with power, to the hearts of the hearers, as the only true foundation to build upon. In my coming down to Wales . . . a necessity was laid upon me to lift up my voice like a trumpet to all professors to examine their profession, and to make a close search in what the foundation of their religion

[1] Diary 115B, s.v. January 22, 1745; e.g. xxxvii. 22 (January 16); HMGC i. 327 (January 17); TM i. 284 (January 18); CMHO, 103 (April 3), 114 (April 24), 126 (July 31).

and faith was seated; whether in the outward man, called the flesh or nature, or whether it had indeed penetrated to the inward man, called the heart or spirit? . . . I went on thus some years through Wales, bearing my testimony to these truths, in the face of carnal professors, Arians, and Socinians, who all railed against me.'[1]

To reprove Rowland and Whitefield for their 'levity' became a frequent and favourite practice on Harris's part during the late 1740's. Increasingly, too, he became critical of their doctrine as 'legal in some expressions', and for being 'contemptible of the Blood' [that is, Harris's usage of the phrase], and particularly sensitive to their denunciation of Antinomianism.[2]

The Neath Association of October 1746 was particularly stormy and acrimonious.

'They agreed at an Association they had together for Mr. Rowland to take my place, and to settle who to go out and where to send all. . . . Am here again called Antinomian and Moravian. When they said how formerly when any jars would arise between me and Brother Rowland, I would cry and fall on his neck, and take his words, and so it would be over, but now it was not so, I was more stiff. . . . As I am called so much to England I was free to resign my place to Brother Rowland, but could not without sinning against the Lord give him any authority over my ministry so as to order me where to go or how to preach.'

There were charges and counter-charges: 'Brother Rowland laboured to declare me a changeling, self-contradicting and a liar and Antinomian. . . . I said I did not know of anything I opposed him in unless it was in reproving his licentiousness in eating, drinking, laughing, beating etc. withal, I know I am by far the worse.' As to suspicions of Harris's orthodoxy, he said, 'When they charged me with worshipping the Blood of Christ, I said I did not as separate from Him but as part of Him, how the propriety of the one nature is often reckoned to the other, that God bled and died because the man that suffered was God.' At this point Harris was departing from the sound, accepted theological usage of phrases relating to the death of Christ. As Edward Morgan says in his biography of Harris, 'He did not sufficiently bear in mind that the divine and human natures of Christ were perfectly distinct. It is true that they are so united, that what was done by the one for man's salvation, was attributed to the

[1] Diary 145, s.v. June 22, 1750; *A Brief Account*, 62, ff.
[2] HVL, 8; HVP, 138.

other, as when we read of "the blood of God", Acts 20:28.' Harris, regrettably, was going further than this communication of attributes, and the idea conveyed by his language was that God the Father had suffered in the Son, thereby advocating the related heresies of Patripassianism and Sabellianism.[1]

These ideas were widely propagated by Harris, and they prompted the publication by the Methodist leaders of a brief but weighty theological treatise under Rowland's name, *Ymddiddan rhwng Methodist Uniongred ac un Camsyniol* (Dialogue between an Orthodox and an Erroneous Methodist). The two debaters in the book obviously represented Rowland and Harris. Certainly this is how Harris saw it when he first read the book in November 1750: 'I saw dear Brother Rowland's charge against me as holding four heresies; denying the term "Person"; holding that the Father suffered; and that God suffered and died; and that Christ's body is everywhere.' Harris's conscience acquitted him, he was unrepentant, and continued to use the same phrases as before. A second edition was called for almost immediately, and a third edition was issued in 1792 'to make known the orthodox views of the fathers, labourers, and helpers at the Association's beginning, especially those of the Rev. Mr. Daniel Rowland'.

In this brief work Harris is represented as charging his opponents with Arianism, the heresy which denied the eternity of Christ, and therefore His equality with God. Rowland defends the usage of 'Person' by appealing to Scripture [Hebrews 1:3, among others]. To the question, 'Do you believe that God died?', Rowland replies, 'God is a Spirit, without body, parts, or sufferings, and so He cannot suffer or die. He is called the immortal God, and therefore cannot die.' To explain the death of Christ, Rowland first refers to His one Divine Person in two distinct, unmixed natures, human and Divine. In His human nature He could suffer and die; by virtue of the two natures being united in the One Person, His death has infinite worth to make satisfaction for man's sin before God's justice. Harris erred in failing to distinguish the two natures in Christ and seeing their respective properties. Rowland's faith confesses 'that the union of two natures in one Person remains, so that our Lord was God-man in the womb, God-man on the cross, God-man in the grave'. Ultimately, Harris

[1] xxxi. 88–93; HH, 188. For a discussion of the rupture of Welsh Methodism, see Alun Wyn Owen, 'Howell Harris and the Trevecka Family' in xliv. 2–10; and in HMGC i. Pennod ix.

takes refuge in a rejection of book-knowledge and a retreat to the claims of a special revelation. Rowland concluded: 'I appeal to you once more, keep within the limits of Truth. I advise you to read books, rather than burn them, especially the best of all books, the Bible. Add to this much prayer, and then I trust, you may be delivered from the pride . . . and rash spirit which now rules you.'[1]

Another stumbling-block to Harris's credibility at this time was his defence of James Beaumont, the mid-Wales exhorter. Beaumont had been accepted by the Association in 1743, but by 1748 he was dabbling with Antinomian and Moravian errors. A complaint was made that he, with others, taught that 'if a man presses Sanctification or the marks . . . of the Spirit, then these they call "knick-knacks", or "by the way". Only simple believing, no duties, commands, etc. will be allowed of, no growth in grace etc.' In 1744 Harris had led the Association in the expulsion of one who held Antinomian principles. During 1748, however, his opposition to this heresy was noticeably muted. A comment in his diary for February reveals how he admired Beaumont's emphasis: 'Brother Beaumont goes before [that is, leads] in seeing the oneness in the Godhead, etc., and I am sent after him to soften, moderate, mollify.' Both Harris and Beaumont spent part of the summer together in London, during which time Harris reproved Beaumont of pride, but he seems to have been silent as to his principles. Subsequently, when Beaumont appeared before the Association early in 1749, Harris argued in his favour.

This may have been the reason for the appearance about 1750 of *Ymddiddan rhwng Methodist ac Antinomian* (Dialogue between a Methodist and an Antinomian). Both its timing and title suggest that it was the work of Rowland and his supporters. At the very Association that Beaumont was admitted as 'Public Exhorter', he had been impressed by Rowland's sermon on Romans 8:1, 'There is therefore now no condemnation to them which are in Christ Jesus, who walk not after the flesh but after the Spirit.' In the sermon, Rowland had mentioned how the doctrine of justification by faith without works was open to abuse and misunderstanding. He also

---

[1] xxviii. 50; *Ymddiddan . . .* is in Morris Davies, *Deuddeg Pregeth*, tt. 332–9. For a discussion of Patripassianism, Sabellianism, and Arianism see Herman Bavinck, *The Doctrine of God*, 1977, pp. 285–96; and in Welsh, John Gwili Jenkins, *Hanfod Duw a Pherson Crist*, 1931, Pennod VI–VIII. See also John Gill, *Treatise on the Doctrine of the Trinity*, published in 1731.

spoke of the inseparable evidences in those who had been justified by God's grace: they neither live in sin, nor have pleasure in it; they 'walk in the Spirit', and the signs of that walk are to be found in their lives. The pamphlet against Antinomianism might well have been an amplification of that very sermon. It also set out faith as an active principle implanted in the believer by the Holy Spirit, and working a personal and progressive sanctification. By these means Welsh Methodism preserved the doctrinal balance of the societies against the sad deviation of Harris and others on this crucial issue, so much so that Whitefield felt that 'the Welsh brethren continue steady'.[1] Sadly, however, they would have to fight the battle again another day.

On these matters of discernment and discipline Harris was being increasingly distanced from his brethren. His approach was entirely subjective, while they insisted on objective criteria for determining a person's spiritual standing. Harris writes, 'When the brethren (Rowland and Williams) offered to cast out the Spirit's light, and that we had no rule to go by but outward fruits to cast people out, I insisted on it that there is an eye in the body and spiritual light, and the spiritual man judges, according to his measure, all things.'

Richard Tibbott considered both sides to be at fault, and later shared his sentiments with Harris. While he acknowledged Harris's reproof of the ministerial brethren as timely and necessary, he also intimated that Harris had been too dogmatic about some things. Tibbott's chief complaint against him, however, was on this very issue of subjective judgment. It resulted, he said, in a failure 'to distinguish between people and their opinions. There is some bad in good men, but it is wrong to regard good men as bad men on account of their faults.' He said further, that there were other serious consequences to Harris's harsh, hasty judgment:

'You failed to distinguish between some and others of those you opposed, and accused all indiscriminately. You took things to extremes against those you withstood, their persons and actions, depicting them as the blackest rebels. . . . You failed to use all the means for their recovery, and by dealing harshly with them as enemies, you hardened them in their faults; you concentrated too

[1] For Beaumont see DWB; Trefeca Letter 1836; xlviii. 76; HVP, 142; HVL, 208, 210; xxxi. 115; xli. 34; Derec Llwyd Morgan, *Y Diwygiad Mawr*, 1981, tud. 197; TM i. 198; GW ii. 79; cf. also R. T. Jenkins, 'The Moravian Brethren in North Wales' in *Y Cymmrodor*, xlv. pp. 38–41.

much on words at the expense of sense and substance. . . . You were too hasty in taking suspicion for fact.'

This led to direct confrontation between the leaders, Harris expelling some from the society according to his subjective principle, Rowland admitting them as before on the grounds of his more objective assessment of their condition. 'I see', said Harris, 'there is one thing yet to be settled of the Lord which is dark to me till Brother Rowland is heartily united. When I turn out of the society, where I feel I have authority, much of the reproof is lost by his keeping them in the Sacrament afterward.'[1] This confused state of affairs could not long continue. Almost exactly a year later, on May 9, 1750, Rowland and Harris were together at an Association for the last time for many years.

Another matter involving Harris also contributed to the disruption of Welsh Methodism. From the summer of 1749 one of the North Wales converts, Mrs Sidney Griffith, had been travelling with Harris on many of his journeys, with his wife's knowledge if not with her approval. She had come under Gospel influences through the preaching of Peter Williams in 1747, and had been at the Association when Beaumont's teachings were discussed. Her husband, William Griffith, was a country squire whose religious convictions fell far short of those of his wife. Harris came to regard her spiritual insights as having prophetic significance for him and for his ministry: 'I find a total change since I met Mrs. Griffith, raised to new life with God in everything; knowing none after the flesh, my dear wife being given me alone of all the daughters of Eve for my wife, feeling her placed in her place in my soul. Mrs. Griffith being my nearest counsellor friend, and Brother Beaumont as the nearest brother and fellow labourer.' When Harris married Anne Williams on June 18, 1744, she became his travelling companion whenever possible, and certainly his spiritual confidant. At that time, too, Rowland had been his 'nearest brother'. Now both had been replaced: the break with Rowland was an unworthy step and caused dismay, the relationship with Mrs Griffith was a grave error of judgment and gave considerable offence.

Many sought to reprove him for his folly, Rowland and Whitefield among them. It is highly significant that, throughout the protracted controversy, Whitefield supported Rowland. In the absence of

[1] HVP, 139; MTU, 210–11; HVL, 181.

Rowland's manuscripts, the matter has to be weighed in the light of Harris's reactions. As one who knew both protagonists intimately, and lived through the trauma of the disagreement between them, Whitefield's stance is important. He had every opportunity at the time to gauge personal attitude as well as doctrinal orthodoxy. His consistent agreement with Rowland must carry great weight in apportioning blame. As far as Whitefield was concerned, that clearly lay with Harris.

Thus, in August 1751, while Harris was in London, as on other occasions, Whitefield 'said that he did not approve of Madam Griffith being with me, that it was contrary to God's Word, and spoke with great authority in his spirit. I told him his speaking and acting with such authority, when he knew he had none from God or man, was not right, and that though I am a great sinner, her being with me is not among my sins, that I act in it out of conscience toward God.' This betrayed an attitude of self-justification in Harris, and a sad abdication of responsibility to God's Word and God's people. It also displayed a naïve ignorance of human nature, both his own and that of his wife: 'I took Madam Griffith from the Lord in the spirit, and not outwardly; the whole matter was a matter in the spirit out of and above nature, and did not interfere with any tie of nature'.[1] In effect, Harris was laying claim to a super-spirituality which none of them possessed. By this lack of submission to God's Word and ordinances Harris put the whole of the Welsh Methodist movement at risk. It would take several years to repair the breach.

Matters moved rapidly in 1750 to that conclusion. Following the Llanidloes Association of May 9, 'Rowland's people' and 'Harris's people' went their separate ways. Rowland had the advantage that such buildings as were already available for the societies usually included his name as one of the Trustees, and Whitefield supported him in this by writing a letter to Marmaduke Gwynne for the use of the House at Builth.

During one of their debates, Rowland had made it clear that he had no ambitions to be organiser of the work. In this respect he admired Harris's gifts. He had only one reservation about Harris's leadership: all too often he jettisoned his reason in favour of the

[1] Gomer M. Roberts, *Portread o Ddiwygiwr*, 1969, tud. 112; HVL, 235, 14, 17. For a discussion in Welsh of Mrs Griffith's part in the Separation, see Gomer M. Roberts, *ib.* (Pennod IX); and Alun Wyn Owen in HMGC i. 334–53.

impulse of the moment. Still, Rowland recognised that the time had come when the work must be preserved, and, with the support of the other leading ministers, a meeting was arranged for that purpose in Llantrisant on July 4, 1750. Four ministers, seven public exhorters, and four private exhorters attended. Harris's dictatorial attitude, however, soon lost him considerable support, and gradually Welsh Methodism rallied behind Rowland. It seems likely that Peter Williams acted as intermediary between the two parties for a while, but nothing came of his efforts to keep them together.

By the middle of August 1750 Harris had received a request from Rowland's Association for the return of moneys to be used for Methodist purposes. Harris, for his part, hesitated to respond, being reluctant to concede that Welsh Methodism lay with Rowland, rather than with himself. Of twenty causes of the Disruption listed by Harris afterwards, most of them, significantly, had to do with Harris's authority. Two of them summarised the issue: 'My spiritual light in private and preaching even had on them become a burden, and they called me a Pope, and trampled on my authority. They had also left the teaching of the Spirit to lean on and study books.'[1] His brethren, however, acted on a different principle. No work of God, however ecstatic its experiences or impressive its progress, can survive at the expense of the Word of God.

An indication of this is the fact that Rowland included, at the end of his pamphlet against Harris, Articles 1, 2, and 4 of the Thirty-nine Articles. These were confessional statements on the Trinity, the Incarnation, and the Resurrection, fundamental doctrines of the Christian Faith. Deviation from these would have reduced Welsh Methodism to a visionary sect with its own amorphous mixture of individualism and extremism. Most basic of all was Harris's unconscious elevation of his own authority above that of Scripture, whether in matters of belief or behaviour. There is no question about Harris's sincerity and intensity. His doctrinal imbalance, his authoritarian impatience, his reliance on 'prophetic' utterances, and his indifference to the reproach brought upon the cause of God by his unwise relationship with Mrs Griffith: all these were ultimately a refusal to bow to the authority of God's Word. God rules His people by His Word, and that Word has to be applied without respect of persons, and in every area of life. No-one is exempt from this

[1] STL ii. 47–8, 46–7; Gomer M. Roberts, *Bywyd a Gwaith Peter Williams*, tud. 44; MTU, 175; HVP, 182.

principle, and leaders are to obey it above all others. For the Welsh Methodists this was a necessary lesson to learn. In spite of the defection of friends and the taunts of enemies, Rowland was the one who faithfully led those who persevered in applying it to the people and teaching of the Great Awakening in Wales.

'Tears and prayers are our weapons.'

JOHN CALVIN

'In a clock there are several wheels, which run counter to one another; some move slowly, and others whirl about with great velocity; yet all unite in keeping the clock in motion, and contribute their share to make it a true index of the flight of time. So is every event, however opposite it may seem, disposed by the secret, impelling hand of God, to promote His glory, and to further the salvation of His chosen.

DANIEL ROWLAND
in a sermon on Hebrews 1:9

26

Testimonies from the 1750's

The most immediate effect of division among the Welsh Methodists was polarisation. People inevitably apportioned blame to one or other of the leaders and took sides. Some of the Methodist societies availed themselves of the prevailing confusion to turn to the Dissenters.[1] Rowland laboured on, with Harris torn between loyalty and jealousy towards him. From this time the reports that Harris received of the progress of the Gospel beyond his own sphere were often distorted by prejudicial party spirit. Thus, at the beginning of 1751 Harris 'heard that poor Brother Rowland goes on triumphing, opposing and blaspheming with Davies too'. Harris was in Carmarthenshire at the time, and was severe in his denunciation of the 'professors [that is, those who professed faith], how they were never awakened', a deliberate rebuke to those who owned allegiance to his former colleague. With as much vehemence Harris, when he heard in June 'of Rowland being near dying', felt 'vast love to him, and was willing to give' his life for him. In December Harris was pleased to note that Rowland was in the congregation on two occasions when he was speaking in Pembrokeshire, even though they made no personal contact.[2]

The plain fact is, that while Rowland's labours in preaching, organising and instructing the societies, maintained their momentum, Harris was gradually losing his vision and authority. Throughout 1751 he was trying to secure the allegiance of the societies for himself and his party, but his unorthodox views and his dictatorial attitude alienated many. In October 1751 he set out for his last journey north, but his preaching was defensive in tone and dwelt much on the themes of suffering and death. He still found time to pray for Rowland, and in March the following year he preached

[1] xxxii. 27; cf. HMGC i. 388, ff.
[2] HVP, 191, 193, 205; MTU, 213.

for over two hours to some thousands of 'Rowland's people' at Llanddewibrefi.[1] A three-week visit to London followed, but when he came home in May, he was a sick man. In July Harris did not think it likely that he would 'go about any more', adding, 'I think my work is done.' The final token of the withdrawal of the evangelist from his labours was that he gave his horse away on December 1, 1752. For the next seven years he supervised an agricultural community at Trefeca, adding to the buildings, setting up a printing press, and organising its spiritual life with strict discipline. During that time his Methodist friends visited him from time to time for different reasons. After one such visit in January 1755, Charles Wesley sent a poetic appeal for Harris's return to evangelism:

> Awake, old soldier! – to the fight half-won,
> And put thy strength and put thine armour on!
> Nor dream thyself a vessel cast aside,
> Broken by stubborn will, and marred by pride.
> Most proud, self-willed, and wrathful as thou art,
> Yet God hath surely seen thy simple heart . . .
> If thou art Harris still, – awake, arise,
> Renew the fight, re-labour up the skies.

When John Wesley visited him in March of the following year, Harris told him 'he preached till he could preach no longer, his constitution being entirely broken'. Shortly afterwards John wrote him a letter, and he, too, warned him against self-will.[2] William Williams probably expressed the sentiments of most of the leaders about Trefeca when he asked in his elegy to Harris many years later:

> Why seek shelter in a castle?
> Or a cave that man devised?
> Why forget the very many
> To the fold of Christ you led?

[1] xxx. 2–18, 73; HVP, 214; xxx. 77; MTU, 217–18.
[2] HVL, 218, 222, f.; Diary 159, s.v. July 5, 1752; HVL, 272; HMGC i. 393; *John Wesley's Journal*, iv. 153; Trefeca Letter 2827b. For the Trefeca Community see HVL, 266–80; Alun Wyn Owen, unpublished M.A. Thesis (Wales), 'A Study of Howell Harris and the Trevecka Family (1752–1760)', and in xliv. 2–13; Eifion Evans, *Howel Harris, Evangelist*, pp. 58–9; and in Welsh, HMGC i. Pennod X. The Trefeca Printing Press was bought in 1753, see iv. 24–6 and Ifano Jones. *A History of Printing and Printers in Wales to 1810*, 1925, p. 76.

Harris saw things differently. As the building progressed at Trefeca he compared it to the 'Inn mentioned in the Parable of the Samaritan. This was an Inn, and till the Awakening becomes general, the Lord would send such as are wounded here, and I must receive them and go to Him for work for them, as He ordains that as the means for maintaining them'.[1] Even Harris's sympathisers had misgivings with this arrangement. Richard Tibbott wrote to Harris in November 1752 with that very clear message:

'All our accusations against the ministers for being legalistic, leading the people to bondage, leaving them in the wilderness, and turning men's eyes from Christ to themselves, can now be turned on you and those who are with you. . . . The whole country has been filled with prejudice against religion on account of our heavy, unevangelical controversies, which are as contrary to the Gospel as darkness to light, and depth to height. . . . Don't give up the land or professors until God has given them up. . . . You must listen, and look around from your tower, whether there is any voice from heaven in this, and do what is right before the day has passed. It would be quite contrary for you to let those souls die that you should be nourishing, instead of arguing. You are as though you have excommunicated yourself from the work. . . . Beware lest that spirit which you complain of as lacking in others, should be lacking in you also. Follow after it always, and let it not be too hard for you to turn back each step that you have followed another spirit.'[2]

With such constraints in their hearts, men like Tibbott would have found the appeal of Rowland's persistence in the work hard to resist. But there was no response from Harris, and the responsibility for extending the work of the Gospel in Wales was borne for the next decade by Rowland and his 'people'.

One positive gain from the 'Disruption' was its tendency to produce a clearer definition of Welsh Methodism. It was seen to be Trinitarian in doctrine and moral in practice. Its teachings on the way of salvation were manifestly in agreement with the Thirty-nine Articles of the Church of England. Justification by faith was not the door to Antinomian excesses. Vigorous insistence on a careful, worthy profession of the Gospel under accepted norms of discipline tolerated no deviation, even on the part of the most distinguished leader. Mutual submission to one another in close fellowship was regarded as obligatory among these 'Society People'. Their very

[1] CYN i. 494; HVL, 268.   [2] MTU, 225–9.

human failures even served to reinforce their teaching on the sinful corruption of the human heart and the resulting need for the sovereign and free grace of God. Amid the dismal set-back of Harris's withdrawal, these factors were definite assets in the over-all situation, not easy to quantify, but assets nonetheless.

Another encouraging aspect concerned the nature of the work. This had not changed, though the success which attended it fluctuated from time to time. The ministry of God's Word was still paramount, and still, on occasions, extraordinarily powerful. Consolidation was an urgent priority at this stage, and for this the Welsh brethren had the help of Whitefield. During the fifties Wales was regularly included in his 'rounds', usually for a two or three weeks' 'circuit'. This gave the Welsh work cohesion, as also did his published works. Welsh and English Calvinistic Methodism were seen as one movement, a readily identified piety which centred on the doctrines of grace propagated in the life and power of the Holy Spirit.

Whitefield's initial reaction to the Welsh divisions was one of caution. 'I would gladly fly to Wales', he had said in September 1750, 'but perhaps my coming had better be deferred to the cool of the day. Let us not fear. This storm will blow over.' Rowland visited Bristol the following April 'on a visit to Lady Huntingdon'. Whitefield was also in Bristol at the time, and they preached together in the open-air to vast crowds. The Countess, as ever, rejoiced in this faithful proclamation of the Gospel:

'It is delightful to see such multitudes flocking to hear the Word. Mr. Whitefield and Mr. Rowland are greatly owned and honoured of the Lord in the conversion of notorious profligates and self-righteous formalists. Very many have been compelled to lay down the arms of rebellion, and submit to the all-conquering sword of the Spirit.'

Rowland doubtless took the opportunity to press on Whitefield an invitation to Wales. One thing in particular was on Rowland's mind: the opening of a new Methodist chapel in Pembrokeshire where Howel Davies was labouring so diligently. Whitefield at the time was thinking of a visit to Ireland, and the two purposes providentially coincided. Rowland's appeal was heeded.

After arriving in Dublin, Whitefield could write of his time in Wales: 'In about three weeks I rode perhaps above five hundred miles, and preached generally twice a day. Congregations were as large as usual, and I trust an unusual power accompanied the Word.'[1] As for 'Woodstock Chapel', it was to become a strategic preaching centre in Pembrokeshire. It also provided a place for the administration of the Lord's Supper for the Methodist converts.

Whitefield's next tour was in July 1752, and lasted for two weeks. Once more he went as far west as Haverfordwest, and found the fields 'white, ready unto harvest'. He wrote triumphantly to Lady Huntingdon, 'Abundance of souls, especially in Pembrokeshire, have attended, and I hope that seed has been sown which will spring up into eternal life.' Again in May 1753 on the same 'circuit' the familiar pattern of preaching was followed, and the success was even more encouraging: 'congregations were large, and a gracious melting seemed to be among the people'.[2]

While at Haverfordwest on this occasion Whitefield met John Cennick, who by this time was labouring for the Moravians. Cennick was on a preaching tour through Wales, responding belatedly to an invitation by Harris in 1749. The incident at Haverfordwest is recorded in Cennick's Journal for May 20, 1753:

'This afternoon at four Mr. Whitefield preached to many people; and that no appearance of opposing him might appear in me, I stayed till near six o'clock till we began our meeting, all which time some hundreds stayed in our room who did not choose to hear him. We had a blessed time. . . . But it was extremely hot because I preached inside, for the weather threatened rain.'

The next day Cennick and Whitefield spent an hour together in conversation. At the end of his tour, in September 1753, Cennick wrote about his impressions of the Welsh scene:

'I have now been in every county in Wales; and observed everywhere the fruits of the indefatigable labours of Howel Harris, which have been wonderful, though now he has but few with him, and those chiefly about North Wales. I also observed a great spirit of devotion through all the Welsh people, and almost an universal respect for the ministers, whether laymen or clergy, and this has been amiable in them, and without doubt a work of God. I wish a few solid preachers who understand Welsh could be sent by our Saviour yet through this

---

[1] GWL ii. 373; [A. C. H. Seymour], *The Life and Times of Selina Countess of Huntingdon*, vol. i. 1844, p. 172. For Woodstock Chapel see HMGC i. 384–5.
[2] GWL ii. 438, 437; iii. 14.

pretty country, and water and help the good seed already sown there, but this is not my plan or place.'[1]

It was this shortage of Welsh-speaking Gospel labourers which made Harris's absence all the more regrettable.

The reaction to Whitefield later in 1753, at Wrexham, North Wales, was quite different from the 'respect' which Cennick's Journal might have led him to expect. 'Upon my coming, the town was alarmed, and several thousands came to hear. Several of the baser sort made a great noise and threw stones, but none touched me, and I trust I can say, our Lord got Himself the victory.' Few particulars are preserved of Whitefield's visit in May 1756 or of his travels through North Wales on the way from Ireland to London at the end of July 1757, but his tour of June 1758 'was one of the most prosperous' that he could remember. 'Twice every day, thousands and thousands attended in various towns in South Wales, and on the Sundays the numbers were incredible. Surely they fled like doves to the windows.' When he returned again in June 1760, it was for the same purpose of 'inviting souls to come to Christ'.[2]

While Harris's withdrawal had been damaging to the Revival, it had not led to its conclusion. The scenes of exceptional spiritual activity which Whitefield witnessed in Wales throughout these years showed that the work was of God. Even though some of His instruments might be removed from the task, the Holy Spirit's power was still very much in evidence, on occasions remarkably so, as will appear shortly.

Unlike Harris, the Welsh Methodists at large were convinced of the importance of building chapels for the convenience of young believers. Woodstock Chapel was one of seventeen chapels built between 1751 and 1762. Rowland's name appears in many of the Title Deeds. Whitefield was faced with the same need, in June 1753 opening his new Tabernacle in London, and in November the Tabernacle at Bristol. Nor was that the end of the matter for Whitefield: his new chapel in Tottenham Court Road, London, was opened in November 1756. Of this building Whitefield reported, 'A neighbouring doctor calls the place, "Whitefield's soul-trap". I pray the Friend of sinners to make it a soul-trap indeed, to many

---

[1] Moravian Church Archives, London, Box A/3, Archives Book p. 45, 'John Cennick's Journals 1748–1753'.
[2] GWL iii. 35, 178, 209–10, 234–5, 262.

wandering creatures.'[1] The Welsh Methodists would heartily have echoed the same prayer for each of their 'Society Houses' as the chapels were mostly called at first.

Perhaps the most important building of all for Rowland was the chapel erected at Llangeitho. The first of these was intended to house the Llangeitho society, and was built on land belonging to Rowland's brother-in-law, Peter Davies. That was in 1756. Another building was raised on the same land in 1760, described as

'a primitive structure of mud walls and thatched roof, measuring ten yards by six. It was replaced in 1764 by a peculiar building in the shape of a double house, the roofs resting in the centre on four stone pillars. The walls measured 45 feet square on the inside. The chapel had four doors, one in each pine end of the two sections, or "houses" as they were called, the one being known as "the house nearer the pulpit" because it contained the pulpit, and the other "the house nearer the altar", as the communion seat was placed in it [there was no altar at all; Cardiganshire usage of the word applies it to the area surrounding the communion table]. To make room for hearers the communion table was hoisted on pulleys. The pulpit could only be entered by a small door leading from outside. . . . In the old chapel Daniel Rowland, on a communion Sunday, had to leave the pulpit by the little door and walk round the house to the door which led to the "altar" in the other section.'

Part of the roof was of straw, and the other part of slates, while the floor was of earth. The few seats were for mothers and children, and even those would be taken out when exceptionally large numbers were present.[2]

Building chapels was a necessary part of the work, given the success of the Awakening. It was far more vital, however, to build up people in the faith. Rowland's emphasis, as always, was on preaching. Together with Whitefield, he was increasingly helped in this ministry by Howel Davies, William Williams and Peter Williams. The 'exhorters' played their part, too, through the earlier arrangements decided at the Associations. There was even an Association of Rowland's people at Bala, North Wales, in 1751,

[1] Harris disapproved of the Methodists building their own chapels because, in his opinion, it gave the impression of schism, cf. HVL 199; TM i. 401; MTU, 213–14; HMGC i. 382, 387–8; MC ii. 60, 141; xxxiv. 5; John Gillies, *Memoirs of . . . George Whitefield*, 1811, pp. 178, 195, n; TGW ii. 310, 317, 374.

[2] HMGC i. 384; ii. 13–14; *Archaeologia Cambrensis*, vol. xcix. p. 155.

though whether Rowland himself was present is not clear. John Thomas, the Carmarthenshire exhorter converted under Harris's ministry, was accepted by an Association at Carmarthen about 1752 'in an upper room where the brethren (Mr. Rowland among them) were gathered', and was reminded of the disciples gathering in a similar place.[1] Harris's organising genius was missed at these meetings and in the societies up and down the country. Repeated attempts by the Methodist leaders failed to entice him away from Trefeca. Rowland and Williams visited him in September 1754, followed by Peter Williams in December. Rowland was back again in February 1755, William Williams and Howel Davies in 1756. A positive response had to await three more years.[2]

Testimony to Rowland's ministry during this period comes from John Thomas, a Carmarthenshire man who eventually settled at Tre-main in Cardiganshire. He kept a diary from 1756–1759 which narrates the typical experiences of a faithful Methodist of the time. When he was about thirteen a cataract developed in his right eye. Four years later he had the first opportunity to attend a Welsh school, the teacher, William Christopher, being a godly Methodist. This man often reproved his class for Sabbath-breaking, dancing, and taking the Lord's name in vain. He also warned of death, the day of judgment, and hell, commending the means of grace to all. Gradually, Thomas found the Lord's grace working a spiritual appetite in him that he had never known before. It brought to his soul a relish for sermons and hymns. 'I looked on some men as messengers from God to me, namely, Mr. Daniel Rowland and Mr. Howel Davies, and others.' He would take every opportunity to hear such 'commending the Lord Jesus, and His way'. In time he was given assurance of his salvation and laboured as one of the Circulating schoolmasters.

John Thomas's diary is particularly valuable because it shows the tireless activity of Rowland's Methodists in West Wales at what might otherwise have been thought of as a period of decline. There was regular preaching by the clergymen and exhorters, fervent society meetings with some exalted occasions, Associations with a sense of close fellowship, and much fervour. The diary effectively

[1] cf. MTU, 193, 200; xiv. 94; xxvii. 146; xxx. 77; J. Dyfnallt Owen, *Rhad Ras Ioan Thomas*, 1949, tud. 89. For a list of Associations from 1751 to 1811, see lv. 24–32.

[2] HMGC i. 393–5.

reflects the Scriptural teaching of the leaders and mirrors the profound experiences of the Methodism of the day. Its greatest value, however, lies in another, though related, direction. It is a warm personal record of spiritual pilgrimage and soul culture, and as such the diary is an exquisite gem.

Thomas spent Christmas 1756 at Llangeitho. On Christmas Day he heard Rowland preach on Luke 2:7, 'And she brought forth her firstborn son, and wrapped him in swaddling clothes, and laid him in a manger; because there was no room for them in the inn.' The theme was the blindness of the natural man, 'that he cannot perceive the Godhead of the Lord Jesus through the swaddling clothes. Great is the mystery of godliness!' Another opportunity to hear Rowland came the next day, a Sunday, when Rowland showed from Matthew 11:28 'how God in a wonderful way gives rest to His people in the midst of weariness'. By this time, however, Thomas's soul had been richly fed, especially at his lodging-place the previous night:

'On the Saturday night I was staying at a house with several other brethren. They were praying and singing, and in the Lord were rejoicing like David before the Ark. I was labouring under a sense of estrangement, but before dawn the next morning – I shall never forget the 26th December – I was trying to sing with the brethren, and felt my spirit being quickened somewhat with this word, "He saved multitudes before I ever lived". One of the brethren went to prayer, and with that I experienced such a charge being wrought in my entire being that my heart melted in tears before God, and as I afterwards went to prayer, God came down among us! Praise His name for ever!'

These elevated experiences made a lasting impression. The measure of their authenticity and edification was assessed in a stringent, searching manner through the society meeting, and under the preaching of the Word, as Thomas would have known from a sermon of Rowland's on Matthew 13:11 a month previously:

'The knowledge that God's children have of the Kingdom of Heaven is such that no natural man can attain to it by any means other than through God's Spirit alone. Someone outside the covenant of grace may have much knowledge about God in his head, and this knowledge may affect his heart just as the devils tremble from their knowledge of God. Indeed, a man through learning may talk in a very enlightened manner about God and about God's grace in His people, and yet be a stranger to Him. . . . Men under the sound of the Gospel may be no better, and even be worse, because 1, they are wandering and fickle in their minds. . . . The sun may not be seen properly in running water; 2, because men are not standing on rock, that is on God, when they hear the Word. When someone hits a cork floating in the water, the blow has no effect because the cork sinks under it; but when the cork is on rock, one blow is sufficient to disintegrate it completely. So it is with that man who stands on rock, that is on God, when hearing the Word, that Word in the Spirit's hand breaks his heart. 3. Because men hear God's Word in their natural state without God's nature in them. The sun cannot be seen except in its own light; even so God may not be seen or known other than by His own light.'

Searching seasons were not confined to preaching occasions. Some of Thomas's most penetrating experiences came at a society meeting.

One of these meetings must have been quite extraordinary. The date was Wednesday, March 2, 1757, the time about 9 or 10 at night, the place was a Methodist's house in Tre-main. At first Thomas had been 'unconcerned about God's glory and the cause of my own and others' souls' while one of the exhorters spoke. When one of the brethren gave out some verses of a hymn on 'the lamentation of a sinner', a paraphrase of Psalm 130, Thomas felt his soul crying with increasing earnestness that the Lord should set him free from his chains, and he was enabled to triumph in some measure through believing prayer. More, far more, was to come. He felt a strong measure of unity with his brethren in Christ, and verses on that theme were powerfully sealed to his soul, John 17:21–23 among them. At that moment he was walking from one house to another, a mere yard or two apart, but suddenly he was as if rooted to the spot by a mighty power:

'It was as if lightning flashed into my spirit, and I thought in my heart that the people around me had seen it, too, but they had not, and with the light such a powerful peace and joy came into my heart. In one moment I felt as if wholly revitalised by some infinite power, so that my body would be shattered like an earthen vessel. I saw God's work in my soul and God's Word weaving harmoniously together the peace which passes all understanding, the exceeding greatness of His power etc. I could gladly seal with my blood the truth of those words. . . . At that time my soul was uttering these words: 'Holy! Holy! Holy! Wonderful! Wonderful! Eternally wonderful! I felt as though my body and soul were being lifted from the earth, and being dissolved to go to heaven. . . . Tears of joy flowed spontaneously from my eyes in torrents. . . . This lasted about an hour or more as far as I can gauge. Indeed, it lasted amazingly with me all that night; I could neither eat nor drink; I felt a fulness within me. If I slept it was but little all night, I could only praise and wonder at God, and who could do less? Because it had become heaven to me on earth; thank God from my heart! . . . I cannot reckon it as one of the days of earth, only as one of the days of heaven.'

The sequel was sobering: 'I had thought I would henceforth be left alone by unbelief, the devil, the flesh, the world, and by sin and corruption, and at present these enemies are subdued, but I fear and tremble at them more than ever before.' His record of this extraordinary experience closes with a prayer that God would enable him to bring about the fall of his spiritual enemies, as God's Ark brought about the downfall of Dagon.[1]

Six months later at yet another society meeting God met him again in a similar way. He had been more inclined to stay at home that particular night, and even as he went he was sceptical of receiving any blessing. His heart accused him of many things: failure, unbelief, hypocrisy, dead formality, lack of preparation for the meeting. After some praying and hymn-singing, and when another of the brethren went to prayer,

'such a ray of dazzling light shone on my soul that I did not know what to say or what to do. I felt glory! glory! glory! thanks! thanks! thanks! murmuring and echoing throughout my soul. Indeed, I never thought that so much heaven was to be had the other side of the grave as what I had now, by free grace, proved this side of the grave! I now see that the Kingdom of Heaven is righteousness, and peace, and joy in the Holy Spirit, and that it is within believers.'

He might well have been repeating the sentiments of Whitefield in 1749, 'Alas! to what a heaven are they strangers, who deny the influence of the blessed Spirit, and cry down the felt and abiding joys of the Holy Ghost as fancy, enthusiasm, and delusion. You poor, dry Rationalists! I honour your parts in other respects, but pity your ignorance in the things of God.' Other great writers on experimental theology have spoken of such seasons of refreshing as an immediate, powerful influence of the Spirit on the believer's soul, John Owen, the great Puritan writer on the Holy Spirit, among them:

'When He so sheds abroad the love of God in our hearts, and so fills them with gladness by an immediate act and operation (as he caused John the Baptist to leap for joy in the womb upon the approach of the mother of Jesus), then the soul even from hence, raises itself to a

---

[1] *Y Drysorfa*, 1931, tt. 281–4, 391–7, 432–4.

consideration of the love of God, whence joy and rejoicing also flow. Of this joy there is no account to be given, but that the Spirit works it when and how He will. He secretly infuses and distils it into the soul, prevailing against all fears and sorrows, filling it with gladness, exultations, and sometimes with unspeakable raptures of mind.'[1]

The glory of God had not yet departed from the land.

Rowland's preaching of that love was quite overwhelming. John Thomas heard the latter part of his sermon on John 3:16 at Nantcwnlle in November 1756. 'He was nearly finishing when I arrived', he wrote afterwards. 'As soon as I went into the church I believe I heard God's voice in these words, "many waters could not quench it", the devil's malice and the rage of men failed; even the wrath of God failed to hinder Christ from finishing the work of redemption. Blessed be His name for ever!' One of the North Wales preachers, Robert Jones, was also present on that occasion. His account conveys a similar impression of wonder and ecstasy:

'He dwelt with such overwhelming, extraordinary thoughts on the greatness of the love of God, and the vastness of the Gift, that I was swallowed up in amazement. I did not know whether my feet were on the ground. I had no idea where I was, whether it was on earth or in heaven! Presently, Rowland cried out with a most powerful voice, "Praised be God for keeping the Jews in ignorance respecting the greatness of the Person in their hands. Had they known who He was, they would never have presumed to touch Him, much less to drive nails through His blessed hands and feet, and to put a crown of thorns on His holy head. For had they known they would not have crucified the Lord of Glory."'

Jones was so 'lost in wonder, love, and praise' at the sight of the exquisite vistas of God's love exposed to the gaze of his soul that he left the church without his hat![2]

Thomas Charles of Bala enlarges upon the effects and attractions of a visit to Llangeitho:

'From Llangeitho the fructifying streams flowed all over the country in those blessed days. The sermons heard there, being repeated by many persons on their return, to the country people, and being related again by them to their neighbours, were wonderfully blessed. Divine truth was gaining ground and spreading through all the

---

[1] *ib.* 1932, tt. 388–9; GWL ii. 277; John Owen, *Works*, vol. ii. 1851, p. 253.
[2] *Y Drysorfa*, 1931, tud. 391; MR, 62; *Y Llenor*, cyf. xv, Gorffennaf 1898, 'Gwaith Robert Jones Rhoslan', tud. 16.

country. Many were consequently stirred up and induced to go and hear the extraordinary preacher at Llangeitho for themselves. . . . The multitude, having heard a sermon or two from him, would go their various long and tedious journeys with great gladness, praising God for His unspeakable gifts received at Llangeitho.'[1]

Evidently the Methodists unfailingly travelled home from Llangeitho with something of heaven in their hearts and the songs of Zion on their lips.

The great difference between Rowland and Harris, between Llangeitho and Trefeca during that decade is significant. People journeyed to Llangeitho for Rowland's powerful ministry fully resolved to return to live out their Christian lives in the place and calling chosen for them by God. Those who went to Trefeca did so with the intention of withdrawing from the world into a spiritual community. Rowland took the conflict into 'enemy territory' with the conviction that the Gospel message is to be proclaimed in all circumstances, foul or fair. Harris confined the conflict to the arena of his own soul and the souls of those who joined him. In these respects, Rowland displayed the God-centred quality of a vigorous Calvinism, while Harris practised a more subjective and individualistic Pietism. It was not surprising, therefore, that Rowland was the one who tenaciously carried on the work of the Gospel during this critical period. And there was still much to be done.

[1] MR, 145.

'He was given ten full talents,
    And he traded them each one;
Making from them many hundreds
Ere his working day was done.'

WILLIAM WILLIAMS, *Elegy to Rowland*

'The hymns of William Williams are packed with theology and experience. . . . William Williams was the greatest hymn-writer of them all. You get greatness, and bigness, and largeness in Isaac Watts; you get the experimental side wonderfully in Charles Wesley. But in William Williams you get both at the same time.'

D. MARTYN LLOYD-JONES

27

'To Make up a Breach in God's House'

It is astonishing how the Methodists ever found time for everyday affairs. Sermons and society meetings seem to stretch from one Sunday to another in John Thomas's diary. Rowland was obviously involved in much of this kind of activity, making his absences from home frequent and sometimes prolonged. At home, he supplemented the meagre income he derived from ecclesiastical sources by keeping sheep, sending them for the winters of 1752 and 1753 to his brother-in-law. His wife capably and bravely managed these domestic affairs in his absence. Only occasional glimpses of Rowland's participation in the social life of the community have survived. One example of this belongs to the year 1759, when Rowland was admitted a burgess of Lampeter, often in those days a political strategy on the part of the candidate to gain votes. The person responsible for Rowland's admission may have been John Lloyd of Lampeter, who had been at least sympathetic to Methodism, and had been returned unopposed for the County of Cardigan at the 1754 General Election.[1] More of Rowland's social activities can only be surmised, although his ministerial labours would have kept them to a minimum.

Rowland's family was growing, too. Nathaniel, the younger son was born in 1749, and John, the older son was ordained deacon in September 1757, and priest in August of the following year. Sarah, one of Rowland's four daughters, was born in 1757 and was to survive until her 82nd year. Very little is known of their spiritual state, except in the case of Nathaniel, who came to know

---

[1] xxx. 84; Bethan Phillips, *Peterwell*, 1983, p. 76; xii. 112.

the Lord about 1762.[1]

Rowland's diligent, untiring ministerial labours might give the impression of a man who was unencumbered with the cares of family life. The truth is that he fulfilled his ministry against the background of family and social responsibility outlined above, and was by no means insulated from these demands upon his time and energy. Indeed, during the period of Harris's withdrawal the other Methodist leaders worked harder and more closely together, and did so without tension.

Each had a distinct contribution to make. William Williams by his writings gave popular expression to Rowland's theology as well as his own. Between them there appears to have been the closest theological harmony during the whole time of their Methodist association. They also shared the gift of simple, homely, popular, and memorable application of the truth. Rowland used that gift in his sermons, Williams in his writings. Howel Davies devoted his gifts and energies to Pembrokeshire. By his preaching and teaching the county was preserved for Calvinistic Methodism at a time when the Moravians were making determined attempts to establish a base, especially in that English-speaking area. In this respect Davies received considerable support from Whitefield's visits, and in turn was able occasionally to minister in his chapels in England. Peter Williams gave himself to much travelling, making his home in Carmarthenshire. In later years he became a writer, translator and Bible commentator, but during the 'fifties his great contribution was to supply, in some measure, the itinerant ministry of preaching and counselling the societies which Harris had previously fulfilled.

A fruitful literary ministry was also exercised by the Methodists in this period. Some of it was apologetic in nature, but much of it was intended to provide edifying material for young believers. In defending the Methodists against charges of enthusiasm and Romanism, Whitefield in 1749 had issued *Some Remarks on a Pamphlet Entitled, The Enthusiasm of Methodists and Papists Compared.* Methodist 'field preaching' was nothing new, merely an attempt at following the example of Christ and His disciples, Paul on his

---

[1] For Nathaniel Rowland see DWB, s.v. Daniel Rowland; and xlv. 60, 67; xlvi. 10; For John Rowland see DWB, s.v. Daniel Rowland; and xxxvi. 25; D. Worthington, *Cofiant y Parch. Daniel Rowland*, 1923 'Pedigree'; *Glamorgan, Monmouth, and Brecon Gazette*, July 20, 1839; CH 1978, p. 37.

missionary journeys, and subsequent practice in the history of the Church. Assurance of salvation, a particular target for criticism, was clearly taught in the Church's Homilies, and, in contrast, hotly disputed by the Council of Trent. Other Methodist doctrines, such as justification by faith, and works as the fruit of faith, were diametrically opposite to those of the Church of Rome. Finally, Whitefield asserted that all Methodist endeavour centres on the need

'to awaken a drowsy world to a sense of this, to arouse them out of their formality, as well as profaneness, and put them upon seeking after a present and great salvation, to point out to them a glorious rest, which not only remains for the people of God hereafter, but which by a living faith the very chief of sinners may enter into even here, and without which the most blazing profession is nothing worth.'

This prompted the appearance, two years later, of *A Second Letter to the Rev George Whitefield* ..., which also viciously attacked Rowland for allegedly countenancing immorality and deception. In 1752 Theophilus Evans issued another attack on Methodism, *The History of Modern Enthusiasm*, a second edition of which appeared in 1757. Here again, the classic teachings of Methodism were derided as leading to Antinomianism, immorality, madness, delusion and pride.

During the fifties Williams issued several collections of hymns. The first part of *Hosanna i Fab Dafydd* appeared in 1751 and a collection of English hymns with this title translated into English was published in 1759 as *Hosanna to the Son of David*. The first of the sixteen hymns which appeared in 1757 under the title *Rhai Hymnau a Chaniadau* (Some Hymns and Songs) spoke of Christ as 'The Rose of Creation', and notice was given in the work that a revised selection of hymns would shortly appear. This would make the collection

'more profitable and edifying to all degrees of believers, having modified some lessons which were beyond those believers who have only an ordinary measure of faith and feeling, either to a prayer for such grace, or to admire the Lord who gave it; or else to take away the selfish boasting in the lesser part that Jesus alone should be exalted. Further, they have been stripped of that small abominable word "I" which was in a few of them, putting Jesus and His grace instead, "not I, but Christ who lives in me", etc. Not quite taking away, either, but rather confirming the "I" of believing, that is the personal application of faith, without which faith is no longer faith.

In short, as far as possible to put the sound of Christ, and His free Gospel as blood in their veins, and to bring man, his understanding, his power, his light as nothing.'

This collection of 242 hymns appeared in 1758 under the title *Alleluja*. In an important preface he sets out his conviction on the matter of writing and singing hymns.

'I acknowledge that there are some of these first hymns, on the assurance of faith, longing to be dissolved, spiritual joy, together with triumph over enemies, which weak Christians cannot easily sing. This happened not so much because the Lord kept my own soul in good spirits at the time, but chiefly because the Spirit had been so plentifully poured out on those godly people for whom they were written. . . . When I came to know myself better, and saw what an Egypt of darkness, a sea of uncleanness, a world of pride is man, I determined to exalt the salvation which is in Christ far more, and to abase man and his gifts more. I did my utmost, whatever the nature of the hymn – complaint, plea, holy boasting, or praise, for Christ to be the centrepiece of it all. . . . I am constrained to give a little advice to those who give out these hymns. . . . Some give out verses full of assurance and delight to a congregation that denies the first and has not experienced the second. . . . Others give out verses of complaint and questioning to a people who have been elevated to the heavenlies, and who feel life in their faith, and Satan under their feet, as if to urge people to sing about the cold of winter while the sun blazes in hottest summer.'[1]

Sound principles, and sound advice for the 'spiritual songs' in which the Methodists believed so passionately, and used so effectively in their societies! Griffith Jones had been a strong advocate of Psalm singing, and the Methodists used these widely, but the hymns which Williams wrote gave fuller, Gospel expression to the glories of the Redeemer and 'the wonderful works of God' in Him. The genius of Williams' hymns lay in the unobtrusive blend of teaching and experience. They were at once both biblical and experimental. The act of singing them was proclamation and profession, objective and subjective. They were pure Calvinistic Methodism, extolling the free grace of God and expressing the full heart of man.

[1] WW ii. 62–3, 64, 65. For a discussion of Williams, see J. Gwilym Jones, *William Williams Pantycelyn*, 1969 (bilingual); Glyn Tegai Hughes, *Williams Pantycelyn*, 1983 (English); and in Welsh, WW ii. Pennod II; T. H. Parry-Williams, 'William Williams, Pantycelyn-Ei Emynau', yn Dyfnallt Morgan (gol.), *Gwŷr Llên y Ddeunawfed Ganrif*, 1966, tt. 83–91; Derec Llwyd Morgan, *Williams Pantycelyn*, 1983. The hymns are in CYN, ii.

Williams' next contribution in that period showed much study and discernment. *Golwg ar Deyrnas Crist* (A View of the Kingdom of Christ) drew heavily on the works of William Derham (1657–1735) and, to a lesser extent, James Hervey (1714–1758). This was a long poem, shortened for its second edition in 1764. It was, like the vast majority of Williams' literary efforts, written entirely in Welsh, expounding Colossians 3–11 and I Corinthians 15:25. Although its intended title was changed from *Buddugoliaeth yr Efengyl* (The Triumph of the Gospel), its purpose was the same: 'to urge my own soul, and the souls of others, to love the Great Captain of our salvation', and to reprove others 'for their public neglect of Christ and their wilful indifference to relying on Him for the soul's justification'. 'Christ is all and in all' is the theme, and He is shown to be this in God's Eternal Counsel, in Creation, in Eden's Promise, in Providence, and in the Salvation of His Saints (Christ's Particular Kingdom). In the second edition another chapter is added, 'Christ is all in the Bible, (the Statute Book of Christ's Kingdom)'.[1]

Whether in setting out the Truth or in exposing error, Williams' standards are 'the Holy Scriptures, the foundation of all Truth', 'the Church of England's Articles, the (Westminster) Assembly's Catechism, the Puritan Writers'. The particular errors which Williams had in mind were those held by eighteenth-century Rationalists and Deists: 'those who destroy the whole body of revealed religion . . . who deny the Godhead of our Blessed Lord, the value of His blood, the merit of His death . . . who say that it is by the Father's Purpose or Appointment alone, not through any infinite worth and efficacious merit in Christ's sufferings, that sins are forgiven.' The work tends to be tedious because Williams never varies the metre of his verses, but in dealing with the last theme of all, 'Christ is all in the Saints' salvation', that same metre becomes inspiring and elevating.

Chapter one deals with the glory of God's electing grace as the determinative principle of all God's operations, and he extols 'the

[1] For this work see CYN i; GWP, i. An English translation appeared in 1878. For a discussion in Welsh see WW ii. 144–55; and Derec Llwyn Morgan, *Y Diwygiad Mawr*, tt. 207–224. The two works of Derham which Williams used were *Physico-Theology: or A Demonstration of the Being and Attributes of God from His Works in Creation*, 1713; and *Astro-Theology; or A Demonstration of the Being and Attributes of God From a Survey of the Heavens*, 1715. For Derham and Hervey, see *Dictionary of National Biography*.

plan of grace', 'the infinite scheme' which 'resolved to raise me up'. For the second chapter he draws on Derham for facts about the marvels of Space, the revelations of the microscope, and the curiosities of Natural Science. 'Creation is a book of countless pages, setting out the endless glory of the Second Adam', and the crowning work in that natural creation is man:

> But man himself's a cosmos, the great King may be seen
> More visibly in Adam, than all that's ever been;
> If nothing else had shown us what God is really like,
> God then in man's creation that likeness plain did strike.

This is followed by an account of man's fall by sin and his recovery through Christ. The satisfaction which He rendered is complete, unique, and effective. Nothing else will do to bring man to God. Anything else, either as a substitute for or as a supplement to Christ's atonement, is offered in vain:

> God takes no heed of praying, God heeds no righteousness;
> No sacrifice or incense, no praise or alms impress;
> Nor conscientious effort, nor zeal or holy fast,
> Nor aught to pardon sinners; Christ's death alone will last.

> Like lighting one small candle to supplement the sun,
> Is adding man's weak merit to what our Lord has done;
> For He the books of heaven has cleared by His blood,
> Our righteousness is in Him, His Name the Son of God.

Where Christ reigns all is changed. The believer is not only restored to fellowship with God, he is indwelt by the Spirit, and finds his sufficiency altogether in Christ:

> This now the place from morning and on into the night
> I look to be the victor, my idols put to flight;
> Thy Spirit, gracious Jesus, can make me fully clean,
> A thousand times more able than hell has ever seen.

> To see Thy face, Beloved, makes my poor soul rejoice,
> O'er all I've ever tasted, or ever made my choice;
> When they all disappear, why should I grieve or pine
> While to my gaze there opens the sight that Christ is mine?

> He's greater than His blessings, He's greater than His grace,
> Far greater than His actions, whatever you may trace;
> I'll plead for faith, gifts, cleansing; for these I'll yearn quite sore,
> But on Him only, always, I'll look and lean far more.

This, then, was intended as a popular presentation of 'the Methodist Way'. Revelation was held to be the organiser of reason and the interpreter of nature. The Kingdom of Christ was the unifying principle for the whole range of man's culture in this world. On this principle man could live in harmony with God, with himself, with the physical world around him, with others, with natural phenomena, with social institutions, with his history and with his destiny. The One who gave life cohesion and fulfilment was Christ, God's Elect, His people's King. 'The Methodist Way' was nothing if not convincing, wholesome and comprehensive.

Methodists were in the created world of time and space, but not of it in its corrupt, immoral ethos. This growing awareness of the vast knowledge, phenomena, customs, achievements, and wonders of the world was a sign of the times. It was an exciting age to live in, a kind of information revolution, with seemingly endless facts and figures about man and his world becoming more and more accessible. There was only one snag, as far as the Christian Faith was concerned. The dissemination and interpretation of that revolution was all too often in the hands of Rationalists and Deists. The French philosophers of the day were decidedly anti-Christian, led by Voltaire, Rousseau, Diderot. Permeated by their ideas, a French counterpart of Ephraim Chambers' *Cyclopaedia; or a Universal Dictionary of Arts and Sciences* (1728), from its first appearance in 1751, was seen as an attack on supernatural and personal religion. The whole universe was a stage on which was enacted the natural and social drama of life, a great spectacle to be observed, measured, admired, repudiated, and classified, but at best only a mechanistic process. God, if He existed, was not involved.

Already, in his 'View of Christ's Kingdom', Williams had shown his encyclopaedic interest, and how God's revelation and Christ's Kingship together resolved the believer's relationship to the world in which he lived. More came from his pen from 1762–1779 with the publication in seven parts of *Pantheologia, Neu Hanes holl Grefyddau'r Byd* (Pantheologia, the History of all the Religions of the World). It was more than a study in comparative religion, it included geographical details, and cost him a great deal of labour.[1] Above all, its intention was to bring to Welsh Methodists a realisation of the

[1] For a discussion of this work see WW ii. 221–5; and Alwyn Prosser, 'Diddordebau Lleyg Williams Pantycelyn', in *Llên Cymru*, iii. 201–14.

uniqueness of Christ amid man's blind quest for God. Divine revelation was still enthroned as the only rule of faith and practice.

Rowland's translations in this period belong to the same category of literature, a kind of apologetic in the face of new knowledge. *Aceldama, Neu Faes y Gwaed* (Aceldama, or The Field of Blood), was Rowland's translation into Welsh of a work that Whitefield had issued as a translation from the Dutch. It set out the cruelties and uncertainties of a war in which the Russians were involved. In the 'Preface' by Peter Williams, the readers are urged to pray for those who are fighting for the Protestant Religion, and to flee from all danger to Christ for safety and acceptance.[1] Three years later Rowland translated another work, John Wetherall's 'Fifteen Orations', under the title *Pymtheg o Areithiau ar Amryw Destynau*. Once again Peter Williams obliged with a 'Preface' saying that Wetherall's purpose in the Orations, delivered to a very mixed audience, was 'to convince his hearers of original sin and the need for justification by an imputed righteousness: his weapons were not carnal, and I know that his translator has done him no injustice'. The subjects dealt with 'in fifteen minutes' were: the beginnings and progress of idolatry; what is meant by the Tree of Life; the visit of the Queen of Sheba to Solomon; the significance of the curse on the serpent; God's justice in pardoning the sinner; Nebuchadnezzar's conversion; how the world was turned upside down by the apostles; how the world was peopled; the conversion of the dying thief; and the parable of the children in the market-place. It is an amorphous work, the context in which the orations were delivered determining the manner in which they were presented. Throughout, there is an attempt to confront the hearer not only with convincing argument but also with personal application. Apologetic is combined with the prevalent encyclopaedic interest and delivered with Methodist fervour. Here lay the reason for Rowland's interest in the work. The Gospel was not for spectators of the drama of life, it spoke of an immediacy, a relevance, and a reality in which every man must participate. In the face of imminent, and even violent, death, or of the greatest issues of life, Methodism came into its own.

Two other translations illustrate the comprehensiveness of the leaders' emphasis. The first of these, in 1752, was the sermon on Genesis 5:24, 'And Enoch walked with God', that Whitefield had

[1] HMGC i. 416.

preached over ten years earlier at the opening of the Watford joint Association. It was a call to holiness, love and zeal: 'In order to walk closely with God, His children must not only watch the motions of God's providence without them, but the motions also of His blessed Spirit in their hearts'. The other work, which appeared in 1760, had been a favourite with Calvinists since its appearance in the previous century with recommendations by Thomas Goodwin and John Owen. This was *A Practical Discourse of God's Sovereignty* by Elisha Coles. The 'other material points derived thence' and discussed in the book dealt with God's Righteousness, Election, Redemption, Effectual Calling, and Perseverance.[1] Each Methodist was expected to live out his life in the world within these two polarities: personal holiness and the sovereignty of God.

Rowland and Williams were using the years of consolidation to create and influence a truly 'Methodist Mind'. It was not to be shaped after Harris's image of a subjective, Pietistic withdrawal, but rather in terms of a God-centred Calvinistic involvement. Welsh Methodism would be Calvinistic in practice as well as in doctrine and worship.

As they entered the new decade of the seventeen-sixties there were gains and losses for the Welsh Methodists. Philip Pugh and Griffith Jones died within a year of each other (in 1760 and 1761 respectively), and their wise counsel was undoubtedly missed. However, others were joining their ranks, men of similar conviction and zeal. Two of these, David Jones and William Davies, were ordained deacons at the same time as Rowland's son, John (1757), and laboured in Glamorganshire (at Llan-gan and Neath respectively). Even Harris was feeling a constraint to join with his Methodist brethren once more. After tentative moves towards a reconciliation between them during 1759 the realisation of his re-instatement had to wait three years while he served with the Breconshire Militia. A letter from Rowland and the other leaders in May 1762 signalled the passing of the unhappy episode of their separation:

Dear Sir,
    We understand by E. Moses that you intend to resign your present Commission and (God willing) once more to fill up your place among us, which we sensibly [that is, feelingly] acknowledge

[1] GW ii. 13; *Select Sermons of George Whitefield*, 1959, pp. 98–109; HMGC i. 416, f.; WW ii. 240.

has been long vacant. We have followed you with our prayers through your various tours, and are satisfied you generally appeared doubly armed, to the furtherance of the Gospel, glory be to free, sovereign grace! And we unanimously conclude that your inclination to visit our several counties again is the voice of Heaven, and we doubt not but all animosities will and must subside, and a spirit of love take its place. Amen. Amen.

Within a few months Harris seemed to be a different man, seeing himself 'less by millions of degrees than Whitefield, Wesleys, and Rowland'. He was humbled as he read the works of Rowland and Williams, and found 'special love to Rowland' in his heart. The most convincing evidence of harmony came when Harris saw Rowland's mission as being 'to make up a breach in God's house', and that he was clearly 'set as head of all this work'.[1] This was both a sign and an earnest of unparalleled blessing.

[1] HMGC i. 399; HRS, 136, 172; WW i. 136; xxxii. 42, 43.

'...a little of the Llangeitho fire to keep my soul from freezing....'

IOAN THOMAS
Rhad Ras

'It will be a wonderful thing if Wales should be favoured with such gracious operations as these, instead of the awful judgments that afflict many countries these days! Oh may we long more earnestly, and ardently for the gracious visitations of the Lord to our country and neighbourhood, but especially to our own souls.'

JOHN ELIAS
on Revival, 1832

'The influences of the Spirit are compared in the Scriptures to the rain: "He shall come unto us as the rain, as the latter and the former rain unto the earth". Would you object to the rain, and say, it cannot be rain, because it sometimes comes suddenly and in so many drops? We are given to understand that a nation will be born in a day.... It is said that it is all enthusiasm. If the distress of sinners is greater than the case demands, then call it enthusiasm. But if the sinner is in danger of losing his soul, not to be distressed is blockish stupidity. Is it rational to brave the terrors of the Almighty, and to slumber on the brink of eternal perdition? It is said, the sudden joy manifested in revivals is irrational, and cannot be the effect of divine influence. What shall we find to answer these expressions in the Bible? – "The peace of God that passeth all understanding"; "Rejoicing with joy unspeakable and full of glory"? ... Would not a criminal, who should be reprieved on his way to the gallows, rejoice? ... When Philip preached in Samaria, was there not great joy in that city?'

ASAHEL NETTLETON (died 1844)
'Thoughts on Revivals'

28

1762: 'Blessed Summer's Day'

In historical perspective it is possible to see evidence of real achievements even during the period when the Welsh Methodists were separated by the Disruption. There were effusions of the Spirit's power from time to time, like scattered showers, as well as a rich dew of heavenly ministry through the regular means of grace. None could have foreseen, however, the exceptional and torrential flood of blessing which was experienced at Llangeitho in 1762.

Under God three factors brought it about. Harris mentions Rowland's ministry as one of these in the same statement that acknowledges his leadership of the work in general: 'seeing this revival also begun by him'. Another factor that Harris mentions in bringing about what he calls 'these late showers' was 'some of the meanest [most ordinary] of all the exhorters'. One of them, William Richard, in speaking of 'this last revival in Cardiganshire', had told Harris that 'when they first cried out at Llangeitho' [during the 1762 visitation], in the midst of the general response, 'that word had gone through him, "I will once more shake the heavens" [Hebrews 12:26, Haggai 2:21].' The third contributory element was the appearance of another collection of hymns by Williams, *Caniadau y Rhai Sydd ar y Mor o Wydr* (The Songs of Those Who are on the Sea of Glass). Such was the popularity of these hymns that twelve hundred copies had been sold within a few months, and the call for another edition was urgent. The hymns set forth in vivid imagery the believer's longing for the enjoyment of God's presence, and the power of His love: 'The light of Thy countenance brings life . . . it is everything'; 'One little spark of Thy love breaks all my chains.'[1] Several hymns are based on the Song of Solomon, expressing the joy and confidence of the believer's union with Christ.

[1] For the 1762 Revival see R. Geraint Griffith, *Revival and Its Fruit*, 1981; HRS, 187, 189, 209; WW ii. 66–72; CYN ii. 131–87.

In retrospect, people spoke of the time preceding the 1762 revival as 'the long winter'. Williams does the same through one of his Methodist characters:

'One time there were just a few of us, professing believers, gathered together, cold, and unbelievably dead, in a meeting which we called a special service, so discouraged as to doubt whether we should ever meet again. Some . . . were usually absent from every meeting, some in deadly apathy with nothing to say of God nor of their own souls, some given over to the world and its cares, some backslidden completely from all the means of grace and the ordinances of the Gospel, some give over to the flesh and its lusts . . . and I myself well nigh disheartened. . . . These services were conducted in an incredibly lifeless manner. There was no encouragement for anyone to carry on the work, save only the promise of God, that wherever there were if only two or three coming together in His name, if their purpose were right, however lifeless their present state, He would come to them and bless them. This alone made us come together to pray, but our prayers were not much more than groans.'[1]

When the revival came it was like the healing of heaven for the ills of earth to their souls. Their graces were invigorated and their longings were fulfilled to an unusual extent. The life which God had planted in their souls was quickened afresh. This was not a different, but the same Gospel experience, powerfully heightened by the Holy Spirit. The manifestations of that power were intensified, certainly, but it served the same purpose of advancing the holiness of God in His people.

Preaching was as central during this revival as it was before it. The doctrines preached, now as before, were the doctrines of grace. Each of the leading ministers was proving a measure of authority in his preaching, even in the years leading up to that 'acceptable year of the Lord'. John Thomas of Tre-main faithfully recorded his impressions under the ministry of those days. He bears consistent witness to the solid nature of the teaching he heard and the depth of the work wrought in his soul. On April 1, 1759, he heard Howel Davies at Llechryd on Zechariah 2:13. 'He was given unusual power in this meeting. Praise be to God for supporting His beloved and faithful servants in such manner, Amen! I feel deep wounds in my soul these days.' A fortnight later he was at Llangeitho for the Easter services. On the Saturday afternoon from Lamentations 1:12, Rowland

[1] R. *Geraint Gruffydd, op. cit.*, p. 22; William Williams, *The Experience Meeting*, 1973, p. 8.

'showed that God's infinite wrath fell on Christ for the sins of all the elect'. Easter Day morning and afternoon Rowland preached on Matthew 28:5.

'He said that the three Mary's, with the same name, set forth the church of the living God, which is one. This sets out the excellence and honour of the church, and yet that she is still liable to meet bitterness. Magdalen signifies a castle, which speaks of the safety of the church. Mary the mother of James sets out the fruitfulness of the church; and the meaning of the word "Salome" is "peace" or "peaceable", setting out the peace of the church. How amazing is the sight of these godly people at Llangeitho! The outward appearance of their pleasant faces reflects hearts within that burn with joy. I am not sorry that I took this journey, because there is no price to be paid for Mr. D. Rowland's preaching.'

In the summer under an 'authoritative sermon' by Peter Williams, Thomas felt fearful on account of the hardness of his own heart. The Llechryd Association on the last day of October gave him an opportunity to hear both Rowland and Williams. 'These two men strike exactly the same chord, namely, God is everything; man, and all to do with him, is nothing; God is eternally exalted and glorious, and man down in the dust as dung under foot, with all the best that belongs to him. This is the chord that all the saints have ever struck; my spirit feels it, too, and its sound is exceedingly sweet.'[1]

Rowland's sermon on Revelation 3:20, 'Behold, I stand at the door and knock' was published in 1762, but it was preached at Llanddewibrefi on November 1, 1761, at much the same time as the publication of Williams' hymns. In English translation its title was 'The Redeemer's Voice', but its Welsh title is 'The Voice of the turtle-dove, that is, Christ's gracious invitation to sinners'. That occasion might well have been the sounding of the 'silver trumpet' that proved to be the first clarion call of the revival. The sermon is nothing if not urgent and immediate, piercing and direct, appealing and compelling:

'O conscience! conscience! conscience! awake from thy deadly stupor and ponder, intensely ponder on the height and depth of redeeming love. Behold! the ever-blessed Immanuel hath pity on those whom none else will pity. Nay, He who sits enthroned above, encircled by myriads of His obedient creatures, who never opposed His will or resisted His authority, has pity on those who have no pity on themselves, and have been all their days flying in His face, and

[1] lvi. 60, 61, 88–9; lvii. 16.

fighting against Him with His own weapons. O what compassion is this! O what tenderness is here shown to sinners, the chief of sinners, the worst, the vilest who tread the earth, and can hardly be matched in hell!'

Preaching with God's truth as his matter, and with God's love as his constraint, Rowland depended solely on God's Spirit for success:

'Though you have lost the power of obeying, and, like Samson, are shorn of your strength, yet with God all things are possible. When He said, "Let there be light", there was light. When He sends out His Word, He can heal you. His Spirit can quicken your dead souls, and enliven your dullest frames. It is in the belief of this that I now address you, and if a Divine energy will accompany the Word, I make no doubt of rousing you, dead as you are, to a sense of your danger and to an earnest longing after Jesus Christ. O that He would speak to you, as He spoke to Lazarus, saying, "Come forth!" or in the language of the prophet, "O ye dry bones, hear the Word of the Lord!" O that this might be the "hour in which the dead among you shall hear the voice of the Son of God and live!" (John 5:25) It is His voice alone that has this vivifying power in all ages of the world. Let not ministers therefore imagine that they can convert souls by their gifts and persuasive eloquence; but let them rely altogether upon His promise who said, "Lo, I am with you alway, even unto the end of the world". And if any are brought to the Lord, it is this "I" who stands at the door and knocks that is the efficient cause of it. It is the Holy Spirit that convinces the world of sin.'[1]

---

[1] *Eight Sermons*, 23, 43–5. Among the Vincent Manuscripts at NLW [Cwrt Mawr MS 859C], one writer claims that 'the observations on the word "Behold" in the sermon on Rev. 3:20 were taken from Gill's *Remains*'. The writer adds, 'Indeed I have seen the actual volume with the name of Daniel Rowland on the title page from which the said observations had been translated. When I mentioned this circumstance to an old clergyman who was well acquainted with, and a great admirer of, Daniel Rowland, he replied that Mr. Rowland was in the invariable habit of preaching from short notes all his lifetime, and that the only sermons in his possession must have been written by him when very young. When Mr. T. Davies of Fishguard applied to him for sermons to be published, he took some of his early sermons out of a box and gave them to him, not remembering and probably not caring whether they were all original or not.' It has not been possible to verify this statement. Besides the published sermons, Rowland's son Nathaniel reported that his father had prepared another for the press, but that it had been lost. The text was 1 Cor. 15:32, 'If after the manner of men I have fought with beasts at Ephesus . . .', and the theme portrayed the character of the believer's spiritual conflict, especially against Satan's temptations and attacks. See *Casgliad o Bregethau a Hymnau y Diweddar Barch. Daniel Rowlands*, 1864, tud. xxii.

Such were the convictions which lay behind the 1762 revival and the explosive rejoicing which accompanied it. Those who have ignored the solid base of sound teaching which preceded and accompanied the revival have often regarded what took place as emotional excess or even worse. Both the essence of that revival and its excellence, as of any other true work of God, are to be understood, rather, in terms of a manifestation of God's free grace to undeserving sinners communicated through preaching and in song.

As always, the precise manifestation of God's presence awaited His sovereign time. Men had been preaching and praying before, congregations had been longing and singing and sighing for God to come, but God's intervention is always sovereign. Rowland and the other ministers had laboured diligently and with a measure of success during the previous years, but in 1762 the Holy Spirit was poured out in exceptional profusion. Williams relates His coming to a despised, dispirited prayer meeting:

'At last, forced by cowardice, unbelief, and the onslaughts of Satan, we resolved to give up our special meeting, and now we were about to offer a final prayer, fully intending never again to meet thus in fellowship. But it is when man reaches the lowest depths of unbelief that God imparts faith, and when man has failed, that God reveals Himself. So here with us, in such straits, on the brink of despair, with the door shut on every hope of success, God Himself entered into our midst, and the light of day from on high dawned upon us. One of the brethren, yes, the most timid of us all, the one who was strongest in his belief that God would never visit us, while in prayer, was stirred in his spirit and laid hold powerfully on heaven as one who would never let go. His tongue spoke unusual words, his voice was raised, his spirit was aflame. He pleaded, he cried to God, he struggled, he wrestled in earnest like Jacob, in the agony of his soul. The fire took hold of others, all were awakened, the coldest to the most heedless took hold and were warmed; the spirit of struggling and wrestling fell on all, we all went with him into the battle; with him we laid hold upon God, His attributes, His Word and His promises, resolving that we would never let go our hold until all our desire should be satisfied.'

This was another factor in the revival: believing, persistent, agonising prayer. Its life and vigour, too, must come from the Holy Spirit, and as Williams showed, His coming is unexpected, and irresistible. The promises of God's Word were pleaded, their fulfilment awaited, and God's people were not put to shame:

'And this came to pass, for there fell upon us the sweet breath of the love of the Lord. We were filled as if with fulness of the bowls and horns of the altar. The fire was kindled and we gave voice with our tongues. The cloud melted away, the sun shone, we drank of the fruit of the vines of the promised land, and we were made to rejoice. Gone was unbelief, gone guilt, gone fear, gone a timid, cowardly spirit, lack of love, envy, suspicion, together with all the poisonous worms that tormented us before; and in their place came love, faith, hope, a joyful spirit, with a glorious multitude of the graces of the Holy Spirit. Up till now the service was only beginning, for prayer, singing, praise and blessing were redoubled, and no one felt like bringing things to an end. Now some were weeping, some praising, some singing, some filled with heavenly laughter, and all full of wonder and love and amazement at the Lord's work – to my mind like the time of the Apostles, when the Spirit descended from on high on a handful of fearful people, and strengthened them mightily. . . . As it was then, so it was here now.'

What followed was glorious and heavenly. The blessings spread like a flood, carrying all before it. 'The sermons were a delight, the listeners plentiful, thoughtful, and eager to listen. There were some convicted in every service. . . . Now the tone of the whole district was changed.'[1] It was all reminiscent of the prophecy of 'that Scripture in Joel 2:29–30' which found its initial fulfilment on the Day of Pentecost.

The Awakening now became virtually general throughout Wales. Something of the fervour of revival comes through in the writing of a Caernarfonshire exhorter, Robert Jones:

'About the year 1762, in the face of great unworthiness and baseness, God remembered His covenant by graciously visiting a great number of sinners in several parts of Wales. . . . There was a great difference between this revival and that which began at first through the agency of Mr. Harris. The mode of proceeding in that was sharp and very thunderous; but in this, as in the house of Cornelius long ago, great crowds magnified God without being able to cease, but sometimes leaping in jubilation as did David before the Ark. Sometimes whole nights were spent with a voice of joy and praise, as a multitude that kept holy day. I heard from a godly old woman that it lasted three days and three nights without a break in a place called Lôn-fudr in Lleyn, Caernarfonshire, one crowd following the other. When some went home, others came in their place, and although they went to their homes for a while, they could stay there hardly any time before returning. When these powerful outpourings descended on several

[1] William Williams, *The Experience Meeting*, pp. 8–10.

hundreds, if not thousands, throughout South Wales and Gwynedd, there arose much excitement and controversy concerning the matter; many were struck with amazement and said, "What can this mean?" "They are drunkards", said some. Others, very like those on the Day of Pentecost long ago, said "They are mad".'

In May 1763 Harris could bear witness to the vast congregations, mentioning figures up to 12,000 attending the Word. 'Now a great awakening in several parts of the country', he says, adding 'vast singing and rejoicing'. He had first heard in February about 'the spirit of singing that is fallen on various parts, and of several hundreds awakened in Cardigan, Carmarthen, and other shires, and the vast flock coming to hear'. He advised caution about owning or denying these outward manifestations, saying that they should be judged by their moral influence upon the heart and life, looking especially to see whether they produced poverty of spirit. At the same time, it was perfectly understandable and inevitable that God's people should rejoice:

'This work of singing, if God comes in this way for a time for some wise purpose, who will hinder Him? His saving and usual way is to come without any outward appearance, calmly, quietly, and still. If a man was in Carmarthen jail for debt, and never hoped to come from there, and beyond expectation a relative from the East Indies, hearing of his circumstances, would come and pay his debt and release him, would you blame him much if he could not contain himself for some time, but did leap as David before the Ark? Would you not excuse him? The case here is beyond this! . . . This spirit of singing is not as yet attended with levity and self as the last was.'[1]

As the revival progressed, criticism and censure followed. From Carmarthenshire came this letter to a London Newspaper:

'There is here what some call a great Reformation in Religion among the Methodists, but the case is really this. They have a sort of rustic dance in their public worship, which they call religious dancing, in imitation of David's dancing before the Ark. Some of them strip off their clothes, crying out "Hosannah!" etc. in imitation of those that attend our Saviour when He rode into Jerusalem. They call this the glory of the latter day; and when any person speaks to them of their extravagance, the answer they give is, "You have the mark of the enemy in your forehead!" Such is the delusion and uncharitableness of this people!'

[1] HRS, 156, 157, 172, 173; TM i. 407.

Even a year later one correspondent was reporting the 'wild pranks' of the Methodists to his brother: 'The worship of the day being over, they have kept together in the place whole nights, singing, capering, bawling, fainting, thumping, and a variety of other exercises. The whole country for many miles round have crowded to see such strange sights.'

What was at first the object of curiosity and debate soon became matter for distortion, caricature, and sheer fabrication. Comment was often as false as the description which the poet Edward Williams later offered of the effects of the preaching of one of the English Calvinistic preachers, Rowland Hill:

> Come, all ye true believers
> Of Calvin's ranting sect;
> Tho' deemed by some, deceivers,
> We are sure the Lord's elect
> And a-jumping we will go.
>
> In Antinomian beauty,
> Our gospel we display;
> We teach no moral duty,
> No reasoning laws obey.
> But a-jumping we will go.
>
> With mad fanatic jumping,
> With folly bawled aloud,
> Wild rant and pulpit thumping,
> We charm the silly crowd,
> When a-jumping we do go.

At the end of the century an observer who understood no Welsh attended a meeting of the so-called 'jumpers' at Caernarfon. After the 'raving' of the preacher, interspersed by noises from the congregation, a psalm was sung, during which – it was claimed – 'part of the assembly' were seen 'jumping in small parties of three or four together, and lifting up their hands, beating their breasts, and making the most horrid gesticulations'. The same 'sect' was shortly afterwards accused of disloyalty to the throne, as 'instruments of Jacobinism', and distributors of Thomas Paine's treasonable literature. Such a bad press in 1799 drew from Thomas Charles a careful defence. He pointed out that monoglot English accusers were hardly in a position to judge the content of Welsh sermons, and emphasised that 'the doctrines preached, and the morality inculcated by the Methodists are drawn from the pure fountain of inspiration, and are in exact conformity with the Articles of the Established Church'.[1]

So much for the word of foes: what of friends? At Carmarthen on August 27, 1763, John Wesley was given a report of revival phenomena 'in the congregations attended by Mr. William Williams and one or two other clergymen'. 'It is common', alleged the reporter, 'after the preaching is over for anyone that has a mind, to give out a verse of a hymn. This they sing over and over with all their might, perhaps over thirty, yes, forty times. Meanwhile the bodies of two or three, sometimes ten or twelve, are violently agitated, and they leap up and down in all manner of postures, frequently for hours together.' Wesley, for his part, gives his own views of the report in his *Journal*.

'I think there needs no great penetration to understand this. They are honest, upright men who really feel the love of God in their hearts. But they have little experience, either of the ways of God or the devices of Satan. So he serves himself of their simplicity in order to wear them out, and to bring a discredit on the work of God.'

Wesley had a short memory. A mere eighteen years earlier he had written these words about excesses at a time of revival: 'Do you delay fixing your judgment till you see a work of God without any stumbling block attending it? There never was yet, nor ever will. . . . And scarce ever was there such a work of God before, with so few as have attended this.'

Spiritual discernment, charity, and patience are required to assess the reality of revival phenomena. At a time of great emotional experiences there is the possibility of a worked-up joy as well as that of being overcome with joy. Speaking for the Welsh Methodists, Williams affirmed, 'I am convinced that the Spirit of God is the author of this present work, however many hypocrites mix their voices with those of genuine believers. . . . But you must expect great trials in the days to come, a bitter winter after such a glorious

---

[1] *Lloyd's Evening Post and British Chronicle*, June 27–29, 1763; G. Eyre Evans (ed.), *Lloyd Letter (1754–1796)*, 1908, p. 52, quoted in R. Geraint Gruffydd, *op. cit.*, pp. 23, 24; lx. 53; D. E. Jenkins, *Life of Thomas Charles*, ii. 360–1, 362, 364, 366. For Rowland Hill (1744–1833) see J. D. Douglas (ed.), *The New International Dictionary of the Christian Church*. For Edward Williams ('Iolo Morgannwg', 1747–1826) see DWB.

summer.' It was in such testing times that the real was to be distinguished from the counterfeit. Meanwhile, the leaders recognised that, as God was at work in their midst planting the wheat, so also the enemy would sow his tares.

Another Englishman, the kind, evangelical philanthropist John Thornton, expressed his concern about these manifestations. Rowland's reply was apparently quite effective: 'You English blame us, the Welsh, and speak against us and say, "Jumpers, jumpers". But we, the Welsh, have something also to allege against you, and we most justly say of you, "Sleepers, sleepers".'[1]

Williams' own appraisal appeared during the heat of the 1762 revival, when he wrote two of his most effective works in its defence. Before the end of 1745 he had read Jonathan Edwards' book, *Some Thoughts Concerning the Present Revival of Religion in New England*, and concluded that it was 'the best book I have seen to that purpose; it gave me more light in some things'. By 1762 he had also read Edwards' *The Distinguishing Marks of a Work of the Spirit of God*. From Williams' own pen, then, came 'Martha Philopur's Letter' in 1762, and 'Philo Evangelius's Reply' in 1763, from which his salutary comments are taken. The latter concludes with a quotation from *The Distinguishing Marks*, with the promise that Williams would publish the full work if any objected to his own. Such an issue, he added, would also serve as a rebuke to the Nonconformists who scornfully claimed that revival manifestations were to be found only among the Welsh Methodists!

The opening sentences of *The Distinguishing Marks* show the relevance of the work to the Great Awakening.

'In the apostolic age, there was the greatest outpouring of the Spirit of God that ever was; both as to his extraordinary influences and gifts, and his ordinary operations, in convincing, converting, enlightening, and sanctifying the souls of men. But as the influences of the true Spirit abounded, so counterfeits did also abound: the devil was abundant in mimicking, both the ordinary and extraordinary influences of the Spirit of God, as is manifest by innumerable passages of the apostles' writings. This made it very necessary that the church of Christ should be furnished with some certain rules, distinguishing and clear marks, by which she might proceed safely in judging of the true from the false without danger of being imposed upon.'

[1] John Wesley's *Journal*, v. 27–8; Luke Tyerman, *The Life of John Wesley*, i. 469; GWL ii. 30; JO, 35.

With great lucidity Edwards pursues his theme, starting from the premise, 'That there are some counterfeits is no argument that nothing is true: such things are always expected in a time of reformation.' Scripture prophecy like Isaiah 66:8, says Edwards, gave notice that extraordinary manifestations may be expected to accompany an outpouring of the Spirit. However, 'a work is not to be judged of by any effects on the bodies of men, such as tears, trembling, groans, loud outcries, agonies of body, or the failing of bodily strength'. Rather, 'the distinguishing evidences' of a genuine work, gathered from 1 John are a conviction of Christ's deity and saving uniqueness, an aversion to every manifestation of sin, a greater regard for God's Word, and God's love at work in the individual. Edwards was at pains to demonstrate the superiority of the Spirit's grace over His gifts:

'God communicated his own nature to the soul in saving grace in the heart, more than in all miraculous gifts. The blessed image of God consists in that and not in these. The excellency, happiness and glory of the soul immediately consists in the former. That is a root which bears infinitely more excellent fruit. Salvation and the eternal enjoyment of God is promised to divine grace, but not to inspiration.'[1]

Such wise counsel was available to Rowland and Williams as they faced the responsible task of safeguarding the 1762 work from error and excess.

The 'Martha' of Williams' writings is an imaginary but typical young convert of the 1762 revival. She is made to say what the revival has meant for her:

'O blessed hour, when my soul was in the greatest extremity, the day dawned upon me. In a moment I felt my sins forgiven. I received the Word in fullest ecstasy, fuller than any prisoner would feel on being released from sentence of hanging. . . . Like the woman of Samaria, fire is kindled in me, which I can no more extinguish than she could, without exploding! While you preach the Word of Life, I do my utmost to restrain myself, lest I cause others to stumble . . . and I

---

[1] *Select Works of Jonathan Edwards*, vol. i. 1965, pp. 86, 90, 91, 104, 138. For a discussion of Edwards on 'Revival' see the excellent paper by J. I. Packer in *Increasing in the Knowledge of God* (read at the Puritan and Reformed Studies Conference, London, December 1960), and by Dr D. Martyn Lloyd-Jones in *The Puritan Experiment in the New World* (read at the Westminster Conference, December 1976).

often cannot stop my tongue from crying out, "God is Good!" . . . The earliest opportunity I get, while Christ's love burns within me, and I give vent to my spiritual emotions, it is inevitable that I shout the Lord's praises; I bless and magnify God; I leap and shout for joy, in so great salvation, that I never knew before. . . . At such time my memory is more alert, and innumerable Scriptures flood my mind, all of this one strain – praising God for His free grace. My senses are sharpened; I understand the things of God in clearer light; my reason and emotions are so disciplined, that I am careful not to say or do anything which would cause my brethren to stumble, or the ungodly to blaspheme.'

That is what the 'jumping' was about: the unmixed, fresh, irresistible joy of salvation. Energy, emotion, understanding, memory, natural senses, spiritual desires, all – and more besides – were transposed to hitherto unimaginable heights of reality in the enjoyment of God. And the result?

'After sermons, the entire afternoon and well into the night, the time is spent in praying, singing, praising the name of the Lord for His coming, and in holding on to the heavenly breeze lest it be withdrawn. The place for the whole time was full of the presence of the Lord . . . some singing, while others were laughing, many weeping, gnashing their teeth and trembling in fear of the wrath to come.'

But she is deeply concerned lest her intense spiritual experiences were the heightened excesses of nature, and seeks her pastor's advice.

Accordingly, in his 'Reply', 'Philo' first gives a summary of what had happened:

'Now the day has dawned, the Lord has breathed on the dry bones and they move. Multitudes flock to the Word of Life, who can count them? North and south seek one King, and His name is One, Jesus, King of Saints! When the Sun of Righteousness arose with healing in His wings, and He flew towards us from on high with wonderful suddenness, the country was kindled by His brightness. Many ministers desired to see that hour; a thousand cried for that Sun to rise. At last He came. Our mourning turned to dancing; hearing the Word of Life is sweeter than market or fair. The six work days have turned to Sabbaths, and the Sabbath extends from one end of the year to the other. Salvation in Christ is the only pleasure of hosts of people. The country's young people have become estranged from fancy clothes. Sleep has fled. Craving for meat and drink is swallowed by praise and song. Hymns and Psalms and spiritual songs are the only nourishment at the saints' love feasts. Pride of honour and name are forgotten. Prayers, sermons, and especially singing praise to God cover the land. This is more wonderful than earthquakes and all the wars of the world. Blessed summer's day! It is come! it is come!'

Finally, Williams makes 'Philo' address himself to evaluation, and provide an answer to the question, 'How can it be said to be a genuine work of God?'

'It is not only by means of outward manifestations, such as verbal expressions of the tongue or physical movements of the body, shouting, jumping, and laughing, that I conclude that God is in the Church and is visiting His people. Apart from the heavenly inclination on their spirits inciting their tongues to a lively praising of God, this fire burns in the life and behaviour of so many of them. . . . They are zealous, not for secondary matters of faith, but for the essential issues of salvation. Faith and love are the chief graces they cry for. . . . They all acknowledge that Jesus of Nazareth is the true God . . . their Prophet, Priest, and King.'

The work's closing remarks belong to Edwards. 'We need not be sorry for breaking the order of means, by obtaining the end to which that order is directed. He who is going to fetch a treasure need not be sorry that he is stopped by meeting the treasure in the midst of his journey.'[1]

Certainly, life would not be lived in the perpetual heat of revival. True grace planted in the soul, however, would have a permanent and enabling quality. 'The children of promise', Rowland had said in a sermon on Caleb from Numbers 14:24, 'are the very ones who will believe and rest in God's promise even though Providence seems contrary. A man's spirit is sharpened all the more by means of obstacles and trials.'[2] As Williams had so judiciously pointed out, the true vindication still lay in the future, in the persistent Christian living of its leaders and followers. The same joy in the Holy Spirit which produced on occasions 'unspeakable raptures of mind' also provided unshakeable strength for living, whatever trials and 'contrary providences' there might be.

[1] GWP ii. 2, 3, 16, 28, 31.   [2] lvi. 64.

'The bishop permitted Rowland to continue preaching at Llangeitho as curate to his son, warning him at the same time that the Welsh clergy were constantly complaining of his irregularities, and that he could not long look over them. . . . To the bishop's threats Rowland replied, "that he had nothing in view but the glory of God in the salvation of sinners, and that as his labours had been so much blessed he could not desist". At length, in the year 1763, the fatal step was taken. The bishop sent Rowland a mandate, revoking his license. . . . Rowland was shut out of the Church of England, and an immense number of his people all over Wales followed him. A breach was made in the walls of the Established Church which will probably never be healed. As long as the world stands, the Church of England in Wales will never get over the injury done to it by the preposterous and stupid revocation of Daniel Rowland's license.'

BISHOP J. C. RYLE

29

'Herald of the King of Glory'

'If God is going to give you a heavier burden, He will also give you the shoulders on which to carry it.'[1] The saying is Calvin's, and its truth was wonderfully demonstrated in Rowland's experience. The very power and scale of the 1762 revival astonished its instruments and its critics alike. Rowland had witnessed scenes of intense spiritual activity before, but this manifestation of God's presence surpassed them all. God was giving him 'the shoulders on which to carry' the 'heavier burden' of expulsion from his curacy at Llangeitho.

Ecclesiastical disapproval was not new to Rowland, of course. The latest expression of this had been the appointment of his own son to succeed Daniel's brother to the living of Llangeitho. This was clearly intended as a rebuff to the father who had served as curate there for 25 years! John Rowland, Daniel's brother, had held the living since 1730, shortly before the death of their father. Now, on July 5, 1760, John had drowned while swimming at Aberystwyth. Rowland's son, also John, was collated and instituted to the Rectory of Llangeitho on September 24.

Neither the ties of family nor those of faith were important to Rowland's son. For the rest of his life he distanced himself geographically from Llangeitho, and made no attempt to hide his disapproval of his father's evangelical stance. Two other appointments affected Rowland, that of Isaac Williams to the Nantcwnlle living, and the licensing of a David Davies to curacies at Llanddewi-brefi and Llanbadarn Odwyn. This was an attempt to curtail Rowland's activities and influence. Its immediate effect, however, was financial rather than ecclesiastical. It drove his son, John, to seek more lucrative posts elsewhere, leaving his father to perform the

---

[1] G. E. Duffield (ed.), *John Calvin*, 1966, p. 86.

necessary parish duties. In October 1760 John was resident in the English border county of Hereford and by 1767 he had moved north to Shropshire, where he remained for the rest of his life. For a short while Daniel Rowland had a free hand at Llangeitho and Nantcwnlle. David Davies was either negligent, or indifferent enough to allow Rowland to preach at Llanddewi in November 1761 (the printed sermon on Rev. 3:20), and in 1768 a complaint was entered against him 'for scandalous living'. Isaac Williams resigned Nantcwnlle in 1764 and was succeeded in the following year by a John Thomas.[1]

The failure of Rowland's son to secure Nantcwnlle was a bitter disappointment to him. When a Bishop's visitation was arranged at Cardigan in 1767 he pleaded ill-health as the reason for non-attendance, adding his personal grievance:

'I am Rector of Llangeitho in that county, but have always lived in Shrewsbury, curate of St. Mary in that town. When I was inducted to Llangeitho, Bishop Ellis purposed in a little time to bestow upon me the adjoining church of Nantcwnlle, that it might be worth my while to reside there, but he soon after died, and then all my hopes were gone, for your predecessor, Dr. Squire, would bestow no favours upon me nor would he hear any solicitations for any one that went by the name of Rowland, believing, as I suppose, that the iniquity of the parents is entailed upon the child, whether he abhors the idolatry of the father or not. I need not inform you of anything concerning my father for I suppose by this time that you are well informed of his character, etc.'[2]

For Anthony Ellis, the Bishop in 1760, to appoint Rowland's son to Llangeitho was a useful compromise. On the one hand he did not want to be seen lending support to Rowland, and on the other he could not ignore the almost exclusive allegiance which Rowland commanded in the parish. Bishop Samuel Squire replaced Ellis in the year 1761, shortly before the powerful effects of another revival became a matter of public amazement and debate. Squire was no friend of the Methodists, and he was either unwilling or unable to

---

[1] xii. 58; NLW Church in Wales SD/BR/5, p. ix; NLW Cwrt Mawr MS 182B, 'Freehold Book for the Manor of Lampeter, 27 October 1760'; NLW Church in Wales SD/Misc/1826, and DWB, s.v. Daniel Rowland; NLW Church in Wales SD/Let/1198; SD/BR/5, pp. 29, 30; Shropshire Public Library, Shrewsbury. Deed 57.

[2] xlv. 77–8.

evaluate the joyful phenomena which accompanied the work at Llangeitho.

It is possible that political pressures precipitated the bishop's expulsion of Rowland from his curacies in July 1763. There is evidence that Herbert Lloyd of Peterwell, who had been friendly to the Methodists previously, was on favourable terms with the Bishop in the matter of ecclesiastical preferments. A complaint from Lloyd would have provided the Bishop with a sufficient reason for removing Rowland. Whatever the reason, the responsibility was clearly his, and on August 5 a 'licence was granted to the Revd. William Williams, Clerk, [not Williams, Pantycelyn] to perform the office of curate in the parish churches of Llangeitho and Nantcwnlle in the County of Cardigan, upon the several appointments of the Revd. John Rowland, clerk, Rector of Llangeitho, dated 30 July 1763, and the Revd. Isaac Williams, clerk, Vicar of Nantcwnlle, dated August 3, 1763'.[1]

Harris heard of the event on arriving at Llangeitho for an Association on August 3: 'Mr Rowland is cast out of the churches.' A month later he told Rowland that he should feel honoured at being the first to suffer such persecution. In typical Harrisian fashion, he pleaded with Rowland and the others to stay within Anglicanism despite the provocation to separate:

'1. Not to turn to the Toleration Act [seeking legal status as another religious body] to trust to that, for that may be removed also, and is an arm of flesh; 2. Not to think of leaving the Church on this account lest it be malice, or seem so, and as a revenge on the Bishop for his severity; 3. Not to speak bitterly or evil of the Bishop, lest the seed of evil or rising against the Government be found among us.'

By October 1763 the full significance of the event was beginning to dawn even on Harris: 'The Bishops are going to ruin the Church of England by turning out so many thousands.'[2]

The Bishop's action inflicted untold damage on Anglicanism, both locally and nationally, at the time and for many generations to come. A letter in 1764 reflects contemporary judgment on the issue: 'Rowland is turned out of his cures by the Bishop, and now keeps up public worship in a house built hard by after the Form of the Church Liturgy. He has, however, the satisfaction of drawing the crowd after

---

[1] Bethan Phillips, *Peterwell*, p. 59; NLW SD/BR/5, p. 18.
[2] HRS, 188, 196, 200.

him, and of seeing his late churches almost vacant.' Subsequent history confirmed this. 'So completely did his parishioners follow Daniel Rowland, that the Sacrament of Holy Communion was not administered at the church for nearly fifty years. The people, it is true, remained faithful to the customary public service at the church every Sunday morning, but they took communion with the hosts of Wales at the New Chapel Gwynfil [built for Rowland nearby in the old village of Gwynfil, that name having been superseded by "Llangeitho"] every month from the hands of Daniel Rowland and his assistants.'

Two attempts were made to reinstate Rowland within Anglicanism. One was by the churchwardens and principal inhabitants of Nantcwnlle in 1767, who petitioned the Bishop for his services, John Thomas being non-resident. The latter, at their earnest request, had 'applied to the Reverend Mr. Daniel Rowland to be our curate (who faithfully served our church upwards of thirty years) to which Mr. Rowland agreed to, provided your Lordship would be pleased to give your consent (otherwise he will not).' No official appointment followed, and the parish register entries for 1770–71 are by 'John Lewis, clerk', except for one, a baptism at which 'the Rev. Daniel Rowland' officiated.[1]

The other attempt was in the form of an offer by John Thornton of the living of Newport in Pembrokeshire in November 1769. There were conditions: 'provided you will reside and are satisfied to proceed regularly as a minister of the Church of England. You may see by this that I know how to make all proper allowances for those irregularities that ministers are too often forced into by being shut out of the Church, but when they receive an offer of work sufficient to employ them in the pale of the Church, I think their whole strength ought to be devoted to it, as I hope yours will be henceforward'. It was a tempting offer. Rowland had been more than thirty years in the same parish without any ecclesiastical preferment. On the contrary, he had been repeatedly harassed by the authorities, and he was now, humanly speaking, isolated and without any support. God alone had honoured him, and in turn he found God's people were doing the same:

[1] George Eyre Evans (ed.), *Lloyd Letters (1754–1796)*, pp. 52–3; *Archaeologia Cambrensis*, xcix. 154–5; D. Edwardes, *Plwyf Nantcwnlle* (1913), tud. 4; xxxv. 72–3.

'When his people around Llangeitho heard of it, they were greatly distressed. They flocked in great numbers to his house, and their entreaties, their importunities, and their weepings, were such as can hardly be conceived. They were like children, on the eve of being left by a beloved father, the staff of their support, and the supplier of their comfort.'

Their importunity prevailed, and the conditions were found to be unacceptable. Before the end of the 1769, Thornton reluctantly and affectionately had to withdraw the offer: 'I have got a letter from your son Nathaniel mentioning the concern your people are under at the thoughts of losing you, and that you proposed sometimes doing duty where you are at present. That can't be, as it is not an ordained Chapel, and unless you resolve to reside at Newport and be wedded to your parish, we can't stand before the Bishop.' So much by letter; in private to Nathaniel, Thornton said, 'I had a high opinion of your father before, but I have now a still higher opinion of him, though he declines to accept my offer. The reasons he assigns are highly creditable to him. It is not a usual thing with me to allow other people to go to my pocket, but tell your father, that he is fully welcome to do so whenever he pleases.'[1]

It was at Llangeitho that Rowland remained for the rest of his life. Far from being curtailed, his usefulness as well as his freedom were considerably enhanced by doing so. Now in his 59th year, Rowland was still one of those who 'turned the world upside down'. The evil expectations and intentions of his eviction were thwarted and reversed by the Sovereign power of an Almighty God. By the miracle of His grace, even set-backs were transformed into successes.

Rowland was by no means isolated on account of this ecclesiastical blunder. The Methodist ranks were augmented by a number of godly, able ministers, both from within Anglicanism and from without. On his travels through Cardiganshire early in 1764, Harris learned that Rowland's defence of the revival to the Bishop had been rejected on the grounds that it estranged people from the Established Church and belittled the clergy. At the same time Harris made the acquaintance of one of the sympathetic Nonconformists. This was Thomas Grey, successor to Philip Pugh in the neighbouring Independent churches, and living in Nantcwnlle. He had worked for a time as a coal miner, but while preparing for the ministry at Abergavenny

[1] xxix. 34; xix. 125; JO, 76.

Academy, had been blessed by Rowland's ministry. He was evidently of a 'Methodist Mind', attended Association meetings, and on occasions helpfully supplied Rowland's pulpit during his absence. However strongly attracted Grey may have been to Methodism, Rowland counselled him to continue his labours within Independency: 'You had better continue working that side of the mountain where you are, and I will go on here; we may meet in time, undermining the kingdom of Satan.'[1]

William Williams had been free of episcopal restraints for over twenty years. He was still Rowland's chief ally, living with his wife and two sons at his mother's old home of Pantycelyn, but free to assist at Llangeitho and to travel widely throughout Wales. Howel Davies and Peter Williams were also 'in the field', exercising fruitful ministries in their respective spheres, Davies mainly in Pembrokeshire, Williams itinerating in England as well as in Wales.

As Davies laboured in a more English-speaking part of the country, he continued to be favoured with visits by Whitefield. In 1767 there were unforgettable memories for Whitefield after one such visit. Apart from the crowds, 'life and light seemed to fly around', and the general cry was 'for more of the Bread of Life'. Davies was not well at the time, but Whitefield advised him to preach in spite of it: 'I have been pushing on dear, sick Mr. Davies to go out and preach six miles off. He is gone finely mounted, and I am persuaded will return in high spirits. Who knows, but preaching may be our grand, universal remedy again? This is the good Methodistical, thirty-year old medicine!'[2] Whitefield's next visit to Wales was for the opening of a College at Trefeca in August 1768.

Of the clergy who were now coming into prominence as the 'second generation' of Methodists, two have special significance, David Jones of Llan-gan and Rowland's own son, Nathaniel. Jones had been at Llan-gan since 1767 and was present at the third College Anniversary. The Countess of Huntingdon used him as often as possible to supply her chapels. He preached at the opening of her Swansea building in 1789, and at her funeral in London on July 3, 1791, he preached on Genesis 50:24, 'And Joseph said to his brethren, I die, and God will surely visit you.'

'You will say, we have lost a great mother in Israel, but the God of

[1] TM i. 415; HMGC ii. 19; MR, 150. For Thomas Grey see DWB.
[2] GWL iii. 348, 349.

Israel lives. If He takes away a Moses, He will give a Joshua. There is no loss at the hands of our God. . . . If He takes away a humble and resigned Eli, He will soon favour the Church with a Samuel. If He takes away an eminent Elijah, behold in His hand, for the comfort of the Church, Elisha with a double portion of his spirit. . . . God has honoured me with her acquaintance for nearly thirty years, and I have been with her in many of her public excursions for the spread of the Gospel. We have often met with the enmity and scorn of the world, yet for our support, Jesus, the Leader of His despised host, has frequently refreshed our souls with the sweet cordials of His Gospel of peace, and thus enabled us to hold on in the day of battle. . . . Not many days before her last illness, she said to me, "O, Jones! my soul is filled with glory, my soul is filled with glory!" . . . Remember! Jesus lives, though friends die; Jesus our Head and Captain said, "Because I live, you shall live also." This will turn our mourning into joy, our black cloth into white robes, and our hosannas into hallelujahs for ever and ever.'

What impressed many people about David Jones was his tenderness. Christopher Bassett, at one time curate to William Romaine, said of him, 'I have never seen one who appeared in the pulpit imbued to such a degree with the spirit of the Gospel. His ministry seemed to me singularly adapted to conciliate enemies to the truth, to strengthen the weak, and to decide the wavering. He was well-skilled in administering the "Balm of Gilead" to the wounded conscience.' He travelled extensively in North Wales, and was instrumental in the conversion of that eminently useful preacher, Robert Roberts, Clynnog.

Llan-gan became in Glamorganshire what Llangeitho had become in Cardiganshire, a centre of Methodism, and more importantly, the scenes of extraordinary visitations of God's Spirit. A contemporary describes the kind of zeal which stirred people to attend David Jones' ministry: 'The travellers increased all the way as we went until we arrived at Llan-gan, about eleven miles distant; and many coming from a greater distance overtook us on the road. Such was our desire for spiritual food, that we could not be prevented by any weather, however severe'.[1]

[1] Seymour, ii. 112, 115, 504–07; Griffith Parry (gol.), *Cofiant a Phregethau Robert Roberts Clynnog*, 1884, tud. 13; xx. 99; For David Jones see DWB. Also Eifion Evans, 'David Jones of Llan-gan in *The Gospel Magazine*, April 1967, pp. 152–163; and R. Brian Higham, unpublished Thesis M.Th. (Wales, 1980), 'The Life and Work of the Rev. David Jones, Llan-gan, 1736–1810.'

Several factors account for the fact that Jones did not attain during his lifetime the eminence among his countrymen that he deserved. One was his commitment to the Countess of Huntingdon, necessitating some periods of absence from Wales. Another was the fact that Nathaniel Rowland, after his father's death, exploited his father's name to lever himself into positions of power and prominence. A third reason, more personal and more gratifying, was his own gracious, meek spirit.

In contrast, Nathaniel Rowland was proud and domineering, living very much on the capital of his father's prestige. He was educated at Oxford and ordained deacon by the Bishop of Oxford on May 26, 1771, and priest by the Bishop of London on September 21, 1773. He spent some three years as a curate in Essex under William Unwin, an evangelical clergyman who was familiar with the Countess of Huntingdon. In 1776 Nathaniel married Howel Davies's daughter, Margaret, and settled in Pembrokeshire. From 1778 he pastored the Methodist flock in Haverfordwest, and served as clerk of the Association until 1797. As long as his father was alive, Nathaniel showed enough diligence to find general acceptance with the Methodist fraternity. Williams, in his elegy to Rowland, goes so far as to address Nathaniel as 'the servant of heaven', urging him to be a father to the Association, and to shepherd the flock which his father had gathered. He added, 'if you feel weak, you will get help from that true evangelist, honest David of Llangan'.

Regrettably, this was the last thing that Nathaniel was capable of doing, and the Pembrokeshire flock, which came under his care after the death of Howel Davies, suffered as a result. He was favoured with the Countess of Huntingdon's patronage while she lived, but by the turn of the century there was a marked decline in the quality of his spiritual ministrations as in the moral quality of his life. The former degenerated into a zeal for maintaining Anglicanism when the Methodist societies longed for the satisfaction of a greater need, the nourishment of their souls. In the area of personal discipline, drunkenness and gluttony proved his undoing. The Association with great reluctance finally expelled him from their midst in 1807.[1]

When Howel Davies died in 1770 these sad events were still in the distant future. The extra burden of oversight in Pembrokeshire would have fallen on Rowland particularly, and on Williams

[1] See DWB; xxxvi. 33; xlv. 67–70; xlvi. 10–16, 60–70; TM ii. 328.

Pantycelyn and Peter Williams to a lesser degree. Nathaniel's marriage and settlement in Pembrokeshire eased that burden considerably and even satisfactorily in the eighties. In his Welsh elegy to Davies, Williams consoled the Pembrokeshire flock who mourned his passing, 'Jesus Himself is the physician who will make the plaster as big as the wound.' His English elegy is both poignant with grief, 'Poor Wales has lost a bright, laborious man', and yet full of promise:

> Cease, Pembroke, cease, 'tis sinful to lament,
> As hopeless men for pious souls that went
> To Realms of Bliss, to reap what they have sown,
> And for their toil receive Eternal Crown.
> Thy God will send, thy God knows all thy need,
> Some faithful pastor all thy flock to feed;
> When Moses's gone to mingle with the blest,
> A Joshua shall lead Jacob to his rest.[1]

Within three years God had called a 'Joshua' of His choice 'to lead Jacob to his rest'.

This was Thomas Charles, a Carmarthenshire man, whose name became inseparably linked with Bala, Sunday Schools, and the Bible Society. The instrument of his conversion was Rowland, the occasion, a preaching service at Llangeitho, the date, January 20, 1773, and the text, Hebrews 4:15, 'For we have not a high priest which cannot be touched with the feeling of our infirmities, but was in all points tempted like as we are, yet without sin.' Charles was eighteen at the time, studying at Carmarthen Academy, and already under some religious impressions. Then came 'the day of his espousals' and 'the day of the gladness of his heart':

'A day much to be remembered by me as long as I live. Ever since the happy day I have lived in a new heaven and a new earth. The change a blind man who receives his sight experiences does not exceed the change I at that time experienced in my mind. . . . Then I was first convinced of the sin of unbelief or entertaining narrow, contracted, and hard thoughts of the Almighty. I had such a view of Christ as our High Priest, of His love, compassion, power, and all-sufficiency, as filled my soul with astonishment, with joy unspeakable and full of glory. My mind was overwhelmed and overpowered with amazement. The truths exhibited to my view appeared too wonderfully

[1] CYN i. 478, 655.

gracious to be believed. I could not believe for very joy. The glorious scenes then opened to my eyes will abundantly satisfy my soul millions of years hence in the contemplation of them. I had some idea of Gospel truths before floating in my head, but they never powerfully and with divine energy penetrated my heart till now. The effect of this sermon remained upon my mind above half a year, during which time I was generally in a comfortable and heavenly frame. Often in walking in the fields, I looked up to heaven with joy and called that my home, at the same time ardently longing for the appearance of the glorious Saviour to take me for ever to Himself. At times doubts would come into my mind, and I would say within myself, "Can it possibly be that these things are true?" The Lord would reply, "I will not execute the fierceness of my anger, I will not return to destroy Ephraim, *for I am God and not man.*" Praise the Lord, O my soul, and forget not all His benefits! About this time also Luther's exposition of Galatians 1:4 was very much and particularly blessed to me, as it has been many times since.'

From that time Charles was no stranger to Llangeitho: 'When at school at Carmarthen my excursions there in the holidays, twice a year, were more profitable to me than all the sermons I heard in the intervals between. I had therefore every possible reason to think highly of that great and good man of God.' Rowland later came to regard Charles as 'the Lord's gift to North Wales', faithful in his labours, wise in his counsel, and solidly biblical in his teaching.

With regard to Gospel usefulness, Charles exemplified in his practice what he firmly believed,

'that it is not sufficient, to make a minister of the Gospel, to have a system of wholesome doctrines in the head, except he is led by the Holy Spirit to see and feel the glory of the person of Christ, and the excellency of the work accomplished by Him for sinners. The truths which he preaches must be his *own* food and nourishment, and not food to be talked of to others only. What need we have to be humble and fervent in prayer for divine illumination and teaching! If we ourselves live far from God in daily communion, we can do but little good to others with our refined notions.'

Those sentiments were written in 1787. Charles evidently shared 'the Methodist Mind' of Rowland and Williams.

Thomas Charles never tired of owning that Rowland's ministry had been God's means of bringing him to whatever usefulness in the work of the Gospel had been his portion. 'Wales . . . is a highly favoured country. That aged herald of the King of Glory, D. Rowland, is, and will be an eternal honour to it. I seldom can speak of him in moderate terms. I love him dearly and honour him as my father in Christ, and not without reason, for to him, under God, I am indebted for whatever light I have, and experience I have of the glorious salvation through Christ.'[1] During the crucial years of Welsh Calvinistic Methodism's emergence from Anglicanism, Charles' wise contribution was invaluable. To a wider Christian public his printed works, particularly *Geiriadur Charles* (a Scripture Dictionary) and *Hyfforddwr* (an extended catechism), became household names. Rowland's influence would live on for another generation through the life and witness of such men as Charles.

[1] D. E. Jenkins, *The Life of the Rev. Thomas Charles B.A. of Bala*, 1908, vol. i, pp. 35, 173, 542, 569; William Hughes (ed.), *Life and Letters of the Rev. Thos. Charles, B.A.*, 1881, p. 130.

'*I have no objection, if you will print the lightning, thunder, and rainbow with it.*'

GEORGE WHITEFIELD
when asked about printing one of his sermons.

'*Thank God the Spirit can use a written sermon, but it does not compare with a preached sermon.*'

D. MARTYN LLOYD-JONES

30

'Theomemphus, Seeker After God'

While the ecclesiastical authorities sought to curtail Rowland's influence, other events were taking place which both established and widened it. In addition to the fact that God was raising a number of godly preachers to carry on the work, the biblical message which they sought to propagate was made available in the literature which the Welsh Methodists produced. Rowland also found fresh support and opportunity in his ministry through closer acquaintance with the Countess of Huntingdon.

In 1764 the Countess had visited Trefeca. A plan which had been in Harris's mind for some years was now agreed upon, and the Countess initiated the setting up at Trefeca of a College for training men for the ministry. While it was a new venture, and distinctly Methodist, it served to distance Trefeca from the Welsh work, its contribution being mainly to the Chapels of the Countess in England. Ordination in the Countess's Connexion did not take place until March 1783. Its first President was John Fletcher, and as a 'School of the Prophets' its aim was to produce godly preachers of the Gospel.[1]

From its opening on August 24, 1768, it did, however, provide a grand 'Anniversary' preaching occasion every August, at which Rowland often preached. From 1781 the same event was to be used for a joint Association between Welsh and English Calvinistic Methodism. In this way the whole of August became for Rowland a feast of preaching opportunities, one of the Welsh Associations

[1] See Eifion Evans, *Howel Harris, Evangelist*, pp. 62–3; xxvii. 66–75; liii. 88–9; Geoffrey F. Nuttall, *The Significance of Trevecka College, 1768–91*, 1969; *Transactions of the Honourable Society of Cymmrodorion*, Session 1967, Part ii. 1968; Seymour, ii. 78–86 (which mentions the books used); Edwin Welch, *Two Calvinistic Methodist Chapels*, 1975, p. 67; Seymour, ii. 436, ff.

[335]

being held regularly at Llangeitho in the same month.

The Countess of Huntingdon also prevailed upon Rowland to preach in England. He did so at Bath in September 1766, and again in 1768 before returning to Trefeca in time for the College opening. The journey took him through Gloucestershire, in company with the Countess and Mr Shirley, both men preaching 'several times in the pulpits of the Established Church.' At Tewkesbury, 'the audience was exceedingly large and deeply attentive'. When Rowland preached in the afternoon on Hebrews 9:27, 'It is appointed unto men once to die, but after this the judgment', the congregation was even larger, 'and there was not an inattentive hearer'. The Countess felt that 'a remarkable power from on high accompanied the message of His servants, and many felt the arrows of distress'. The College opening lasted several days with a cluster of preachers taking part, Howel Davies, Peter Williams, and John Wesley among them. Rowland preached on August 19, taking as his text Luke 13:23, 'Lord, are there few that be saved?' The glowing report that Whitefield received prompted the comment to Wesley, 'I am glad to hear that you had such a Pentecost season at the College.' Each Anniversary duplicated the fervour and expectancy of that inaugural gathering, and was seldom unworthy of being called a 'Pentecost season'. Rowland was present in 1770, 1771, 1774, and 1776, and he may have been there in other years as well. Something of the same power evidently persisted over a sustained period, and on April 1, 1777, the Countess of Huntingdon was writing: 'one of our Welsh ministers, Mr. Rowland, has been at Bristol and set it all on fire', adding, 'I keep the Association of all the Welsh ministers in South and North Wales on the 21st of May; I suppose a hundred will meet, of the clergy and others.'[1]

Another aspect of support for Rowland from the Countess was a chaplaincy to the Duke of Leinster. The title, 'Chaplain to the Duke of Leinster', first appeared on the title-page of his three sermons in Welsh, published in 1775. On the 1778 English issue of the three sermons the Duke is called 'one of His Majesty's most Honourable Privy Council in the Kingdom of Ireland'. Such chaplaincies were tokens of favour, and in Rowland's case the influence of the Countess in securing it is quite obvious. Nevertheless, Rowland

---

[1] Seymour i. 476, 428; ii. 98–100, 85, 107, f.; 112, 120, 122; TGW ii. 570; Letter Countess of Huntingdon to Mr Wills, April 1, 1777, from College (NLW Microfilm; original in Rylands Library, Manchester).

remained the same man, in spite of such aristocratic recognition. An anecdote preserved by Edward Morgan, one of Rowland's early biographer's, illustrates this.

'Rowland knew that the value of the Lord's people, however poor, is inestimable, and that their destiny is most glorious. He would own them as his most beloved friends on all occasions. He was honoured at times with the company of persons of distinction. Some great folks whom he knew, came to see him one day, and he was disposed to show a little facetiousness towards them at the time. He told them, in course of conversation, that he could introduce them that day to the company of the king's son. They were much pleased with this good news, and were very anxious to have the favour of such an interview. At last Rowland sent for a truly godly man, that was engaged in the field, preparing the ground for seed. The good man returned home by and by, and went into the house. He was desired to walk into Rowland's room as he was. "Well", said Rowland, when he made his appearance, "here is the king's son; yea, a son of the King of kings, before whom all the kings and princes of the earth shall be gathered one day, to give an account of what was done in the body". It is supposed that the circumstance had its desired effect, in leading these high persons to think better of the children of God, though poor and humble; that they are even kings now in disguise, and that they shall be hereafter highly exalted, Revelation 1:6.'[1]

Rowland considered that the advantages of such a chaplaincy were to be measured primarily in terms of the occasional opportunities of Gospel ministry to the aristocracy which it offered. Financial benefits and prestige were of secondary importance.

However, there was something more important to Rowland than the nominal privilege of a chaplaincy. This was the responsibility to secure the witness of Methodism for the future by arranging settled places of worship for the emerging societies. This did not please everybody. Edmund Jones complained of his policy in 1778:

'Daniel Rowland lately with great solemnity consecrated two places of worship in Pembrokeshire in which no layman of the Methodists is to preach. But there is an adjoining room to that building with a little pulpit in which such as are in connection and communion with Mr. Rowland shall preach. In the consecrated church the whole service of the church is to be performed by ordained clergy. . . . How proud and uncharitable the Methodists are!'[2]

[1] MR, 154–5.
[2] NLW MS 7028A, 'Diary of Edmund Jones, 1778: Sayings and Doings of Erroneous Men'.

Rowland's view of what was involved in a properly equipped and regularly ordained ministry was different from that of Jones. If its order was unacceptable to the latter, it did not follow that its spirit was necessarily 'proud and uncharitable'. Rowland was still in Anglican orders even though he lacked an Anglican benefice. The truth is, that throughout Rowland's lifetime Methodism was cast in an Anglican mould.

Nevertheless, Rowland frequently fulfilled this role of 'consecrating' new church buildings, in North as well as in South Wales. A typical Trust Deed stipulated that the building was 'to be used and occupied as a Meeting-house or place of religious or divine worship for the use of the said Protestants called Methodists, and wherein such teachers or ministers only are to be admitted as shall preach and embrace the Doctrine of Salvation contained in the Ninth, Tenth, Eleventh, Twelfth, Thirteenth, Fifteenth, Seventeenth and Eighteenth Articles of the Church of England.' The choice of Articles is significant. They referred to original sin, free will, justification, the place of good works, the sinlessness of Christ, election, and 'Of obtaining eternal Salvation only by the Name of Christ.' In this way the Methodists safeguarded their doctrinal future.

The fact that, at the opening of such a building there would be preaching, was an indication that the future lay as much with the people who believed the message as with the statement which embodied that message. Edward Morgan gives an account of one such occasion relating to a chapel in Flintshire, North Wales, in 1775:

'The good man that built it, named John Owen, went over to Llangeitho, a distance of seventy miles, to solicit Rowland to favour them at the opening of it. But this excellent man did not live to enjoy the much-anticipated pleasure; he died at Llangurig, Montgomeryshire, on his return home from Llangeitho. . . . Rowland had the mournful office of preaching at his funeral, on his way to open his chapel.'

That was neither the first nor the last of Rowland's journeys to North Wales for the purpose intended by men like Owen. He had been to Denbighshire in 1771 and went to Caernarfonshire in 1777, allegedly his last tour in the north. While in Denbighshire in September 1772, his sermon on Genesis 49:18, 'I have waited for thy salvation, O Lord', and another sermon the next day proved contributory to the conversion of Thomas Jones, another North

Wales Methodist leader whose great contribution lay in steering the Methodism of the following century safely between the rocks of Arminianism and High Calvinism. Together with Charles he published a periodical, *Trysorfa Ysbrydol* (Spiritual Treasury), and personally translated into Welsh William Gurnall's *Christian in Complete Armour* and a history of the martyrs.[1]

In their literary efforts, both Thomas Jones and Thomas Charles were following in the tradition of Rowland and Williams. The latter, for the last twenty-five years of their lives continued to nurture the Welsh Methodists by this more permanent means. Their output forms a rich and varied legacy.

If North Wales held the prospect of advance, in the south there was once more the threat of doctrinal error. At the Woodstock (Pembrokeshire) Association in May 1764, Rowland preached from John 12 on Mary's anointing of the feet of Jesus. The crowds were larger than ever and there was great harmony. A note of discord, however, was struck by the exhorter John Popkin, and it was a very dangerous one. Popkin had been influenced by the teaching of the Scotsmen, Robert Sandeman and his father-in-law John Glas. This limping, unbalanced teaching undermined the true nature of saving faith, alleging a bare intellectual assent to the truth to be sufficient and neglecting the aspects of personal application to the heart and the will. The benefit of Christ's death, Sandeman affirmed, 'is conveyed to men only by the Apostolic report concerning it; (so) that every one who understands this report to be true, or is persuaded that the event actually happened as testified by the Apostles, is justified and finds relief to his guilty conscience; (further), that he is relieved not by finding any favourable symptoms in his own heart, but by finding their report to be true'.

William Williams, particularly, opposed Popkin on that occasion, charging him with being fickle and unstable. He told him that previously Elisha Coles had been his favourite, then Erskine, followed again by James Hervey, and now Sandeman was every-

---

[1] xl. 43; MR, 115; HMGC ii. 91, 61, 73; John Jones, *Cofiant ... Michael Roberts*, 1883, tud. 151; Jonathan Jones, *Cofiant ... Thomas Jones*, 1897, tud. 41. For Thomas Jones see DWB. Jones wrote an Elegy on the death of Rowland in which he refers to him as 'the bright, exalted star', and 'the candle of Wales', an 'authoritative spirit' whose 'enlightened, heavenly proclamation' delighted to dwell on 'the salvation which free grace had planned for guilty, helpless sinners'. Jonathan Jones, *op cit.* 410, 411, 387.

thing. Popkin was unrepentant and proceeded to disseminate his views in print, several items appearing between 1764 and 1781, translations of Glas and Sandeman's works among them. His preaching tours also sowed dissension and confusion, and one notable preacher, David Jones from Llangeitho, was strongly influenced by him. Their heretical teaching was diametrically opposed to everything for which Methodism stood, and they were both expelled from the Methodist ranks, not without causing much pain to Rowland and others.

In his elegy to Rowland, Williams compares Popkin and his followers to Lucifer, aspiring to climb to Rowland's chair, 'proud Sandemanians, boasting their light and power, inflated like bladders with wind, until they burst and come to nothing'. It was this jealousy to which they, and others, were so prone that Williams condemned as in *Crocodil Afon yr Aifft* (The Crocodile of Egypt's River), which was published in 1767. In this work he exposed the havoc wrought by jealousy, referring to biblical examples, from the jealousy of Cain and of Ahab in the Old Testament, to that of the elder brother of 'the Prodigal Son' and the gifted members of the church at Corinth in the New. Jealousy was a poison which had produced a 'black gang of fiends, which follow jealousy as smoke follows fire'. It had only gained access to the town of 'Mansoul' by a temporary neglect on the part of the watchmen on the walls, the chief of whom were 'Lively Ministry, Close Discipline, Sharp Reproofs, and Spiritual Oversight'. The only effective antidote was love, and the graces which accompany it: humility, unity and patience. In an 'Appreciation of the Bible', published in 1766, Williams had depicted Sandemanianism as 'bare believing, believing without the Spirit, without power', and denounced its belittling of conviction and broken-heartedness. 'Pentecost, baptism with the Spirit, baptism with fire' do not belong to Sandemanianism, 'any more than Lapland belongs to Guinea'.[1]

The most powerful presentation in print of Methodism, as an all-round 'believing with the Spirit and power', appeared from William Williams' pen in 1764, the very year he began opposing Popkin. The influence of that great Methodist classic, *Theomemphus* was both

---

[1] TM i. 416. For John Popkin see DWB; for Sandemanianism see D. Martyn Lloyd-Jones in *Profitable for Doctrine and Reproof*, 1967 Westminster Conference Papers; MR, 97–9; In Welsh see xxxix. 30–3; WW i. 144; ii. 160; GWP 11.36, 95, 99; David Williams, *Cofiant J. R. Jones, Ramoth*, tt. 754–9.

profound and lasting. It traced the believer's pilgrimage from nature's night to heaven's glory by drawing vivid sketches of people and teachings.

'Theomemphus' is first a representative sinner who has sinned his way through every conceivable transgression, and then a representative saint who by grace is delivered out of every conceivable temptation. Of special significance are the would-be and genuine soul-physicians. On the one hand the blind guides, Seducus, Orthocephalus, Schematicus, have nothing of Christ's righteousness and nothing of the Spirit's saving power. Only the preaching of Boanerges and Evangelius, and the counsels of Dr Alethius bring conviction and life to the soul. God's grace in the believer sees him through the trials of life, enables him to triumph over temptation, compensates his disappointments, and guides him in all his decisions, including that of marriage. Here Williams depicts Theomemphus as having to forego one courtship because there was too much of the flesh in it, only to find that the woman he eventually marries turns out to 'have more bitterness than grace', and to be a veritable 'thorn in his flesh', a 'serpent in his bosom', and 'gall on his table' for her acid tongue and complaining, whining spirit. This side of glory there is no perfect home, no perfect marriage, even for the most illustrious saint. The believer's ALL is to be found in God. Heaven alone provides perfection, but that is most certainly gained through the living and dying grace which God provides.

The work served to neutralise all kinds of erroneous teaching. Above all it established that, in terms of believing, living, and dying, 'the Methodist Way' was no more and no less than the Christian Way in timeless dress with only a hint of eighteenth-century fashion.[1]

Confirmation of Welsh Methodism's part in and identity with The Great Awakening, if it were needed, appeared in 1766 with Williams' translation of Samuel Buell's *Copy of a Letter . . . to the Rev. Mr. Barber of Groton in Connecticut* published in America two years previously. Buell had supplied Jonathan Edwards' pulpit at Northampton while he was away preaching in February, 1742. At that time he was a raw recruit, fresh from college, a kind of firebrand preacher, with very little experience but with much of heaven about

---

[1] 'Theomemphus' is in GWP i. For a literary discussion of the work in English see Glyn Tegai Hughes, *Williams Pantycelyn*, 1983, pp. 22–42; and in Welsh, Derec Llwyd Morgan, *Williams Pantycelyn*, 1983, tt. 27–44.

his soul and ministry. It was a time of revival and one of those whose soul was blessed was Edwards' own wife: 'She remained in a kind of heavenly elysium, and did as it were swim in the rays of Christ's love, like a little mote swimming in the beams of the sun that come in at a window.' The powerful working of God's Spirit then was attended, says Edwards, with 'an extraordinary sense of the awful majesty, greatness, and holiness of God, so as sometimes to overwhelm soul and body'. Such an experience would have appealed to the Welsh Methodists. Williams found Buell's account of the success of the Gospel in New England irresistible, and was convinced that it would be useful in Wales by way of confirmation and encouragement.

Edwards, too, was prompted to write of the general revival which was taking place in those days, making special reference to his own town of Northampton, and to his wife's experiences. When *Some Thoughts Concerning the Present Revival of Religion in New England* appeared in 1743, it was seen as another remarkable documentation of events and a convincing defence of their authenticity. One section in this work expresses a conviction that 'The latter-day glory is probably to begin in America'.[1] Unusual luminous activity in the night sky prompted Williams Pantycelyn to write on the theme of the latter-day glory in Welsh in 1774 under the title *Aurora Borealis*.[2]

Two other translations by Williams were designed to have the same effect of giving Welsh Methodism historical perspective and experimental identity. These related God's dealings with two very different persons, Thomas Goodwin the Puritan preacher and writer, and Ukawsaw Groniosaw an African Prince.[3] Goodwin's experience was translated 'to tell the whole Church how far men may go in some kind of warm affection, burning zeal, joy, and pleasure in religious duties, and yet be without any acquaintance with God, or genuine transformation'. Such was the triumph of God's sovereign grace that it had sought out Groniosaw in America by Whitefield's instrumentality. Nothing was impossible with God! He is no respecter of persons, nor is His grace limited by time or culture. Historically and doctrinally, then, Methodism traced its source through Puritanism to the Acts of the Apostles; experimentally and

[1] Jonathan Edwards, *Works*, i. cvii. 376.
[2] *ib.* i. 381; WW ii. 228–30; GWP ii. 161–79; Glyn Tegai Hughes, *Williams Pantycelyn*, 70–75; cf. Iain Murray, *The Puritan Hope*, 1971.
[3] WW ii. 242–3, 258; HMGC ii. 475–6.

geographically, it was the realisation of Christ's Great Commission in the power of the Holy Spirit.

Two works were issued in translation by Williams in this period with a more controversial purpose. *Emmanuel; or a Treatise on the Incarnation of the Son of God* was written by James Ussher in 1638 to set out the glory of Christ's Person. Its appearance in Welsh in 1786 coincided with concern over Peter Williams' remarks on John 1:1 in his monumental Bible Commentary, issued in parts on a bi-monthly basis from 1768. Peter Williams had received some help in the work from Rowland. Controversy raged for twenty years over the tendency to Sabellianism (a confusion of the Persons in the Godhead) in the comment on that verse. Rowland's control of the situation, and his proverbial orthodoxy kept the controversy from hardening into confrontation. By 1791 other factors aggravated the situation, and Peter Williams was expelled from the Methodist ranks.[1] The other work was aimed at exposing the sterility and subtlety of Antinomianism, calling it in the title the 'bogey of the formal part of the Christian Church'. It was a translation of Joseph Hart's spiritual pilgrimage, and served to show the true bounds of Christian freedom with regard to God's law.[2]

William Williams' Welsh works of this period dealt with very practical issues. His 1768 work 'Three men from Sodom and Egypt' dealt with the very different attitudes and destinies of three people living in the same world of material wealth and pleasure. Their names betray their characters: Fidelius, 'God's soldier', aiming to be faithful to the One who called him; Avaritius, fiercely consumed by greed; Prodigalus, indulging in all kinds of wantonness and vanity. To each there is an elegy.[3] The true Methodist, like Fidelius, lives in sight of death and eternity.

The other two works both appeared in 1777. *Drws y Society Profiad* (The Experience Meeting) is the classic work on Methodist soul culture and close spiritual dealing in the context of Christian fellowship. It is the full-dress presentation of the earlier manuals and rules for the societies, modified and presented with true Pantycelyn genius. Consider, for example, its description of the ideal society

---

[1] WW ii. 243; Gomer M. Roberts, *Bywyd a Gwaith Peter Williams*, 64, 74, 94; John Gwili Jenkins, *Hanfod Duw a Pherson Crist*, 1931, Pennod VIII. See also DWB.

[2] WW ii. 241.

[3] Glyn Tegai Hughes, *op. cit.*, pp. 60–3; GWP ii. 117–60; WW ii. 225–8.

leader: 'A good counsellor perceives what sin keeps the one being counselled from God. He can discover the murky lairs where Satan and sin, the flesh, and lust for the world and its idols, are lurking; as an angler knows where the fish are, and the mole-catcher the paths of the mole, and the fowler the haunts of the partridge.'[1] Its aim was to show Methodism in its spiritual environment of soul concern and shared experience, of worship, instruction, and praise. Supremely, it showed Methodists together in the presence of God, open, honest, eager, and expectant.

Williams had sought to portray the Methodist in the world and the Methodist before God in fellowship with His people. Now he sought to describe the Methodist at home, and the three together make an attempt at an all-round Christian perspective on life. The third of these works bore the title *Cyfarwyddwr Priodas* (A Marriage Guide), and drew heavily on Robert Snawsel's *A Looking Glasse for Maried Folkes*, published in 1610. Williams' reasons for writing it are given at the outset: it was to place marriage firmly in the context of Christian self-denial and discipline. For its time it was a bold, but mature, presentation of a woman's power and weakness:

'Our sex has power, Martha, especially when we have beauty and purity, and no little subtlety to tempt the wisest, the most discerning, the strongest of men, so that it is hard to escape our nets, unless heaven's grace prevails. Our hearts are nets all the time; and we use all the ability and means at our disposal to make our bodies the same as well. . . . Our hands and arms are a mighty double-chain. . . . With this chain we can snuff out wrath and spark off love; we turn bears into babes, and wolves into lambs.'

The implications of marriage, whether social, spiritual, or sexual, are set side-by-side in the light of biblical principles. 'The reason why I composed this dialogue was a survey of the corruption of this present age with regard to the courtship and marriage of religious professors.' Williams exposes the prevailing evils of a heady disregard for Christian counsel and for the biblical precept not to marry an unbeliever. The distinctive place of men and women, as well as their spiritual equality, are discussed, as are matters like the strength of love and lust, harmony in the home, and the purpose of married life.[2]

[1] GWP ii. 181–242. The quotation given is on p. 208.
[2] GWP ii. 243–303. The quotation given is on p. 268. cf. Alwyn Prosser yn *Llên Cymru*, v (1958), tt. 70–85.

Methodist life and love in the home was to be regulated by the Word of God.

Provision was still being made for the societies' love of song. 'In singing hymns we were so set aflame that we could not part', was an early experience of the Welsh Methodists.[1] When Williams made the observation in 1763 'that Mr. Rowland did shine in the pulpit, but was not fit for any other place or work', he was referring to his organising, rather than to his poetic gifts.[2] Some more of Rowland's hymns were published together with 'Five Sermons' in Welsh in 1772. In the 'Preface' it is claimed that 'No introduction is necessary to recommend the author's work, since his sound doctrine and vast success is known throughout the country, and the sermons already published have had such a warm reception.' In another volume, three more of Rowland's sermons appeared during 1772, the publisher acknowledging that Rowland had no time to check or correct the proofs, partly on account of his labours, and partly because the public were urgently pressing for the sermons. In the 1775 Welsh collection of *Tair Pregeth* (Three Sermons), it is said that 'there is wide acceptance to his doctrine even by those who have never seen him in the flesh, and some London merchants have sent the books, like so many pearls, across the oceans to far away India and other places'.[3]

Eight of Rowland's sermons appeared in English translation in 1774. Introducing them, John Davies the translator, said:

'The following Sermons are the productions of an eminent clergyman in the Principality of Wales, who has been for nearly forty years a zealous and indefatigable labourer in the Lord's vineyard. He is still alive, and, notwithstanding his advanced age, as active as ever. . . . His audiences are very large wherever he preaches, and the stated number of communicants at the monthly Sacrament in his own church is seldom less than two thousand, and sometimes more than four thousand. . . . Yet, being convinced that no human persuasion can prevail with them to accept of a free and plenteous redemption, he with earnest supplications recommends them to the Spirit of grace, and to the efficacious influences of His power. . . . Having learned by happy experience that faith is a vital principle, wrought in the soul by the Spirit of God, he not only inculcates universal holiness in heart and life, as an evidence of its being a genuine faith, but insists upon it as an indispensable meetness for communion with God both in time and eternity.'

[1] xxvii. 107.   [2] xxxii. 44.
[3] D. J. Odwyn Jones, *Daniel Rowland Llangeitho*, 1938, tt. 84–5.

Among the list of subscribers are a number of well known evangelical clergymen: William Romaine (100 copies), John Berridge, Rowland Hill, Andrew Gifford; and an impressive number of titled people including the Countess of Huntingdon. Rowland's boast, however, was not in any of these things. His chief concern was simply to be an ambassador for Christ whose time was short and whose message was urgent. In a sermon on Jude 9 he makes this constraint clear:

'The service of God is man's most honourable distinction: nothing else can make him great. St. Paul attests this truth when he says, "I have laboured more than they all", 1 Corinthians 15:10. He does not say, I have reigned or conquered more than any of the other apostles; no, but "I have laboured". What labour? was it to preach the Gospel, to plant churches, and to set them in order, or to do some extraordinary feat of the like import? No, but he laboured in the meanest offices most abundantly, "in stripes, in prisons, in journeyings, in perils, in hunger and thirst, in cold and nakedness, etc.", 2 Cor. 11:23–25. . . . To be a servant to, and a messenger for, Jesus Christ is the highest dignity that any created being can aspire to!'[1]

It was in the capacity of a servant and a messenger for Jesus Christ that God so abundantly used Rowland, sustaining him in the work even to the closing years of his life.

[1] *Eight Sermons*, 107–108.

'I feel my spirit leaving all, places and men, here below, and going to my Father, and to my native country, home; yea my own home. And though I am here below in his kingdom, yet, whilst I wait to be called home, my longings and cries are insatiable indeed. And when the Lord of Glory answers me, that I shall soon go to him . . . I must have the Saviour indeed, for he is my all; all that others have in the world, and in religion, and in themselves, I have in thee: pleasures, riches, safety, honour, life, righteousness, holiness, wisdom, bliss, joy, gaiety, and happiness. . . . And if a child longs for his father, a traveller for the end of his journey, a workman to finish his work, a prisoner for his liberty, an heir for the full possession of his estate; so, in all these respects, I can't help longing to go home.

HOWEL HARRIS
in his last illness

31

'The Old Grey-headed Elijah'

The closing years of Rowland's life were remarkably active. There was the familiar pattern of preaching and travelling, the communion Sundays once a month at Llangeitho, the outbursts of occasional, local revivals, the great Association occasions. Rowland must have derived considerable satisfaction from seeing scores of young men who showed the promise of being 'able ministers of the New Testament'. They would compensate, in some measure, for those who were being taken to glory from the Methodist ranks, Harris and Whitefield being chief among them.

It is Harris who, as before, provides glimpses of Rowland's powerful preaching from the time of the Llangeitho revival of 1762 until the next decade. In 1768 at Llangeitho 140 children were meeting weekly to pray, sing, and open their hearts to one another, so that others came under conviction as they witnessed these things.[1] A year later Harris saw 'Mr. Rowland at the head of all the work in Wales', and heard how it spread everywhere, 'especially in the north about Bala and Montgomeryshire'. As far as Llangeitho was concerned, there was 'very strict discipline', which would have pleased him, and good news as well: 'About 1,500 communicants, and great glory among the children who meet to pray weekly.'[2] When Harris went to Woodstock, Pembrokeshire, in February 1770 to meet Rowland, he heard of Rowland's extraordinary success, with 'over 2,000 people coming to the Sacrament at Llangeitho every Saturday, many coming over 40 miles'. At the beginning of September Rowland was preaching at Trefeca College with 'much light', a Harrisian short-hand phrase for penetrating spiritual insight, freshness, warmth and authority. His text was Colossians 1:19, 'For it pleased the Father that in Him should all fulness dwell',

[1] TM i. 423.   [2] HRS 233.

and he spoke of 'man's folly in seeking things where they were not to be had; such as go to fish on the top of the hill, or catch fowl in the ocean's bottom. He showed how man seeks happiness in the world and creatures here. He showed how all is vanity, and that even bread and water have nothing in them without the Lord.'[1]

From that time on, Harris's diary entries were fewer and scantier. One of his last references to Rowland was that of November 4, 1771, when a huge audience came to hear Rowland preach at Trefeca.[2] Harris died on July 21, 1773, and was buried inside Talgarth church on the 24th. It was estimated that twenty thousand attended his funeral, six ministers preaching nine sermons 'with great power and freedom' while 'hundreds' of the hearers were 'dissolved in tears'. Part of the inscription on the monumental tablet to him in Talgarth church states, 'Here, where his body lies, he was convinced of sin, had his pardon sealed, felt the power of Christ's precious blood at the Holy Communion. Having tasted grace himself, he resolved to declare to others what God had done for his soul. . . . His end was more blessed than his beginning. Looking to Jesus crucified, he rejoiced to the last that death had lost its sting.'[3]

Rowland must have felt deeply the loss of his fellow-soldier in the Gospel battle. They had laboured together for more than a quarter of a century. Both of them in their beginnings had been insignificant and despised, living in hamlets that were unknown and obscure. Both, in their calling and their usefulness, displayed the Gospel principle, 'that no flesh should glory in His presence' (1 Corinthians 1:29). Although during their lifetime there had been diversity in their gifts, doctrines, and success, in their deepest conviction there was the most complete harmony: 'we have this treasure in earthen vessels, that the excellency of the power may be of God, and not of us' (2 Corinthians 4:7). Harris had outlived Whitefield, their common brother and friend, by almost three years. It was Williams who summarised, in his elegy to Whitefield, what was dear to them all as Methodists, the Gospel message which they preached:

> O Faith! ne'er faint while the Redeemer reigns!
> By death, by life, the Gospel strength regains;
> Let mountains high to foaming billows fall,

---

[1] TM i. 425, 427; HH Diary No. 262, s.v. September 2, 1770.
[2] Itinerary, iii. 46.
[3] HH, 271; Hugh J. Hughes, *Life of Howell Harris*, 1892, p. 436.

And monarchs chain'd in miserable thrall;
If the earth would blaze in one ethereal flame,
And the upper worlds would also feel the same.
The Gospel promise, and the Gospel sound
Shall never lose a single inch of ground.
Therefore, my soul, with sadness ne'er repine,
But take thy comforts from the page divine;
Hold fast thy faith, the promises have cost
A thousand times more than the Church hath lost.[1]

The passing of such mighty men of God could only have been viewed with a mixture of personal grief and joyful hope by Rowland.

There was, however, one consideration which compensated for Rowland's trials during this later period of his life. Not a single decade went by from the time of the 'great awakening' at Llangeitho in 1762 until the end of the century without some part of Wales experiencing revival. Sometimes the outpouring of God's Spirit would be localised, at other times more general. Like the mustard seed of Christ's parable, the work from small beginnings had blossomed into a tree, its branches providing shelter for all who were called to lodge in them.

Such was the profusion of religious blessing in the Caerphilly area in 1772 that Edmund Jones reckoned it an 'uncommon work' transforming the beautiful country into 'a Beulah.'[2] While some took that sympathetic view of revival, however, others were disturbed by its being a 'mixed' work, often with blemishes, and therefore open to misinterpretation. A letter to John Wesley, dated December 18, 1772, suggests uncertainty or misunderstanding with regard to the revival's fruit in the writer's area of Cardiganshire. It was written by a clergyman, John Rees, from Llangrannog:

'You must know sir, that I live in a neighbourhood where there is more noise about religion than practice. . . . I live also within less than thirty miles of the famous Mr. D. Rowland, whom I admire as an extraordinary preacher; and doubt not of his being very useful in Wales; yet most of his followers are too ready to pass an uncharitable sentence on all who differ from them. I am sure I should love them dearly was it not for this.'[3]

---

[1] CYN i. 655.
[2] xxi. 112.
[3] *Arminian Magazine*, 1785, p. 604.

A little closer investigation or enquiry would have provided him with first-hand information for a more biblical assessment.

Not much further east from John Rees than Llangeitho another revival was in progress seven years later. This took place in a remote, mountainous area, where the Methodists occasionally preached.

'A homely exhorter, of very ordinary preaching talents, but of great piety, Jack Edwards Watkins by name, was preaching at the place on a Sabbath afternoon, when suddenly the fire kindled, and numbers who had been so far hearers only became deeply concerned for their everlasting safety. Daniel Rowland heard the glad tidings, and he resolved to ascend the mountain to see this thing which the Lord had wrought. He preached, and *the power* was still present, and even mightier than on the preceding Sabbath. On his return home he said to his friends, "It is a heath fire and will spread abroad." And it *did* spread from these dreary mountains to the valleys and plains around, until it had reached many and far-distant localities in South and North Wales, and thousands were brought earnestly to seek everlasting life.'[1]

Thus there was proliferation as well as profusion. Dafydd Morris, one of the newer labourers, was God's instrument of revival in the Llanwrtyd area of Breconshire in 1789.[2]

Llangeitho, however, continued to attract multitudes, and that for a very simple reason: Rowland's ministry was as powerful as ever. The years 1780–81 were exceptionally fruitful throughout South Wales, the blessing radiating from Llangeitho. For a year Rowland had been preaching on the same text. The commencement, according to Rowland's son Nathaniel, was when Rowland referred in his sermon to Matthew 11:25–26, 'I thank Thee, O Father, Lord of heaven and earth, because Thou hast hid these things from the wise and prudent, and hast revealed them unto babes; even so, Father, for so it seemed good in Thy sight.' 'The entire chapel seemed as if it was filled with some supernatural element, and the whole assembly was seized with extraordinary emotions, hundreds of them, with tears streaming down their faces, some evidently from excess of sorrow, others from the overflowing of joy; some broken and contrite with penitence, and others rejoicing with the hope of glory.'[3]

By this time there was considerable traffic between north and

---

[1] William Williams, *Welsh Calvinistic Methodism*, 1872, p. 155.
[2] *Ychydig o Hanes Bywyd y Parch. H. Bevan*, 1840, tud. 7.
[3] JO, 49; cf. MC i. 249, ii. 17.

south Wales in terms of religious interest. The numbers of people that regularly travelled to Llangeitho for the monthly sacrament bore ample witness to the blessings received on those occasions:

'There were on some Sundays at Llangeitho . . . persons from almost every county in Wales. On sacrament Sundays, which were observed monthly, the multitude assembled was immense, filling an area of about sixteen hundred square yards. One or two sermons from this great and good man, it seems, fully satisfied them for the toilsome journey of fifty, sixty, seventy, or eighty miles, (for many of them came on foot), so that they went home rejoicing, and often made the hills and valleys echo with their hallelujahs. . . . It is well known that some hundreds of these pilgrims used to meet at a well within about two miles of Llangeitho on the morning before divine service, to take some refreshment, drinking water from the well, after long and tedious journeys through the night. After asking a blessing upon their food, and returning thanks, and praying, they would then sing a hymn, and proceed towards Llangeitho in this happy frame of mind, praising the Lord. Rowland was generally struck with their heavenly singing, as he was walking out musing on his sermon before the service. He would stop, listening, then observing, "Well, here they come, bringing heaven along with them."'

Such 'pilgrims' often braved considerable persecution and ridicule on their journey. Nevertheless they came.

It was a period of increasing awareness of the vast scale of the Holy Spirit's visitation in the land. There was, at times, an expectancy and eagerness for God to work, that could almost be felt. A close-knit network of societies throughout the land was straining to be kept informed of the latest evidence of God's saving work. Preachers, ministerial and lay, moved in ever-widening circuits. For this reason Sally Jones could write to Thomas Charles (her future husband) in May 1780: 'I suppose you have heard of the great Revival that is in South Wales, the last crop probably that the first Reformers shall here upon earth reap of their labours. . . . I hear that some clergymen in South Wales are called and made flaming ministers of the Sanctuary, and that there have been upwards of three hundred received into the Society at Llangeitho since Christmas.' Revival influences persisted at Llangeitho for another year, and Charles could write in May 1781:

'It does my heart good to hear that the Lord's work prospers in any part of the Globe, especially in Wales. How refreshing must the pleasing prospect be to those aged servants of the living God, now just ripe for glory! I am afraid the prosperous gale will carry some of them to heaven where they would be. I should be very glad, if the will of the Lord were so, to see once more the old venerable Prophet before he takes his flight.'[1]

He was, of course, referring to Rowland.

At Bala, too, in 1781, there was unusual spiritual activity. Sally Jones, wrote of it in June as having begun at an Association:

'We had many preachers from South Wales, but Mr. Rowland could not come. There were more people assembled this time than ever before, the Spirit of rejoicing was poured abundantly on a great many. I believe there were many hundreds singing and praising in the streets; their voice at some distance from them was like a sound ascending to the clouds. Some that went among them, to hear the words, were taken captive and joined with them; and others that went to oppose them like mighty giants whom none could resist, were obliged to retreat in disgrace; every stripling flung his stone at them, and their threatening was no more regarded than the chaff which the wind scatters. I was but a spectator upon the scene, only I felt some inward desire that the Name of the Lord should be glorified, for there is much disorder in it. Yet in all probability the Lord works powerfully upon some and takes them as it were into the third heavens.'

She was understandably cautious, but also optimistic as to the eventual outcome, convinced that in every genuine work of the Holy Spirit, fruit would remain to God's glory:

'Some young people that were never religiously affected before met the first night after the Association in a room where someone prayed, and there they spent the night in prayer and praises. The next night they met in the chapel, and it was between 4 and 5 in the morning before they parted. If they take root downward as they spring upward, much fruit may be expected. But I have much more to suspect myself on account of my deadness than anybody else. Yet this I believe, that good and bad are now caught in the net, and that a time of separation will come, when there shall be a difference between those that serve the Lord in spirit and in truth, and those that serve Him not. I believe that there is a danger of serving self in every outward show, at least to me there is.'[2]

Sally Jones was twenty-eight years of age at the time, and her

---

[1] MR, 62–64; D. E. Jenkins, *The Life of the Rev. Thomas Charles*, i. 178, 267–8.　　　[2] *ib.* i. 274–5.

objectivity shows either a cold detachment or a remarkable maturity towards these extraordinary manifestations.

Further north in Caernarfonshire there were similar scenes some four years later, again affecting children and young people. One of them, Robert Roberts, later became a powerful preacher, but at the time he was twenty-three, physically handicapped, and finding the sweet influences irresistible. His mother admonished him for his shouting and singing, fearful of the weakness of his body, but to no avail. The ecstasy of the Spirit triumphed over the limitations of the flesh, and he kept crying 'glory' in an uncontrollable flood of tears.[1]

At the beginning of 1791, William Williams wrote to Thomas Charles: 'A great revival has taken place in many parts of our country. From 500 to 600, to my knowledge, have been added to the number of those who profess religion, during the last two years.' By the year's end Bala, too, was in the midst of revival:

'For some time back we have had a very great, powerful, and glorious out-pouring of the Spirit of God on the people in general, especially young people. The state and welfare of the soul is become the general concern of the country. Scores of the wildest and most inconsiderate of the people have been awakened. Their convictions are very clear, powerful, and in some individuals, very deep, till brought for a time, to the brink of despair; their consolations also, which soon follow, are equally strong.'

It began on a Sunday when Charles was preaching on Romans 15:33, 'Now the God of peace be with you all.' Charles's account continues:

'Towards the close of the evening service, the Spirit of God seemed to work in a very powerful manner on the minds of great numbers present, who never appeared before to seek the Lord's face; but now, there was a general and a loud crying, "What must I do to be saved?", and "God be merciful to me a sinner." And about nine or ten o'clock at night, there was nothing to be heard from one end of the town to the other, but the cries and groans of people in distress of soul. And the very same night, a spirit of deep conviction and serious concern fell upon whole congregations in this neighbourhood, when calling upon the name of the Lord. In the course of the following week we had nothing but prayer meetings; and general concern about eternal things swallowed up all other concerns. . . . The work has continued to go on ever since with unabated power and glory,

[1] Griffith Parry (gol.), *Cofiant a Phregethau Robert Roberts, Clynnog,* 1884, tud. 34.

spreading from one town to another all round this part of the country... In the course of the eight years I have laboured in this country, I have had frequent opportunities of seeing, and feeling also, much of the divine presence in the Lord's work and ordinances, and great success attending the ministration of the Word, but nothing to equal the present work.'

Thus, from the first pouring out of God's Spirit on Harris and Rowland in 1735, the Kingdom of Christ had spread in Wales by successive periods of revival. The glory of 'The Great Awakening' was its Divine origin and sustenance. This was the conviction that prompted Charles to issue a solemn and salutary reminder of the great means of carrying on God's work. Reviewing the progress of the Gospel in 1792 he said: 'Within these fifty years there have been five or six very great awakenings. . . . I am persuaded that unless we are favoured with frequent revivals, and a strong, powerful work of the Spirit of God, we shall, in a great degree, degenerate, and have only "a name to live"; religion will soon lose its vigour; the ministry will hardly retain its lustre and glory; and iniquity will, of consequence, abound.'[1] Whatever the discouragements from without or within, Rowland and the other leaders wholeheartedly shared that conviction.

Of course, Rowland's whole ministry testifies against any idea that he only laboured at a time of revival. On the contrary, he and his brethren laboured on, vigorously and prayerfully, 'in season and out of season', believing that God would bless the means of grace. So they assaulted the kingdom of Satan with their preaching, arranged for the supervision and nurture of the societies in their Associations, instructed their people by means of literature, wrote hymns so that believers could give expression to the praise and longing of their hearts, and when some of the labourers died they encouraged others to take their place. All the while they trusted God to prosper His work. They walked by faith. Such were the considerations which kept Rowland in the forefront of Gospel activity despite the approach of old age.

During the 'seventies and 'eighties both Thomas Charles and Sally Jones availed themselves of every opportunity to hear Rowland at Llangeitho, usually at the August Association. Rowland preached more than once from Jude verse 20, 'Praying in the Holy Spirit', in December 1782. Charles had failed to see 'the old grey-headed

[1] D. E. Jenkins, *op. cit.*, i. 178, 267–8; ii. 54, 88–90, 98; *Y Geiniogwerth*, 1847, tud. 61.

Elijah' in the summer and he was eager for news, pleading repeatedly for a long letter from Sally. She obliged with this description of Rowland's anointed ministry and matter:

'There was something solemn and awful in the place, and I thought that perhaps the greatest divine since the time of the Apostles was then undertaking his glorious employment. . . . [He] showed that lip service is not respected, that cursers and swearers were more justified than those who mocked God with their lips, while their hearts were far from him; that the saints could be in no state in this world that their prayer would not be heard; that the promise of the Comforter in the 16th of St.John is now accomplished; that the Spirit of God in the saints makes them conquerors over God Himself, as in Jacob's case; that it is not difficult to prevail for spiritual blessings, but if we ask for riches, or honour, things hurtful, they are given like the flesh to the Israelites; but to those that ask for the Holy Spirit, He is given abundantly, proved in Luke 11:13 and John 4:10, 14, being the water spoken of to the woman of Samaria that springeth up to everlasting life. He dwelt much on the 14th and 16th [chapters] of St.John, about the three Persons in the glorious Trinity, and of Christ's humiliation and abasement, and upon those words, "I *will* pray the Father, and He shall give you another Comforter." He would not exempt Himself from being engaged for His people, but would send another also. He observed that Christ had prayed in different ways; sometimes with strong cries and tears, not that this was necessary to prevail, but like the cry of a man whose house was on fire, venting the grief that was in him, that He prayed by shedding of His blood, which cried louder than the blood of Abel; that He made one sacrifice of Himself, and that the prayers of His people are for ever acceptable in Him; that the Spirit teacheth to pray in His name; that Isaac and Jacob called upon God as the God of their fathers; Elisha called Him the God of Elijah, but now the Antitype being come, we have greater confidence in His name. But alas! alas! I am but darkening the lustre of the fine gold.'

Charles heard Rowland twice at the Association in August of the following year 'proclaiming the deep things of God with that pathos, perspicuity and energy peculiar to himself'. Nor was Charles the only preacher to go to Llangeitho so consistently to attend Rowland's ministry and counsel. One of the editors of his printed sermons testified that 'above a hundred preachers in Wales esteem him as their father, most of whom meet four times a year to consult with him about the most likely means of promoting the Redeemer's interest'.[1]

[1] D. E. Jenkins, *op. cit.*, i. 382, 426; *Three Sermons*, 'Advertisement', dated May 9, 1778.

An anonymous contemporary letter speaks of Rowland's ministry in his old age:

'Saturday morning by 12 noon to Llangeitho to hear Saturday's noon sermon from old Mr. Rowland. There were that day about 4,000 souls, but on Sunday, when the father and son preached, they were obliged to have a pulpit erected in a field, where, by a moderate computation of those who were pretty good judges, there were at least 14,000 people, which was a very wonderful sight, and withal very comfortable to hear the neighbouring hills and valleys ring with the joyful sound of salvation and praises to the Lamb. When they retired after the sermons to the chapel to receive the Sacrament, though the chapel will contain above 3,000 people at once, and there were four clergymen employed in administering, yet the genteeler sort could not attempt to press forward into the chapel, or be able to go up to the Communion Table in less than an hour's time after they began.'

Even in his seventies, Rowland's faculties still showed no signs of decline.

'The river Aeron flowed within a few yards of the house of Daniel Rowland. He walked along its banks thousands of times, and saw it in sunshine and storm. After the rain this river rushed rapidly down through Llangeitho. It is said that Daniel Rowland, even in his old age, innocently amused himself on these occasions by throwing leaves into the rushing torrent; then he would run along the banks, and when he outran the leaves on the water he would say, "There! I have beaten thee, though I am an old man of seventy years of age."'

His mental, as well as his physical faculties were also active. On one occasion Rowland met William Romaine, the English evangelical clergyman, in a bookshop, probably at Bristol. It was said that Romaine considered Rowland to be 'the greatest minister in the whole world'. '"What", said Romaine, "do you, the most eminent divine, come here to buy books? I thought you had the Spirit of God to study his Word and compose your sermons!" Rowland answered him thus, "I find that Romaine lately published some to be read, and how are they to be got, unless purchased from booksellers, where they are to be sold?"' Rowland was not only buying books at this period of his life, he was giving some away, and also borrowing some![1]

[1] i. 33, 34; *Transactions of the Carmarthenshire Antiquarian Society.* ii, 193; Owen Jones, *Some of the Great Preachers of Wales*, 1886, p. 68; JO, 4; MR, 90–1.

One recipient of books from Rowland, a man who visited Rowland often in 1782, was Thomas Richards, a Cardiganshire man later to settle in the North Wales living of Darowen. In one sermon that year Rowland spoke about the nature of 'true Scriptural fasting', namely, '1. sadness, 2. displeasure, 3. fervent expectation of victory, and 4. fear.' He also heard Rowland twice on Colossians 4:2, 'Continue in prayer, and watch in the same with thanksgiving', once in September and then a month later. On the first occasion Rowland's headings were:

'(1) That a multitude of graces should in a Christian precede, support, and follow prayer; (2) That a man in prayer has extensive views of two things, of the infinite glory of God; and a clear view of his own diabolical temper and damnable estate and entire impossibility of recovery without the tender mercy of God. . . . Comparing a man long in prayer to a man on horseback; he will travel most that uses his horse most sparingly. Christ prayed often, not long. . . . Comparing a man preparing his ground, plowing, sowing, and harrowing, yet leaving (though well fenced) the field's gate open for all the swine and other devouring creatures to come in; to a man meditating before and having a good frame in prayer, yet never watching afterwards or expecting answers ever. . . . Therefore watch in and after prayer.'[1]

According to Edward Morgan, 'Rowland used to say in his last days, that he had been endeavouring to learn four lessons all the time he was in the vineyard and service of the Lord, but notwithstanding that, he was yet but a very dull and imperfect scholar in his old age. They were the following truths: To repent without despairing; to believe without presuming; to rejoice without levity; to be angry without sinning.'[2]

Even in 1790, the year of his death, Rowland was still active. 'The Reverend Mr. Rowland enjoys his usual health', wrote one of the exhorters to Charles, 'and preaches, as far as I am aware, as clearly, lively, powerfully and with as much authority as ever he did. The substance of his present doctrine is, "In everything give thanks".' David Jones (Llan-gan) was with him in the summer and reported to the Countess of Huntingdon, 'I have seen dear old Mr. Rowland, and heard him with much pleasure and comfort.'[3]

1 NLW Llwyngwair MS 16986 (a).   2 MR, 172–3.
3 D. E. Jenkins, *op. cit.*, ii. 47; Cheshunt College MS 628, David Jones to the Countess of Huntingdon, July 26, 1790.

Two men who heard him often during the latter end of his ministry recorded their impressions. Christmas Evans, a Baptist, gave this vivid description of a typical Llangeitho experience:

'I see him now, entering in his black gown through a little door from the outside of the pulpit [with access directly into it], and making his appearance in it thus on a sudden to the immense congregation. His countenance was in every respect adorned with majesty, and it bespoke the man of strong sense, eloquence and authority. His forehead was high and prominent; his eye was sharp, quick and penetrating; he had an aquiline or Roman nose, proportionable comely lips, projecting chin and rising a little, and a sonorous, commanding, and well-toned voice. It was the general practice for some minister to read and pray before Rowland made his appearance in the pulpit. He then frequently gave out . . . a stanza . . . to be sung. Then Daniel Rowland would stand up and read his text distinctly to the hearing of all. . . . He had, at the commencement of his discourse, some stirring, striking idea. . . . He would divide his text, and then proceed with the first division. . . . Having glanced at his notes . . . [he] would go on with his discourse in a calm and deliberate manner . . . but he would gradually become warmed with his subject, and his voice became at length so elevated and authoritative, that it resounded through the whole chapel! The effect on the people was wonderful; you could see nothing but smiles and tears running down the faces of all. . . . There was very little if any inference or application at the end of Rowland's sermon, for he had been applying and enforcing the glorious truths of the Gospel throughout the whole of his discourse. He would conclude with a very few striking and forcible remarks . . . and then he would make a very sweet short prayer and utter the benediction. Then he would, full of perspiration, make haste out of the pulpit through the little door.'

The other man, Thomas Jones, a Church of England clergyman, had the advantages of being brought up in Cardiganshire. He summarised 'the peculiar excellencies of Rowland as a preacher' as being 'depth and fervour'.[1]

Both Rowland and his wife seem to have enjoyed exceptionally good health throughout their lifetime. Not until the eighties of the century was there any sustained concern about their physical wellbeing. On Sunday December 22, 1782, Rowland was indisposed in bed, but managed to assist Williams at the Communion later. He was still unwell on January 8 of the new year, when Richards visited him

[1] MR, 125–8; JO 59.

again, but had recovered enough to preach on the 18th of that month. The text was 1 Thessalonians 5:8, 'Let us, who are of the day, be sober, putting on the breastplate of faith and love; and for an helmet, the hope of salvation.'

'In the realm of nature there is a proverb, "birds of a feather flock together", and so it is in spiritual and substantial things. Where there is one true grace, there is every true grace; by allowing one sin we receive thousands of sins, they are like beggars, once you receive one you must receive many, the second more persistent than the first, so that there is no way to get rid of them but to close the door against them. A thousand sins lie in the womb of one sin, and they are like bees, one lot swarming from another.'

His ministry had lost none of its vigour or clarity, familiar comparisons falling over one another in profusion as usual:

'It is hard to get anyone to turn traitor or betrayer against his king as long as he thinks that the king is well-disposed towards him (2 Sam. 20:1–2); so also when one is on the ladder of preferment he is far from turning traitor. . . . Go on, then, in hope of the King's good pleasure towards you! . . . As to the Christian's helmet, that is the hope of salvation, it will make him triumph over all his enemies, since hell has no weapon that can shatter it, the devil has no instrument to succeed against it; because it is not the salvation of the body, but of the soul. Lift up your heads! lift up your heads! though all others bow theirs! Your sun rises while theirs goes down, your heaven begins when theirs ends . . . so shall it be as long as you have the hope of salvation as your helmet. It will keep your head above the water as Noah's ark was kept in the flood, because God had designed it, and sealed it, and kept it; so also David lay down and slept. Where? among hosts of enemies, because the Lord sustained him. There was a Wall within a wall, his enemies a wall around him at a distance, God a Wall around him close by. . . . Some say that good archers can shoot the falcon or kite and yet keep the chick alive; be that as it may, God can shoot sin and keep the soul alive. Faith believes God's Word, and hope believes faith. Abraham "against hope believed in hope" (Rom. 4:18), that is the hope of faith against the hope of reason. The breastplate of faith and love keep the Christian in this world, and at the last he will be received into the "eternal habitations".'[1]

The faith in which Rowland lived, and the grace which God supplied enabled him to deliver such messages with undiminished conviction and strength.

[1] i. 33–4; NLW Cwrt Mawr MS 239A.

With the prospect of those 'eternal habitations' coming into clearer view, Rowland made his last will. 'First, I give my gracious God an entire sacrifice of body and soul, whose merit I humbly beg, and constantly rely upon in Jesus Christ.' A substantial proportion of the 'real and personal estate which the Almighty conferred' upon him, including plots of land and two houses, is left to Nathaniel. Sarah, the youngest daughter, was to receive one hundred pounds, the rest of the children forty pounds each. 'To the poor, the sum of sixty pounds, to be distributed to them by the elders of Gwynfil Society.' The executors were to be Nathaniel and his son Daniel.

It was Nathaniel that kept the Countess of Huntingdon informed of affairs at Llangeitho. Writing to the Countess of Huntingdon in August 1789 he commented, 'My father was much pleased to find the work prospered in your Ladyship's hands, and talked often about you.' Two months later he was reporting of his parents, 'My mother's extreme illness had almost discouraged me from undertaking a journey at this time, but she is something better, and my father able to preach very frequently.' His mother's health improved a little and she lived until August 1792, her 79th year.

Rowland's closest friend was ailing, too. From the time of Rowland's death until his own in January 1791, William Williams was confined to his bedroom. At the request of many he composed an elegy to Rowland, in spite of great physical weakness. Writing to Charles of Bala he also mentioned his spiritual comforts:

'I have come to see that true religion consists in three parts. First, true light respecting the plan of salvation; God's eternal covenant with His Son to pay the debt of believing sinners, all the truths of the New Covenant by which He becomes all in all in creation, in all-embracing providence, and in redemption. . . . The other . . . being in intimate communion with God in all our dealings. . . . Lastly . . . life and conduct, such as would reveal to the ungodly that there is a great difference between us and them.'

The letter breathes the spirit of revival, too, rejoicing in that which was taking place in South Wales. It also breathes the spirit of submission. 'Think what a disappointment it must be to a man who has travelled nearly three thousand miles every year for over fifty years, to be now without moving more than forty feet in a day, from the fireside to the bed! This is how God wishes to deal with me, and it is well.'[1]

[1] xii. 63–4; lvii. 44; CH 1978, p. 32; D. E. Jenkins, *op. cit.*, ii. 51–3.

The Countess of Huntingdon had a high regard for Rowland, and it found expression in a special request in the summer of 1790:

'My Christian love to your dear old father, and tell him I have passed my word that in one thing he will oblige me. Mr. Bowyer, the King's Painter and Mr. Fittler, the King's Engraver, have requested your father's picture; and as the greatest compliment Mr. Bowyer could pay, will go down to draw it, to Llangeitho. I did answer for your father's friendship to me on those conditions, your father would indulge me. Many English friends would be obliged, while neither trouble or expense could be incurred to your father or his family by it. A positive answer must be sent as soon as possible, as Mr. Bowyer has such multiple engagements, and he will set out for Wales in September for this purpose only. The Engraving will be very fine and the Picture, like, I can be sure, and therefore no unkind refusal to me!'

There was no refusal, and Robert Bowyer finished the work just a week before Rowland died.[1] The miniature portrait is now deposited at the National Library of Wales.

One of the children supplied Edward Morgan with this account of Rowland's frame of mind in the weeks preceding his death:

'My father made these remarkable observations in his sermons the two Sundays before his departure. He said, "I am almost leaving, and am on the point of being taken from you. I am not tired of the work, but in it. I have some presentiment that my heavenly Father will soon release me from my labours, and bring me to my everlasting rest. But I hope that He will continue His gracious presence with you after I am gone."'[2]

On the last Sunday before his death, he told his family, 'I have no more to say by way of evidence of my acceptance with God, than I have always stated: I die as a poor sinner, depending fully and entirely on the merits of a crucified Saviour for my acceptance with God.'

Rowland died on Saturday, October 16, 1790, and was buried on the following Wednesday at Llangeitho church cemetery. The previous Wednesday he had felt some change in himself, and by Friday he had weakened considerably. When someone at the time spoke to him of his instrumentality in the conversion of thousands to Christ, and that he had laboured in the Gospel for over fifty years, he

---

[1] xliv. 35; xxxii. 77.   [2] MR, 161.

merely said 'It is nothing'. He owned that the only foundation on which he rested was 'the blood of Jesus Christ, His Son, which cleanses us from all sin'.

When the congregation worshipping in Llangeitho chapel heard of his passing, there was much grief and weeping, and the people dispersed, spreading the news of their great loss. That grief was shared by many, far and wide. The young John Elias wept with disappointment at not having heard Rowland preach; the Countess of Huntingdon shed many bitter tears of grief at the remembrance of the 'great and faithful servant of God'.

Two funeral sermons were preached. David Jones of Llan-gan preached at the graveside on Revelation 14:13, 'And I heard a voice from heaven saying unto me, Write, Blessed are the dead which die in the Lord from henceforth; yea, saith the Spirit, that they may rest from their labours, and their works do follow them.' John Williams, another Cardiganshire Methodist preacher, had expounded the text 2 Timothy 4:8: 'Henceforth there is laid up for me a crown of righteousness, which the Lord the righteous judge shall give me at that day; and not to me only, but unto all them also that love his appearing.'[1]

It was a fitting text, as Rowland had often spoken of the Christian's pilgrimage and conflicts, and of God's crowning grace: 'Be our allotment here ever so afflictive and uneasy, we can lift up our eyes to the hills from whence comes our salvation; and can amidst our sorest conflicts, even of death, say, 'Yonder is my home; here I am only a pilgrim, and it signifies little what hardships I shall endure by the way during my passage through this dreary wilderness, when this short winter day shall so soon end in a long eternal day of rest and happiness. My crown is almost in view. I will therefore maintain the fight unshaken, against a host of corruptions, strong in the Lord and the power of His might; that being refined from all my dross, and made white in the blood of the Lamb, I shall dwell for ever with the God of my salvation.'

For Rowland, leader of the Great Awakening in Wales, 'the old, grey-headed Elijah', that enticing prospect had been turned into glorious possession.

[1] D. Worthington, *op. cit.*, tud. 156–7; Owen Jones, *Some of the Great Preachers of Wales*, p. 70; *Goleuad Cymru*, Chwefror 1826, tud. 316; Goronwy P. Owen (gol.), *Hunangofiant John Elias*, 1974, tt. 55–6; Alfred H. New, *The Coronet and The Cross*, 1858, p. 360; MR, 161–2, 164.

'I am one of these Methodists; and blessed be God, I have had the honour of being one of them for about thirty-five years. . . . A real Methodist is one of those whom God hath chosen in Christ out of mankind, to bring them by Christ to everlasting salvation, as vessels made to honour; wherefore, they, who be endued with so excellent a benefit of God, are called according to God's purpose by His Spirit working in due season; they, through grace, obey the calling; they be justified freely; and made the sons of God by adoption; they are conformed to the image of His only begotten Son, Jesus Christ; they walk religiously in good works; and at length, by God's mercy, they attain everlasting felicity.

GEORGE WHITEFIELD

'The Rev. Daniel Rowland . . . was a very distinguished minister of the Gospel, as he was much followed as a popular preacher during more than half a century. He began to claim attention at twenty-five years of age, and continued rising in the public esteem until his death. . . . He was much noticed by the Countess of Huntingdon, who, it is said, kept a carriage purposely for him. He was reputed among the Calvinistic Methodists; but he taught particular tenets, and was the founder of a distinct sect, which still is pretty numerous in this part of the country, and denominated "Rowlandists" after his name. This conduct drew upon him the censure of the bishop, and he was suspended from his office. After this he built a very large meeting-house in the centre of the village, where he could, unmolested, vent his doctrines. His sister, however, maintained her church principles; and when his meeting-house was thronged with people, the only congregation in the church consisted of his successor there, the clerk, and his sister. He is buried in the church-yard, and a plain stone is affixed against the outside of the church wall to his memory.'

SAMUEL RUSH MEYRICK
description of Llangeitho in 1810

32

'The Power of Heaven in the Word of Life'

The Great Awakening was about power and life. It is Williams of Pantycelyn who makes his would-be ideal Methodist convert say, 'Unless I have the power of heaven in the Word of Life I shall die.' The power of human oratory would not bring about the needed change in his corrupt heart, however orthodox the words might be. Only the power of heaven in conjunction with the Word of Life would serve the purposes of a sinner's salvation. People all over Wales as well as the crowds at Llangeitho, in one generation after another, bore witness to the presence of both in Rowland's ministry to an eminent degree. He would have been the first to acknowledge that heaven was their source, and that they were evident in others as well as himself.

What made the Great Awakening so remarkable was that these conditions lasted so long and were found in so many places at once. Virtually the whole of Rowland's ministry was exercised during this period and in this way. The same manifestations of extraordinary power and life were found in England and America, with similar effects and similar results, over the same time scale.

The list of places so affected could be multiplied, the dates surprisingly repetitive. People in one area knew nothing of happenings in another area at the time, but in historical perspective it can be seen that the theatre of divine activity in the eighteenth century was vast indeed. Furthermore, in those days, more success sometimes attended one sermon than had been accomplished in a lifetime's ministry before. The interval between the sowing of God's Word through preaching, and reaping the harvest of people coming to faith in Christ was shortened. The numbers of those whom God 'added to the church' were large. It all seemed to be a fulfilment of Isaiah's prophecy, 'Shall the earth be made to bring forth in one day? or shall a nation be born at once?' (Isaiah 66:8). This was the Lord's doing and it was marvellous in His people's eyes.

If the success was so general, so were the problems associated with it. Do these accounts of revival scenes sound familiar?

'Was dejected before the evening sermon, and when I came into the pulpit, I could have chosen to be silent rather than speak. After I had begun, however, the Spirit of the Lord gave me freedom, and at length came down like a mighty rushing wind, and carried all before it. Immediately, the whole congregation was alarmed. Crying, weeping, and wailing were to be heard in every corner; men's hearts failing them for fear, and many were to be seen falling into the arms of their friends. . . .

'Then I began to pray, and give an exhortation. In about six minutes, one cried out, "He is come, He is come!", and could scarce sustain the manifestation of Jesus to his soul. The eager crying of others, for the like favour, obliged me to stop; and I prayed over them, as I saw their agonies and distress increase. At length, we sang a hymn, and then retired to the house, where the man that received Christ continued praising and speaking of Him till near midnight. My own soul was so full that I retired and wept before the Lord, under a deep sense of my own vileness, and the sovereignty and greatness of God's everlasting love. Most of the people spent the remainder of the night in prayer and praises. It was a night much to be remembered.'[1]

The words are not those of a Welsh 'enthusiast', but of George Whitefield, and the scene 3,000 miles away in the New York area in the 1740's. The work of the Holy Spirit in revival in both countries had manifestations of power and life in common. They were irresistible, and glorious, yes, but controversial and troublesome too. They demanded from the spiritual leaders of the day a wisdom and discernment, a compassion and determination which only a settled exposure to the situation could provide.

The Methodists were at pains to demonstrate that the Awakening was not a new and different kind of Christianity. It was true Christianity heightened and elevated by the Holy Spirit to an exceptional degree of power and glory. Hence the leaders insisted on an illustrious ancestry, through the Puritans and Reformers to the Apostles, the Day of Pentecost, and the Old Testament prophecies of spiritual profusion in Gospel days. In explaining and evaluating the

[1] *George Whitefield's Journals*, 1960, pp. 484–5, 487.

Awakening their frame of reference was, quite simply, biblical.

Throughout Rowland's life the tensions of life and power were apparent. The Methodism to which they gave rise could not be anything but fluid. It was a fluidity which produced many responses, from discussion, as between Calvinistic and Arminian Methodism, to division, as between Methodism and Moravianism. Tensions spilled over into the wider church, causing some bitterness, much misunderstanding, and a great deal of controversy. Methodism was defining its own identity throughout this time, feeling strongly conservative in its affiliation to Anglicanism, and yet aware of glaring, widening differences of outlook. The 'Methodist Way' was increasingly at variance with the Established Church, not over superficial issues but in its basic ethos. Anglicanism was almost boastful of its formal, institutional, sacerdotal and theoretical mould: detached, objective, distant and inflexible. Methodism was in almost every respect its opposite. Even so, Welsh Methodism did not establish a separate ecclesiastical existence until a little more than twenty years after Rowland's death.

In its relationship with Nonconformity, 'the Methodist Way' found other tensions. If the Establishment's prime concern was over matters of ecclesiastical canons and ministerial orders, not so with Dissent. The Welsh Dissenters were mainly concerned about 'head-knowledge' and congregational independence. 'The Methodist Way' attained a more biblical balance in its view of the relationship between law and Gospel, mind and heart, faith and love, life and the evidence of life, the individual believer and the believing community.

Separation was avoided by Methodism throughout the eighteenth century for one very good reason. So long as the societies were able to nurture the spiritual life of their members in a disciplined and effective way, a formal ecclesiastical identity mattered little. It was enough that in the societies Christ was enthroned supreme, ruling His people by His presence, His Word, and His servants. Their order was new, their orthodoxy old, but their life was incomparably sweet. It was life that undergirded their doctrine, their discipline, and their order. In this way, Welsh Methodism provided a lasting cohesion to its people, so that when Welsh Methodism and Anglicanism finally separated in 1811, it was on account of the needs of its life as well as the extent of its growth. The guidelines and the discipline laid down by Rowland, Harris, and Williams Pantycelyn safeguarded the transition from 'the Methodist Way' to 'The Calvinistic Methodist Church of Wales'. Well might David Griffiths say 'that Rowland and Williams possessed talents sufficient for the government of a kingdom'.[1]

The heritage which 'the Methodist Way' bequeathed to the Calvinistic Methodist Church was a rich one. It was both doctrinal and experimental, truly Calvinistic in its content and motivation, truly Methodist in the mould and vigour of its nurture. As such, it was a harmonious blend of 'the Methodist Mind' and 'the Methodist Ideal'. The alignment of 'Calvinist' and 'Methodist' may surprise some, but not so Rowland and the others who had lived through the eighteenth century with both. For them it was neither more nor less than New Testament Christianity.

'The Methodist Mind' was unashamedly biblical. For Rowland, as for the other Welsh Methodists, the Bible was God's Word. As such it was authoritative, determinative, and final. Its precepts were binding, its promises were reliable, its values were real, and its categories were valid. Its truth and its power were corollaries, so that authentication went alongside effectiveness. In matters of history, theology, and morality alike it was entirely trustworthy. Throughout Rowland's sermons there is an implied rather than an expressed acknowledgment of biblical priority and infallibility. His illustrations are predominantly biblical, but he freely uses Greek classical authors and the early Church Fathers as well. Rowland's teaching, however, is based firmly and exclusively on textual exposition.

Rowland's theology was built on the conviction that the Bible was a reliable storehouse of absolute truth concerning God and man, this world and the next. 'I notice that this is the sum and substance of Mr. Rowland's teaching all the time', says John Thomas, 'namely, to exalt God, setting God as wonderful and eternally glorious at all times and in all things'.[2] 'The Methodist Mind' was capable both of delving into the deep things of God, and of submitting to the mysteries of Divine revelation. It was the Bible which drew the boundary between the two. Thus Rowland makes this affirmation of the different 'operations', or work of each, of the Persons in the Trinity:

'Behold! here are three Persons in one God. For though, in this wonderful dispensation of grace, He appears under three different

[1] MR, 46.   [2] lvii. 13.

characters, yet still it is the same God, rich in mercy to His offending creatures. . . . In this whole economy, the one supreme God is represented by three different operations, which can no more be separated from the Divine essence, than heat, light, and air can be separated from fire. . . . This is one of the deep mysteries of the Gospel, which infinitely transcends human comprehension, and can only be received by faith on the credit of the eternal I AM, who has revealed it.'

Having established the truth of the doctrine, Rowland proceeds to demonstrate its necessity:

'Our salvation is so closely connected with the belief of it, that, on Scripture principles, it is utterly unattainable without it. We had sinned; and like the fallen angels, were alienated from the life of God. Being in this state, it was absolutely necessary that One of infinite merit should make atonement for us, before God *could*, consistently with the rights of His moral government, and the honour of His attributes, be reconciled to us; and that this atonement should be applied to our souls before we *would* be reconciled to Him. Is it not therefore a matter of great consequence to maintain this essential doctrine, since our eternal salvation stands or falls with it? Must we not insist upon this grand peculiarity of the Christian religion, since it is the foundation of all our hopes?'[1]

This was in a sermon preached on Hebrews 1:9, 'Therefore God, even Thy God, hath anointed Thee with the oil of gladness above Thy fellows.' For Rowland there was no dilution of the message for the sake of popular appeal. Men would be won for Christ not by a modification of the Bible's message, but by the Holy Spirit's illumination of the sinner's heart.

The Bible's message also sets forth Jesus Christ as the eternal Son of God through whom the Triune God could be savingly and personally known. The same sermon spoke of Christ in His three offices as Prophet, Priest and King of His people. 'He was anointed with the oil of gladness that he might be a Prophet to teach us the will of His Father, a Priest to atone and intercede for us, and a King to rule over us and to protect us.'

This Christ 'is without parallel. Neither all the men upon earth nor all the shining myriads of glorified angels in heaven can, in any

---

[1] *Eight Sermons*, 216–17. All references to Rowland's sermons are from this work unless otherwise indicated. References to the hymns are from D. J. Odwyn Jones, *Daniel Rowland Llangeitho*.

degree, equal Him who is the Great Messiah, the God-man.'
Rowland is preaching this time on Revelation 3:20, 'Behold, I stand
at the door and knock', and so he elaborates on the wonder of the
Person who speaks to the sinner with such compassion. 'He was
perfectly happy before we had being. The Father rejoiced in the Son,
and the Son in the Father, and both mutually in the Holy Ghost. . . .
To whom does He show this wondrous love? Not to angels, but to
men, to poor worms, who dwell here in houses of clay; to sinful,
polluted dust and ashes, viler than any beasts of the field, and
abundantly more contaminated, fuller of filth than the Augean stable
of old, and more difficult to be cleansed.' Rowland expresses the
same amazement in some of his hymns:

> He stooped our flesh to wear,
> Our Elder Brother dear;
> To make us thus His sons by grace
> That were of Adam's fallen race.
>
> O! wondrous gift, free love t'impart,
> And send Christ from His Father's heart
> In time to suffer in our place,
> To bear in full our sins' disgrace.

It is not strange, therefore, that some of the warmest and most
heart-stirring passages in his sermons are found in the sections
dealing with the Person and work of Christ.

In a variety of ways, therefore, and especially in his treatment of
Christ's three-fold offices, Rowland's affinity with Reformed theology cannot but become apparent. He follows the mainline Calvinist
treatment of the plan of salvation, applying it closely and relevantly
to his hearers:

'He [Christ] is a prophet to instruct us. . . . Other prophets only
taught a part of the will of God, but he has declared to us His whole
counsel. . . . Hear Him, therefore, and attend to his heavenly
instructions. Be it your study to treasure them up in your hearts. . . .
2. Jesus was anointed that he might be the Priest of His people. . . . In
the discharge of this Office His first work was to make atonement for
sin, and to reconcile God to man. . . . Another branch of the priest's
office was to make intercession. . . . He took upon Him our nature,
that He might have a fellow-feeling of our infirmities. . . . He, the
glorious Head in heaven, sympathises with His weary and pinched
feet on earth. . . . 3. His Kingly Office. . . . The Kingdom of Christ is
full of every desirable thing that pertains to life and godliness, and is

rich in every privilege that can make life comfortable and death triumphant. . . . Seeing the Father has anointed the Son, we ought likewise to anoint Him. . . . Anoint His feet with tears, His head with love, and His body with brotherly kindness. . . . The Holy Spirit always melts those into tears of penitence whom He condescends to exalt into the happy number of Christ's fellows. . . . To the tears which you shed for the distress of your bodies and the untowardness of the times, may some be added for the sins of your souls! Some must be wrung from you on this score, before you can be anointed with the oil of gladness. . . . Our next step is to anoint His Head with the oil of true piety and love unfeigned. And when we are enabled to love Him who is the anointed of the Father, we shall then love them who are anointed of Him, and be kindly affectioned one to another.'

To Rowland, the doctrine of Christ's Person and work was no abstract, theoretical treatise. Exalted and profound these truths certainly were, mysteries even, but revealed and transforming, too. He shunned the trap, which the Dissenters fell into all too often, of thinking that the declaration of the doctrine was the preaching of Christ. For him, there must be the immediacy and power to make the living Christ real to the soul.

For this, Rowland relied on the ministry of the Holy Spirit. 'Mankind have brazen foreheads, adamantine necks, and ribs of marble around their hearts, they bleed not, they bend not, they blush not. Now the Word is a hammer, which breaks the rock within them; and the Holy Spirit is the Fire, which dissolves and melts it.' In his sermon on 'The Happiness of the godly' from Romans 8:28 he addresses the 'miserable worldlings' who 'lie under the serpent's curse': 'You have no eyes to look towards heaven, no heart to seek those things which are above. Wretched beyond description is your state, and horrible must be your end, if you continue in it. Flee, flee instantly, O generation of vipers, from the wrath to come. But I can only warn you. It is the Lord that must be your deliverer. May the power of His grace be this moment felt in all your souls!' No statement of 'the Methodist Mind' could be more comprehensive than that. All the ingredients are there: total dependence on the truth, grace, and power of God.

Several people testified to occasions when Rowland was reluctant to preach unless he was granted some prior assurance of the Spirit's assistance in the great work. David Griffiths found him one Sunday morning still in bed, and urged him to get ready for the pulpit. 'I am not quite ready', he replied. 'I have nothing from the Lord to say to the people! I was looking up for divine help in preparing my discourse all last night, and had no sleep!' Rowland was not merely referring to the matter of sermon preparation, he was also thinking of the Holy Spirit's preparation of the preacher's heart. Griffiths was told that he should go ahead, and that Rowland would follow him into the chapel, which he did. 'He went like lightning into the pulpit, full of the Holy Ghost and the heavenly treasure. He was not ten minutes into his sermon . . . before the gracious influence came from above upon him and the vast assembly. The people were overcome with feelings, the most keen and powerful; some were filled with intense joy, and others with the deepest sorrow.'[1] The coming of the Holy Spirit in this way was an 'anointing' without which no preaching would be effective.

'The Holy Ghost and His influences are called "rivers of water", the Comforter, "the Finger of God", "the earnest of our inheritance", and . . . "the Oil of gladness". And indeed this last is a very proper emblem of the Spirit for various reasons. Oil will not easily mix or incorporate with other ingredients: so the Spirit of God is holy, and separated from all creatures in His nature, though He is essentially present everywhere. . . . Oil supples that which is hardened and grown inflexible, so doth the Spirit soften our callous and stiff hearts. Oil assuages wounds and sores, and mitigates their raging pains: so doth the Spirit heal our wounded consciences, and alleviate the bitter remorse of our awakened minds.'

In the matter of turning men to God, Rowland had no illusions: 'If God does not pluck us, as brands out of the burning fire, by His free grace, and remove by His Spirit the veil of darkness and ignorance from our minds, none can be saved.' Salvation is of God, not of man.

Preaching on Matthew 10:7, 'The kingdom of heaven is at hand', Rowland 'showed how "kingdom of heaven" here means all the privileges of the New Covenant, or all the profusion of graces which are in the Lord Jesus Christ. He also showed how God has the initiative in man's conversion, that it is God who seeks man, to work on his soul by His Holy Spirit, before it ever enters man's mind to seek God.'[2] This did not eliminate the sincerity of the Gospel invitation or man's responsibility to respond. No preacher was more earnest in calling men to Christ than Rowland;

[1] MR, 135–6.   [2] lvii. 18.

'Consider the sufficiency which is in Jesus to save the vilest of sinners. . . . Sinner! cry, and say to Him, "O Lord, I do not come to Thee for what is not to be had; there is plenty with Thee; look on the Christ who is at They right hand! is there not enough righteousness in Him to answer for all my unrighteousness? is there not sufficient wealth in Him to supply all my poverty? Oh! must I die for want of forgiveness, when the blood which is always before Thee pleads better things than that of Abel? . . . Bring all your misery into the open, learn from the beggars, who show their blind eyes, and emaciated feet, and bent back to solicit the compassion of those who see them, and to receive something from them. . . . Come, then, through fire and water; if you cannot fly, Isa. 40:31, run, Heb. 12:1; if you cannot run, walk; if you cannot walk, crawl to Him. . . .

'Hold out your hand to receive, even though it shakes!' [Welsh sermon on John 5:6].

It was for the Gospel preacher to issue the call as convincingly and urgently as possible. It was for God to make the call effective.

In the work of regeneration and effectual calling, God is both sovereign and active. The Methodists dwelt much on the new birth, and suffered a great deal for it, from religious hypocrites as well as from worldly scoffers. Their insistence on the need for a man to 'be born again' was only the echo of Christ's statement to Nicodemus in John 3. The public outcry against the Methodists on this score, as on so many others, was merely a reflection of man's rebellion against revealed truth. The Methodists held that in regeneration, therefore, man was passive, and the Holy Spirit's acting was immediate and enlivening. 'It is a strange disposition that men have,' says Jonathan Edwards, 'to thrust God out of the world, or to put Him as far out of sight as they can, and to have in no respect immediately and sensibly to do with Him. . . . And therefore these doctrines are so much ridiculed that ascribe much to the immediate influence of the Spirit, and called enthusiasm, fanaticism, whimsy, and distraction.'[1] The same was true with regard to the Methodists' preaching of justification by faith. This again was a doctrine which was unacceptable to the natural man. It was the death-blow to man's pride of achievement as well as to the licentiousness to which he was prone. Equally repugnant was the Methodist teaching on sanctification as stemming from an inner principle rather than as consisting in outward duties and ceremonies. All these doctrines held together in the Methodism of Rowland as related and liberating truths.

[1] *Treatise on Grace*, London, 1971, p. 53.

The first evidence of regeneration experimentally and consciously in the sinner was a measure of repentance. Preaching on Acts 2:37, 'When they heard this, they were pricked in their heart, and said to Peter and to the rest of the apostles, Men and brethren, what shall we do?', Rowland showed:

'1. That the root of repentance is in heaven. The reality of their repentance was shown, 1. from the time of their conviction, namely, when Christ's religion was everywhere spoken against. Had it been esteemed and respected at the time, it would not be a strange thing to see three thousand converted, and turning to it; but now, when Christ, and His religion and His followers are despised by all, it is clear that their repentance and conversion was of God, and for that reason, real. 2. From the second cause of it . . . not from fear of hell, or fear of judgment, since the apostles were not addressing them in a threatening manner, except to tell them about their sin; they turned from sin from a true hatred of it, not on account of its penalty. . . . 3. . . . they made no excuse for their sin, when they heard that it was their rulers and leaders who were responsible for putting Christ to death; they could also have blamed Judas's sin, and even Peter's, but they did not do so. 4. On account of the great change which was evident in their understanding and regard for the apostles; 5. because they knew that the Spirit possessed the apostles.'[1]

It was on these evidences of God's grace in the heart, rather than on any outward manifestations of the body, that the Methodists placed emphasis. Their societies were designed to assess and evaluate the beginnings of a work of grace, and to encourage its growth and progress. Repentance and faith belong together.

'The law was our schoolmaster to bring us unto Christ, that we might be justified by faith', says the Apostle Paul. The aim of reproving men of sin and breaking up the foundation of any apparent goodness on which they might rely, was to compel them to flee to Christ and trust in Him alone. Setting before men the excellence of His Person and the surpassing merit of His death was therefore central to the Gospel message. It was Rowland's chief delight to do just this, in his hymns as well as his sermons:

> The Heavenly Lamb's own precious blood
> Was shed to cleanse and free me,
> With painful anguish from His heart.
> O God! my soul must praise Thee.

[1] lvi. 24–5.

> Your debt is paid;
> You family of grace
> Your freedom trace
> And give Him praise!
>
> Come listen to Good News!
> Healèd shall be
> Whoever he
> On Christ his soul has rested.
>
> To hell's black pit turn, Satan, see
> How Christ has fully ransomed me;
> This solid Rock my faith will bear,
> The dragon's rage no more to fear.

Man's redemption was accomplished, then, by Christ's dying as a substitute in his place. Crucifixion on a Roman gibbet was a historical fact, but it was also a divine transaction. It was both the responsibility of man and the plan of God. Its meaning and relevance also were to be seen in the relationship between sinful man and a holy God. The cross, with its shadow of death and light of life, must be planted in the hearts of people at Llangeitho, as well as on the hill of Calvary. The application of its reconciling, restoring power was the province of the Holy Spirit, the occasion of its realisation was the preaching of Rowland. An extended extract from his sermon on the dying thief shows the connection:

'Now all these things, very contrary extremes, did wisdom unite and converge in the conversion of the thief. Behold! he is born to Christ, and dies to the world. Behold! grace is planted in his soul, and sin is plucked by the roots from it. Behold! the Son of God receives deadly wounds in His own Body, and heals *his* wounded heart. Behold! the body of death is broken down, and the work of grace built up. Behold him weeping for his sins, and yet rejoicing at the reviving news that he should be so soon with Jesus in paradise!'

The imagery of exchange, between sin and righteousness, wounding and healing, death and life, finds vivid expression in the hymns of Williams, too:

> He came to heal the wounded,
> Being wounded in their stead;
> The heir of heaven was pierced
> For those through sin made dead.
> He sucked the awful poison

The serpent gave to me,
And from that deadly venom
He died on Calvary.

But for both Rowland and Williams this was no mere poetic expression. They were in deadly earnest, dealing with real issues between men and God. Real, yes, and intimate, too. Without powerful, personal dealings between a man and his God, religion is a sham. So Rowland's sermon proceeds:

'In this wonderful transaction the Omnipotence of God is displayed. St. Chrysostom declares, "that this was a greater miracle than that the sun was darkened, that the earth was shaken, that the rocks were cleaved asunder, and that the vail of the Temple was rent in twain from the top to the bottom". What was the darkening of the sun when compared with the enlightening of a dark understanding? What was the cleaving of rocks in comparison with the softening of a hard, stony, adamantine heart? or the rending of the Temple vail, with the removal of the vail of ignorance from the soul? The rod with which Moses evidenced his divine mission is a strong confirmation, as well as a pertinent illustration of this truth. It had authority over the earth, and the sea, and the elements; light, darkness, and every creature within its reach were subject to its command. But it had no power or influence over Pharaoh's hard heart. Behold! it is easier to tear the rock in pieces, than to melt the human heart. Oh Jesus! none but Thy Spirit can do it.'

Repentance and faith, wrought in the soul by the Holy Spirit, evidence a personal and genuine conversion. This, however, was the beginning of the Christian life, not its end.

The continuance of that life is God's unbreakable intention, and to fulfil it He makes full provision. Faith is a sanctifying principle in the soul working nearness to God and distance from sin. Its presence is a guarantee of its culmination when ultimately it will give way to the sight of God, but its exercise is a matter of constant ministerial exhortation. The Christian is to 'live by faith, not by sight': 'It should be our aim, not to be great, but to be useful to our generation; not to be distinguished by our wealth and splendour, but by our meek and lowly spirit, which is the characteristic of all true Christians.'

Another area of concern for 'the Methodist Mind', had to do with the tension between perseverance and presumption. Every believer lives in a hostile environment, and yet he is assured of his safety. He is a pilgrim facing all manner of dangers, yet he will most certainly arrive at his destination. Rowland often talks of the Christian in the world, facing affliction, temptation, deceitfulness, and opposition. Yet he consistently reminds his hearers of God's sovereign control, so that afflictions are 'God's messengers', and 'sanctified affliction is a choice blessing'. They are 'the avenues through which the faithful are conducted to the possession of that which is good'. Rowland's hymns on this theme affirm the unchangeableness of God's covenant and promise to His people. 'Dark hell holds no terror, it's locked, pass by without fear'; 'the dragon's skull is cracked, God has publicly triumphed'.

So the Christian travels on, in humility and hope, giving God the glory. 'Every faithful servant will deposit the money, which he receives for his master's goods, in his master's till. . . . I have read of a bird whose feathers are so light, that he is obliged to carry a stone in his bill lest the wind should blow him away. Be that as it may; it is certain that we do all stand in need of a stone, or rather, of the rock out of which we were hewn, lest the whirlwind of pride should catch us up hastily, and carry us where we shall no more be seen'. Fortified with promises such as Romans 8:28, 'We know that all things work together for good to them that love God, to them who are the called according to his purpose', the Christian can face all present events and future emergencies. 'This is the parent of spiritual courage. The hopes of victory embolden the soldier in the day of battle; and the prospect of a happy voyage entices the mariner to the raging waves; yet neither of these knows what the end may be . . . but we, who believe, do not run so uncertainly. Among all the sorts of men which can be named, or the various occupations which they follow, none have the like promises with believers.' 'The Methodist Mind' fostered by Rowland's preaching produced a progressive and attractive godliness.

Methodism also stood for a disciplined godliness. Much of that discipline was exercised in 'the experience meeting', and Rowland practised it as well as preached it. Conscious that the critical eyes of the world were always on the believer, Rowland counselled, 'Judge your own selves. . . . Look upon the behaviour of others through the spectacles of love. . . . Intreat the Lord to set a watch before your mouth. . . . Do with another man's name as you would wish that he should do with yours.' If it is necessary to reprove another Christian it must be done with great caution and wisdom. 'It must be the combined work of a cool head, and a gracious, compassionate heart', says Rowland; 'deal as tenderly . . . as if you were handling

Venice glass, or the thin and brittle ware of China'. No Methodist could afford to be without 'the spectacles of love'. Rowland's tenderness was proverbial. He maintained that 'the discipline of the Gospel is like a golden hayrake, that gathers and draws all to it for succour and protection, and not like a fork that throws away and scatters'.

Lively preaching and close discipline together constituted a 'Methodist Mind', but they prospered chiefly when the Holy Spirit was poured out in profusion upon God's people. Listen to John Thomas describing the effect of one of Rowland's preaching services: 'Some souls in this meeting were feasting at their heavenly Father's table. Some were drunk, and that with the best wine, namely, the gift of the Holy Spirit, God's peace, God's love shed abroad in their hearts by the Holy Ghost. Some prominent people scorn and deride this, but it is the substance of religion.'[1] This was 'the Methodist Ideal', the blessed fountain from which all other blessings flowed.

In both America and Wales the effects of that power and glory were phenomenal. The Awakening's friends were amazed, embarrassed even, by them. Because of those ecstatic manifestations, their enemies showered upon them contempt and abuse. Williams defended them with insight, discrimination, and conviction.

'Some professors ranted and raved, heatedly gnashed their teeth and bit their tongues, and the whole cause was because this people loved the Christ whom they did not love.... They spend the whole afternoon with other ladies, and the parish clergyman to entertain them over a cup of tea.... And the main subject of conversation all afternoon was the people who rejoiced and sang praises to God. "A bunch of hypocrites" was the best name for them . . . (in church the same people appeal to all and sundry to praise God) . . . and yet they pour out their wrath upon those people who did so from their hearts.... The only reason . . . was the Spirit which possessed them, that zealous spirit of loving and praising God. . . . Because they follow the Lord with all their heart.'[2]

This was the Spirit's doing. Under His influences the senses of the soul were elevated and quickened, and the physical body on occasions felt His power as well. Temperament and emotion had their part, more so in some than in others. But the Methodists

---

[1] *Y Drysorfa*, 1933, tud. 53.   [2] GWP ii. 26–7, 29.

insisted that the authenticity of these manifestations did not lie in how much, or how strong or how often they were in evidence. It lay, rather, in the lasting fruit of the Spirit in personal and social behaviour.

Methodism profoundly influenced the history of Wales. Not only did Methodist people take an interest in learning to read, keeping the Sabbath, setting up family worship, showing integrity and compassion to their neighbours, and spreading the Gospel by missionary endeavour. They also made an impact on the standards and values of their contemporaries, exercising a preserving and purifying influence as 'the salt of the earth'. As David Williams, the historian, concluded:

'It would be difficult to analyse fully the influence of methodism on the development of the Welsh Nation. Not only did it contribute to the growth of nonconformity by the establishment of a new denomination; it led also to the expansion of the other dissenting bodies. . . . It gave an impetus to the study of the Welsh language and produced a considerable literature in Welsh. . . . The moral fibre of the people was stiffened, and they became more law-abiding. . . . The methodist insistence on uncompromising integrity of character, on honesty, temperance, industry and thrift, together with their belief in the sanctity of the individual and the equality of all men before God, led in time to the rousing of the social conscience and the sweeping away of many abuses.'

On the other hand, Professor Williams alleged that Methodism had deprived the common people of a 'carefree joyousness' in their social gatherings. He added, 'the people's concern with the world to come, while it may have saved the country from social disturbance and anarchy, rendered them apathetic to the need for reform'.[1] The Methodists, however, gave real and lasting 'joy' a different dimension by speaking of Christ as its only source, while at the same time giving to Welsh culture a wholesomeness that was beneficial. If Methodism was in the main conservative in its social conscience, it was usually so from the biblical considerations of submission to 'the higher powers'. It expressed misgivings, for instance, at the tendency to personal intimidation and public disorder in the Trade Unionism of the 1830's. At times it may have been misguided, but its insistence on such biblical principles provided guidelines for conduct and much-needed stability in a time of change.

All good achievements, however, were to be attributed to God's

---

[1] *A History of Modern Wales*, 1951, pp. 156, 157.

visiting the land in revival. During the eighteenth century in Wales several human instruments had been used of God to bring about those achievements. Furthermore, if 'Revival' was 'the Methodist Ideal' for the church, Rowland came closest to being the ideal instrument of its propagation. His was a ministry attended with power and glory *par excellence.*

William Williams has a character, Fidelius, which depicts such a man. He is 'the same man within and without', whose life was lived on an even keel. His home was God's temple, his family 'as well learned in their Bible as a student in his grammar', and their singing at family worship the best of any. He was generous, 'as God brought in, so his hand went out', and totally devoted to the well-being of God's church. His chief delight, next to the Bible, was in the works of the Reformers and the Puritans. His trials came from three main directions: the direct, fiery assaults of Satan; the warm, enticing allurements of the world; and those corrupt inward tendencies which are so easily fuelled, baked, and set on fire by worldly objects.

Coming closer again to this ideal Methodist, Williams examines his inner experiences. First, he laboured to keep his conscience void of offence; secondly, open to 'the sweet influences of the heavenly Spirit'. This 'heavenly breeze lifted him above the creature so that he lost count of hours, and seasons, and, filled with the Holy Spirit, he partook of unspeakable and glorious joy, the beginning, he believed, of heaven this side of the grave'. Thirdly, he had much heavenly light to discern his own heart and the hearts of others. Fourthly, he had 'the spirit of power and might which heaven supplied to his need'.

His chief delight, however, was Christ, the Prince of Peace. 'He cared not for sermons, or hymns, or discourses in which Christ was not exalted in the highest degree.' It was not surprising, then, that 'his last hours were hours of preaching as well as hours of prayer'. So much for Williams' picture of Fidelius, 'one of the closest to heaven that ever I saw on my pilgrimage'.[1] Whether Williams intended it or not, as a picture of the ideal Methodist preacher, 'Fidelius' portrayed Rowland well.

Rowland's ministry was attended with power and glory from God. Its grand object was 'to show the nothingness of man and the glory and greatness of God'.[2] He once spoke of 'how the Christian's endeavours terminate in the glory of God', and illustrated this by the

---

[1] GWP ii. 137–57.   [2] MR, 171–2.

progress of drops of water from the mountain to the sea. At first they merge into a trickle, then join a stream, and a large river, which flows eventually into 'the immense ocean . . . and there they are completely swallowed up and lost in the great deep for ever! How delightfully and sweetly does this set forth the believer ending his journey in the everlasting ocean of love and glory!' Rowland's usefulness, as well as his greatness, must be measured in terms of that ideal.

Index

Aberllolwyne
Lloyd Esq
Llany Gwnnion
Llanil
Pentre Dd
Tavern Spite
Morris Esq
Carrog
Llandinol
Melivor
Philipps Esq
Llanrusted
Lla
Rhos
Aberywith
Mabws
Gwyre Vach
Gwyre Vawr
Llanvanfrayd
Llansanfrayd vill
Llanparos
Llany Gwynion
Pon y Gevenin
Pens Brook
Llyn Aeyidwen Mowdi
PEN
Pugh
Cledar Broke
Llech Ran
Blaynpenel
Chap
Llaindden
Aberarth
Aberayrron
Manachty
Llanbaidern
Rheala
Pandy
C
Gwynne E
V vach
Duffrin
Vdangytho
Ucyny Glyn
Llanbaa
Henvenien
or Llanvenien
Ornant
Iron R.
Tru Christ
Capel Bettu
Edeyri
Y Llanuchaim
Novadd
Llinarth
Griffiths Esq
Typlyn Lha
Jones Esq
Brigile
Vaintywillo
Edachly
LewisGent
Typlyn Ucha
James Tg
Killkenyn
Llanller
Lewis
Trevelan
Barwood
Myrrick
Deheny d
Capel Gorthe
Mydur Oilin Mill
Killyaron
Gove
Talsorn
Abermyrick
Vimare
Yotrred
Lloyd Jack
Lloyd Esq
E
Blaen y Wern
Blaen y Wern
Llangubly
Lloy
Novadd Mountain
H
Blaeny Wern
White well
Gent
Tudding
Capell Mowddyn
Pen y Baer
Dery Wermod
Lloyd Esq
Bettus
Galt y Creey Park
Closter Vach
Castell Howel
Peny Bron Goleu
Llansilian
Llansilian vill
Entry
pel Llantisved
UNDRED
Lampiter
Pont Stephen
Ichan Veil
Millfield
Lloyd Bart
Cly
Trauley
Garow
Llanumen
Camnant
Llanvenog
V
Peter well Lloyd
Bole Gwrddon
Tu
Llanvenag
Galts yr Odin
Mountain
Place Lloyd
Doll Wen
Llanbadtnan
Lloyd Esq
Nole woll
Pencarreg
Bulch Buchan
Bulch Manvr
Llan Dudder
R.